The Korean Economy in Transition

The Korean Economy in Transition

An Institutional Perspective

O. Yul Kwon

Korea Foundation Chair in Korean Studies
Director, Australian Centre for Korean Studies
Griffith Business School
Griffith University, Australia

Adjunct Professor
Korea University Business School
Korea University, Korea

Edward Elgar
Cheltenham, UK • Northampton, MA, USA

Published by
Edward Elgar Publishing Limited
The Lypiatts
15 Lansdown Road
Cheltenham
Glos GL50 2JA
UK

Edward Elgar Publishing, Inc.
William Pratt House
9 Dewey Court
Northampton
Massachusetts 01060
USA

A catalogue record for this book
is available from the British Library

Library of Congress Control Number: 2009940977

ISBN 978 1 84064 268 1

Printed and bound by MPG Books Group, UK

Mixed Sources
Product group from well-managed
forests and other controlled sources
www.fsc.org Cert no. SA-COC-1565
© 1996 Forest Stewardship Council
FSC

Contents

Abbreviations

ADB	Asian Development Bank
APEC	Asia–Pacific Economic Cooperation
ASEAN	Association of South East Asian Nations
ASIC	Australian Securities and Investments Commission
BAAR	Basic Act on Administrative Regulation
BDRC	Business Difficulties Resolution Center
BIS	Bank for International Settlements
CD	certificate of deposit
CGQ	corporate governance quality
CPI	Corruption Perceptions Index
CSC	Civil Service Commission
DDA	Doha Development Agenda
DFAT	Department of Foreign Affairs and Trade
DMZ	Demilitarized Zone
DPRK	Democratic People's Republic of Korea
EAAU	East Asia Analytical Unit
EAFTA	East Asia Free Trade Agreement
EAIR	East Asian Integration Regime
EDI	electronic data interchange
EFTA	European Free Trade Association
EIS	Employment Insurance Scheme
EITC	Earned Income Tax Credit
EIU	Economist Intelligence Unit
EU	European Union
FDI	foreign direct investment
FIPA	Foreign Investment Promotion Act
FKI	Federation of Korean Industries
FKTU	Federation of Korean Trade Unions
FSC	Financial Supervisory Commission

FSCMA	Financial Investment Services and Capital Markets Act
FSS	Financial Supervisory Service
FTAs	free trade agreements
FTC	Fair Trading Commission
GATT	General Agreement on Tariffs and Trade
GCI	Global Competitiveness Index
GDP	gross domestic product
GFC	global financial crisis
GMI	GovernanceMetrics International
GNI	gross national income
GNP	Grand National Party
GNP	gross national product
HF	Heritage Foundation
ICG	International Crisis Group
ICRG	International Country Risk Guide
ICT	information and communication technology
IEF	Index of Economic Freedom
IMD	International Institute for Management Development
IMF	International Monetary Fund
IPR	intellectual property rights
IT	information technology
KAMCO	Korea Asset Management Corporation
KBE	knowledge-based economy
KCCI	Korea Chamber of Commerce and Industry
KCSPI	Korean Composite Stock Price Index
KCTU	Korean Confederation of Trade Unions
KEF	Korea Employers Federation
KEI	Knowledge Economy Index
KERI	Korea Economic Research Institute
KFSB	Korean Federation of Small and Medium Business
KFTA	Korea Foreign Trade Association
KFTC	Korea Fair Trade Commission
KI	Knowledge Index
KICAC	Korean Independent Commission against Corruption
KIEP	Korea Institute for International Economic Policy
KIET	Korea Institute for Industrial Economics and Trade
KIHASA	Korea Institute for Health and Social Affairs
KILF	Korea International Labor Foundation

KLI	Korea Labor Institute
KNSO	Korea National Statistical Office
KOFEX	Korea Futures Exchange
KOSBI	Korea Small Business Institute
KOSDAQ	Korean Securities Dealers Automated Quotations
KOSPI	Korea Composite Stock Price Index
KOTRA	Korea Trade-Investment Promotion Agency
KREI	Korea Rural Economic Institute
KRW	Korean won
KRX	Korea Exchange
KSDA	Korea Securities Dealers Association
KSE	Korean Securities and Exchange Commission
KSE	Korean Stock Exchange
KTC	Korea Tripartite Commission
LMC	Labor-Management Council
LRC	Labor Relations Commission
M&As	mergers and acquisitions
MDP	Millennium Democratic Party
MIHWAF	Ministry of Heath, Welfare and Family Affairs
MKE	Ministry of Knowledge Economy (formerly MOCIE)
MNEs	multinational enterprises
MOCIE	Ministry of Commerce, Industry and Energy
MOFAT	Ministry of Foreign Affairs and Trade
MOFE	Ministry of Finance and Economy
MOSF	Ministry of Strategy and Finance
MOU	memorandum of understanding
MPB	Ministry of Planning and Budget
NBLSS	National Basic Livelihood Security System
NGO	non-governmental organization
NII	Korea's national information infrastructure
NPLs	non-performing loans
NPT	Nuclear Non-Proliferation Treaty
OECD	Organisation for Economic Co-operation and Development
PC	personal computer
PCER	Presidential Commission on Education Reform
PDS	Public Distribution System
PSI	Proliferation Security Initiative

R&D	research and development
RIA	Regulatory Impact Analysis
ROA	return on assets
ROE	return on equity
ROK	Republic of Korea
RRC	Regulatory Reform Committee
RRTF	Regulatory Reform Task Force
S&T	science and technology
SAR	Special Administrative Region
SEZs	Special Economic Zones
SFC	Securities and Futures Commission
SMBA	Small and Medium Business Administration
SMEs	small and medium-sized enterprises
SOEs	state-owned enterprises
TFP	total factor productivity
TI	Transparency International
UNCTAD	United Nations Conference on Trade and Development
UNDP	United Nations Development Programme
UR	Uruguay Round
WEF	World Economic Forum
WFP	World Food Programme
WMD	weapons of mass destruction
WTO	World Trade Organization

Preface

This book investigates the transition in the economy of South Korea (hereafter Korea) from a state-led system over the three decades of unprecedented economic success preceding the financial crisis of 1997 to a market-oriented system of the post-crisis period with sluggish economic development. From the early 1960s through to the 1997 financial crisis, the Korean economy continued to surge. After a serious economic setback over one year in 1998, it recovered quickly, unlike other crisis-afflicted economies in East Asia, and became the world's 11th-largest economy in 2003. Korea thus stands as proof that one country can leap from being one of the poorest in the world to joining the ranks of the richest in just one generation.

In the immediate aftermath of the 1997 crisis, outdated economic policies and institutions were regarded as the primary culprit. The Korean government therefore vigorously pursued profound reforms of the nation's economic institutions, in response to both the crisis and the transition under way in its geopolitical and global economic environments as well as domestic political and social changes. These sweeping institutional reforms have in turn been the main drivers of the transition in the Korean economy from being heavily controlled and state-led to a liberalized, knowledge-based economy anchored in market principles. Consequently, Korea presents a fascinating case for enquiry into the evolution of a national economy with its distinctive experiences of apparently miraculous success over three decades since the early 1960s, tumultuous financial crisis in 1997, swift recovery through sweeping institutional reforms, and remarkable economic transition into the twenty-first century.

Despite rapid recovery from the crisis over one year and the sweeping institutional reforms that were introduced as the remedy, the Korean economy entered a low potential growth phase. Clear signals of sluggish performance from the dawn of the twenty-first century have raised concerns in all walks of life in Korea about the consequences of a stagnant national economy, and the dimming prospect of crossing the threshold to advanced-economy status. What explains the sudden economic slowdown and unpropitious prospects of the Korean economy for the decades ahead? In order to reinvigorate and fortify the economy for national well-being and to achieve the popular Korean aspiration to live in an advanced economy, what should be done, by whom, and how? This book is an attempt to address these critical questions through analysing the dynamics of institutional changes and economic operations in Korea across the transition period.

This volume has a number of distinctive features. First, it adopts an institutional perspective in exploring the evolution of the Korean economy in the emerging globalization era because of the nation's idiosyncratic institutional framework. The Korean economy maintains *sui generis* characteristics even while drawing, with most national economies, towards a global standard. As the world has witnessed through the collapse of socialism, differences in per capita income across countries are due mainly to differences in the quality of institutions, and the persistence of relative institutional inefficiency is frequently a major source of long-run economic stagnation. This book therefore examines the Korean institutional context through the multiple lenses of history, society, culture and politics, and analyses various aspects of the Korean economy in this light.

Second, the comprehensive approach of this study explores a rich array of pertinent topics across its 12 chapters to present an informative and across-the-board picture of the Korean economy in transition. It explores the evolution of institutions to investigate the impacts of economic policy, culture and politics on macroeconomic development, and the nation's economic transition toward a knowledge-based economy. Recognizing the now relatively wide open nature of the economy, the book discusses recent developments in institutions that relate to Korea's external economic relations. These include inter-Korea economic relations and the North Korean economic reforms in 2002, both of which are of major significance for the Korean nation and its economic performance. Micro-level analysis takes up institutional reforms related to three main sectors: business, finance and public administration. The book also includes detailed discussions on labour and social welfare issues, recognizing sustainable and equitable economic development as the Korean people's preferred course for the nation. This volume therefore provides valuable, comprehensive information for those seeking to understand the Korean example of national economic development and transition, whether for scholarly purposes or for active engagement in economic development policy.

Third, this volume draws extensively not only from sources in the English and Korean languages, including electronic as well as published materials, but also from my experiences as both scholar and consultant. I have many years of experience involving frequent visits to Korea for academic purposes and as consultant on projects concerned with the Korean economy. I have also conducted surveys and interviews with foreign business people in Korea in the recent past, and these have contributed to my understanding of the Korean economy from foreign perspectives.

The need for this book became clearer to me while teaching a course entitled 'The Korean Economy' at Griffith University in Australia since 1996, and at the International Summer Campus of Korea University, Korea in the recent past. There was no comprehensive treatment of this subject in a single volume; the sources of pertinent information were scattered and inadequate for presenting a well-rounded picture of the recent development of the Korean economy. As the 11th-largest economy in the world and located in a strategically dynamic region of Northeast Asia, Korea plays an important role in the regional and global economy. Yet it has eluded the careful examination that it deserves. All chapters have been rewritten a number of times as the speed of institutional reforms and their consequences overtook production of this book. A number of former students and other colleagues commented on some chapters of the book over the several years of its creation.

Indeed, many people have made valuable contributions to producing this book. Its preparation has been part of a research project funded by the Korea Research Foundation in Seoul, to which I express sincere thanks. I thank Steve Johnson at Sam Houston State University, Dr Hun Soo Kim at Korea's Ministry of Labor, David Schak and Byung Min at Griffith University who commented on draft chapters. Daniel Halvorson deserves special mention for his excellent research assistance and for meticulous editing of this volume. Thanks are also due to Robyn White for her careful attention to detail and her efficiency in preparing the manuscript to meet the exacting specifications of the publisher. Perhaps most importantly, I express deep thanks to my wife, Joanne Kwon, whose patience and caring prevailed while I was buried in researching and writing this book over what seemed like day and night for several years. I therefore dedicate this book to her with warmest thanks and affection. I of course remain solely responsible for any errors and shortcomings in the content of this book.

Introduction

This book uses an institutional approach to analyse the distinctive phases of Korea's economic transition across roughly four decades. It traces national economic development from a state-led system across three decades of miraculous economic success to the 1997 crisis, and the shift this crisis inspired to a market-oriented system with sluggish economic development in the post-crisis period. The transition of the Korean economy has not been analysed comprehensively in the context of the institutions that influence economic performance, particularly during the globalization era. This book seeks to help fill the void by providing critical analysis of the dynamics of institutional evolution and the operations of important economic sectors as well as the overall Korean economy in the recent past.

Korea's economic success is well documented. It stands as proof that a nation can leap from being one of the poorest in the world to one of the richest in just one generation. Over the period from 1963 to 1996, the economy recorded an annual growth rate of 8.7 per cent, per capita income increased more than 100-fold from $100 to $10 548, and GDP rose from $2.3 billion to $520 billion (KNSO various years). In 1996, Korea became the 29th member of the OECD. The Korean economy had become a textbook example of successful economic development. As the vast literature on this subject attests (Kwon 1997), Korea's economic success story has stimulated broad international discussion regarding the Korean development model, the sustainability of the development momentum, and the applicability of this model to other developing countries.

The financial crisis in November 1997 that engulfed much of East Asia temporarily crippled the Korean economy and closed the curtains on three decades of 'economic miracle'. In 1998 negative growth of 6.7 per cent was recorded and unemployment soared to 7 per cent from 2.6 per cent in 1997. Inflation increased from 4.4 to 7.5 per cent, and the US dollar value of the Korean won plummeted from 951 to 1415 (KNSO various years). However, unlike all of the other crisis-afflicted economies in East Asia, the Korean economy recovered swiftly, recording 10.7 per cent growth in 1999 and 8.8 per cent growth in 2000, and establishing Korea as the world's 11th-largest economy by 2003. The Korean economy once again stimulated broad international discussion, this time regarding the diagnosis of, remedies for and recovery from financial crisis, the institutional and structural changes that were implemented in response, and the implications of the Korean example for other countries.

Although it recovered rapidly from the crisis over the ensuing two years, the Korean economy has since shown clear signs of sluggish performance. Over the six years 2001–08, the economy achieved an annual growth rate of 4.4 per cent, which is far below the average over the previous three decades. A number of studies estimate that Korea has entered a low potential-growth phase with a rate of 4–5 per cent over the next ten years up to the mid-2010s, and per capita income remaining one-third below the OECD average (Park and Huh 2004; J.G. Park 2003; Bank of Korea 2005; OECD 2007). This assessment has raised concerns among people in all walks of life in Korea about the consequences of a stagnant national economy and the prospect of failing to cross the threshold to advanced-economy status.

External factors do not explain the Korean economic slowdown, as the global economy and the economies of Korea's major economic partners including the United States, China, and even Japan, performed reasonably well at least up to the 2008 global economic crisis. Soon after the 1997 financial crisis, a consensus formed among analysts that outdated economic policies and institutions and the corresponding economic structure were the primary causes of the crisis in Korea (Kwon 1998; J.M. Lee 2003; Harvie and Lee 2004).[1] Hence, soon after the crisis, sweeping institutional and structural reforms were undertaken to rebuild and fortify the Korean economy. How then should one explain both the sudden economic slowdown early in the new century and the unpropitious prospects of the Korean economy for the decade ahead? What should be done to reinvigorate the national economy for the well-being of the Korean people and to achieve their aspirations for Korea to be one of the world's advanced economies? This book attempts to address these critical questions from an institutional perspective.

The Korean economy has been in transition in many respects from the early 1990s, and in particular since the 1997 crisis. International geopolitical environments have figuratively – and literally – changed the ground on which Korea's economic spectacle is played out. The close of the Cold War has ended the advantage Korea enjoyed as a Western ally from its geostrategic location. The world economy has moved unremittingly toward globalization, heralding intense global competition and the weakening of national economic boundaries. As a signatory of the WTO and a member of the OECD, Korea has firmly embraced its position on the path of globalization. The Korean economy, which depends on international trade and capital mobility for its own survival, is now maturing such that Korea is no longer a developing country. Indeed, commensurate with its size and stage of development, the Korean economy has become a vital cog in the wheel of the global economy.

The global trading system is in transition. In 2001 the Doha Development Agenda (DDA), a new round of multilateral trade negotiations, was launched in the WTO. However, the negotiations have been in deadlock since 2006, and the prospect of WTO-based multilateralism for trade liberalization looks dim. In contrast, regional trade agreements have been multiplying particularly since the mid-1990s, thereby deepening regionalization within the global trading system.

Climate change is now recognized as one of the critical issues faced by all of humankind wherever they live. As a result, carbon emissions trading has emerged as one more vital issue in international trade, compelling all countries to pay proper heed to the impact of economic operations on all aspects of climate and the geophysical environments. In recent years, the world has witnessed instability of energy supply and a sharp rise in energy prices, intensifying competition for energy. Securitization of energy resources has become a vital national concern. Rising anxiety about climate change internationally, greater growth in demand for energy, and acute concern over the supply of energy resources in unstable global markets will exert pressure on national governments to reduce fossil fuel use through carbon markets.

International financial markets have expanded dramatically since the mid-1990s. Cross-border flows of financial assets globally tripled during the past decade to $6.4 trillion, reaching about 14.5 per cent of world GDP by 2005 (Pazarbasioglu et al. 2007). Dramatic growth of international capital flows can be attributed to the increased importance of new financial instruments and the globalization of international financial markets. These new financial instruments include hedge funds, private equity funds and sovereign wealth funds, each of which has expanded greatly in recent years. Global capital markets are becoming more integrated, thereby enhancing linkages between national financial systems. The internationalization of financial markets and growing links between national financial systems have led to the highly unpredictable world of global financial systems and capital markets, which in turn have increased the volatility and subsequent contagion in financial markets. The global financial crisis in the wake of the US financial crisis in September 2008 bears witness. Hence, national policy-makers must be vigilant in taking into account developments in global financial markets as well as in the national context when planning and implementing policy.

Another epochal change in the international economic environment looms on the horizon for Korea. North–South Korean relations, political and economic, have been changing dramatically since the historic summit between the two national leaders in June 2000, followed by another in October 2007. In 2002, North Korea began economic reform through market liberalization, and a number of signs suggested the possibility of further opening to the world outside. However, in 2006 and 2009 North Korea conducted nuclear tests, which provoked UN sanctions, to which North Korea responded with further expansion of its uranium enrichment programme. These developments have important bearings not only on South Korea, its economy and its relations with North Korea, but also on geostrategic and thus economic developments right across the Pacific Rim.

Domestically, too, Korea has experienced a period of transition. The Korean political system has been transformed since 1988 from a series of authoritarian regimes to a vibrant and fully fledged pluralistic democracy headed by a civilian president. Stakeholders in the new political system are not just the president, the bureaucracy, politicians and *chaebol* conglomerates that dominated national economic development strategy and politics through the high-growth period until the 1997 financial crisis. Now workers, consumers, interest groups and other members of the general public are recognized as political stakeholders and they participate actively in the nation's political economy. Korean society and culture have inevitably changed in tandem with the economic and political transformation. As in most nations that have moved towards a more neoliberal system, patriotism and loyalty toward authority have faded, individualistic pursuit has changed the nature of group-oriented society, and the work ethic of the Korean people has weakened. Demographically, as in most industrialized nations, the population is ageing quickly and its growth rate is declining.

Another major transition driven by technological innovation is shifting the Korean economy from industrial to knowledge-based at a time when the global economic paradigm is making a similar shift. In recent years, Korea has been increasingly squeezed between Japan and China in economic competition due to China's exponential improvement in technology as well as its industrial and manufacturing prowess. Thus, international as well as domestic circumstances propel this shift within Korea to a knowledge-based economy.

Importantly for this study, Korea's response to the 1997 financial crisis and to the subsequent shifts in both domestic and international environments has brought metamorphosis to the nation's economic institutions. In compliance with the conditions attached to the IMF rescue package, the Korean government has relentlessly undertaken institutional and structural reforms to liberalize and internationalize the national economy. These major systemic reforms of the nation's institutions have in turn been the main driver of the transition in the Korean economy since the crisis. Liberalization has induced transition from a state-led to a market-oriented economy. Opening the economy to foreign competition has undergirded the transition to a competition-based market economy. Consequently, Korea presents a fascinating case for enquiry into the evolution of a national economy. The Korean case shows progression from a heavily controlled, protected and remarkably successful economy, to a liberalized, internationalized, knowledge-based economy anchored in market principles.

The national economic drama unfolding particularly since the 1997 crisis begs critical interpretation. This requires re-evaluating the earlier literature on the Korean economy since it reports on studies undertaken before the recent developments in domestic and external policy environments. In particular, there is a paucity of in-depth and comprehensive analysis of the Korean economy in the twenty-first century when economic sluggishness became evident. The sudden and unexpected nature of the downturn that followed the brief interlude of strong recovery in the final years of the 1990s means that knowledge of Korea's institutional and structural reforms, and concomitant economic transition in the longer term, are still in the early stages of development. A few analyses such as Kwon (2005, 2007), Harvie and Lee (2004) and OECD (2004, 2005, 2007) have attempted to explore some aspects of this rich analytical terrain. However, no study has comprehensively drawn together detailed information to capture the 'big picture' of Korea's economic transition and future prospects. One important aspect to which the existing literature has paid little attention is the dynamics of the institutional environments and economic operations of Korea under globalization. The comprehensive nature of topics addressed in this book is a direct response to these information needs.

The institutional approach taken up in this study is an integrated and conceptually comprehensive tool for economic analysis (Olson and Kahkonen 2000). This book uses the concept of institutions proposed by North (1990), Williamson (2000) and others, which sees institutions as the 'rules of the game' in society and includes unwritten informal rules or culture, formal written rules, and enforcement mechanisms. Institutions play critical roles within an economy, as they profoundly influence the behavioural patterns of its actors: individuals, the business sector and government. In particular, institutions determine the level of transaction costs through processes of negotiation between economic agents, the valuation of goods and services to be exchanged, and enforcement of contracts.[2] For instance, as the world witnessed through the collapse of socialism, institutions help determine economic performance by governing the level of property rights protection and characteristics of the market. Olson (2000) argues convincingly that differences in per capita income across countries are due mainly to differences in the quality of institutions and economic policies.

All this indicates that economic operations are clearly sensitive to changes in institutions.

The institutional approach is openly interdisciplinary, recognizing insights from political science, sociology and anthropology as well as economics. It is also evolutionary rather than attempting to generate all-embracing general theories. Hodgson (1998) points out that the institutional approach enables one to delineate the transition of social, political and economic institutions and to focus on the impacts of institutional transformation on the economy. Understanding the importance of institutions and the appropriateness of the institutional approach to its task, the present study focuses on institutions as one essential factor that helps to determine the overall performance and prospects of the Korean economy.[3] Here the logical loop of the influences of economic operations on institutions is not ignored. Nevertheless, the focus is on the flow of causality from institutional changes to the transition and operations of the Korean economy, to keep the task of analysis manageable.

As North (1990: 110) argues, economic systems are specific to particular constellations of institutional frameworks that vary both over time and across countries. In other words, institutional differences result in differences between economic systems. The Korean economy maintains its *sui generis* characteristics largely because of the nation's idiosyncratic institutional framework. North (1990: 7) also argues that persistence of relative inefficiency in institutions is the source of long-run stagnation of an economy. This book therefore examines the Korean institutional context through the multiple lenses of history, society, culture and politics, and analyses aspects of the Korean economy in this light. In particular the book seeks to explore the primary causes of the current sluggish state of the Korean economy through the dysfunction of institutions.

An extensive survey of English- and Korean-language literature has inspired a set of nine propositions concerning the dynamics of institutional changes and their impacts upon the Korean economy.

1. The external context of the Korean economy has changed remarkably in the recent past, including emergence of the globalization and information era, liberalization of the international financial market and changes in international geopolitics. Profound institutional reforms responding to these external changes and to domestic circumstances from the 1997 financial crisis have become the main force for determining the transition path of the Korean economy.
2. In conjunction with institutional reforms, Korea's economic policy paradigm has been shifted from a state-led industrial economy toward a market-oriented and knowledge-based economy.

3. The shock of the financial crisis and institutional reforms implemented in response in the late 1990s, alongside the process of globalization, has generated changes in Korean society and culture consistent with the neoliberal economic paradigm. Patriotism and loyalty toward authority have faded, individualism has risen at the expense of collectivism, and the work ethic has weakened.
4. Fully fledged, pluralistic political democratization has been developed along with and through institutional reforms in Korea. This has increased the range and extent of activity by political stakeholders, making the political process more complex.
5. Liberalization and internationalization of the Korean economy resulting from institutional reforms have provided a more level playing field for foreign competitors in the Korean market, enhancing the attractiveness of Korea's international business environment to foreign businesses. This has facilitated not only trade in goods and services but also inflows and outflows of foreign direct investment (FDI).
6. Even North Korea, with its tightly controlled economy, has undertaken profound institutional and economic reforms in response to changes in both international geopolitics and domestic circumstances. This development has major implications for the South Korean economy.
7. Institutional reforms have been undertaken across the economy and in particular in the business, financial and public sectors. The operations of each of these sectors have been changed remarkably.
8. Labour market reforms and demographic changes have altered the characteristics of the labour market and improved its flexibility.
9. Remarkable changes in Korean society and culture as well as the economic system have transformed society's view on equity, and the need for equity and for an improved welfare system have become more highly valued and actively sought.

These propositions recur across the following 12 chapters where they are explored carefully. A variety of topics of particular relevance to the Korean economy are explored in these chapters, taking the analytical reach of this book beyond that of most conventional analyses of an economy. This book considers not only traditional topics concerning external relations and individual sectors of the economy but also North Korea's 2002 economic reform, inter-Korean economic relations and the impacts of culture and politics upon the economy.

Using an institutional approach for this study gives rise to the question of how to evaluate institutional reforms, a significant issue given the scope of these reforms and the functional changes they have delivered. Choice of the most appropriate institutions and policy paradigm for national economic policy is predicated on the economic objective that a nation seeks given its perspective of internal and external environments. This study postulates that sustainable and equitable economic development anchored in market principles within a pluralistic political democracy is the Korean people's preferred course for the nation, as reflected by the policies and actions of their fairly elected national government. The question that follows is whether the institutional reforms governments have implemented are adequate and appropriate for achieving such an economic objective. To address this question, the present study undertakes a three-pronged approach.

First, it analyses the internal operations of the organizations that are established to implement institutions. North (1990: 5) observes that organizations are developed in consequence of the institutional framework, and include political, economic, social and educational agencies. He distinguishes between institutions and organizations by using the analogy of the rules of the game and the teams in it, and emphasizes the interaction between institutions and organizations. Certain organizations like regulatory agencies are established to implement and improve institutions. These organizations in turn contain the organizational structure and operational process. Organizational structure includes organizational goals, strategy and governance as well as stakeholders. Operations include processes that enforce and refine institutions through interactions among stakeholders under the prevailing social, political and economic environment. The present study questions whether, in the Korean case, organizational structures are properly constituted in the light of organizational goals and whether these structures function efficiently to meet national policy objectives and the interests and concerns of stakeholders.[4]

Second, the operational outcomes of institutional reforms are evaluated in light of their contributions to achieving reform objectives and other economic policy goals. Even though institutional reforms may be well designed, their implementation may not be effective due to cultural inertia, path-dependence or other unforeseen or poorly appreciated circumstances.

Third, the current state of Korea's institutions is assessed against those of advanced countries. Given that Korea has embraced open market principles under globalization, and seeks to attain advanced economy status, comparative assessment is vital for understanding the Korean institutional framework. To this end, institutional indicators are compared across countries to indicate the performance and relative efficacy of institutions within the Korean economy.

The book has four sections that each take up one of its four interrelated lines of enquiry. The four chapters in Part I explore the evolution of institutions to investigate the impacts of economic policy, culture and politics on macroeconomic development and the economic transition to a knowledge-based economy. Part II comprises three chapters that examine the reforms of institutions related to Korea's external economic relations, with one chapter assessing recent moves to reform the North Korean economy to understand inter-Korean economic relations better. The three chapters in Part III discuss the evolution of institutions related to three important sectors of the economy: business, finance (banking and securities) and the public sector. Part IV, which contains the last two chapters, examines labour and social welfare issues that are closely related to each other through the national objective of achieving equity for its citizens.

In light of the paramount importance of economic policy for Korean development over the last four decades, Chapter 1 opens discussion of Part I with a critical examination of Korea's economic policy from the 1960s to the present, and consideration of possible future directions. This chapter examines why Korea's economic policy was successful for three decades but ultimately underpinned all the causes of the crisis that struck the national economy in 1997. The chapter then critically examines the transition of the national economic policy paradigm after 1997, and proposes a policy framework consistent with the nation's objective of sustainable and equitable economic growth under the emerging policy environments.

Culture, or informal institutions, has an important bearing on the economy not only by directly affecting the behavioural patterns of individual economic actors but also by influencing formal institutions. Chapter 2 explores the role of Korean culture in national economic development and in particular for future prospects of the economy, by focusing on the impact of culture on individuals' economic behaviour. To this end, this chapter introduces the concepts of transaction costs and creative capacity of all citizens as the intermediary between culture and economic development. It then examines the salient aspects of traditional Korean culture and how it has changed in recent times, to consider possible impacts on transaction costs and the nation's creative capacity. In addition, a variety of Korean cultural facets relevant to economic developments are also analysed comparatively, using social indicators developed by well-known international organizations.

The political system in Korea has transformed remarkably in the recent past from the authoritarian regimes of the 1960s and 1970s to a fully fledged democratic system. Chapter 3 examines the impacts of these political systems on the nation's economic development. To this end, a set of evaluation criteria have been developed which include: the establishment of proper institutions to minimize transaction costs and promote competition; and the implementation of national economic policy with a high degree of deliberation of the nation's aggregate social interests, decisiveness, consistency, credibility and a long-term orientation. Although the formal structure of the Korean government now differs only minimally from the politically advanced Western models, the Korean political system maintains some distinctive characteristics, many of which are products of history associated with the nation's idiosyncratic Confucian-influenced culture. This chapter discusses the underlying weakness of Korea's political system as it has evolved, including deficiencies in democratic consolidation and civic culture, and the system's inherent instability resulting largely from the factionalism of political parties and single five-year presidential terms. Ways to address these weaknesses are also suggested.

Chapter 4 assesses Korea's transition to a knowledge-based economy (KBE) as an ineluctable development given recent demographic changes and external developments. It uses the analytical framework proposed by Dahlman and Andersson (2000), which recognizes that successful transition to a KBE involves coordinated and complementary development of four pillars: institutions; human resources; information and communication technology (ICT) infrastructure; and innovation system. The Korean government laid out its strategy and programmes in 2000 to promote a KBE more or less in line with this framework, including programmes to address the digital divide that are intrinsic to nationwide KBE development. This chapter assesses Korea's progress across these four pillars by comparing it with world-leader KBEs and emerging economies in East Asia. It identifies substantial progress but also areas of deficiency.

Chapter 5 takes us to Part II to consider Korea's external economic relations. Features of Korea's trade policy such as trade liberalization, the tariff system and free trade agreements are assessed *vis-à-vis* the key policy objective of sustainable and equitable economic development. The chapter then considers specific aspects of trade policy that require further improvement. One is the underdeveloped trade in services, with the service sector characterized by lack of specialization, weak supply capacity and small-scale operations – the result of domestic regulations and barriers that hinder the entry of domestic as well as foreign companies. Assessment in comparison with other countries helps to identify weaknesses and limitations of the Korean trade regime.

Chapter 6 examines and evaluates the systems and institutions involved in Korea's inward and outward FDI, with focus on the former. The 1997 financial crisis forced the Korean government to recognize the value of inward FDI and to pursue a paradigm shift in national FDI policy from 'restriction and control' to 'promotion and assistance'. Nevertheless, inward FDI in Korea has been waning in recent years while outward FDI has been robust. Despite a spurt of FDI soon after the crisis, Korea's capacity to attract FDI is still low by international comparison. This chapter discusses a variety of causes of the sluggish rate of inward FDI, including the impacts of excessive and opaque regulations, lack of transparency and consistency in FDI policy, labour market inflexibility and turbulent labour–management relations. Global indicators of inward FDI show that Korea ranks relatively poorly *vis-à-vis* emerging East Asian countries. This chapter proposes policy measures to enhance Korea's attractiveness to inward FDI.

Chapter 7 turns to Korea's northern neighbour whose presence as a hostile territory, rather than as part of a unified Korean nation, powerfully influences all aspects of Korean policy and capacity to achieve national goals. This chapter assesses North Korea's economic reform and inter-Korean economic relations. After the bitter experience of economic and social predicaments that resulted largely from institutional failure, the North Korean regime undertook economic reform in 2002 towards decentralizing the tightly planned economy, bringing prices and wages within the market mechanism, establishing private marketplaces, eliminating the rationing system, promoting autonomous enterprise management and pursuing an open-door policy. The regime's reform moves toward co-existence of planned and free market economy are consistent with what the Chinese government calls market socialism, although the North Korean regime disavows this claim. This chapter observes that, although North Korea will encounter serious difficulties in pursuing economic reform and its economy will remain fragile and dysfunctional until nuclear issues are resolved, the regime is highly unlikely to reverse direction back to the pre-2002 system. Further development of North Korea's economic reform and inter-Korean economic relations are mutually intertwined. The high political and economic stakes for both North and South Korea suggest the strong possibility that inter-Korean economic cooperation will expand further. Nevertheless, further nuclear testing in 2009 suggests the North Korean government may continue to surprise and disappoint outsiders whose world-views differ dramatically from those who dominate the North Korean regime.

Chapter 8 opens Part III, which considers individual sectors of the economy. The business sector, which Chapter 8 discusses, has been marked by the dominance of large conglomerates, or *chaebols*, although it has continued to comprise mostly SMEs. In implementing export-led industrialization, successive governments used *chaebols* as a conduit and provided support and protection through incentives and regulations. *Chaebols* expanded and diversified with debt capital to take advantage of these institutionalized privileges, but this practice ultimately led to making them one of the main culprits of the 1997 crisis. In the wake of the crisis, the government has undertaken dramatic reforms of the business sector and eliminated many of the institutionalized privileges previously bestowed on *chaebols*. This chapter evaluates the reform of the corporate sector in terms of corporate governance, financial structure, efficiency and international competitiveness, and considers the mitigation of economic concentration in *chaebols*. Comparative evaluation of the Korean business sector demonstrates that there is still a long way to go before the reforms are completed. This chapter then explores the causes behind the dismal results of corporate sector reform and their possible consequences in the economy. It also explains the relative underdevelopment of SMEs and the implications of this condition for society and for the economy. Finally, the chapter suggests future directions of the policy paradigm for the business sector and for the SME–*chaebol* relationship.

Chapter 9 examines the transition in the Korean financial sector in the wake of the 1997 crisis and suggests ideas for the sector's future agenda with a focus on the banking sector and securities market. The Korean government used the banking sector as a conduit for financing state-led industrialization throughout the high-growth period. It firmly controlled and protected the banking sector without implementing proper prudential supervision, causing moral hazard and a lack of transparency and of accountability in this sector. These flaws and weaknesses contributed to the 1997 crisis and inspired government to respond with drastic structural reforms to liberalize and internationalize the financial sector and liberalize the capital account. This chapter assesses the banking sector reforms in terms of the reforms' objectives, the operational efficacy of organizations involved, and by comparison with counterpart sectors in other countries.

The Korean securities market played only a minor role in financing economic development through the high-growth period and failed to attract foreign capital. In the wake of the 1997 crisis, however, Korean policy planners have recognized the importance of the securities market and have sought to develop it in line with global standards. Chapter 9 considers and assesses the series of post-crisis reforms to the securities market in terms of financial-market sophistication, efficiency, transparency and openness. Evaluation results suggest failure to transform the financial system toward a market-based model, mostly because of failure in the financial investment services industry, which is the weakest area of the Korean securities market. To boost this industry, the Financial Investment Services and Capital Markets Act (FSCMA) was enacted in 2007 and implemented in February 2009. The FSCMA constitutes a drastic and timely reform of the Korean capital market, aligning the Korean financial investment service industry with counterparts in economically advanced countries. This chapter also suggests ways to improve the efficiency of organizations involved in implementation of the FSCMA.

Chapter 10 turns to the public sector and examines in particular the reforms of public administration undertaken in response to the 1997 crisis. It assesses these reforms, using assessment criteria of effectiveness, efficiency, predictability and transparency. This chapter also considers the far-reaching regulatory reforms that were introduced to align the nation's regulatory system with WTO and OECD frameworks. Rather than examining individual regulations, it assesses the regulatory reform management in comparison with counterparts in economically advanced countries. It then assesses the operational efficacy of the organizations involved in the reform management. The Kim Dae-jung government established a permanent regulatory reform organization – the Regulatory Reform Committee (RRC) – as well as reform mechanisms such as Regulatory Impact Analysis (RIA) for systematically analysing and communicating the impact of new and existing regulations, and the use of sunset clauses to address ongoing scrutiny and review processes. This chapter identifies strengths and weaknesses in the regulatory management system and proposes suggestions for improvement, particularly in the operational efficacy of the RRC.

Chapter 11 opens Part IV which discusses the two closely related subjects, labour and welfare. This chapter presents a critical examination of the serious challenges that Korea faces in its labour force and industrial relations. The labour force has remained stagnant due to slow growth and the rapid ageing of the Korean population, and there is a significant mismatch between job-seekers' preferences and employment demand. The structural changes entailed in liberalizing the economy have weakened capacity for job creation and signal the emergence of a 'jobless growth' economy. Chapter 11 explores ways to address these issues.

Industrial relations have been dramatically transformed since the 1997 crisis, yet remain one of the most contentious and critical issues in Korea. Internationally, Korea is seen to have one of the world's worst circumstances in both labour regulation and industrial relations, as comparative data attest. The Korean style of industrial relations management produces hostile employment relations, relatively higher wage levels than neighbouring competitor nations, and a duality in the labour market between regular and non-regular workers, all of which raise critical social and economic issues in Korea. This chapter investigates the underlying causes of these issues and proposes ways to address them. These suggestions are by nature socially contentious and controversial, and so require strong political leadership and the skills to build up social consensus. The suggestions include ways to improve the operational efficacy of the nation's three organizations that play important roles in industrial relations management.

Chapter 12, the final chapter, evaluates the Korean social welfare system. Introduced in the wake of the 1997 crisis, the system is intended to mitigate the most pernicious aspects of the market-based economy under globalization: persistent poverty of certain groups of people, and rising income inequality. Successive Korean governments implemented the 'growth-first' strategy up to the 1980s and paid little attention to income distribution and social welfare. Nevertheless, income distribution in Korea was among the most equitable in the developing world, and no serious social concerns were raised about the welfare system until the 1997 crisis. However, the crisis and the reforms that governments implemented in response to it have profoundly transformed income distribution and social welfare issues, rapidly exacerbating income polarization and generating an upsurge in the demand for welfare provision by the state. Korea's social welfare system has been transformed so that its framework and types of welfare programmes now differ little from those of Western advanced countries. Nevertheless, the Korean welfare system today still suffers from serious shortcomings, which are reflected in worsening economic polarization, rising poverty rates and an emerging cycle of transgenerational poverty. If left unchecked, these will adversely affect political and social stability as well as the strength of the national economy. This chapter therefore explores ways to tackle these challenges, including measures to improve the operational efficacy of organizations involved in Korea's welfare system.

Overall, the analysis in this book weaves together a rich array of topics considered across the 12 chapters to present an informative and comprehensive picture of the Korean economy in transition. Its institutional approach for this analysis enables examination of both informal (cultural) and formal institutions, while focusing on the flow of causality from institutional changes to the transition of the national economy. This applies to the treatment of many topics discussed throughout this book. The choice of topics most pertinent to this discussion has been guided by the nature and magnitude of the institutional transformation in the Korean economy in the wake of the 1997 financial crisis. The concerns and themes taken up across the 12 chapters provide the underpinnings for continuity across the volume, although each chapter can also be read independently.

This book is shaped by the author's keen awareness of the unremitting nature of globalization and its impact on national economies worldwide. Some observers may argue that the globalization process will precipitate further changes in the Korean economy that keep it on a path of convergence with other national economies. However, this book maintains that the distinctive nature of Korean culture and institutional frameworks will continue to preserve the *sui generis* characteristics of the Korean economy. Like all nations, Korea has been shaped on all fronts by unique experiences. For Korea's economic performance, these include in recent times the tumultuous financial crisis and swift recovery from it, and sweeping institutional reforms in pursuit of a free market economy. These striking developments make knowledge of the transition of the economy as well as its miraculous success story particularly valuable for those seeking to understand recent developments in the Korean economy. This knowledge is also valuable for informing policy-making in any country, from a conceptual and a practical basis.

NOTES

1. For a further exposition of this argument, see Chapter 1 of this book.
2. North (1993) cites an empirical study which found that 45 per cent of US gross national product (GNP) in 1970 was devoted to transaction costs.
3. It is of course acknowledged that economic development is a complex phenomenon shaped by multiple factors.
4. This is an analytical approach proposed by Ostrom (2005) who proposes the 'action arena' as a core unit of institutional analysis. The action arena includes 'action situations' and 'participants'. An action situation refers to the social space where participants interact, exchange goods and services and solve problems under circumstances shaped by exogenous variables including attributes of the society, rules and material conditions. Through interactions within the action arena, outcomes are generated, which are in turn evaluated in light of the exogenous variables.

REFERENCES

Bank of Korea (2005), 'Decline in Korea's potential growth: causes and prospects', *Monthly Bulletin*, September, 23–58.

Dahlman, Carl and Thomas Andersson (2000), *Korea and the Knowledge-Based Economy: making the transition*, Paris, France and Washington, DC, USA: OECD/World Bank Institute.

Harvie, C. and H.H. Lee (2004), 'Towards a new economic development model for Korea', in C. Harvie, H.H. Lee and J.G. Oh (eds), *The Korean Economy: post-crisis policies, issues and prospects*, Cheltenham, UK and Northampton, MA, USA: Edward Elgar Publishing, pp. 286–318.

Hodgson, Geoffrey M. (1998), 'The approach of institutional economics', *Journal of Economic Literature*, **36** (1), 166–92.

Korea National Statistical Office (KNSO) (various years), *Korea Statistical Yearbook*, Seoul: KNSO.

Kwon, O. Yul (1997), 'Korean economic developments and prospects', *Asian-Pacific Economic Literature*, **11** (2), 15–39.

Kwon, O. Yul (1998), 'The Korean financial crisis: diagnosis, remedies and prospects', *Journal of the Asia Pacific Economy*, **3** (3), 331–57.

Kwon, O. Yul (2005), 'A cultural analysis of South Korea's economic prospects', *Global Economic Review*, **34** (2), 213–31.

Kwon, O. Yul (2007), 'South Korea', in A. Chowdhury and I. Islam (eds), *Handbook on the Northeast and Southeast Asian Economies*, Cheltenham, UK and Northampton, MA, USA: Edward Elgar Publishing, pp. 42–60.

Lee, Jaymin (2003), 'Economic crisis and structural reform in Korea', in C.H. Sohn (ed.), *Structural Reforms and Economic Development*, Seoul: Korea Development Economic Association, pp. 35–64.

North, Douglass C. (1990), *Institutions, Institutional Change and Economic Performance*, Cambridge: Cambridge University Press.

North, Douglass C. (1993) 'Economic performance through time', Douglass C. North – Prize Lecture, http://nobelprize.org/nobel_prizes/economics/laureates/1993/north-lecture.html.

OECD (2004), *OECD Economic Surveys: Korea*, Paris: OECD.

OECD (2005), *OECD Economic Surveys: Korea*, Paris: OECD.

OECD (2007), *OECD Economic Surveys: Korea*, Paris: OECD.

Olson, Mancur (2000), 'Big bills left on the sidewalk: why some nations are rich, and others poor', in M. Olson and S. Kahkonen (eds), *A Not-So-Dismal Science: a broad view of economies and societies*, Oxford: Oxford University Press, pp. 37–60.

Olson, M. and S. Kahkonen (2000), 'Introduction: the broader view', in M. Olson and S. Kahkonen (eds), *A Not-So-Dismal Science: a broader view of economies and societies*, Oxford: Oxford University Press, pp. 1–36.

Ostrom, E. (2005), *Understanding Institutional Diversity*, Princeton, NJ: Princeton University Press, pp. 3–31.

Park, Jung Gu (2003), 'Potential growth engines of Korea', mimeograph, presented at the International Conference on Growth Engines of Korea, July, Seoul, Korea.

Park, W.A. and C.G. Huh (2004), *Estimates and Prospects of Korea's Potential Growth Rates*, Seoul: Korea Economic Research Institute.

Pazarbasioglu, C., M. Goswami and J. Ree (2007), 'The changing face of investors', *Finance and Development*, **44** (1), 28–31.

Williamson, Oliver E. (2000), 'The new institutional economics: taking stock, looking ahead', *Journal of Economic Literature*, **38**, 595–613.

PART I

Evolution of institutions and the economy

1. Korea's economic policy in transition: evolution, assessment and future direction

1.1 INTRODUCTION

Korea's economic policy has attracted international attention due to the country's well-documented economic transformation from one of the world's poorest countries to one of the richest between 1963 and 1996. Despite a lack of natural resources, a high population density, severe wartime devastation and heavy defence expenditures, economic growth averaged 8.7 per cent per annum over the 1963–96 period. Per capita GDP, just $100 in 1963, had increased to $12 197 by 1996. Nominal GDP increased from $2.3 billion in 1963 to $557 billion in 1996, establishing Korea as the world's 11th-largest economy (Tables 1.1 and 1.2). In 1996, Korea became the 29th member of the OECD.

Korea's economic miracle ended abruptly in November 1997 during the Asian financial crisis. In 1998 negative growth reached 6.7 per cent while unemployment jumped to 6.8 per cent from 2.6 per cent in 1997. However, unlike other economies affected by the crisis, Korea recovered quickly with 10.7 per cent growth in 1999, followed by an 8.5 per cent growth rate in 2000 (Table 1.1). Once again, Korea's economic performance stimulated broad international discussion, this time as a model for overcoming financial crisis. Over the following six year period, 2001–07, however, this spectacular growth slowed considerably with an average annual growth rate of 4.7 per cent (Table 1.1). Potential economic growth is estimated to be around 4–5 per cent per year over the next ten years (Park and Huh 2004; Bank of Korea 2005a), leading people from all walks of life in Korea to be concerned with the national economy.[1] Over the course of the nation's post-war economic development, no one would repudiate the Korean government's pivotal role in the prodigious growth, the developments through the financial crisis, and the ensuing process of economic restructuring.[2]

Table 1.1 Korea's major economic indicators, 1963–2007

	1963	1970	1980	1990	1996	1997	2000	2003	2004	2005	2006	2007
Population (mill.)	27	32	38	43	46	46	47.0	47.9	48.0	48.1	48.3	48.5
Annual population growth	2.82	2.21	1.57	0.99	0.96	0.94	0.83	0.49	0.49	0.44	0.33	0.33
GDP per capita (US$)	100	250	1673	6151	12 197	11 237	10 888	12 707	14 144	16 306	18 373	20 015
GDP (US$ bill.)	2.3	8	64	264	557	516	512	608	680	787	887	970
GDP growth rate (%)	9.1	7.5	–1.5	9.2	7.0	4.7	8.5	3.1	4.6	4.0	5.1	5.0
Gross saving rate (%)	14.4	17.8	24.7	37.5	35.5	35.5	33.7	32.8	34.9	33.0	31.4	30.6
Gross investment rate (%)	18.1	24.8	31.9	37.4	39.0	36.1	31.1	30.1	30.3	30.2	29.9	29.4
Share of GDP (%)												
Agriculture	43.5	26.5	14.9	8.5	5.8	5.4	4.9	3.6	3.3	3.3	3.2	3.0
Manufacturing	11.6	22.7	29.8	29.6	28.9	26.8	29.8	26.9	25.8	28.8	28.2	28.3
Services	44.9	50.8	55.3	61.9	65.3	67.8	65.3	69.5	70.9	67.9	68.6	68.7
Share of employment (%)												
Agriculture	63.1	50.4	34.0	17.9	11.7	10.8	10.6	8.8	8.1	7.9	7.7	7.4
Manufacturing	8.7	14.3	22.5	27.6	22.6	21.5	20.4	19.1	19.1	18.6	18.0	17.6
Services	28.3	35.3	43.5	54.5	65.7	67.7	68.0	72.1	72.8	73.5	74.2	75.0
Employment (mill.)	7.7	9.6	13.7	18.1	20.9	21.2	21.2	22.1	22.6	22.9	23.2	23.4
Unemployment rate (%)	8.2	4.4	5.2	2.4	2.0	2.6	4.4	3.6	3.7	3.7	3.5	3.2
Inflation rate (%)	20.2	12.8	28.7	8.6	4.9	4.4	2.3	3.5	3.6	2.8	2.2	2.5
Exchange rate (won/US$)	130	317	660	716	844	1415	1260	1198	1044	1013	930	938
Exports (US$ bill.)	0.09	0.8	17.5	65.0	130	136	173	194	254	284	332	371
Imports (US$ bill.)	0.50	2.0	22.3	69.8	150	145	160	179	224	261	302	357
Trade balance	–.41	–1.2	–4.8	–2.0	–20	–9	+17	+15	+30	+23	+30	+14
Exports/GDP (%)	3.9	13.6	32.1	28.6	30.3	26.4	33.7	31.9	37.4	36.1	37.4	38.2
Imports/GDP (%)	16.1	23.8	40.0	29.0	32.6	28.1	31.3	29.4	32.9	33.2	34.0	36.8

Sources: KNSO (2002, various years).

Table 1.2 Trend of the Korean economy

	1963–69	1970–79	1980–89	1990–99	1963–96	1963–2007	2001–2007
Average annual growth rate (%)	9.8	9.7	8.3	6.2	8.7	7.7	4.7
Gross saving rate (%)	16.2	22.3	31.1	35.2	26.4	27.7	32.2
Gross investment rate (%)	19.8	27.9	30.5	34.5	28.9	28.5	29.8
Unemployment rate (%)	6.6	4.0	3.8	3.2	4.1	4.1	3.5
Inflation rate (%)	14.5	15.3	8.4	5.7	11.3	9.2	3.1
Population growth (%)	2.56	1.75	1.24	0.94	1.61	1.35	0.4
Productivity (%)[a]	n.a	8.9[b]	5.2[c]	4.7	5.0[d]	4.6[e]	4.1

Notes:
[a] Labour productivity is measured as the index of constant value-added (net output) divided by the index of labour man-hour input.
[b] Indicates value for 1971–79.
[c] For 1983–89.
[d] For 1983–96.
[e] For 1983–2007.

Sources: KNSO (2002, various years); Bank of Korea (2008a, 2008b); for productivity for 1983–2007: KLI (2008); for productivity for 1971–79: Korea Productivity Center (2008).

This chapter critically examines the transition in Korea's economic policy paradigm over this period, with particular attention to the period since the financial crisis. Here several questions beg special attention. Why did Korean economic policy work well over the three decades of economic success? Why did the economic policy that worked well in the past fail suddenly in 1997, resulting in the financial crisis that briefly crippled Korea's economy? How has the Korean policy paradigm changed since the financial crisis? These questions have drawn some critical examination by observers but they have not been taken up systematically and comprehensively. The specific purposes of this chapter are therefore:

1. to examine the policy paradigm during the period of national economic success (1963–96);
2. to relate the failure of economic policy to the causes of the financial crisis;
3. to examine and appraise the transition of the economic policy paradigm in conjunction with the crisis; and
4. to propose a future agenda and direction for Korean economic policy.

1.2 THE KOREAN ECONOMIC POLICY PARADIGM PRIOR TO THE 1997 FINANCIAL CRISIS

1.2.1 Extensive State Intervention in the Economy

Although Korea adopted capitalism and the market system from the inception of the Republic in 1948, there is a general consensus that the nation maintained a state-led economy during the period of economic success (1962–96). Evidence of state intervention in the economy can be found in every field of economic activity throughout that period (Kwon 1998). Since 1962, economic activities were geared to achieving targets set down in consecutive five-year economic plans, with the economy held under the firm control and extensive intervention of the central government. The underlying thrust of Korea's economic policies and the accompanying plethora of regulations was maximum economic growth, although state directives went through different stages as the economy developed. During the 1960s, the Park regime (1961–79) sought to achieve maximum economic growth through export-led industrialization by developing light, labour-intensive industries. This was the genesis of industrial policy that successive governments implemented as an integral part of Korea's maximum growth policy. The outward-looking development strategy was aimed at overcoming Korea's lack of natural resources and small domestic market. During the 1970s, still under the Park regime, Korea carried out industrial policy to promote heavy and chemical industries (steel, petrochemicals, metals, shipbuilding, electronics and machinery).

In the early 1980s, the Chun Doo-hwan regime (1980–88) introduced structural adjustments and comprehensive stabilization measures as the nation's main policy direction. The new policies were less industry-specific and followed an economic liberalization policy based on a private sector-guided, market-rational economic system. Concurrently, under mounting pressure from trade partners, more serious moves towards trade liberalization were made during the mid-1980s. In the late 1980s, the Roh Tae Woo regime (1988–93) pursued democratization, ending more than three decades of authoritarian rule. The political transition imposed tremendous economic adjustment costs on the country. Labour disputes, which the authoritarian regimes suppressed while pursuing maximum economic growth and political stability, became rampant and violent, and wages rose far in excess of productivity growth. During this adjustment process, the Korean economy lost part of its economic growth vitality and international competitiveness. Against this political and economic background, the Y.S. Kim government (1993–98), the first civilian administration in three decades, was launched under the banner of a 'New Korea through change and reform' with a focus on 'globalization'. This implied further liberalization and internationalization of the economy. One result of these efforts was that Korea was admitted to the OECD as its 29th member in 1996.

With extensive state intervention as an integral part of development strategy, the government mobilized all possible policy tools which may be classified into incentive schemes and domestic market protection. The former included tax, credit, foreign exchange allowances and interest rate policies, and the latter included trade policy, foreign direct investment (FDI) policy as well as other forms of intervention and regulation. Among the incentive schemes, the most powerful tool was the allocation of credit at preferential interest rates for specific purposes such as exports and investments in target industries or projects that government had chosen during the 1960s and 1970s.[3] The government protected the domestic producers of strategic manufacturing sectors – including heavy and chemical industries – by erecting high barriers to imports through regulations, tariffs and non-tariff barriers. It also used a licensing procedure to block the entry of domestic and foreign competitors into target industries.

Government intervened extensively in the labour market until the late 1980s, aiming for maximum generation of employment in line with the maximum growth policy (Kwon 1998). To this end, until the late 1980s anti-competitive institutional arrangements such as minimum wage laws and labour protection laws were not implemented, and organization of unions was prohibited or held back by the state. Labour laws prohibited retrenchment of workers, which was never a serious issue because of the continuous expansion of companies and practices of lifetime employment. Government promoted the rights of management at the expense of labour, suppressing union activities and intervening in labour disputes. Hence, management often relied on the government to resolve labour disputes, instead of developing and practicing appropriate methods of dispute resolution.

1.2.2 Why Was this Strategy Successful?

Economic success under this style of national economic policy involving extensive state intervention raises a critical question: did the intervention contribute to economic development? This question has been discussed extensively in the literature on Korea's economy, with comprehensive surveys by Pack and Westphal (1986), Westphal (1990), Chang (1993), World Bank (1993), Stern et al. (1995) and Cha et al. (1997). However, all of these studies were undertaken before the 1997 financial crisis, and so could not have identified or explained the problems that were generating behind the opaque operation of government, business and banks. We must therefore reassess state intervention in Korea's economic development during the high-growth period in light of the lessons learned from the 1997 financial crisis that forced a dramatic change to economic policy thinking and implementation.

State intervention beyond rectifying neoclassical market failure could be easily justified at the initial stage of Korea's post-war economic development. The market was too small and underdeveloped to function efficiently, and the institutions required for information flow and other aspects of efficient market operation did not exist. Development of the Korean economy required international capital and technology, and overseas financial institutions were unwilling to provide loans to Korea during the 1960s and 1970s without a government guarantee. International markets for technologies were marked by pervasive inequality of bargaining power. These features of underdevelopment, as well as technological externalities and economies of scale, can be held to justify the type and extent of intervention that the government undertook to promote development of the Korean economy.[4]

Not only was the state intervention justified, but it was also highly effective, although its efficacy abated over time. Consecutive authoritarian military regimes maintained the national interest of rapid economic development as their way of legitimizing political power. These authoritarian governments, with presidents at the pivot of authority and policy-makers in tow, managed to maintain political stability through assertive leadership over business, and set up economic policies consistent with rapid economic growth. All this enhanced policy credibility and certainty which in turn stimulated business investment.

From the early stage of Korea's post-war economic development, government established the institutions necessary for economic development and operated them effectively. The powerful Economic Planning Board, established in 1962, was assigned the central economic policy-making role and a broad budgetary authority. Integration of planning and budgeting eliminated possible conflicts of interest among different ministries. The government secured competent economic technocrats through highly competitive civil service examinations and almost every ministry of the government established its own research institution staffed by academics mostly with doctorates from abroad.

A bureaucracy staffed by talented technocrats ensured a high degree of autonomy from political interference under the authoritarian regimes. Shielded by their powerful, prestigious and highly reputable organizations of economic policy-related ministries and affiliated research institutions, and guarded by the respect of society, core technocrats were able to formulate and implement policies in pursuit of national goals. They answered directly to the top regime leaders, maintaining significant independence from the legislature and other sources of political pressure.

Government maintained close and extensive interactions with business, although clearly, government was the assertive leader and the business community was a cooperative follower in implementation of national development policies. Government established a number of deliberation councils under various ministries and for special policy tasks. These councils provided forums for government officials to discuss policy issues with experts from the private sector and academic community, and to exchange views and information. As such, the councils facilitated two-way transmission of information between the government and the private sector. Experts from the private sector and academic community monitored both government and business members in the councils, thereby restraining self-interested behaviour.

The international environment was also conducive to the Korean economic strategy of state intervention at this time. Strategic location enabled Korea to play an important role for the Western allies in the Cold War. The national economy was relatively small and underdeveloped until the mid-1980s, so the export-led economic development strategy coupled with protection of domestic industries did not raise serious ire from advanced countries. This enabled Korean products to penetrate further into advanced economies without resistance, facilitating the success of Korea's export-led industrialization strategy.

Another factor conducive to state intervention was the strong nationalism and zeal for economic prosperity that prevailed in Korean society. This generated a powerful incentive for the citizenry to give high priority to the nation's economic growth. With growth as the overriding objective, the predatory behaviour of state officials and businesspeople for their own self-interest was not a serious issue. It is therefore reasonable to draw a conclusion that under the internal and external policy environments, economic policy and its implementation mechanism reflecting extensive state intervention were all conducive to Korea's rapid economic development over the three decades to the end of the 1980s.[5]

1.3 STATE INTERVENTION AS THE MAJOR CAUSE OF THE FINANCIAL CRISIS

The effectiveness of state intervention in any national economy is shaped powerfully by external and domestic environments and the institutions at work within them. After the Cold War, Korea no longer received preferential trade treatment by advanced Western countries. Under the rising globalization with increasing economic integration and competition, protection of the Korean domestic market and industries by state intervention has become increasingly difficult. Domestically, the organizational capabilities prevalent under the authoritarian regimes have declined. Swift democratization has produced significant change in both the political and economic landscapes. Politically, after the decades of stable but authoritarian rule, democratic regimes with presidents for only single five-year terms have been relatively unstable and less credible than their forerunners. Government has lost its hold on strong policy direction, which is no longer sanctioned by the society at large. Expansion of the size and importance of the business sector has swung the balance in the government–business relationship sharply toward business. The government has lost its advantage over the business sector in collecting and understanding the information required to pursue appropriate economic strategy under the emerging globalization and information era. These changes in government–business relations have rendered government control over the private sector less effective than in the high-growth period. Concomitant democratization of the labour market has led to an increase in labour disputes, but state intervention in the labour market has become politically impossible.

Not only has state intervention lost its efficacy over time, but it also sowed the seed of the 1997 financial crisis in Korea. The causes of the Korean financial crisis, which have been extensively investigated in the literature (Cha 2001; Jwa and Yi 2001; Kwon 1998; J.W. Lee 2004), include:

1. excessive expansion and diversification of *chaebols* by debt capital;
2. an inefficient financial sector afflicted with moral hazard;
3. a lack of transparency in business operation;
4. low productivity and loss of international competitiveness; and
5. rigid labour market practices.

The fundamental factor underpinning each of these causes was state intervention and the attendant economic policies.

Korea has developed a distinctive government–business relation from its export promotion and industrial policy. The government nourished a limited number of *chaebols* with which to pursue its economic development strategy by providing a variety of incentives, protection and institutionalized privileges. These privileges included cross-subsidiary loan guarantees, cross-subsidiary ownership, prevention of takeover by means of hostile M&As by domestic and foreign firms and a lopsided corporate governance system in favour of the majority shareholders.[6] This process brought about collusion between the government and *chaebols*, and generated a perception that *chaebols* were 'too important and too big to fail', or that they would be 'bailed out by the government if needed'.[7] Taking advantage of these privileges and government protection against not only potential domestic and international competitors but also minority shareholders, *chaebols* expanded and diversified excessively. In doing so, they relied on debt capital because of perceived low risk together with readily available loans at preferential interest rates. This was reflected in the high debt–equity ratio of 519 per cent held by the top 30 *chaebols* in 1997 (Joh 2001). It thus follows that collusion with the government and the lopsided corporate governance system has led to a lack of transparency and accountability in the operation of *chaebols*.

The unhealthy structure and financial weaknesses rendered *chaebols* vulnerable to a financial crisis. In 1997, a number of the major *chaebols* became insolvent because of their excessive expansion and diversification with debt capital together with their operational inefficiency.[8] By allowing a few *chaebols* to become bankrupt, the government signalled a message that it would no longer bail out large companies, causing their creditworthiness to crumble. These bankrupt companies eventually dumped their non-performing debt on domestic financial institutions, thereby weakening the already weak financial system. This was part of the genesis of the financial crisis.

The lack of transparency and accountability of financial institutions were among the major causes of the 1997 financial crisis and were attributable to Korea's particular style of government intervention. To control credit allocation in line with the requirements of national industrial policy, government controlled and protected financial institutions as the most influential owner of them as well as their legitimate regulator. From the 1960s until the mid-1980s, the government was the major shareholder in a number of banks and intervened extensively in bank management, including the appointment of managers. It was therefore the government, not the banks, which decided credit allocation. The government imposed measures to protect the financial sector from domestic and international competition, thereby safeguarding the financial sector. *Chaebols* were prohibited from being controlling shareholders of commercial banks. Thus, the ownership of banks was widely diversified, and minority shareholders had little power in terms of management of banks. Since banks were accountable to no one but their political masters, bank operations lacked transparency and accountability. The perception that 'banks will never fail' held firmly because of government protection, which generated moral hazard.

Banking regulation and supervision was fragmented and inefficient over a long period of time. As part of financial policy, a strict separation was maintained between financial industries (commercial banks, securities firms, and insurance companies) until the early 1990s. Regulation and supervision of each of these sectors was separated. As a result, proper supervision and coordinated prudential regulations for the financial sector did not develop. Under these circumstances, Korea started to liberalize and internationalize the financial market in 1994, allowing banks to access the international capital market. The lack of prudential regulation of banks enabled them to borrow excessively from offshore financial markets in the face of domestic interest rates substantially higher than those in the international market and the insatiable demands for funds from *chaebols*.

Korean financial institutions relied heavily on short-term borrowings from abroad rather than long-term funds, because of lower interest rates for short-term foreign loans and the prevailing perception of low risk under government protection. In the presence of mounting short-term foreign debt, foreign reserves held by the Bank of Korea dwindled quickly to $7.3 billion in November 1997 (Kwon 1998). Besides this, the Korean currency was held at an artificially high rate from 1988 by state intervention in the foreign exchange market (Kwon 1998). The Korean financial situation was therefore certainly ripe for speculative financial attack.

Government intervention led to a loss of efficiency and international competitiveness in the Korean economy. With government repression of the labour market until the late 1980s, the flexibility of this market declined, and approaches to labour management through conciliation did not develop. Democratization of the labour market at the end of the 1980s brought about widespread and militant union activities that raised labour costs rapidly. Here a paradox of domestic market protection had materialized. Although government intervention and protection contributed to the rapid growth of industries and banks until the end of the 1980s, they ended up depriving *chaebols* and banks of the imperative to make their operations internationally competitive. In the face of globalization forcing open national markets worldwide, Korea's loss of national competitiveness became key causes of the 1997 financial crisis.

Another important cause of the financial crisis was the government's failure to take appropriate action in advance in response to the emerging changes in the domestic and international environments for several years. Instead the government maintained a policy of extensive intervention in the economy, particularly through a slew of regulations over business and banks, indicating the structural and institutional dysfunction of the policy process.

Several conclusions concerning Korea's policy apparatus can be drawn from the financial crisis that struck the Korean economy in November 1997. First, the Korean government did not recognize that state intervention and attendant policies and regulations would make the national economy so vulnerable to the financial crisis. Second, it did not introduce appropriate measures in time to stem the financial crisis in the presence of numerous emerging symptoms and evidence in Southeast Asia. The actual financial crisis in November 1997 and the ensuing enormous economic damage have made the country understand the multiplying problem of moral hazard, political cronyism and the resulting institutional and structural dysfunction behind the facade of rapid growth under the old policy process. This has led the country to realise the necessity to shift the policy paradigm. This recognition was reinforced through IMF conditionality to secure a rescue package that required replacement of the old state-led paradigm with a new paradigm foregrounding the notion of free market.

1.4 TRANSITION IN THE ECONOMIC POLICY PARADIGM

1.4.1 Transition of Policy Environments

It was demonstrated that the main reason for the 1997 financial crisis was extensive state intervention in the economy and its attendant economic policies and regulations. By the mid-1990s, domestic and international economic policy environments had changed remarkably. As the Cold War ended, international pressure prevented Korea from continuing to protect domestic markets. Korea, as a signatory of the WTO and a member of the OECD, has embraced the emergence of the globalization and information era and the international capital market, leading its economy to be market-based. Rapid development of neighbouring economies in East Asia, particularly China, has narrowed Korea's economic lead. A remarkable demographic change has also occurred in Korea, with the population ageing quickly and its growth rate declining. These conditions in the national and international environment have promoted transformation of the Korean economy from industrialization-based to knowledge-based, in pursuit of sustainable development.[9]

The domestic political system has also changed significantly. The earlier authoritarian regimes narrowly served the President, the bureaucracy, National Assembly members and *chaebols*, who played the overwhelming role in economic development strategy. Since the late 1980s, the pluralistic democratic system headed by an elected civilian president also recognizes the general public, including workers, consumers and interest groups, as important political stakeholders. A single five-year presidential term has diminished the pivotal role of the President in formulating the nation's economic policy, and the consistency and certainty of economic policy have in turn declined. The bureaucracy, which had also played a critical role in economic development, has lost credibility and authority since failing to stem the financial crisis.

The Korean economy is in transition from an industry-based to service-based one. As shown in Table 1.1, the agricultural sector as a share of GDP declined from 43.5 per cent to 3 per cent over the period 1963–2007, and the manufacturing sector expanded rapidly at the beginning and stabilized at around 28.3 per cent. In contrast, the service sector increased steadily from 44.9 per cent in 1963 to 68.7 per cent in 2007, bringing the Korean economy closer to the structure of other advanced economies. Enlargement of the service sector could create a drag effect on economic growth because of the sector's low productivity. Both labour productivity and total factor productivity in the service sector were remarkably lower. Through the 1980s and 1990s, labour productivity grew on average by 8.2 per cent per year in the manufacturing sector, but by 2.2 per cent in the service sector (H.J. Kim 2007). The growth rate of total factor productivity in the service sector declined from an annual average of 1.7 per cent in the 1980s to 0.4 per cent in the 1990s, while in the manufacturing sector the rate increased from 3.5 per cent to 5 per cent (H.J. Kim 2007). The levels of labour productivity in the service sectors in the United States and Japan were respectively 2.4 and 1.8 times higher than those of Korea in 2005 (KIEP 2006b: 68). As further examined in Chapter 5, low productivity in the service sector is largely explained by heavy regulation, narrow opening to international competition and lack of appropriate reform. Other contributing factors are lack of specialization and weak domestic supply capacity, particularly for producer services (H.J. Kim 2007).

Another critical challenge for Korea is substantial decline in the economy's growth potential. The Bank of Korea (2005a) estimates the potential rate of economic growth over the period 2005–14 to be 4.6 per cent, with contributions of labour, capital and total factor productivity by 0.8 per cent, 2.1 per cent and 1.7 per cent respectively. This compares with the potential growth rate of 6.1 per cent over the period 1991–2000. This decline in the potential growth rate is explained by declines in inputs of labour and capital and total factor productivity (Bank of Korea 2005a). The decline in labour input potential can be attributed to slow population growth and an ageing population. Capital input potential is expected to decline due to deterioration of the investment environment, as reflected in low national competitiveness or economic freedom indexes as examined later in this chapter. The low contribution of total factor productivity can be explained by a number of factors such as slow development of high-technology and high-value-added products, inefficient financial intermediation, inefficient R&D activities, the poor quality of education for creativity, and rising social conflict among interest groups (Bank of Korea 2005a; KIEP 2006a: 63–71).

After the financial crisis, society and culture have also changed noticeably. A new trend towards liberalism has gradually emerged, patriotism and loyalty toward authority have faded, group orientation is giving way to a trend of individualism, and the strong work ethic has weakened. Under these evolving domestic conditions, and with the more intense market competition globally, the long-standing policy paradigm of extensive state intervention could no longer work; the transition of economic policy from state-led to market-based had become ineluctable. The 1997 financial crisis made the government ready and willing to steer the metamorphosis of paradigm that it now saw as necessary for a new national economic policy. At the height of the crisis, long-time opposition leader Kim Dae-jung was elected President in December 1997 and inaugurated in February 1998. The Kim Dae-jung government steered a shift in policy paradigm and undertook a series of reforms in the economy. President Roh Moo-hyun, from the same political party, was inaugurated in 2003. He refined and reinforced reforms initiated by his immediate processor.

1.4.2 Shift in the Macroeconomic Policy Paradigm

At the request of the Korean government in December 1997, the IMF agreed to provide financial assistance of $58 billion to save the nation from foreign debt default, under strict conditions. The IMF policy package consisted of three components – macroeconomic policy, financial sector restructuring and other structural reform measures. The package was quite consistent with the policy prescription of the Washington Consensus that included market liberalization, macroeconomic stabilization and privatization, seeking to minimize government intervention and promote a market-based economy.[10] Macroeconomic policy was to restrain aggregate demand, maintain a flexible exchange rate without state intervention and build up foreign reserves.

One important facet of the former policy paradigm was protection of domestic market and industries by imposing restrictions on imports, capital flows and FDI. However the IMF reform package required trade and capital account liberalization. The government fulfilled the trade liberalization requirements by the end of 1998 (MOFE 1998). Korea also complied fully with capital account liberalization to increase Korea's access to foreign capital. All controls on capital movements including Koreans' overseas investment and borrowings, incoming FDI and establishment of financial institutions, have been abolished. Foreign exchange transactions were fully liberalized on 1 April 1999 in a move to open the securities market to foreign investors. Foreigners have also been legally allowed to purchase real estate and invest in local bonds and short-term money market instruments without restrictions. These moves constitute a marked shift in the philosophy of the national economic policy paradigm.

1.4.3 Shift in the Policy Paradigm toward Individual Sectors

In accordance with the IMF policy package, restructuring of individual sectors was intended to remedy their structural shortcomings identified in conjunction with the crisis. The financial sector reform was intended to consolidate and strengthen the supervision of all financial institutions, liquidate and restructure insolvent financial institutions, recapitalize viable ones, and liberalize the financial sector. Liberalization of the financial sector allowed competition from abroad and M&As of banks. New financial bills, passed in December 1997, strengthened and consolidated the multiple supervisory functions of the financial sector (including banks, securities, insurance and trust companies) under the new Financial Supervisory Commission (Kwon 1998).[11]

The government closed or suspended non-viable banks and non-bank financial institutions, reducing the number of banks from 33 in 1997 to 18 in 2006 and the number of non-bank financial institutions from 30 to 2 over the same period (Bank of Korea 2006: 63). The remaining domestic banks were recapitalized to obtain the 'sound bank' status with a Bank for International Settlements (BIS) ratio of 11.29 per cent at the end of 2004 (Bank of Korea 2005b). In achieving this, the government provided public funds to purchase non-performing loans through the Korea Asset Management Corporation (KAMCO).

Under the new financial framework, the transparency and accountability of financial institutions has improved through an enhancement in corporate governance and the penetration of foreign capital. Financial institutions are now required not only to have external audits conducted by internationally recognized accounting firms but also to have members of their board of directors selected by shareholders. The financial sector has been opened to foreign capital not just through the almost complete lifting of barriers against foreign investment but also through allowing M&As of financial institutions. As a result, a number of domestic firms have been taken over by foreign investors, marking a watershed in the Korean financial sector. The government has also changed its policy direction from the separation of banks from insurance, securities and trust firms to universal banking. Banks are now permitted to engage in various businesses, such as the securities business, either directly or through their subsidiaries.

Compliance with the IMF rescue package has forced the Korean government to shift markedly its policy toward *chaebols*. The IMF package required reform of *chaebols* in terms of their financial and business structures, corporate governance and opening of the business sector to foreign capital. One of the most significant achievements in *chaebol* reform is the so-called five-point agreement on corporate restructuring reached between the government and *chaebols* in January 1998. The agreement required: mandatory reporting by *chaebols* of consolidated financial statements; eliminating the practice of cross-subsidiary loan guarantees; improving corporate financial structure; focusing on a limited number of core operations; and making majority shareholders and executives more accountable (Kwon 1998).[12]

Chaebols have complied with all the agreed requirements. To improve business structure, the government ordered credit banks to assess the viability of client firms and to distinguish between the viable and non-viable. Non-viable firms were encouraged to exit through refusing new credit and prohibiting financial assistance across affiliate companies. Viable firms were required to formulate their self-rescue (debt work-out) plans together with their credit banks, with government providing some assistance in implementing the plans. The five largest *chaebols*, because of the preponderance of their market share and economic influence, have been coerced into taking part in the so-called 'big deals', which aimed to make the five *chaebols* focus on their core competencies, and to reduce overcapacity in key industrial sectors through mergers and business exchanges among them.

Chaebols now provide consolidated financial statements beginning in fiscal year 1999 and disclose intra-group transactions, detail cross-shareholdings among affiliates, intra-group guarantees and credit rating (Harvie 2004). They have also complied with the requirements of eliminating cross-subsidiary debt guarantees from March 2000 and had reduced their debt–equity ratio to 163 per cent by the end of 2002, as compared to the required 200 per cent by the end of 1999 (J.M. Lee 2003). To make majority shareholders and executives more accountable, the listed companies in *chaebols* now appoint outside directors. Restrictions on the voting rights of institutional investors were removed, while minority shareholders' rights were strengthened by lowering the representation requirement for class action suits from 1 per cent to 0.01 per cent of the total share in May 1998.

Another important shift in the national economic policy paradigm has been carried out in the labour market. The Tripartite Commission comprising labour, government and business representatives was established to comply with requirements for the IMF rescue package and made it possible for the government to revise labour laws in February 1998. The revised laws instituted labour market flexibility for employers by, for the first time in history, allowing employers to lay off employees in the event of urgent management need.[13]

The financial crisis highlighted the shortcomings of Korea's regulatory structures and the inefficiency in public sector operation. It was recognized that, on the one hand, the regulatory regime in the financial sector was inadequate for the prudential supervision of the industry, and on the other hand, regulations for other areas including trade and FDI were excessive, outdated, anti-competitive, or inconsistent with global standards (Yang 2004). Hence, regulatory reform was pursued to remedy the regulatory defects. The government has established permanent regulatory reform institutions and mechanisms such as the Regulatory Reform Committee (RRC), the Regulatory Impact Analysis (RIA), and 'the sunset clause'. By the end of 1998, of the 11 125 regulations in place during the crisis, 5430 (48.8 per cent) had been removed, and 2411 (21.7 per cent) revised (Yang 2004; Jeong et al. 2005). The OECD (2007: 110–12) argues that 90 per cent of Korean standards related to foreign trade were harmonized with their international counterparts by 2005. The government also undertook reforms in the public sector with the objectives of rationalizing state functions to create a smaller, more efficient and customer-oriented government. To this end, the government downsized the public sector significantly. It also introduced structural reorganizations, a new budgeting system, merit-based human resource management, and a new information system. Serious efforts were also made to improve citizens' participation in public administration.[14]

1.5 ASSESSMENT OF THE REFORMS

1.5.1 Internal Assessment

The paradigm of Korean economic policy has shifted from a government-led economy toward a market economy consistent with international standards under globalization. In doing so, a set of reforms have been undertaken in the financial, business (*chaebol*) and public sectors and in the labour market. A critical question arises as to whether these reforms have met their objective to rectify the causes of the financial crisis, to deter future crises and rebuild the country's economic vigour. Here assessment of the reforms is offered on two grounds. One is the reforms' effects on the business environment and the economy inside Korea. The other is comparison of national competitiveness indicators across countries.

The objectives of macroeconomic policy envisaged by the IMF were achieved in a short period, with interest rates lowered below the pre-crisis levels, the exchange rate stabilized under a flexible system without state intervention, and foreign reserves accumulated beyond the agreed level. However, particularly since 2001, concerns have been expressed about the low economic growth rate, stagnant investment and rising income inequality. Over the 2001–07 period, the Korean economy was sluggish with an average growth rate of 4.6 per cent (see Table 1.1), compared to an annual growth rate of 8.7 per cent over the period 1963–96. The gross investment rate was

29.8 per cent which was substantially less than the gross saving rate of 32.2 per cent, while in earlier years the former was generally significantly higher than the latter. Over the same period, labour productivity was also significantly lower, at an annual average growth rate of 4.1 per cent, as compared to 6.5 per cent per year over the 1971–96 period. Both the OECD (2007: 8) and the Bank of Korea (2005a) have noted the recent decline in Korea's growth potential. Recent developments of these macroeconomic variables may indicate that the reforms are either inappropriate or inadequate.

The reforms and in particular the liberalization of the capital market have been quite successful in weakening government intervention in the private sector. Inflow of foreign capital has contributed to both resolving the bad debt problems of *chaebols* and banks and improving these institutions' efficiency. As foreigners gained control of some of the major financial institutions, government found it increasingly difficult to intervene in management of these institutions. Neither could government allocate credits to special sectors of the economy since it had been forced to surrender its power over credit allocation. And as government no longer provided *chaebols* with protection against foreign competitors or takeovers through M&As, *chaebols* became less cooperative with government.

Restructuring of the financial sector has consolidated and strengthened the function of prudential supervision, making it more independent from government. Substantial progress has also been made in increasing the international competitiveness of financial institutions through enhancing their capital viability, efficiency, stability, transparency and accountability. However, the basic approach to restructuring the financial sector reveals a number of shortcomings. Confronting the urgent need to rebuild international financiers' confidence in the Korean financial sector, the government attempted to enforce structural reforms on financial institutions through the familiar means of coercion and intervention, rather than relying on market principles. It forced amalgamation of non-viable banks with seemingly viable ones. In buying non-performing loans from commercial banks, the government in effect nationalized a number of banks. This approach amounts to an encroachment on the autonomy of the financial sector, creating another type of collusion between the government and banks, as well as the problem of moral hazard. For the long-term health of the financial sector and the national economy at large, the government should first have allowed the financial sector to operate under market principles without the intervention that subjected it to moral hazard, as argued in Chapter 9.

Substantial progress has been made in attaining transparency, securing financial soundness and upgrading corporate governance of *chaebols*, and their cross-debt guaranteeing system has been eliminated. However, evidence indicates that the government's approach to the structural reform of *chaebols* has been inappropriate for the overall development of a market economy. The government attempted to enforce structural reforms on *chaebols* not just through guidelines but with threat, coercion and direct intervention, as is evident in the so-called 'big deals'. The requirement of all *chaebols* to reduce to a uniform 200 per cent debt ratio by the end of 1999 was without a clear economic rationale. Decisions about whether or not to stay in an industry and determination of appropriate debt ratios should have been the prerogative of the companies involved, based on their core competence and their appreciation of market discipline. The government should rather have discarded completely the perception of its bail-out and established a framework to achieve a liberalized market by allowing market forces to bring reform. The government's approach to reform through alternative forms of intervention has led *chaebols* to drag their feet in implementing reform measures, and to seek financial and regulatory support from government, which generates further moral hazard.

Although labour relations have improved since the crisis, instability in the labour market is regarded as one of the biggest factors underlying sluggish economic progress in recent years. Park (2007) attributes labour market instability to government intervention in labour disputes and ineffective enforcement of labour laws. Reflecting the instability in labour relations, Korea records the highest number of work days lost in strikes among all OECD members (Park 2007).

The government has taken significant steps toward reducing the regulatory burden on the economy. However, regulatory reform in Korea has, to date, been carried out mostly in terms of quantity rather than quality (Yang 2004; Hlasny 2008). Some Korea observers, including the OECD (2007), identify as a crucial problem for the national economy the excessive regulations that are still in place, their lack of transparency and consistency, and their arbitrary interpretation by front-line government workers. They also identify as problem areas the fragmented implementation of reforms by a multitude of agencies, the existence of regulatory areas outside the RRC, and the lack of both legislated oversight and strong and consistent enforcement (OECD 2007: 35, 66; Hlasny 2008). The lack of market opening and competition in the services and agricultural sectors comes in for particular criticism from the OECD (2007: 38).

The success of the public sector reforms is mixed. Government effectiveness has improved, although Korea's value in this domain remains far below the OECD averages of recent years. Government efficiency has also improved although there was room for improvement. Predictability and consistency have been low mainly because of the continuous introduction of multiple reform programmes with poor coordination. Some evidence of improvement has been identified in citizens' participation in public administration.

1.5.2 Comparative Assessment

A number of organizations regularly provide 'national competitiveness' indicators, which measure the relative status of economic policy and institutions of individual countries. One is the World Economic Forum (WEF) which develops the Global Competitiveness Index (GCI) based on 12 pillars.[15] One of them is the public institution pillar which forms the framework within which private individuals, firms and government interact to generate income and wealth. This includes the required legal framework, government efficiency, and corporate ethics and accountability (WEF 2008: 4). Korea's performance relative to the other 54 to 67 countries studied for the GCI has fluctuated markedly, from 29th in 2000 to 13th in 2008 with an average ranking of 20.6th over the nine-year period 2000–08 (Table 1.3). The WEF indices show that Korea's relatively high rankings in the recent past are due to its technological prowess.

Table 1.3 Korea's ranks in national competitiveness, economic freedom and globalization, 2000–08

	2000	2001	2002	2003	2004	2005	2006	2007	2008
WEF	29	23	21	18	29	17	24	11	13
Public institutions	n.a.	44	32	36	41	42	47	26	28
IMD	29	29	29	37	31	27	32	29	31
Government efficiency	31	28	26	33	32	28	41	31	37
HF	24	25	30	40	35	38	38	36	41
A.T. Kearney	n.a.	31	31	28	32	30	29	35	n.a.
Transparency International	48	42	40	50	47	40	42	43	40

Sources: World Economic Forum (WEF) (various years); International Institute for Management Development (IMD) (various years); Heritage Foundation (HF) (2009); A.T. Kearney/*Foreign Policy* (various years); Transparency International (TI) (2009).

On the public institutions index, which ranks nations on economic policies and regulations, Korea performed quite poorly with its ranking ranging from 47th to 26th over the eight-year period 2001–08 with an average of 37th (Table 1.3). Korea's rank was extremely low by comparison with other industrialized countries, and was comparable with rankings for the former communist states of Eastern Europe. The poor rankings Korea has scored in public institutions clearly indicate that there is still much to be done with economic policy and institutional and structural reforms in order for Korea to reach par with other industrialized countries.

The International Institute for Management Development (IMD) world competitiveness scoreboard is based on four factors: economic performance, government efficiency, business efficiency and infrastructure. Government efficiency, which reflects results of economic policy measures and reforms, assesses public finance, fiscal policy, institutional framework, business legislation and societal framework (IMD 2005: 621).[16] Korea's relative position on the IMD world competitiveness scoreboard for 55 nations also records erratic behaviour ranging from 27th to 32nd over the period 2000–08 with an average of 30.4th (Table 1.3). In 2008 Korea was placed at 31st. While the top-ranking 15 economies on the IMD scoreboard are similar to those on the WEF list, Korea's performance on the IMD scoreboard was much poorer than its performance on the WEF rankings. A number of Korea's neighbours such as China, Taiwan, Malaysia and India all outranked Korea on the IMD scoreboard for 2008. For the government efficiency index, Korea's ranking was worse than the overall IMD scoreboard and at 37th place in 2008 (Table 1.3). These rankings and, in particular, the rankings of public institutions by the WEF and those of government efficiency by the IMD, indicate clearly that there is much room to adjust Korea's economic policy and regulatory regime if a more liberalized market economy is the nation's true aspiration.

A third useful indicator of Korea's economic liberalization is the Heritage Foundation's Index of Economic Freedom (IEF) which regards economic freedom as 'built on a strong rule of law', and as the key to prosperity (Eiras 2004). The Heritage Foundation uses ten determinants to measure economic freedom, ranking 120 countries.[17] Korea's ranking on the IEF has declined markedly in the new century, from 24th in 2000 to 41st in 2008, although fluctuating over time (Table 1.3). Hong Kong and Singapore have consistently ranked 1st and 2nd respectively for the entire period. Of other Asian countries, both Japan (17th) and Taiwan (25th) outranked Korea (41st) in 2008.

The globalization index (A.T. Kearney/*Foreign Policy* 2007) includes a ranking of 62 countries for 14 variables grouped in four brackets: economic integration, personal contact, technological connectivity and political engagement. This reflects the extent of market opening and harmonization with international standards. Korea consistently ranked poorly on the globalization index with an average ranking of 31st over the period 2001–07. Its ranking declined substantially to 35th in 2007 from 28th in 2003 (Table 1.3).

Finally, the annual Corruption Perceptions Index (CPI) by Transparency International (TI) orders countries according to the degree to which corruption is perceived to exist among public officials and politicians. Wilhelm (2002) points out that corruption is highly correlated with the overabundance of regulations or unnecessary restriction of business activities and with real gross domestic product per capita. Corruption may also indicate the lack of transparency and general observance of rules and regulations and of private property protection (Kwon 2008: 163–83). As shown in Table 1.3, Korea performed quite poorly consistently over time with its ranking ranging from 40th to 50th over the period 2000–08. Korea ranked 40th out of 180 countries in 2008, which was remarkably low by comparison with Western advanced countries. All newly industrialized countries in East Asia outperformed Korea with the CPI in 2008. Korea's rank on the CPI indicates the existence of significant room for improvement in rules and regulations related to business activities.

External evaluation through all four of the indexes as discussed above indicates that Korea does not perform well relative to many other nations in terms of economic liberalization and internationalization. It appears that if the Korean government, society and business sector truly aspire to a free market economy with minimal government intervention, further across-the-board reform and/or deeper reform is required to reduce the government's regulatory role in managing the national economy.

1.6 A NEW ECONOMIC POLICY FRAMEWORK

At this juncture, an important question arises as to what types of policy the government should apply from now on. Choice of the most appropriate policy paradigm must be predicated on the vision that a nation attempts to pursue and its internal and external environments. Identifying a social consensus on the most appropriate national vision for Korea is surely a daunting task. Nevertheless, voters' choices at national elections suggest that sustainable and equitable economic development upholding market principles, alongside an open political democracy, are the people's preferred course for the nation. This is consistent with President Kim Dae-jung's proclaimed dual objective of democracy and a market economy (D.J. Kim 1999) and the Roh Moo-hyun government's Vision 2030 (MOFE 2007; OECD 2007: 27).[18] The bitter experience of the 1997 financial crisis and ensuing economic setback, fortified by a strong feeling of economic injustice, have underscored the importance of sustainability and equity in the process of economic development. Also since the onset of the financial crisis and the presidential elections in 1997, it appears that Korean society has taken the market economy, globalization and political democracy for granted.

Under these circumstances, what can and should the government do to achieve the sustainable and equitable economic growth needed to make Korea one of the world's advanced countries in the near future? As Stiglitz (1997, 1998, 1999) has argued cogently, the government should play a role complementary to that of the private sector.[19] Under the new policy paradigm, the government's role should be to guarantee the economic freedom of the private sector and create environments conducive to the development of both a strong, competitive and efficient private sector, and open markets. This requires government to establish a comprehensive and robust regulatory infrastructure that comprises legal and institutional frameworks to safeguard the key success factors for the private sector. Stronger emphasis on equity is also an important consideration.

The government's complementary and facilitator role will need to be constrained as global economic integration advances. Korea resembles other like-minded nations in seeking to benefit from globalization through the greater efficiencies that can be derived from specialization and competition, and from foreign technology and capital. At the same time, management of the domestic economy and maintaining national sovereignty remain vitally important for the nation. Summers (1999) argues that the three goals are incompatible. If Korea wishes to maintain national sovereignty and accept international economic integration, it must accept an entirely free market at the global level, but this requires abandoning the nation's independent regulatory powers over international flows of goods, services and capital.[20] Already it appears that in Korea economic liberalization has progressed beyond the point of no return, and the nation obviously aims to take advantage of the benefits arising from international economic integration. Under these circumstances, Korea has little choice but to align domestic policy with international standards, including those of the WTO and the OECD. This will require openness, transparency and accountability in the policy-making process domestically, and ensuring that policy content is consistent with international standards. The government should also establish standard rules based on market principles consistent with international standards, and impose them fairly and impartially. This requires corporate governance, transparency, accounting systems of the private sector and business and labour laws to meet international standards. All this amounts to reconfiguring the government's relationship with the private sector, with transparent oversight of *chaebols* and banks and with stronger competition between business entities domestically and internationally. The new policy should also seek to improve labour relations and the flexibility of the labour market to meet global standards.

With demographic change domestically, and the rapid rise of Chinese and other neighbouring economies, Korea should aim toward a knowledge-based economy anchored on market principles, in which innovation is the main source of sustainable economic growth. Innovation requires developments in science and technology and advanced human resources. To this end, improvements are required in the education system particularly in tertiary education with emphasis on basic science. The government should upgrade the R&D and innovation system by enhancing collaborative linkages between business, government, academics and foreign counterparts.[21]

Social development programmes should be an integral part of the new policy paradigm. Korea has paid minimum attention to this area over the past four decades of economic success. In particular, social safety nets have not been developed, partly because of the low priority that government has attached to them, but also because cultural heritage favours family members supporting each other during difficult times. The circumstances surrounding equity issues have changed remarkably, particularly since the 1997 financial crisis. The pluralistic democratic system has fully developed, in which social development has become an indispensable political issue. The Korean tradition of supporting each other among family members has faded to a remarkable extent. Long-cherished lifetime employment practices are disappearing as the lay-off system takes root. All this makes it vital that government provides some support for the rising number of people who cannot support themselves.[22]

Equity should be recognized as an important component of social development programmes for efficiency as well as for social and political stability. Not only do social safety nets protect those adversely affected by macroeconomic shocks like the financial crisis, but they also play the so-called built-in stabilizer role against economic fluctuations. Improvement in income distribution enhances social cohesion which in turn increases 'social capital', an important factor for long-term economic development.[23] A basic level of financial security frees people to take risks such as starting a business, investing in their education or trying an unconventional career, all of which contributes to the development of innovation and a knowledge-based economy.

The new Lee Myung-bak government was inaugurated on 25 February 2008, marking the first peaceful return to a conservative government from two preceding liberal governments. Although specific policy measures by the Lee government remain to be transpired, the underlying thrust is to revitalize economic vigour, as expressed in his election campaign. His economic goals were expressed in the so-called '747 Plan', which referred to a 7 per cent annual economic growth rate for a decade to bring per capita GDP up to US$40 000 and make Korea the world's seventh-largest economy. After the election, Lee's new developmental paradigm for Korea includes five strategic-level goals which appear to be consistent with sustainable and equitable economic development upholding market principles, alongside an open political democracy. His priority is on revitalizing the sluggish economy by a strong drive for free trade agreements (FTAs); an aggressive attitude to attracting FDI; an aggressive deregulation of the private sector in addition to privatization of some public entities; promotion of technological innovation; and the establishment of a harmony between economic development and environmental concerns and between markets and the public interest (Jwa 2008). However, before embarking on any of these strategic drives, Lee's economic policies have been overtaken to a large degree by events surrounding the global financial crisis that commenced in the United States in September 2008. Specific characteristics of his economic policy and their critical evaluations therefore remain to be done.

1.7 CONCLUSIONS

National economic policy has been of overriding importance for Korean economic development throughout the post-Korean War years. This chapter has therefore examined why and how the paradigm of this policy has shifted in the wake of the 1997 financial crisis. It has also assessed the reforms carried out in the nation's major economic structures as a result of the paradigm shift. The paradigm of economic policy before the crisis can best be described as extensive and distinctively styled state intervention through implementation of far-reaching industrial policy and consecutive five-year economic plans. Until the late 1980s, this style of state intervention had appeared to work well. It was based on a firmly grounded social consensus upholding a national vision of maximum economic growth and strong organizational capabilities. From the late 1980s, the effectiveness of state intervention was eroded by adverse changes in the internal and external policy environments. Indeed, by the time the financial crisis erupted in Asia in mid-1997, the Korean economy had become highly vulnerable to its own fallout.

This chapter has demonstrated that the style and extent of state intervention was primarily responsible for rendering the private sector vulnerable to the crisis. The government's firm control of the economy and protection of *chaebols* encouraged the conglomerates to expand and diversify excessively with debt capital, without establishing systems to ensure the transparency and accountability of their operations. The nature and extent of state intervention in the financial market led financial institutions to become inefficient, undercapitalized and heavily reliant on short-term foreign borrowings. Government protection of domestic industries from international competition enabled these industries to hold and expand their domestic markets in the short term but over time resulted in their loss of efficiency and competitiveness against foreign companies. Government repression and intervention in labour markets resulted in inefficient labour management and a lack of flexibility. Due to the structural and institutional dysfunction of the policy process, the government failed to take appropriate actions in advance in response to the emerging changes in the domestic and international environments and as a result could not stem the financial crisis as it spread from elsewhere in Asia. It learned from this experience that the paradigm of the nation's post-war economic policy produced short-term success but dismal failure in the longer term.

The consequent shift in policy paradigm from extensive state intervention toward a freer market economy is reflected in the post-crisis programme that has implemented structural reforms of financial institutions, *chaebols*, the labour market, and regulatory systems as required by the IMF rescue package. As this chapter has revealed, the Korean economy is still in transition. Internal and external evaluations of the reforms indicate that the shift in policy paradigm and attendant reforms are incomplete and inadequate. They suggest that further across-the-board reform is required to rebuild the national economy into a strong, stable and durable condition.

An important question was then raised as to what types of policy the government should apply from now on. This chapter has suggested that the government play a complementary role for the private sector under the premise that the basic objective of the nation's economic policy is to pursue sustainable and equitable economic development upholding market principles, alongside an open political democracy. This in turn requires Korea to align domestic policy in consistence with international standards under the emerging globalization which Korea has embraced. In addition, policy emphasis should be placed on the development of a knowledge-based economy.

The examination in this chapter of Korea's economic policy paradigm since the 1960s makes it clear that the policy paradigm of a nation should be changed over time as the vision of the nation changes alongside change in internal and external circumstances. To maintain economic development over time, a nation must be diligent in identifying changes in its policy environments, and adapting its economic policy paradigm to the emerging changes. Otherwise, the nation is placed to experience economic setbacks, as Korea has experienced in the 1997 crisis and beyond. The chapters that follow from here proceed from the discussion in this chapter of Korea's new economic policy framework that the 1997 crisis experience inspired. The following chapters critically examine recent institutional and policy developments in each of the important sectors of the Korean economy and assess them in light of the new policy framework informed by the free-market paradigm.

NOTES

1. For a further detailed examination of the developments of the Korean economy since the 1960s, see Kwon (2008: 13–33)
2. Olson (2000) argues cogently that the great differences in the wealth of nations are due mainly to differences in the quality of their institutions and economic policy.
3. For the extents of subsidies in the form of preferential loans for the promotion of exports and heavy and chemical industries over the 1961–81 period, see Kwon (1997).
4. Similarly, Stiglitz (1997) argues that state intervention contributed strongly to economic growth in the United States during the end of the nineteenth century.
5. Stiglitz (1997, 1999) argues strongly that government intervention has had an enormous effect in promoting the rapid growth in East Asia as well as in Korea.
6. For a detailed analysis of corporate government of *chaebols*, see Chapter 8.
7. There were a number of incidences since 1972 in which the government actually bailed a number of large companies out of financial difficulties, and large-scale bankruptcy was almost non-existent until the 1997 financial crisis (Joh 2001).
8. The excessive investment and diversification by *chaebols* resulted in a 2.2 per cent rate of return on equity capital in 1996 (Lee and Lee 1998).
9. For a comprehensive examination of the transition of the Korean economy to a knowledge-based economy, see Chapter 4.
10. On the Washington Consensus, see Williamson (1999) and Stiglitz (1998).
11. For a comprehensive examination of the financial sector reforms, see Chapter 9.
12. For a further comprehensive analysis of the *chaebol* reforms, see Chapter 8.
13. For a further comprehensive analysis of the reform of the labour market, see Chapter 11.
14. For a further comprehensive examination of the reforms of the public sector and regulatory structure, see Chapter 10.
15. The WEF defines national competitiveness as 'the set of institutions, policies and factors that determine the level of productivity of a country', the key determinant of economic growth (WEF 2008: 3). For the 12 pillars, see WEF (2008: 3–7).
16. The IMD defines the competitiveness of a nation as those 'facts and policies that shape the ability of the nation to create and maintain an environment which in turn sustains more value creation for its enterprises and more prosperity for its people' (IMD 2005: 608–9).
17. The ten determinants include business, trade, labour, fiscal, monetary, investment and financial performance, property rights and freedom from government and corruption (Eiras 2004).
18. The Roh Moo-hyun government announced its Vision 2030 plan in 2006, entitled 'Vision 2030 – Korea: a Hopeful Nation in Harmony'. This plan is a comprehensive long-term strategy to develop Korea to be a fully advanced country by 2030. Specifically, it envisions Korea enjoying a $49 000 per capita income, ranking among the top ten in quality of life, and bolstering social expenditure to 21 per cent of GDP. This compares to per capita income of $18 000 and the lowest quality of life among OECD member countries in 2006, and social expenditure amounting to 8.6 per cent of GDP in 2007 (MOFE 2007: 32–41).
19. There are debates in the literature on what governments should do as they govern under economic situations similar to those surrounding the Korean economy. According to the Washington Consensus, the Korean government has little left to do for the national economy, as it has more or less fulfilled the IMF policy prescriptions of liberalization, privatization and macroeconomic stabilization. However, the World Bank (1993) as well as

Stiglitz (1997, 1998, 1999) argue that the government must maintain an important and complementary role beyond the policy prescriptions of the Washington Consensus.

20. According to Summers's reasoning, if Korea embraces economic integration internationally while maintaining public economic management domestically (taxes, welfare, pension, labour standards and so forth), it will end up forfeiting sovereignty through relinquishing monetary and other regulatory policies), as member countries of the European Community have done. Further, maintaining national sovereignty and public economic management will render Korea unable to benefit fully from international economic integration.
21. For a further detailed analysis of the Korean economic transition to a knowledge-based economy and its assessment, see Chapter 4.
22. For a detailed examination and assessment of the social welfare system, see Chapter 12.
23. For a further examination of the role of social capital for economic development, see Chapter 2.

REFERENCES

A.T. Kearney/*Foreign Policy* (various years), 'Globalisation Index Rankings', *Foreign Policy*.

Bank of Korea (2005a), 'A decline of Korea's potential economic growth: causes and prospects', *Monthly Bulletin*, September, 23–58.

Bank of Korea (2005b), *Financial Stability Report, 2005.4*, April, Seoul: Bank of Korea.

Bank of Korea (2006), *Financial System in Korea*, Seoul: Bank of Korea.

Bank of Korea (2008a), *Annual Report 2008*, Seoul: Bank of Korea.

Bank of Korea (2008b), *Monthly Bulletin*, **4**, April, Seoul: Korea.

Cha, Dong-Se (2001), 'The Korean economy into the new millennium: reform and revival', in O.Y. Kwon and W. Shepherd (eds), *Korea's Economic Prospects: from financial crisis to prosperity*, Cheltenham, UK and Northampton, MA, USA: Edward Elgar Publishing, pp. 39–59.

Cha, Dong-Se, Kwang Suk Kim and D.H. Perkins (eds) (1997), *The Korean Economy 1945–1995: performance and vision for the 21st century*, Seoul: Korea Development Institute.

Chang, Ha-Joon (1993), 'The political economy of industrial policy in Korea', *Cambridge Journal of Economics*, **17** (2), 121–57.

Eiras, Ana Isabel (2004), 'Why economic freedom, not aid, is the answer to poverty', in Marc A. Miles (ed.), *The Road to Prosperity: the 21st century approach to economic development*, Washington, DC: Heritage Books, pp. 29–52.

Harvie, Charles (2004), 'Corporate restructuring in the wake of the financial crisis', in Charles Harvie, Hyun-Hoon Lee and Junggun Oh (eds), *The Korean Economy: post-crisis policies, issues and prospects*, Cheltenham, UK and Northampton, MA, USA: Edward Elgar Publishing, pp. 38–78.

Heritage Foundation (HF) (2009), '2008 Index of Economic Freedom', http://www.heritage.org.

Hlasny, V. (2008), 'Regulatory climate change', *Korea Policy Review*, **4** (1), 55–8.

International Institute for Management Development (IMD) (various years), *World Competitiveness Yearbook*, Lausanne: IMD.

Jeong, Hakyung, Dae-Ki Kim, Kookhyun Kim and Jeff Rinne (2005), 'South Korea', World Bank Administrative and Civil Service Reform Country Reform Summaries, http://www1.worldbank.org/publicsector/civilservice/rsSouthKorea.pdf.

Joh, Sung Wook (2001), 'The Korean corporate sector: crisis and reform', in O.Y. Kwon and W. Shepherd (eds), *Korea's Economic Prospects: from financial crisis to prosperity*, Cheltenham, UK and Northampton, MA, USA: Edward Elgar Publishing, pp. 116–32.

Jwa, Sung-Hee (2008), '"MBnomics": a review and the road ahead', *International Journal of Korean Studies*, **12** (1), 83–100.

Jwa, Sung Hee and Insill Yi (2001), 'Korean financial crisis: evaluation and lessons', in O.Y. Kwon and W. Shepherd (eds), *Korea's Economic Prospects: from financial crisis to prosperity*, Cheltenham, UK and Northampton, MA, USA: Edward Elgar Publishing, pp. 73–98.

Kim, Dae-jung (1999), 'Toward a parallel pursuit of democracy and a market economy', *Economic Bulletin*, **21** (3), 49–54.

Kim, Hyun-Jeong (2007), 'The shift toward the service economy: causes and effects', *Economic Papers*, Bank of Korea, **10** (1), 169–211.

Korea Institute for International Economic Policy (KIEP) (2006a), *Mid & Long-Term Strategies towards an Advanced Trading Economy*, (in Korean), Research Series: 06-01, Seoul: KIEP.

Korea Institute for International Economic Policy (KIEP) (2006b), *Mid & Long-Term Strategies towards an Advanced Trading Economy: open and globalized economy*, (in Korean), Research Series: 06-02, Seoul: KIEP.

Korea Labor Institute (KLI) (2008), *2008 KLI Labor Statistics*, Seoul: KLI.

Korea National Statistical Office (KNSO) (2002), *Major Statistics of Korean Economy 2002.9*, Seoul: KNSO.

Korea National Statistical Office (KNSO) (various years), *Korea Statistical Yearbook*, Seoul: KNSO.

Korea Productivity Centre (2008), *Labor Productivity Statistics*, Seoul: Korea Productivity Centre, www.kpc.or.kr.

Kwon, O.Y. (1998), 'The Korean financial crisis: diagnosis, remedies and prospects', *Journal of the Asia Pacific Economy*, **3** (3), 331–57.

Kwon, O.Y. (2008), *International Business in Korea: the evolution of the market in the globalization era*, Cheltenham, UK and Northampton, MA, USA: Edward Elgar Publishing.

Lee, Jaymin (2003), 'Economic crisis and structural reform in Korea', in C.H. Sohn (ed.), *Structural Reforms and Economic Development: experiences of the Northeast Asia*, Seoul: Korea Institute for International Economic Policy, pp. 35–64.

Lee, Jong-Wha (2004), 'Lessons from the Korean financial crisis', in C. Harvie, H.H. Lee and J.G. Oh (eds), *The Korean Economy: post-crisis policies, issues and prospects*, Cheltenham, UK and Northampton, MA, USA: Edward Elgar Publishing, pp. 11–21.

Lee, Young-Sup and Jong-Uk Lee (1998), 'Was it possible to foretell Korea's currency crisis?', (in Korean), presented at a symposium sponsored by Korea Finance and Economic Research Institute, Seoul, Korea, 14 February 1998.

Ministry of Finance and Economy (MOFE) (1998), 'Policy issues of the month', *Economic Bulletin*, **20** (12), December, 22–7.

Ministry of Finance and Economy (MOFE) (2007), 'Prime Minister welcomes foreign strategies to Korea's future', *Korea Policy Review*, Seoul: MOFE, **3** (2), February, 31–41.

OECD (2007), *Korea: progress in implementing regulatory reform*, Paris: OECD.

Olson, Mancur (2000), 'Big bills left on the sidewalk: why some nations are rich, and others poor', in M. Olson and S. Kahkonen (eds), *A Not-So-Dismal Science: a broad view of economies and societies*, Oxford: Oxford University Press, pp. 37–60.

Pack, Howard and Larry E. Westphal (1986), 'Industrial strategy and technological change', *Journal of Development Economics*, **22**, June, 87–128.

Park, Won-Am and C.G. Huh (2004), *Estimates and Prospects of Korea's Potential Growth Rate*, Seoul: Korea Economic Research Institute.

Park, Yung-chul (2007), '10 years after the financial crisis: What has Korea learned and where is it headed?', *Korea Focus*, **15** (3), 126–37.

Stern, Joseph D., J.H. Kim, D.H. Perkins and J.H. You (1995), *Industrialisation and the State: the Korean heavy and chemical industry drive*, Cambridge, MA: Harvard University Press.

Stiglitz, Joseph (1997), 'The state and development: some new thinking', www.worldbank.org.

Stiglitz, Joseph (1998), 'More instruments and broader goals: moving toward the post-Washington Consensus', www.worldbank.org.

Stiglitz, Joseph (1999), 'Back to basics: policies and strategies for enhanced growth and equity in post-crisis East Asia', www.worldbank.org.

Summers, Lawrence H. (1999), 'Distinguished lecture on economics in government: reflections on managing global integration', *Journal of Economic Perspectives*, **13** (2), 3–17.

Transparency International (TI) (2009), 'Corruption Perceptions Index 2008', www.transparency.org.

Westphal, Larry E. (1990), 'Industrial policy in the export-propelled economy: lessons from South Korea's experience', *Journal of Economic Perspectives*, **4**, Summer, 44–54.

Wilhelm, P.C. (2002), 'International validation of the corruption perceptions index: implications for business ethics and entrepreneurship education', *Journal of Business Ethics*, **35** (3), 177–89.

Williamson, John (1999), 'What Washington means by policy reform', in John Williamson (ed.), *Latin American Adjustment: how much has happened?* Washington, DC: Institute for International Economics, pp. 7–20.

World Bank (1993), *The East Asian Miracle*, Washington, DC: World Bank.

World Economic Forum (WEF) (various years), *The Global Competitiveness Report*, New York: Oxford University Press and Geneva: WEF.

Yang, Junsok (2004), 'Public sector reforms', in Charles Harvie, Hyun-Hoon Lee and Junggun Oh (eds), *The Korean Economy: post-crisis policies, issues and prospects*, Cheltenham, UK and Northampton, MA, USA: Edward Elgar Publishing, pp. 120–42.

2. Cultural effects on the Korean economy

2.1 INTRODUCTION

As the new institutional economics argues, economic performance is shaped by both formal and informal (culture) institutions (North 1993). Culture has important bearings on the economy not only through its direct effects on the behaviours of individual economic actors but also through its effects on the performance of formal institutions. Whitley (1999) argues that culture underpins formal institutions and is the underlying prerequisite for the success of new arrangements of formal institutions.[1] Post-crisis reform of the Korean economy involved embedding new institutional arrangements with formal rules, which are consistent with advanced Western systems. Yet these arrangements need to be underpinned by values and understanding among members of Korean society that enable the arrangements to operate as policy-makers have planned. Since the underlying cultural prerequisite for success of the new arrangements will take some time to develop within Korean society, the absence or still only nascent state of this required cultural underlay may explain the reform's limited success so far, as examined in Chapter 1.[2]

It is thus imperative to explore the role of culture to understand better the nature of economic development in Korea and how recent cultural changes augur for future prospects of the national economy. This chapter takes up that task. It recognizes that economic development is a complex phenomenon jointly determined by a variety of factors including labour, capital, technology, formal institutions and cultural values. Acknowledging the complementarities of these multiple factors, this chapter first investigates the role of culture, before turning in subsequent chapters to other factors that, in a complementary manner, help to determine the operation of the Korean economy.

The culture of a country, as the learned behavioural pattern shared by its people, is moulded by its prevailing religions, geographic surroundings, predominant social and political systems, and language. Korea, a historically isolated country with unique geographic surroundings, and with its own religions and language, has developed a unique culture.[3]

A broad range of recent literature examines the relationship between culture and economic development in general, and in particular, the relationship between Confucian culture and East Asian economic development. However, in the context of the Korean economy, little attention has been paid to the possible impact of culture on economic progress, particularly in the recent past and even more so following the 1997 financial crisis. As Kwon (2005) has observed, although the Confucian model of East Asian economic development has gained popularity among some observers, the model has a number of serious theoretical and methodological problems. Extending the study done by Kwon (2005), this chapter reviews the problems inherent in the Confucian model and offers suggestions to make the model a viable complementary alternative to the mainstream approach to development economics. The suggested model is then employed to analyse the place of culture in Korea's economic performance.

2.2 CULTURE AND ECONOMIC DEVELOPMENT: LITERATURE REVIEW[4]

Conventional economists have traditionally shied away from analysing culture in economic development. Not only is culture an ambiguous term, but it is difficult to analyse in an economic context primarily because of its complexity, the difficulties in quantification, and the ambiguity of causality in the relationship between culture and economic development. Neoclassical economics assumes that all humans are homogeneous rational actors, and that culture does not matter because through competition only the most efficient culture is sustained within a country or across countries. Culture is thus reduced to a matter of *ceteris paribus*.

Other disciplines of the social sciences, and in particular anthropology, recognize not only the existence but also the functionality of culture. However, most anthropologists in general argue for cultural relativism, which denies the possibility of cultural comparison across countries in terms of economic progress. Contrary to the argument of cultural relativism, many social scientists, particularly sociologists and economists, have argued that cultures can be compared and judged against each other to assess which cultures or which aspects of cultures are more conducive to economic development. Max Weber was among the first observers to consider different cultural influences on economic development. In *The Protestant Ethic and the Spirit of Capitalism* (1950), Max Weber argued that the Protestant work ethic was the basis of Western economic development and modernization, and that the absence of this ethic in Asia was the reason for the region's lower level of economic development.

Interest in culture as an explanatory variable for economic development has since ebbed and flowed over time. In the 1940s and 1950s, much attention was paid to culture as a crucial element in understanding societies and explaining economic development (for example, Schumpeter 1951; Lewis 1955). In the 1960s and 1970s, however, work on culture among scholars of economics declined dramatically with the advent of a quantitative approach to economic issues, although one outstanding exception was Myrdal's *Asian Drama* published in 1968. In the 1980s, interest in culture began to re-emerge in response to the economic success of East Asia. Some scholars rejected Weber's proposition and argued that in East Asia's economic development, Confucian values played a role similar to that of the Protestant work ethic in the modernization of the West (Kahn 1979; Tu 1988; Tai 1989; Berger and Hsiao 1990).

Harrison (1985), drawing from his extensive study of economic development in South American countries over two decades, argued that differences in economic development among countries or ethnic groups arise primarily due to cultural differences. Huntington (1998) strongly affirmed the importance of culture as the primary variable for both national development and the conflicts generated among nations. Harrison and Huntington's (2000) collaborative work has deepened the interest in culture and again heightened the importance of culture for economic development. The publication of books by North (1990) and Eggertsson (1990) gave momentum to neo-institutional economics in the academic community from the start of the 1990s. Although institutional economists include culture as an informal component of institutions, they have in general focused on formal institutions, marginalizing the role of cultural values in explaining economic development.

In particular, swift and unprecedented economic success in East Asia, including Korea, inclined some scholars to take a cultural approach to East Asian economic development, recognizing that economically successful East Asian countries share Confucianism as a common cultural and ethical influence. These scholars argue that Confucian culture is the key to East Asian economic success. They point to specific characteristics of Confucian culture, particularly collectivism with strong notions of hierarchy, emphasis on education with focus on developing humanity (moral virtue) rather than technical information or specialized expertise, and secularism in the sense that leading a moral and virtuous life in this world is an end in itself rather than a precondition for life after death (Leys 1997; Ahn 1996).

Most proponents of the Confucian model of economic development consider that the Confucian trait of emphasizing education has contributed to East Asian economic development. However interpretation of other aspects of Confucianism vary. A number of scholars, including Kahn (1979), Tu (1988), Tai (1989), Levy (1992) and Lipsey (1991), consider collectivism as a force for development on the ground that it emphasizes not only harmony and cooperation but also social cohesion, conformity to hierarchy and loyalty. For Kahn (1979) and Holzer (2000), secularism in Confucian-influenced societies helped economic development by encouraging diligence, frugality and compliance with bureaucratic authority. K.C. Lee (1995) contended that emphasis on duty and cooperation and on the self as the centre of the human relationship produces discipline, diligence and thriftiness that can be instrumental in economic development.

As Gong and Jang (1998) have discussed, one of the serious problems of the Confucian model is its tendency to overgeneralize from failing to take into account cultural differences among different national contexts. Morishima (1982) argued that Confucian culture upholds a mix of ethics and values, and the key values emphasized differ among each of the East Asian nations. Further, the basic methodology of the Confucian model is flawed since it fails to demonstrate empirically, and instead simply assumes, causality from culture to economic development. The Confucian model cannot explain convincingly why collectivism is more conducive to economic development than individualism. It lacks a firm empirical basis since it relates culture, which is by nature a micro-psychological phenomenon and changes relatively slowly, to the ever-changing macro processes of economic development. To investigate the role of culture in Korean economic development, we must therefore adjust the Confucian model so that it is conceptually useful for dealing with Korea as a special case.

2.3 CULTURE AND ECONOMIC DEVELOPMENT IN KOREA: LITERATURE REVIEW[5]

Korean scholars in particular argued during the 1980s and 1990s that national culture contributed significantly to economic development over the three decades from the early 1960s (for example, Jones and SaKong 1982; Cho 1994; S.S. Park 1995; Y.H. Kim 1994; Song 2003; K.C. Lee 1995; Koo 1995; Nam 1994). Korean society has a relatively homogeneous culture. Its key characteristics are hierarchical collectivism, patriarchal familism with filial piety as a central virtue, authoritarianism, strong nationalism, status consciousness, secularism, zeal for education, diligence, frugality, self-discipline and a competitive dedication to improving the relative position of self and family (Song 2003; Jones and SaKong 1982; Kweon 2003; Han 2003; Yi 2003; Hahm 2003).

Nam (1994), who served as one of the major architects and managers of Korean economic development during the 1960s and 1970s in the positions of Finance Minister, Deputy Prime Minister (in charge of the Economic Planning Board) and Prime Minister, has identified six principal factors that accounted for Korea's rapid economic development, and four of them are related to culture.[6] Numerous Korean scholars have pointed out a variety of cultural traits that have contributed to economic development. Y.H. Kim (1994) argues for strong nationalism and secularism, while K.C. Lee (1995) points to the emphasis on group harmony and social cohesion. Some observers argue that the Korean management system based on Confucianism contributed to economic development (Chang and Chang 1994; Song 2003). Many scholars argue that perhaps the most important contribution of culture to Korean economic development was its influence, through education, on human capital development (Y.H. Kim 1994). It should be noted that in Korea, Confucianism is an ethical rather than a religious system and it is more flexible and amenable to other cultures than the rigid religious traditions. Yet it should also be pointed out that the Korean Confucian tradition has some cultural traits detrimental to economic development. These include a distinctive form of social stratification; denigration of manual labour, merchants and businessmen; a weak spirit of personal initiative and fatalism (Cho 1994; S.S. Park 1995; Nam 1994; Oh and Kim 2002; Patterson 2002).

Indeed, serious reservations and qualifications have been put forward against the positive contribution of Confucianism to Korean economic development. Some observers have questioned whether and how state intervention could contribute to Korean economic development under the authoritarianism that hierarchical collectivism fostered. As S.S. Park (1995) argued, authoritarianism can be functional for economic development when it maintains law, order and discipline, but dysfunctional when it suppresses creativity. As examined in Chapter 1, even though state intervention initially worked to produce economic development during the 1960s and 1970s, the style of this intervention had burdened the economy in the longer term and contributed to the 1997 crisis. Collectivism has similarly delivered benefit and cost; in promoting group loyalty and cohesion it has been functional, but in nurturing a dependence mentality and suppressing creativity it has been dysfunctional. When the liabilities of Confucianism are taken into account alongside the rewards, the contribution of Confucianism to management efficiency is debatable. Likewise Koreans' educational zeal has led to fierce competition for university entrance examination, but in so doing has emphasized rote learning and stifled development of the critical thinking skills and creative capacity required for success in the globalization era.

If one accepts that Confucianism has made positive contributions to Korean economic development during the 1960s to the 1990s, important questions beg answers. The three with most significance are:

1. Why did cultural elements with positive influence for economic development post-war fail to produce economic development much earlier in Korea's long history?
2. Why did the Korean economy succumb so quickly to the 1997 financial crisis, given that fundamental cultural values had not changed abruptly?
3. What effects will culture have on the future prospects of the Korean economy?

With regard to the first question, S.S. Park (1995) argues that although culture serves as a trigger for economic development, for the flame of Confucian culture to ignite economic development, certain political and economic preconditions must be met, including a free enterprise system, a competitive environment, international trade, appropriate institutions, and a stable and growing middle class.[7] However, Park does not adequately justify the need for the institutional prerequisites to enable culture to trigger economic development. Cho (1994) argues that an inappropriate focus on cultural and social development has fostered undesirable Confucian values such as social stratification and antipathy toward manual labour, merchants and business people. He does not address the process through which the negative cultural traits work against the economy, and contends that these negative Confucian values lose their strengths as the economy develops and a middle class emerges. He leaves unaddressed the role of culture at the initial stage of economic development until the middle class emerges. The arguments by both S.S. Park (1995) and Cho (1994) are not convincing and are almost impossible to test empirically, as is the Confucian model of East Asian economic development.

The second question of the role of culture uses the financial crisis to challenge the validity of cultural factors for explaining economic development in East Asia. Pye (2000) and Perkins (2000) argue that culture works within context, and since the context changed from the early 1990s, the system that worked well with traditional cultural traits could no longer work well under the changed conditions. Within East Asian cultures, economic and business systems based on personal relationships and close government–business relations (or nepotism and cronyism), opaqueness, and ensuing moral hazards in the domestic banking and business systems, could not survive under the liberalization of capital markets. Lee and McNulty (2003) argue that the inflexibility of the labour market, including no lay-offs, lifetime employment and the seniority system that reflected collectivist Confucian values, contributed to weaknesses in Korea's labour and business markets. They claim that in addition to market inflexibility, the mutual support and guarantees promoted by Confucian collectivism, which until the early 1990s formed the basis of the Korean business system, could no longer sustain the earlier economic performance and set off the chain reaction of bankruptcies that spread throughout the economy.[8]

These arguments not only lack empirical basis, but they also raise another troublesome question. If the pre-crisis system established under the traditional culture did not work under the new context, would the new post-crisis system shaped by the economic reforms undertaken after the 1997 crisis work under the existing cultural background? This leads to the third question: how will Korean culture work to shape future economic prospects? Existing models cannot properly address this question because they are methodologically unsound to relate culture as a micro-psychological phenomenon to the macro aspects of economic development. Therefore, a new approach is required for the cultural analysis of economic development. To make a cultural model more operational and able to identify an readily conceivable causality, an operational intermediary should be introduced between culture and economic development. This is, in essence, the model proposed by Harrison (1985), which is discussed in section 2.4.

2.4 A NEW APPROACH TO CULTURAL ANALYSIS OF ECONOMIC DEVELOPMENT: AN INSTITUTIONAL APPROACH[9]

Economic development is a complex process that depends on multiple factors. According to neoclassical economics, the factors of production such as labour and capital are key determinants, assuming technology as given. Yet neoclassical economics assumes the existence of efficient markets with zero transaction costs. In reality, however, efficient markets do not develop spontaneously and they are not free of transaction costs (Olson and Kahkonen 2000). Transaction costs arise through the processes of negotiation between economic agents, valuation of goods and services to be exchanged, and enforcement of contracts (North 1990).[10] The level of transaction costs is an important determinant of how well markets function. Well-functioning markets lead to a high degree of specialization and division of labour in an economy, which in turn leads to a higher level of productivity and economic progress. Therefore, appropriate institutions (both formal and informal) are required for economic development, as institutional economics argues.

Harrison (1985), North (1990) and Fukuyama (1995, 2000) argue that, in static, culture affects transaction costs through its effect on 'social capital', which is rooted in trust within society.[11] Harrison (1985) argued that culture shapes the radius of trust and identification that people experience, which affects the level of transaction costs.[12] A broader radius of trust and identification lowers transaction costs because in such a fiduciary relationship people generally believe that others will play by the rules. Without trust, economic agents choose inferior strategies as in the so-called prisoner's dilemma, which gives rise to higher transaction costs. If trust is limited to family members or to small-group members, the capacity for cooperation and compromise in a society will be weak, which also results in higher transaction costs. Compromise implies acceptance of dissent, which is in turn critical for the effective working of pluralistic systems within a democracy. As the concept of compromise weakens with lack of trust, confrontation is likely to increase, also raising transaction costs.[13]

Another cultural factor identified by Harrison (1985) is the rigour of a society's system of ethics. The extent of public respect for the rule of law is determined by the ethical system, which is in turn a matter of culture. Strong inclination to follow laws and rules reduces enforcement costs. Harrison also argues that the rigour of the ethical system determines the sense of social justice or fairness. If members of a society expect injustice with respect to enforcement of laws, economic and educational opportunities, and income distribution, then cooperation and compromise among members of society are undermined, corruption and nepotism flourish, and self-discipline declines. All of these consequences raise transaction costs.[14]

In dynamics, Harrison (1985) contends that the creative capacity of all citizens is the main source of economic development. Harrison's creative-capacity contention is consistent with understanding in traditional economics of the role of technology and resulting productivity, although his analysis is more comprehensive. Culture affects economic development through its impact on the creative capacity of all citizens. Cultural traits that foster creative capacity are 'future orientation, rationality and equality/authority' (Harrison 1985: 5). The time orientation of a society is also highly important for economic development. If people's major focus is on the future, and the idea of progress is well established in their culture, the notion that planning, savings and investment will be rewarded by increased income and improved living conditions will dominate. If, however, society's major focus is on the past or the present, with minimal regard for the future, then planning, savings and investment are unlikely to be encouraged. Future orientation also implies the possibility of change, including introduction of new technology and the well-known concept of 'creative destruction' of Schumpeter (1951). Time orientation also affects people's attitudes to work and education. People with future orientation are more likely to undertake education and work hard at the expense of present enjoyment of leisure.

It is readily conceivable that rationality and equality contribute to a nation's creative capacity. Rationality encourages the pursuit of scientific discovery. If people are inclined to believe that humans have the capacity to know and understand the world around them, and that scientific methods can solve apparently arcane problems, beliefs and attitudes are likely to link to the ideas of progress and discovery of new technology. If, however, people rely on supernatural forces and belief systems in solving their problems or believe in fatalism or the afterlife, there is little room for reason and education, which hinders progress. People's orientation toward equality is more conducive to economic development than an orientation toward hierarchy and authoritarianism, as equality encourages free competition, mobility and creativity. Harrison (1985) also argues that authoritarianism has negative consequences for the healthy growth of individuals and societies. Authoritarianism may decrease transaction costs through forcing strict adherence to laws and rules, but it suppresses the creativity of individuals.

In summary, whereas the Confucian model relates culture directly to economic development, the new approach to cultural analysis of economic development introduces the concept of transaction costs in the static sense and people's creative capacity in the dynamic sense. In the former case, both the radius of trust (or social capital) and the ethical system operating in a society affect transaction costs, which in turn influence economic development. Both linkages are operational, and empirical studies support these claims. In the latter case, creative capacity is consistent with the traditional concept of technology and productivity progress, and it requires within society a value system embedded with future orientation, rationality and equality. This new approach is employed below in addressing the three questions identified above regarding the role of culture in the Korean economy.

2.5 NEW ASSESSMENT OF CULTURAL EFFECTS ON THE KOREAN ECONOMY

2.5.1 Why Culture Did Not Produce Economic Growth Historically

Korea absorbed Confucianism in the fourth century as part of cultural exchange with China and adopted the Chinese writing, education and government systems. Over the 500 years of the Yi dynasty (1392–1910), Korea adopted the Confucian canon as the national religion or social ethical principles, and its culture, society and governance systems became profoundly imbued with Confucianism.[15]

Under the prevailing culture, it is not surprising that the Korean economy remained stagnant over the 500 years of the Yi dynasty. Transaction costs were high and the creative capacity of the Korean people was minimal. Society had not established the basic formal institutions required for a market system, such as laws to protect private property rights. In terms of culture, the radius of trust was limited as collectivism centred on the extended family, and the ethical system was loose as attested by the prevalence of corruption and political confrontation. As Harrison (1985) points out, the people's creative capacity could not develop under this society's dynastic rules. People remained unaware of scientific and economic progress around the world as the dynasty applied a strict isolation policy. Even though people were secular in terms of institutionalized religion, they were highly influenced by Shamanism and fatalism that forestalled rational thinking. Together with strong authoritarianism and collectivism, a distinctive form of social stratification prevailed in society, and manual labour, merchants and business people were widely denigrated. These circumstances crippled the spirit of independence and equality and thus the people's creative capacity.

Korea's economic situation improved little under the oppressive Japanese colonial regime from 1910 to 1945. The few established institutions were re-geared to benefit the colonial master. Harsh regulation forced obedience to laws, and the radius of trust narrowed even further. These conditions demolished not only the hopes of the Korean people but also their creative capacity and future aspirations. The education system did not introduce scientific and rational thinking to the general public. With liberation from Japanese colonial rule in 1945, Korea went through a chaotic period. No sooner had Korea become a sovereign independent country, than the nation was divided into two. The 1950–53 Korean War utterly demolished not only the existing industrial base but also the social fabric. Survival as individuals or as family units prevailed as the utmost goal in society for a long while.

2.5.2 Why Economic Development Began from the 1960s

From the 1960s, the Korean economy was set to develop rapidly. The Korean people rebuilt their ethical system, the government implemented appropriate policies, and the new institutions that were established began to operate successfully, all of which contributed to a lowering of transaction costs. A new mood of hope and optimism projected Korean society towards the pursuit of social equality and development of a future orientation. These worked to enhance the nation's creative capacity.

The military regime of General Park Chung Hee that took government in 1961 introduced a strict authoritarian order that raised compulsion to comply with the law, and in so doing reduced transaction costs. The Park regime created a number of formal institutions to strengthen the market system including protection of private property rights, and implemented nationwide a development campaign that cultivated future orientation. Part of this campaign was the so-called Saemaul (community development) Movement.

Park's government introduced the first five-year economic plan in 1962 and consecutive five-year plans were devised and implemented until the beginning of the 1990s. These development plans led the Korean people to look towards the future, which inspired higher national savings and investment rates and the will to work harder and pursue education seriously. Rapid industrialization and rising employment opportunities in urban areas weakened social stratification and the long-held disdain for manual labour and commercial activities, creating conditions that both promoted and enabled aspirations to social equality.

2.5.3 Why, Then, the 1997 Financial Crisis?

Park Chung Hee's was just the first of a series of authoritarian regimes that tightly controlled and intervened extensively in the economy across the following three decades until the early 1990s. While the system had produced spectacular economic growth, it had also bred institutional dysfunction. Private property rights, particularly of *chaebols*, were poorly protected under some of the military regimes. The state had confiscated assets of some of the *chaebols* in the early days of the Park regime, and the Chun Doo Hwan regime (1981–88) did likewise for the *chaebols*' alleged illegal accumulation of property, and the infamous bankruptcy of the Kookje *chaebol*. The military regimes held the banking sector under tight control, enabling the government to control credit lines to private companies. Private companies were forced to collaborate with government to secure their private property and minimize transaction costs, leading to corruption and cronyism. Generally, the more corrupt the society, the narrower the radius of identification and trust within it, which raises transaction costs for the whole society.

Extensive state intervention in the banking and business sectors and government protection of these sectors from domestic and international competition fostered the deluding perception that banks and *chaebols* were economically invincible. It was generally imagined that these bodies were too big and too important for the national economy to be allowed to fail, so the government would bail them out if needed, as discussed in Chapter 1. This perception engendered moral hazard for banks and *chaebols*, which encouraged them to underestimate transaction costs and expand their enterprises with debt capital.

The economic system based on Confucian collective values could not survive under the competitive ethos brought by economic liberalization and globalization from the beginning of the 1990s. Kang (2003) argues that in a situation of 'mutual hostage' among a small and stable number of actors in the government and business sectors, cronyism can actually reduce transaction costs, and that Korean government–business relations were one such case. However cronyism and corruption could not be sustained when the number of competitors reached a certain threshold and competition became more intense with increasing liberalization of markets. Together with reduced state protection as part of economic liberalization, the extant post-Korean War business system based on moral hazard and underestimated transaction costs could not survive.

Another factor inspired by market liberalization was the need for more domestically generated creative thinking. The creative capacity of Korean people had not been so critical for Korean economic development insofar as the country was catching up with advanced countries. With sustained rapid economic development over several decades, Koreans had become quite future-oriented as indicated by their high savings and investment rates, diligence and level of education. Even though the number of religious believers including Christians and Buddhists increased substantially, secularism did not abate and, indeed, rational thinking increased as Koreans became better educated. Pursuit of equality was also enhanced by readily available economic and educational opportunities. This is evidenced by one of the most equitable income distributions among developing countries, as examined in Chapter 12. In terms of technology, Korean enterprises were able to purchase technology from further advanced countries that were willing to sell to them until the surge in economic competition. However, as Korea became a serious contender in many areas of international business, the Korean economy could not survive with technologies imported from competitor nations. International market competition has forced Korea to develop its own technology and to enhance its international competitiveness more than ever. This shift was reflected in low productivity growth and low international competitiveness from the early 1990s, as discussed in Chapter 1.

2.5.4 Cultural Trends and the Future Korean Economy

The last question concerns the role of culture in Korea's future economic development. In the current liberalized and globalized economic environment, the Korean economy must maintain increases in efficiency and productivity to gain or retain competitive edge over foreign counterparts. Minimizing transaction costs and maximizing creative capacity of the Korean people are thus enormously important for Korea to hold its economic performance relative to other nations.

Culture does change over time. While cultural change is usually slow, the government's reform programme in response to the 1997 crisis introduced a raft of institutional and legal reforms that have induced relatively swift cultural change. A variety of sources of decline in trust or increase in social discontent have been developing in the recent past, resulting from changes in culture instigated by institutional changes. All this signals decreases in social capital. First, trust has declined in the labour market. In 1998 the labour law was changed to allow managers to lay off workers for management reasons. This opened the way for banks and other businesses to dismiss a large number of staff as part of business restructuring or as a survival strategy. Such a large-scale dismissal has dramatically diminished the concept of lifetime employment. Companies have also introduced performance-based compensation and promotion to replace the seniority system. These changes in the labour market and in human resource management create uncertainty for workers and inevitably reduce the level of trust between employers and employees. The decrease in trust in turn lowers loyalty toward companies and aggravates labour relations, which raises transaction costs. This reduction of trust in employment relations is reflected in Korea's poor ranking internationally for labour relations, as will be further examined shortly.

Second, also within the context of employment, trust has declined from the rising disparity between full-time and part-time workers. Since the 1997 crisis, many employers have changed employment from full-time to part-time to reduce production costs. The proportion of full-time workers has declined, while that of temporary workers has increased. As examined in Chapter 11, over the 1990–97 period, an average of 56.6 per cent of all employees were full-time, while over the 2000–07 period this figure fell to 50.8 per cent (KLI 2008). The gap between the two groups of workers in their compensation and working conditions has widened in favour of full-time workers. Temporary workers' income was 56.6 per cent of full-time workers' income over the 2000–01 period, but decreased gradually to 50.6 per cent in 2007 (KLI 2008). In response to perceived injustice toward employees, the appeal of such approaches as cooperation, compromise, stability and continuity has declined in Korean society, while confrontational attitudes have strengthened.

Third, changes in employment conditions also appear to have shifted general attitudes to work. Korea introduced a law for five working days per week from 2004, replacing the long-held practice of a six-day working week. The number of hours worked per week has declined steadily from 47.5 hours in 2000 to 43.5 hours in 2007 (KLI 2008). The work ethic appears to be losing ground, with the hallmark diligence of Korean workers now declining. As lifetime employment disappears, workers' loyalty toward their employer declines. More workers are employed on a part-time or casual basis, and these non-regular employees' dedication to their employers, their readiness to take the initiative and their creativity are usually less than those of regular workers. The Roh government's emphasis on social equity over economic efficiency and growth has promulgated a view within society that is less laudatory of entrepreneurs, business and profit. This has discouraged entrepreneurship and creativity, thereby lowering the nation's investment rate.

Fourth, as Harrison (1985) and Josten (2004) argue, increasing inequality in income distribution reduces social capital and thereby increases transaction costs. As discussed in Chapter 12, inequality in income distribution has been rising. As shown in Table 2.1, income distribution measured by the Gini coefficient has somewhat worsened in the recent past. The ratio of income of the richest 10 per cent of citizens to that of the poorest 10 per cent (Q10/Q1) increased from 7.48 in 2000 to 8.75 in 2007, indicating a rising income gap between the rich and poor. This is further supported by the rising poverty rate. The share of households with income below the official poverty line increased from 13.3 per cent in 2003 to 18.1 per cent in 2007 (KIHASA 2008). Perceptions of injustice in society are also on the rise due to rising inequality not only in income but also in wealth distribution. J.W. Lee (2003) points out that disparity in the distribution of wealth is much worse than the inequality of income distribution, because of the heavy concentration of land ownership and the high price of land.

Fifth, another serious problem arising from the growing income disparity is the shrinking middle-income class. The middle-income class declined from 68.5 per cent of the total number of households in 1997 to 63.9 per cent in 2004 (Bank of Korea 2006).[16] Typically, the middle-income group has played an important role in maintaining the stability of Korean society and politics after an extensive history of social instability and clan conflict. Contraction of the middle class alongside increases in the number of households with income under the poverty line augurs poorly for future developments in Korean society, politics and the economy. The trend may well produce more extensive social discontent from an expanding segment of society, further lowering the level of trust in society.

Sixth, it appears that the Roh Moo-hyun government over the period 2003–08 took advantage of rising income polarization for political purposes by emphasizing the social dichotomy between rich and poor and promoting itself as representing the 80 per cent poor at the expense of the 20 per cent rich. As a result, the political culture has developed in such a way that suspicion of, and hostility toward, political opponents continues to escalate. Political confrontation has become the rule of the game, while the concepts of cooperation and compromise have disappeared. One may expect the prevailing wrangling within the political sphere to affect adversely prospects for cooperation and compromise and hence the radius of trust within Korean society at large. The Lee Myung-bak government from February 2008 has been de-emphasizing the income polarization.

Table 2.1 Korea's social and economic indicators, 2000–07

	2000	2001	2002	2003	2004	2005	2006	2007
GDP growth (%)	8.5	3.8	7.0	3.1	4.7	4.2	5.1	5.0
Saving rate (%)	33.7	31.7	31.3	32.6	34.9	32.9	31.3	30.4
Investment rate (%)	31.1	29.4	29.1	29.5	30.4	30.2	29.9	29.4
Population growth rate	0.82	0.65	0.55	0.49	0.49	0.44	0.33	0.33
Fertility rate (%)	1.47	1.30	1.17	1.18	1.15	1.08	1.12	1.25
Divorce rate (%)	2.5	2.8	3.0	3.5	2.9	2.6	2.6	2.5
Gini coefficient	0.296	0.303	0.298	0.298	0.304	0304	0.303	0.306
Q10/Q1	7.48	7.63	7.24	8.24	8.75	8.76	8.70	8.75
% of non-regular workers	n.a.	n.a.	27.4	32.6	37.0	36.6	35.5	35.9
Penal code criminal cases (000s)	523	554	797	857	827	826	828	845

Sources: Fertility rate, population growth rate, divorce rate, and penal code criminal cases: KNSO (2009); Gini coefficients and Q10/Q1: KIHASA (2008); GDP, saving and investment rates: KNSO (2008); percentage of non-regular workers: KLI (2008).

Seventh, another indicator of the deterioration in community life is the rising divorce rate in recent years. This may reflect or be associated with the declining radius of trust in Korea. As shown in Table 2.1, the divorce rate increased rapidly from 1.1 in 1990 to 3.5 in 2003. Although declining to 2.5 in 2007, the Korean divorce rate was one of the highest in the world. Like other recent data on Korean society indicating lower involvement in collective activity and the flagging level of trust within society, this data indicates the ever weaker legacy of the Confucian past on contemporary Korean society.[17]

Eighth, Fukuyama (1995: 310) has argued that the rise of crime and litigation indicates the decline of social trust. In Korea today, the rule of law appears to be losing its regulatory power, as does the prerequisite underlay of trust and ethics that enables, sustains and reinforces rule of law. The source of personal and social ethics appears to be shifting. Many observers have agreed that the moral basis of oriental societies such as in Korea is 'shame' within a collective culture, while the moral basis of Western societies is 'guilt'. Thus, with collectivism fading in Korean society, as already noted, the moral basis of society may be damaged or at least altered. In the recent past, large-scale political corruption cases have been exposed, and illegal activities by corporations, unions and interest groups have been prevalent, vitiating the ethical system and its regulatory capacity over Korean society.[18] As data in Table 2.1 reveal, the number of penal code criminal cases was less than 400 000 by 1997, and had more than doubled by 2007 with 845 000 cases.[19] Joo (2003) found that the overall crime rate in Korea between 1970 and 2000 was not as serious as in Japan and the United States, but warned that Korea's crime rate had increased faster than these two countries' rates.

Finally, nationalism is still prevalent in Korea, although like other emotional responses such as trust, it too is weakening. Relatively strong nationalism by comparison with other national examples helps to explain why many observers from overseas still regard Korean people as xenophobic (O.Y. Kwon 2003). Indeed, the xenophobic attitude of many Koreans in general also reduces the radius of identification and raises transaction costs in commercial dealings, while globalization transforms national economies worldwide.

The future orientation that fosters creative capacity within society also appears to be fading in recent years. Under the Roh Moo-hyun administration, part of the main focus of Korean society appeared to be on political movements seeking 'history corrections', attempting to identify those who sympathized with the Japanese colonial government more than 50 years earlier. Uncertainty perceived by workers after 1997, and uncertainty and instability generated by inconsistent government policy measures in the recent past, have also hindered the future orientation of citizens. Declining savings and investment rates may reflect decline in future orientation. As shown in Table 2.1, over the period 2000–07, the savings rate decreased to 32.4 per cent, compared to 36.5 per cent during the 1990s, and the investment rate decreased further to 29.9 per cent, compared to 35.4 per cent during the 1990s. These decreases in savings and investment rates will adversely affect economic growth potential.

Also relevant for attention here is the rapid decline in fertility rate, taking Korea to the lowest rate in the world in 2002 at 1.17 children, with further declines until 2007 when it increased to 1.25 (Table 2.1). The declining fertility rate may be influenced by families' consumption preferences. Because of the low fertility rate, the population growth rate has declined continuously to 0.33 per cent in 2007 (Table 2.1). It is forecast to decline further to 0.23 per cent in 2010 and continue declining beyond 2020 (T.H. Kwon 2003). Furthermore, the Korean population is ageing rapidly. Those aged 65 and over accounted for 7.2 per cent of the population in 2000, with expected growth to 15.1 per cent in 2020 (T.H. Kwon 2003). All of these demographic trends portend future slowdown for the Korean economy.

2.6 COMPARATIVE ANALYSIS OF RECENT CULTURAL TRENDS IN KOREA

So far the wide-ranging cultural changes within Korean society have been analysed in terms of their possible effects on the future economy through their influences on future transaction costs and the nation's creative capacity. This analysis should be augmented, particularly to comprehend Korean cultural effects on its international competitiveness, by an analysis of a variety of Korean cultural facets relevant to economic development, compared to those advanced countries that Koreans seek to emulate. To this end, recent trends of relevant cultural facets within Korea are examined by comparing pertinent social indicators, which would reflect those cultural facets or their changes, to those of other countries. Table 2.2 shows Korea's global rankings across various indicators of its social framework between the years 2000 and 2008 from an average of 51.6 countries studied by the International Institute for Management Development (IMD), about 103 countries by the World Economic Forum (WEF), and about 180 countries by Transparency International (TI).

Obviously trust has declined in the Korean labour market markedly more than in other countries. As shown in Table 2.2, according to the IMD and WEF, Korea's labour relations were consistently among the worst over time. Over the period 2000–08, the IMD shows that Korea belonged to the worst 95 percentile over the first three years, and then it ranked last among the 30 to 61 countries surveyed for the remaining six years (2003–08). The WEF ranked Korea on average 80.4th out of 102.9 countries over the same period for its own labour relations index. As a result, Korea was one of the countries that had the most industrial disputes, as indicated by Korea's rank of 38.6th on average out of 51.8 countries surveyed over the same period by the IMD for the number of industrial disputes.

As shown in Table 2.2, Korean society's view of individual firms' behaviours is quite low, indicating a relatively low level of trust in companies, compared to other countries. According to the IMD, Korea's rankings for the social responsibility of business leaders held fairly steady between 2000 and 2007, with rankings of 39th and 41st respectively, with a striking improvement to 2nd ranking in 2008, thereby bringing up an average ranking of 28.7th over the period 2000–08.

Corporate ethical practices demonstrated a similar pattern, showing a relative improvement and subsequent decline between 2000 and 2007, before improving again to a rank of 29th in 2008. Korea's average rank for corporate ethical practices was 35.1st from an average of 51.8 countries studied over the period. For ethical behaviours of firms, the WEF ranked Korea 38th in 2002, before declining to 61st in 2004, and recovering to 27th in 2008, resulting in an average rank of 36.7th from 113.1 countries studied by the WEF between 2002 and 2008. The low level of trust in companies together with poor labour relations would be reflected in a relatively low level of work ethics. Unlike the renowned hallmark diligence of Korean workers, the IMD ranked Korea 30.4th out of 51.8 countries on its worker motivation index.

Table 2.2 Comparative stances of Korea's social indicators, 2000–08

	2000	2002	2004	2005	2006	2007	2008	Average (2000–08)
Labour market								
Labour relations (IMD)	44	47	60	60	61	55	55	50.9 (51.8)
Industrial dispute (IMD)	38	44	43	37	38	n.a.	n.a.	38.6
Labour relations (WEF)	56	55	103	81	114	55	95	80.4 (102.9)
Worker motivation (IMD)	33	19	42	37	32	33	30	30.4
Society's view of firms								
Social responsibility (IMD)	39	24	30	30	34	41	2	28.7
Ethical practice (IMD)	38	29	38	36	40	41	29	35.1
Ethical behaviour (WEF)	n.a.	38	61	35	38	25	27	36.7
Observance of ethics and laws								
CPI (TI)	48	40	47	40	42	43	40	43.6 (180)
Favouritism in official decisions (WEF)	27	30	49	26	46	15	22	29.8
Justice (IMD)	32	35	41	35	42	30	31	32.9
Judicial independence (WEF)	44	41	48	45	51	35	45	45.0
Public trust of politicians (WEF)	44	39	85	38	67	22	25	45.9
Attitudes and values								
Social cohesion (IMD)	37	42	46	34	48	25	25	35.2
Quality of life (IMD)	33	32	40	41	39	38	31	33.6
Social attitudes to globalization								
Attitudes to globalization (IMD)	n.a.	16	14	7	13	32	13	14.8
National culture (IMD)	47	44	49	53	55	55	55	48.4

Sources: IMD (various years); WEF (various years); TI (various years).

The level of trust, rigour of ethics and law observance level are remarkably lower in Korea than other advanced countries. As shown in Table

2.2, Korea's ranking on the Corruption Perceptions Index (CPI) developed by TI remained more or less steady over the period between 2000 and 2008 with an average rank of 43.6th out of 180 countries. This indicates a high prevailing perception that the corruption level in Korea is relatively quite high, compared to advanced countries. The WEF survey on corruption supports the TI results with Korea's ranking of 29.8th out of 103 countries over the period 2000–08 on favouritism in official decisions. According to the IMD and WEF, the perception that social justice is not fairly administered prevails quite highly. Over the period 2000–08, the IMD ranked Korea on its social justice index 32.9th on average out of 51.8 countries. The WEF ranked Korea on average 45th out of 103 countries on its judicial independence index. In particular, the WEF shows that public trust of politicians is relatively quite low. Korea's ranking was 45.9th out of 103 countries over the period between 2000 and 2008 on the index of public trust of politicians by the WEF, although Korea's ranking has improved overall, from 44th in 2000 to a rank of 25th in 2008 (Table 2.2).

The perception is relatively widely held that the Korean government does not put a priority on social cohesion. Korea ranked on average 35.2nd over the period from 2000 to 2008 on the social cohesion index of the IMD, although Korea's ranking has fluctuated from 37th in 2000 to 48th in 2006 before improving to 25th in 2008 (Table 2.2). Table 2.2 also shows that the perception of Koreans' quality of life was quite low between 2000 and 2008 at an average rank of 33.6th out of an average 51.6 countries studied by the IMD. As compared to Korea's ranking of 14th and 23rd respectively, with its GDP and per capita GDP in 2007, the satisfaction level of quality of life is relatively low.

Finally, as compared to other countries, Korean society has relatively opened toward globalization, yet people's mindsets have remained quite closed to it. According to the IMD survey, Korea's rankings for social attitudes to globalization between 2000 and 2008 were relatively high at 20th in 2001, improving to 7th in 2005, before declining to 13th in 2008, with an average rank of 14.8th over the period. By contrast, Korea ranked very poorly in terms of the national culture being closed to foreign ideas. Korea was worst ranked in 2000, 2003, 2007 and 2008, with an average rank of 48.4th from the total average of 51.8 countries over the nine-year period. This vindicates the arguments that nationalism and xenophobia as its corollary are still prevalent in Korea.

The above comparative analysis of social indicators reinforces the argument that the recent cultural trends within Korea society would be unfavourable for future economic development by raising transaction costs. The relative rankings with the above social indicators provide comparative assessment of the nation's business environments and are critically important in informing foreign investors and businesses when considering opportunities. Therefore, for the nation's strategic goal of achieving the status of advanced countries, Korean mindsets, which are the underpinning of formal institutions and economic development, have to adjust towards those of advanced countries and the advent of globalization.

2.7 CONCLUSION

This chapter has explored the role of Korean culture in national economic development, with an eye to future prospects. Economic development is a complex phenomenon influenced by capital, labour, technology, and formal and informal economic, social and political institutions. Cultural values underpin both formal institutions and the behavioural patterns of individual economic actors. Recognizing the complementarity of the multiple factors for economic development, this chapter has focused on cultural values as one particularly important factor.

A wide-ranging literature has recently been developed concerning the relationship between Confucian culture and East Asian economic development. However, the Confucian model has a number of serious theoretical and methodological problems since it does not take into account cultural differences between national contexts and relates the micro-psychological phenomenon of culture directly to the macro aspect of economic development. This chapter has refined the shortcomings of the Confucian model to explore the relationship between Confucian culture and Korea's economic development by drawing on the model proposed by Harrison (1985), among others. This model introduces an operational intermediary between culture and economic development to make the model more operational and the causality readily conceivable. Under this model, culture affects economic development through its impacts on transaction costs in the static case and through its impacts on creative capacity in the dynamic case.

Using this model, this chapter has found that a variety of cultural changes in the recent past have decreased the level of trust and thus social capital in Korean society, thereby increasing transaction costs. Changes in political and economic institutions in response to the 1997 crisis have promoted individualism and reduced the sense of community and the radius of trust. The perception of injustice in society has risen. Trust between employers and employees has decreased markedly, and the divorce rate has jumped to one of the highest in the world. Inequality in income and wealth distribution has risen, the middle-income class has shrunk, and the number of households below the poverty line has increased. Inequity between full-time and part-time workers in their working conditions has worsened, and more workers have been forced into part-time employment. The rising social injustice has fed into national political life, making for a more confrontational politics. Rule of law has lost regulatory strength, partly as a consequence of large-scale political scandals, corruption in *chaebols* and illegal activities of unions. This is reflected in the substantial increases in the national crime rate. These developments have contributed to a declining sense of community and trust, a weaker appreciation of cooperation and compromise, and a stronger inclination towards confrontation. These outcomes all serve to raise transaction costs and socio-economic instability, which will adversely affect the Korean economy in the future.

Other findings are also consistent with this inauspicious economic trajectory. The future orientation that fosters citizens' creative capacity has faded, as suggested by decreasing savings and investment rates. The fertility rate has declined rapidly to be one of the lowest in the world, which will intensify the problems associated with an ageing population and lower the growth potential of the economy. The strong work ethic that characterized Korean workers has weakened, alongside decline in workers' diligence, loyalty and dedication to their employer companies. Furthermore, a social view tending to disparage entrepreneurs and business has evolved, discouraging entrepreneurship and creativity.

This chapter has also analysed a variety of Korean cultural facets relevant to economic development, compared to those of other countries by means of social indicators developed by a number of well-known international organizations. Trust in the Korean labour market has declined markedly more than in other countries. Korean society's trust in private business is relatively low, which, together with low trust in labour relations, has weakened worker motivation more than other countries. Again as compared to advanced countries, the level of trust, the rigour of ethics, and law observance in Korea are all relatively low. This is reflected in a higher corruption level in Korea, that is detrimental to the country's international competitiveness as well as social harmony and integration. Further, Koreans are relatively intransigent to foreign cultures and ideas. All this would adversely affect Korea's international competitiveness and make it difficult for Korea to take full advantage of globalization.

As this chapter makes clear, the complex and wide-ranging changes in Korean culture in the recent past are serving to raise transaction costs and curtail the Korean people's creative capacity. The effects of these cultural changes on the Korean economy are likely to be negative in the future, compared to the largely positive influence of culture upon Korea's economic development in earlier decades from the 1960s. This is further reinforced when relevant facets of Korean culture are compared to those of advanced countries. Culture, the underpinning of formal institutions and behaviours of economic actors, is therefore not *ceteris paribus*. Even if all else remains the same, the prospects of the Korean economy will be weakened by the influence of culture as Korean society adjusts to the advent of globalization and economic liberalization. To improve Korea's economic prospects in the emerging globalization era, careful attention needs to be paid to the cultural changes now under way in response to recent policy and institutional changes. Clear understanding of these changes and their causes will be necessary for informing public campaigns and future national policies. Government, business and society as a whole will need to work together to redirect what appear to be deleterious cultural changes to a direction conducive to economic development.

NOTES

1. Pejovich (2004) argues that inconsistency between formal institutions and culture have increased transaction costs in Central and Eastern European countries after their transition to free market economies.
2. J.C. Lee (2001) argues that political culture has inhibited institutional reforms required for economic liberalization in Korea after 1997, as it has dragged down the consolidation process of democracy.
3. For a further exposition of Korean culture, see Kwon (2008: 64–85).
4. This section draws heavily on Kwon (2005).
5. This section draws on Kwon (2005).
6. The six principal factors identified by D.W. Nam (1994) are:
   a. ethnic and cultural homogeneity and a strong Confucian tradition that places great emphasis on education and loyalty to the nation;
   b. the national security threat from communist North Korea, which helped the government forge greater national cohesion and consensus in favour of economic development, while simultaneously preserving authoritarian rule;
   c. strong and effective leadership by an authoritarian government;
   d. the faith of the South Korean people in the free-enterprise system, as opposed to the communist system operating in North Korea;
   e. an outward-looking, export-oriented development strategy; and
   f. the favourable international economic climate that prevailed during the 1960s and 1970s.
7. Institutional prerequisites for favourable cultural traits to work for the Confucian model of East Asian economic development are also pointed out by Clegg et al. (1990), Morishima (1982), Levy (1992) and Pye (2000).
8. After Lee and McNulty (2003), very few studies examined the Korean financial crisis from a cultural perspective.
9. This section draws on Kwon (2005).
10. North (1993) cites an empirical study which has found that 45 per cent of US gross national product (GNP) was devoted to the transaction sector in 1970.
11. There are numerous studies on effects of social capital (or trust) on transaction costs (Putman 1995; Moore and de Bruin 2004; Dyer and Chu 2002).
12. The radius of trust and identification discussed by Harrison (1985) is equivalent to the 'social capital' discussed by Fukuyama (1995: 23–32).

13. The radius of identification and trust indicates the danger of dysfunctional aspects of collectivism, familism and parochial nationalism under Confucianism.
14. Josten (2004) argues similarly that an increase in inequality in income distribution reduces social capital and increases transaction costs.
15. For detailed examinations of historical developments of Confucianism, culture, society, politics and economy in Korea, see Han (1969) and Grayson (2002).
16. According to the *Dong-A Ilbo* (2006), the middle class shrank further to 58 per cent in 2005.
17. C.M. Park (2003: 313) found that about 80 per cent of individuals had no affiliation with any social organization, and 6 per cent of people had only one affiliation in 1999. Park's findings indicate that the social participation rate in community activities or voluntary civic cooperation, which could enhance social capital, is extremely low.
18. Soon after the 2002 presidential election, the Grand National Party was engulfed in political corruption because of illegal political contributions. Over the 2002–07 period, chairmen/owners of two *chaebols* (Doosan and Hyundai Automobiles) were sentenced to prison. A special prosecutor was set up to investigate alleged illegal activities by the Chairman of Samsung, the largest *chaebol* in Korea. Over the same period, there were 91 illegal and militant demonstrations per year in Korea (*Hankyoreh* 2008). From the late 2008, the country has been seized again by a corruption scandal associated with a businessman (Yeon-Cha Park), implicating the former President Roh Moo-hyun and numerous politicians.
19. The Korea National Statistical Office (KNSO) (2009: 541) shows from its nationwide surveys that Koreans perceived the law-observance level by other Koreans as decreasing from 28 per cent in 2005 to 26 per cent in 2008, and that over the same period the law-observance level by themselves declining from 64.3 per cent to 56.9 per cent.

REFERENCES

Ahn, Byung Wook (1996), *The Analects of Confucius*, (in Korean), Seoul: Jayumoonwhasa.

Bank of Korea (2006), 'Effects of changes in income distribution on consumption', (in Korean), *Monthly Bulletin*, April, 23–56.

Berger, Peter L. and H.H.M. Hsiao (eds) (1990), *In Search of An East Asian Development Model*, London: Transaction Publishers.

Chang, Chan Sup and N.J. Chang (1994), *The Korean Management System: cultural, political and economic foundations*, Westport, CT: Quorum Books.

Cho, Lee-Jay (1994), 'Culture, institutions and economic development in East Asia', in L.J. Cho and Y.H. Kim (eds), *Korea's Political Economy: an institutional perspective*, Boulder, CO: Westview Press, pp. 3–41.

Clegg, Steward R., W. Higgins and T. Spybey (1990), 'Post-Confucianism, social democracy and economic culture', in S.R. Clegg and S.G. Redding (eds), *Capitalism in Contrasting Cultures*, New York: Walter de Gruyter, pp. 31–78.

Dong-A Ilbo (2006), 'Rising the households under the poverty line', 26 September.

Dyer, Jeffrey H. and W. Chu (2002), 'The role of trustworthiness in reducing transaction costs and improving performance: empirical evidence from the United States, Japan and Korea', mimeograph.

Eggertsson, T. (1990), *Economic Behavior and Institutions*, Cambridge: Cambridge University Press.

Fukuyama, Francis (1995), *Trust: the social virtues and the creation of prosperity*, New York: Free Press.

Fukuyama, Francis (2000), 'Social capital', in L.E. Harrison and S.P. Huntington (eds), *Culture Matters: how values shape human progress*, New York: Basic Books, pp. 98–111.

Gong, Y.S. and W.H. Jang (1998), 'Culture and development: reassessing cultural explanations on Asian economic development', *Development and Society*, **27** (1), 77–97.

Grayson, James Huntley (2002), *Korea: a religious history*, revised edn, London: RoutledgeCurzon.

Hahm, Hanhee (2003), 'Korean culture seen through Westerners' eyes', *Korea Journal*, **43** (1), 106–28.

Han, Kyung-Koo (2003), 'The anthropology of the discourse on the Koreanness of Koreans', *Korea Journal*, **43** (1), 5–31.

Han, Woo-Keun (1969), *The History of Korea*, Seoul: Eul-Yoo Publishing Company.

Hankyoreh (2008), 'Resurrection of suppression of demonstration as in the 5th Republic', 17 March, www.hani.co.kr/popups/print.hani?ksn=276231.

Harrison, Lawrence E. (1985), *Underdevelopment is a State of Mind*, Cambridge, MA: Harvard University Press.

Harrison, L. and S.P. Huntington (eds) (2000), *Culture Matters: how values shape human progress*, New York: Basic Books.

Holzer, B. (2000), 'Miracles with a system: the economic rise of East Asia and the role of sociocultural patterns', *International Sociology*, **15** (3), 455–78.

Huntington, S. (1998), *The Clash of Civilisations and the Remaking of the World Order*, London: Touchstone Books.

International Institute for Management Development (IMD) (various years), *World Competitiveness Yearbook*, Lausanne: IMD.

Jones, Leroy P. and Il SaKong (1982), *Government, Business and Entrepreneurship in Economic Development: the Korean case*, Cambridge, MA: Harvard University Press.

Joo, H.J. (2003), 'Crime and crime control', in D.C. Shin, C.P. Rutkowski and C.M. Park (eds), *The Quality of Life in Korea: comparative and dynamic perspectives*, Boston, MA: Kluwer Academic Publisher, pp. 239–63.

Josten, Stefan D. (2004), 'Social capital and transaction costs in a growing economy with heterogeneous agents', Working Paper, Institute of Public Finance at the Helmut-Schmidt University Hamburg.

Kahn, Herman (1979), *World Economic Development: 1979 and beyond*, Boulder, CO: Westview Press.

Kang, David C. (2003), 'Transaction costs and cronyism capitalism in East Asia', *Comparative Politics*, **35** (4), 439–58.

Kim, Yoon Hyung (1994), 'An introduction to the Korean model of political economy', in Lee-Jay Cho and Yoon Hyung Kim (eds), *Korea's Political Economy: an institutional perspective*, Boulder, CO: Westview Press, pp. 45–62.

Koo, Bon Ho (1995), 'Sociocultural factors in the industrialisation of Korea', in B.H. Koo and D.H. Perkins (eds), *Social Capability and Long-Term Economic Growth*, New York: St Martin's Press, pp. 181–202.

Korea Institute for Health and Social Affairs (KIHASA) (2008), *2008 Poverty Statistics Yearbook*, Seoul: KIHASA.

Korea Labor Institute (KLI) (2008), *2008 KLI Labor Statistics*, Seoul: Korea Labor Institute.

Korea National Statistical Office (KNSO) (2008), *2008 Korea Statistical Yearbook*, Seoul: KNSO.

Korea National Statistical Office (KNSO) (2009), *2008 Social Indicators in Korea*, Seoul: KNSO.
Kweon, Sug-In (2003), 'Popular discourses on Korean culture: from the late 1980s to the present', *Korea Journal*, **43** (1), 32–57.
Kwon, O.Y. (2003), *Foreign Direct Investment in Korea: a foreign perspective*, Seoul: Korea Economic Research Institute.
Kwon, O.Y. (2005), 'A cultural analysis of South Korea's economic prospects', *Global Economic Review*, **34** (2), 213–31.
Kwon, O.Y. (2008), *International Business in Korea: the evolution of the market in the globalisation era*, Cheltenham, UK and Northampton, MA, USA: Edward Elgar Publishing.
Kwon, Tai-Hwan (2003), 'Demographic trends and their social implications', in D.C. Shin, C.P. Rutkowski and C.M. Park (eds), *The Quality of Life in Korea: comparative and dynamic perspectives*, Boston, MA: Kluwer Academic Publishers, pp. 19–38.
Lee, Ho-Chul and M.P. McNulty (2003), 'Korea's economic crisis and cultural transition toward individualism', Economic and Social Research Institute, Discussion Paper Series No. 71.
Lee, Jong Chan (2001), 'Political institutions and reforms for economic liberalisation: central issues of neo-institutionalism and Korean cases', (in Korean), in S.H. Jwa and D.Y. Yoon (eds), *Korea's Institutional Reforms: issues and direction*, Seoul: Korea Economic Research Institute, pp. 177–220.
Lee, Joung Woo (2003), 'Income, consumption and poverty', in D.C. Shin, C.P. Rutkowski and C.M. Park (eds), *The Quality of Life in Korea: comparative and dynamic perspectives*, Boston, MA: Kluwer Academic Publisher, pp. 197–209.
Lee, Kwang-Chun (1995), 'Back to the basics! New interpretation of Confucian values in Korea's economic growth', *Korea Observer*, **16** (2), 97–114.
Levy Jr, Marion J. (1992), 'Confucianism and modernization', *Society*, **29** (4), 15–18.
Lewis, Arthur W. (1955), *The Theory of Economic Growth*, Homewood, IL: Richard D. Irwin.
Leys, Simon (1997), *The Analects of Confucius*, New York: W.W. Norton & Co.
Lipsey, Richard G. (1991), 'Economic growth: science and technology and institutional change in a global economy', Canadian Institute for Advanced Research, Toronto, mimeo.
Moore, Chris and A. de Bruin (2004), 'A transaction cost approach to understanding ethical behaviour', paper presented at the Eleventh World Congress of Social Economics – Social Economics: a Paradigm for a Global Society, 8–11 June, Albertville, France.
Morishima, Michio (1982), *Why has Japan Succeeded? Western Technology and the Japanese Ethos*, Cambridge: Cambridge University Press.
Myrdal, Gunnar (1968), *Asian Drama: an inquiry into the poverty of nations*, New York: Pantheon.
Nam, Duck Woo (1994), 'Korean's economic takeoff in retrospect', in S.Y. Kwack (ed.), *The Korean Economy at a Crossroad*, London: Praeger, pp. 1–19.
North, Douglass C. (1990), *Institutions, Institutional Change and Economic Performance*, Cambridge: Cambridge University Press.
North, Douglass C. (1993), 'Economic performance through time', Douglass C. North – Prize Lecture, http://nobelprize.org/nobel_prizes/economics/laureates/1993/north-lecture.html.

Oh, Tai K. and E.S. Kim (2002), 'The impact of Confucianism on East Asian business enterprises', in Z.S. Rhee and E.M. Chang (eds), *Korean Business and Management: the reality and the vision*, Elizabeth, NJ: Hollym, pp. 207–26.

Olson, M. and S. Kahkonen (2000), 'Introduction: the broad view', in M. Olson and S. Kahkonen (eds), *A Not-So-Dismal Science: a broad view of economies and societies*, Oxford: Oxford University Press, pp. 1–36.

Park, Chong-Min (2003), 'Quality of local government and democratic citizenship', in D.C. Shin, C.P. Rutkowski and C.M. Park (eds), *The Quality of Life in Korea: comparative and dynamic perspectives*, Boston, MA: Kluwer Academic Publisher, pp. 291–319.

Park, Sang-Seek (1995), 'Culture and development: the Korean experiment', *Korea and World Affairs*, **19** (3), 510–21.

Patterson, Dennis P. (2002), 'Asian management styles? The evidence from Korea', in Z.S. Rhee and E.M. Chang (eds), *Korean Business and Management: the reality and the vision*, Elizabeth, NJ: Hollym, pp. 227–48.

Pejovich, Svetozar (2004), 'Understanding the transaction costs of transition: it's the culture, stupid', Working Paper No. 24, International Centre for Economic Research.

Perkins, Dwight H. (2000), 'Law, family ties and the East Asian way of business', in L.E. Harrison and S.P. Huntington (eds), *Culture Matters: how values shape human progress*, New York: Basic Books, pp. 232–43.

Putman, Robert (1995), 'Bowling alone: American's declining social capital', *Journal of Democracy*, **6**, 65–78.

Pye, Lucian W. (2000), '"Asian Values": from Dayamos to Dominoes?', in L.E. Harrison and S.P. Huntington (eds), *Culture Matters: how values shape human progress*, New York: Basic Books, pp. 244–55.

Schumpeter, Joseph A. (1951), *The Theory of Economic Development*, Cambridge, MA: Harvard University Press.

Song, Byung-Nak (2003), *The Rise of the Korean Economy*, Hong Kong: Oxford University Press.

Tai, Hung-Chao (ed.) (1989), *Confucianism and Economic Development: an oriental alternative?*, Washington, DC: Washington Institute Press.

Transparency International (TI) (various years), 'TI corruption perception index', www.transparency.org.

Tu, Wei-Ming (1988), 'A Confucian perspective on the rise of industrial east Asia', *Bulletin of the American Academy of Arts and Sciences*, **42** (1), 32–50.

Weber, Max (1950), *The Protestant Ethic and the Spirit of Capitalism*, New York: Charles Scribner's Sons.

Whitley, Richard (1999), 'Competing logics and units of analysis in the comparative study of economic organisations', *International Studies of Management and Organization*, **29** (2), 113–26.

World Economic Forum (WEF) (various years), *The Global Competitiveness Report*, New York: Oxford University Press and Geneva: WEF.

Yi, Jeong Duk (2003), 'What is Korean culture anyway?', *Korea Journal*, **43** (1), 58–82.

3. The Korean political system and its effects on the economy

3.1 INTRODUCTION

The political system in Korea has transformed remarkably in the recent past: from an authoritarian system during the 1960s and 1970s, to democratization in the late 1980s, and further to a liberal-democratic political system. The system through which political decisions are made has an important bearing on the economy, as these decisions have direct impacts on the behaviours of all economic actors and entities. The purpose of this chapter is to assess the effects of Korea's political systems on its economic development since the establishment of the Republic of Korea (ROK) in 1948 with a focus on recent years.

Theories of economic growth abound. Given the well-known theories on promoting economic growth, a burning question arises as to why certain countries are able to take advantage of these ideas to achieve economic growth, while others fail. In this regard, Olson (2000) argues convincingly that differences in per capita income across countries are due mainly to differences in the quality of institutions and economic policies. It is thus the government that plays a critical role in economic performance as it implements economic polices and establishes formal institutions. The nature of government is in turn reflected in the political system, which for this study refers to a system of political decision-making. Political decisions are made through the interactions among political stakeholders (such as politicians, political parties, bureaucrats, business, labour, interest groups and the general public) under a set of institutions such as legal, constitutional and party rules. Under such a decision-making framework, another critical question arises as to what kind of political system will implement development-oriented policies most successfully. Economic development is a complex phenomenon jointly determined by a variety of factors. Acknowledging the complementarity of these multiple factors, this chapter examines the political system as one essential factor for economic operation, and assesses the impacts of political systems on Korean economic development.[1]

3.2 EFFECTS OF POLITICAL SYSTEMS ON ECONOMIC PERFORMANCE: LITERATURE REVIEW AND ASSESSMENT CRITERIA

A vast literature in political science and political economy is dedicated to the causality running from economic performance to political systems, arguing for a certain level of economic development as a prerequisite for the transition from authoritarianism to democracy (Przeworski and Limongi 1993). This chapter reviews the relatively small literature on the effects of regime type on economic performance. For most theoretical and empirical studies in this area, political systems or regimes are generally characterized simply as authoritarian or democratic. The arguments in favour of one type of political system are in essence based on critiques of the other system. The effects of presidential versus parliamentary democratic systems on economic performance are almost totally absent from the literature.

3.2.1 Authoritarian Regimes and Economic Performance

With the collapse of communism and the end of the Cold War in 1991, it has become a moot point to suggest that authoritarian regimes may produce economic outcomes superior to those of democracies.[2] Yet a contrast between the authoritarian and democratic regimes on their impacts on economic performance is relevant particularly to the Korean case. With regard to property rights protection, which institutional economists regard as one of the critical elements for economic development, Przeworski and Limongi (1993) argue that there is nothing in principle to suggest that authoritarian regimes cannot protect property rights to the same degree as democracies. One of the positive arguments that authoritarianism is beneficial to economic growth revolves around the assumption that authoritarian regimes have a greater propensity to accumulate investment than democracies (Kohli et al. 1984; Cohen 1985). As authoritarians are not concerned much with democratic elections, they are better equipped to force savings due to their greater coercive ability to hold down wages and consumption for investment (Rao 1985). They can also pursue growth policy decisively without concern about policy ramifications on society. Another argument is that authoritarian regimes are better able to pursue development policy as they enjoy autonomy from distributionist or other social pressures (Haggard 1990: 261). All these propositions depend on the nature and competence of the authoritarian regime and the time horizons authoritarians take. An authoritarian could be a benevolent dictator or a predatory one surrounded by corrupt political elites. The time horizon and moral probity of authoritarian elites cannot be judged *ex ante*, although authoritarianism has been seen to promote short-run growth in developing countries. For a country with a reasonably high level of development, further development may be achieved through the creativity, innovation and entrepreneurship of society. For such a country, democratic regimes appear to provide for better economic performance. Harrison (1985) argues that authoritarianism, as compared to democracy, suppresses the creativity of individuals.

3.2.2 Democracy and Economic Performance

Arguments in favour of democracy as beneficial to economic performance maintain that, while authoritarianism may promote short-run growth, democratic rule is more conducive to a sustained and equitable growth in the long run. Autonomous authoritarian elites are regarded as predatory on the society and thus sources of economic inefficiency (Przeworski and Limongi 1993; Sirowy and Inkeles 1990). Under democracy, lesser distributional conflicts will arise because democracy, by its very nature, must accommodate to some degree the claims of the poorer and more numerous sectors of society. Political pluralism in democracy provides the underlying conditions for a market economy in which members are free to accrue and dispense their resources as they see fit. Only under these competitive conditions will innovation and new technologies emerge. It is also argued that the erosion of hierarchical privileges and vested interests, and the greater flows of public information implied by democracy, contribute to a participative mentality that flows into the economic sphere of life (Sirowy and Inkeles 1990). Arguments for democracy for high economic growth hold only in institutionalized plural political systems with safeguards against predatory government interference, requisite levels of political stability and predictability, maintenance of proper economic governance, and secured civil liberties and basic freedoms. Only with these conditions met will the democratic political system motivate companies and citizens to undertake business, work, save and invest.

3.2.3 Results of Empirical Studies

As the arguments for either authoritarianism or democracy are in essence based on critiques of the other system, it is difficult to choose a favourable one from the theoretical perspective. Hence, a number of empirical studies have been undertaken. After the world witnessed the failure of authoritarian socialism in the early 1990s, it has become somewhat unfashionable to suggest that authoritarian regimes may produce economic outcomes superior to those of democracies. Hence, the majority of empirical studies available in the literature were undertaken before the early 1990s.

The findings of empirical studies vary widely depending on the period and the regions of the studies, and are inconclusive.[3] Most empirical studies undertaken after the early 1990s are in favour of democracy for better economic growth (Helliwell 1994; LeBlang 1997; Almeida and Ferreira 2002; Milner and Kubota 2005; Chaudhry and Garner 2007). Rodrik (1992) finds that the East Asian authoritarian regimes provided for better economic performance, while Feng (1995) finds that military regimes in Latin America had a negative effect on growth. In the sub-Saharan African context, Tiruneh (2006) finds no correlation between political regime types and economic growth, while Beaulier and Subrick (2006) find a positive correlation between democracy and economic development. A number of empirical studies find no relationship or only qualified relationship between democracy and economic performance (Burkhart and Lewis-Beck 1994; Weede 1996; Ersson and Lane 1996; Przeworski et al. 2000; Gerring et al. 2005).

The above survey of the literature indicates that the study of the effects of political systems on economic performance is a highly contested and underdeveloped area of political economy scholarship. The evidence suggests that regime type, in itself, may not be that important in determining economic outcomes. Although most statistical correlations were weak, qualified or conditional, the overall impression is that autonomous and effective authoritarian states without predatory elites who are also committed to national economic development will be beneficial to economic performance in developing countries. By contrast, at higher levels of development, where innovation and entrepreneurship become more important, democratic regimes appear to provide for better economic performance.[4]

3.2.4 Assessment Criteria

Most of the surveyed studies in the literature do not articulate the mechanism and process through which the political system affects the economy. For this chapter, the influence of political systems on economic development is looped by the types of economic policies and institutions that are made through the structure of the political decision-making system. Hence, the first task of public policy is to establish proper formal (laws and regulations) institutions that will minimize transaction costs, secure property rights, and promote competition for efficient markets. Given the institutional framework, which is in turn a key element of successful public policy (Beeson 2002), evaluation of economic policies (including institutional reforms) must be predicated on a widely accepted set of objectives that the nation is seeking, and on knowledge of the potential role that economic policies can play in the achievement of these objectives.

From the causality relationship between the political system and economic development linked by economic policy, a few successful factors for the political system can be identified. First, perhaps the most important part of the logical loop between the political system and economic performance would be how well the political system reflects the nation's economic objectives. That is, success of economic policies depends on how comprehensively the government represents the aggregate social interest of the nation or the extent of nationally 'encompassing interests'. In this regard, McGuire and Olson (1996) point out that countries with 'encompassing interest' group structures grow more rapidly than those with a high density of narrow special-interest organizations.[5] The existence of nationally accepted objectives may be regarded as exogenous to the political system. However, to the extent that the political system may contribute to the difficulty or ease with which a nation nurtures collective actions by influencing, say, social unity or fragmentation, national policy objectives are affected by the political system.

With respect to the effective decision-making system of policy objectives, Cox and McCubbins (2001) argue that the design of democratic political institutions has a profound effect on economic performance. They argue that state decisiveness, referred to as the ability to decide effectively on policy objectives, is a function of the political system including the electoral system. They go on to argue that the more 'veto points', or contesting points within the political system, the greater its indecisiveness. Presidential systems typically have more veto points than parliamentary systems, often leading to legislative deadlock, and rendering policies under the former system less decisive.[6] Cox and McCubbins (2001) appear to focus on 'veto powers' within the political system, while McGuire and Olson (1996) focus more on those narrow special-interest groups outside the system. This chapter argues that the decisiveness of economic policy should take into account 'veto powers' both in and outside the political system.

Another important criterion for policy success is its consistency over time. This will provide policy certainty and credibility based on which the private sector undertakes its economic activities. The time horizon the political system takes has a bearing on economic development. If the political system of a nation takes short time horizons, the economy will grow less rapidly than those otherwise comparable nations (Harrison 1985). Policy consistency is equivalent to 'resoluteness' according to Cox and McCubbins (2001), which refers to the ability to stick to a policy decision. They argue that once policy has passed more and exhaustive veto points, it is likely to be more resolute. Conversely, the lack of policy credibility is more likely to occur in a political system with few veto points. They thus conclude that the presidential system provides a higher policy consistency or resoluteness than the parliamentary system. Cox and McCubbins (2001) suggest that regardless of the political system, policy will be both decisive and resolute under a single strongly hierarchical political party. Finally, as Moberg (2000) points out with regard to the Swedish economy, the flexibility and adaptability of economic policies to international policy environments are required for policy success in a small and open economy such as the Korean economy.

In summary, a set of criteria for a successful political system for economic development include: the establishment of appropriate institutions and implementation of national economic policy with a high degree of deliberation of the nation's aggregate social interest, decisiveness, consistency, credibility, flexibility and a long-term orientation. Against these conditions for economic policy success, this chapter examines the impact of the Korean political system on its economic development. To this end, a brief descriptive overview of the evolution of Korean politics and its salient characteristics since independence is provided, with a focus on recent years.

3.3 EVOLUTION OF KOREAN POLITICS

3.3.1 Recent Developments of Political Regimes

Korea had no experience of governing itself as a modern independent state until its liberation from 35 years of Japanese colonial rule in 1945. Upon liberation, the country was divided into two parts, becoming one of the main battlegrounds of the Cold War ideological conflict. This led to the formation of two separate states in 1948: the Republic of Korea (ROK) in the southern portion of the Korean Peninsula and the communist Democratic People's Republic of Korea (DPRK) in the north. This section reviews political developments in the Republic of Korea (hereafter Korea) since 1948.

Korea has, in principle, always had a democratic form of government based on the separation of powers and a system of checks and balances from the inception of the Republic.[7] Syngman Rhee was elected as the first President of the Republic in 1948, governing the country throughout the Korean War and ensuing difficult times. Korea's democracy was not mature at the time and President Rhee stepped down in 1960 in response to strong opposition against his authoritarian and corrupt government by students and citizens. In the same year, the Chang Myon government was established under a parliamentary system. It was subsequently removed in a military *coup d'état* led by General Park Chung Hee in 1961. He led the country until he was assassinated in 1979. Chun Doo Hwan was then elected President in 1980 for a seven-year term after a short transition period under martial law.[8] In the presidential election held in 1987, Roh Tae Woo was elected for a five-year term. Both Chun and Roh were former generals.

The democratic advances made during the Roh administration set the stage for the election of Kim Young Sam in 1992 for a five-year term 1993–98, ending the three decades of authoritarian rule under successive military dictatorships. The Kim Young Sam administration heralded a democratic transition and a new era of a pluralistic democracy in Korean politics headed by the first civilian President in 32 years. The new political system comprised a larger number of important political stakeholders than before including not only the President, bureaucracy, politicians and *chaebols* who had been major political players in the past, but also trade unions, strong interest groups, the general public and local governments.

Long-time opposition leader Kim Dae-jung was elected President in December 1997 and was inaugurated on 25 February 1998 for a five-year term. In addition to guiding the country through the financial crisis of 1997–98 relatively successfully, the election of Kim Dae-jung marked a watershed for Korean politics in that it was the first-ever peaceful transfer of power from the ruling conservative government to a liberal-democratic opposition party in Korean constitutional history. In December 2002, Roh Moo-hyun was elected from Kim Dae-jung's Millennium Democratic Party (MDP), and was inaugurated on 25 February 2003 for a five-year term. In December 2007, Lee Myung-bak from the main opposition party, the conservative Grand National Party (GNP), was elected and was inaugurated in February 2008 in the second peaceful transfer of power from the ruling to an opposition party. President Lee Myung-bak, a former Chief Executive of Hyundai Construction and former Mayor of Seoul was expected to lead a business-friendly and growth-oriented government. At the time of writing in 2009, however, the Lee government had been beset by a series of political crises throughout 2008 resulting from its own ineptness, before being engulfed by the global financial crisis that began in the United States in September 2008.

3.3.2 Constitution and Government

Korea's Constitution was first adopted in 1948 when the Republic was established, and amended nine times throughout the last five decades until the current constitution of 1987. The first eight amendments were made largely for the political expediency of the then presidents. The ninth amendment was approved in a 1987 referendum with bipartisan political support. This amendment provided for the direct election of the President for a single five-year term and for the institution of a system of local autonomy for the first time in 30 years. This Constitution endures to the present (2009) and has ensured the last four peaceful transfers of political power.

The Constitution provides for a liberal democratic political order and for basic individual rights and freedoms, the separation of powers and the rule of law. The Constitution assumes a free-market economy by declaring that the state guarantees the right to property and other economic rights, such as the right to work, freedom of choice of occupation and the right to free association and collective bargaining. It also encourages the freedom and creative initiative of enterprises and individuals in economic affairs.

Korea has a presidential system of government based on the separation of powers and a system of checks and balances. The government consists of three branches: the executive, legislature and judiciary. The President stands at the apex of the executive branch, serving as the head of state and representing the state in foreign affairs. The President is elected by a nationwide, equal, direct and secret ballot, and serves a single five-year term, with no additional terms being allowed as a safeguard against any individual holding the reins of power for a protracted period of time.

Legislative power is vested in the National Assembly, a unicameral legislature. Five-sixths of National Assembly members are directly elected by popular vote – one candidate from each electoral district, with the remaining seats distributed proportionately among parties winning five seats or more in a direct election. The term of office for members of the National Assembly is four years. In addition to the function of making laws, the National Assembly has the right to inspect all aspects of state affairs on a regular basis as a check on executive power. The President cannot dissolve the National Assembly, but the National Assembly has the powers to recommend the removal of the Prime Minister, and of impeaching the President, Prime Minister and any officials in cases of violations of the Constitution or other laws in execution of official duties.

Korea's judiciary consists of three levels of courts: the Supreme Court, High Court and District Court, and also includes a specialized Family Court and Administrative Court. The President, with the consent of the National Assembly, appoints the Chief Justice of the Supreme Court for a single six-year term. The President upon the recommendation of the Chief Justice also appoints the other justices. The Constitutional Court was established in 1988 as an independent, specialized court dealing with issues such as the impeachment of politicians, the dissolution of a political party, the constitutionality of legislation, and for the safeguarding of human rights.

According to the Constitution, local governments deal with matters pertaining to the welfare of local residents and property issues, and also establish, within the limit of national laws, rules and regulations regarding local autonomy. A local government is required to have a council. Laws at the national level determine the organization and powers of the council. The chief executives and members of local government councils are elected by direct vote for four-year terms.

3.3.3 Salient Characteristics of Korean Politics

Korea's latest Constitution follows closely the norms of advanced democratic countries, and the formal structure of government with a system of checks and balances between the three branches of government is little different from those of Western models. However, salient characteristics of Korea culture have shaped the development of politics in a unique way. The culture underlying the developments and changes in Korean politics over the last five decades since 1948 has been Confucianism, which still remains the single most important influence in contemporary politics. Although Korean society has changed significantly, Confucian values, such as an emphasis on personal relationships, hierarchical social structures and respect for authority, still remain strong.

Confucian influence on Korean political development can be traced back to the Yi Dynasty (1392–1910). Political leaders since the Yi Dynasty have relied on ideas found in Confucianism and have transmitted these ideas to subsequent generations through education in the Confucian classics in an attempt to mould society in line with Confucian doctrine. Through this process, Korea's political culture has emerged with the characteristics of a Confucian hierarchical view of life, submission to authority and reluctance to embark upon changes in the political structure. Despite the imposition of Western democracy from the beginning of the Republic in 1948, Confucianism has remained influential in shaping political development in Korea, maintaining some *sui generis* characteristics as follows.

Paternalistic political leadership

Further to being hierarchical, Korea has also been a paternalistic society under Confucian influence. In such a society people, including politicians, are often judged according to Confucian values of good morals, humanistic attitudes and educational achievements. Political leaders are expected to be morally strong, benevolent and knowledgeable, humble-minded, compassionate and virtuous. Such an emphasis on leadership has rendered Korean politics largely personality-based, rather than institutionally based. Nowhere is the importance of personality in Korean politics more obvious than in the political party system. The main political parties in Korea are largely recognized through their leaders. They do not represent contesting ideologies such as conservatism and liberalism as found in Western advanced countries. It is thus almost impossible to distinguish between the platforms and programmes of the various political parties. Nor do political parties represent different social classes or ideological cleavages.[9] In addition to being indistinguishable on policy platforms, political parties in Korea are subordinate to their leaders. Rather than acting as channels for political dialogue between society and political leaders, political parties are seen as followings for political leaders (Helgesen 1998: 250). This leads to the instability of political parties.

The 'personality charisma' approach in Korean politics has been reinforced by various political systems and culture. Candidates for the election of National Assembly members are nominated by the party leader – not by the local party members as in Western advanced countries. Therefore, any party member who is interested in running for national office cannot dare to challenge his or her party leader. This type of party political system is vulnerable to corruption. As people vote essentially for a person or personal background, legitimate considerations such as 'policies' are secondary. Under these circumstances, institutionalized party politics or disciplined political parties have never taken root, and a number of them have come and gone as attested by several new parties created in conjunction with the 2007 presidential election alone. The prospect of developing a limited number of encompassing parties in Korea looks dim.

Power concentration

Confucianism has contributed to the development of a concentration of political power in Korea. Reflecting the Confucian influence, political power in Korea has been highly concentrated in the President, who is also typically the leader of a political party. The President is surrounded by an interconnected elite group comprising of big businesses, bureaucrats and politicians all bound together by regional affiliations and educational and friendship ties (Helgesen 1998: 246; J.C. Lee 2001). At the same time, Confucianism has been used by this elite group to preserve their position, power and privileges in society through educational institutions (K.O. Kim 1988).

Regionalism

Another influential and visible characteristic of politics in Korea is a regionalism that has had a destructive effect on post-Korean War political developments. In Korea's family- and clan-orientated society, strong emphasis is also placed on one's place of origin; a descendent of a particular place will always belong to that place despite being born in another. Regionalism can thus be seen as a natural outcome of the Korean collective mentality. In the post-Korean War period, successive authoritarian regimes exacerbated the problem through utilizing regionalism as a means of maintaining state power. Dictatorships relied on trust and loyalty, values closely associated with regionalism. Furthermore, the unequal distribution of economic and political wealth – products of Korea's rapid economic development – further reinforced regionalism and its political influence. Accordingly, regionalism is embedded in Korean politics, and people often make important political decisions based on their regional affiliations.

Regionalism continues to plague Korean politics and is manifested in many different forms. The most explicit example of regionalism is the practice of 'voting along regional lines' as demonstrated in the 1987, 1992, 1997 presidential elections and in the 2000 general election (Kwon 2000). If a presidential candidate comes from a particular provincial area, people from the region will support that candidate because he or she 'represents their interests'. Since a political party is identified by its leader and the leader is identified by the region where the leader was born and raised, the region of a party is identified by the region of the party leader.[10] Regionalism and the 'personality cult' mentality exert significant influence over politics and continue to impede the capacity for democracy to function efficiently.

The role of non-government organizations (NGOs)

Korean politics entered a new landscape in 2000 when the Integrated Election Laws changed, allowing non-governmental organizations (NGOs) to participate in election campaigns, although banning them from holding rallies for or against particular candidates (*Asiaweek* 2000). There were nearly 70 000 NGOs registered with the central and local governments as of 2000 and a number of them are financially supported by the government. It is generally believed that these NGOs had a significant influence on the outcome of the 2000 general election. Under the Roh Moo-hyun administration, prominent NGOs enjoyed direct access to the President, who demonstrated his willingness to integrate their concerns into government policy. Former prominent NGO leaders held many key government posts in his administration (H.Y. Lee 2004). Under the Lee Myung-bak government, a number of cabinet positions and key positions at state-owned enterprises are held by members of one NGO which supported him during the 2007 presidential election (*Chosun Ilbo* 2009). As Korea transits from an industrial society to an information society, political participation of NGOs will be expedited as networking among their members and NGOs will be further facilitated.[11]

Prevalence of large-scale social movements

Mass civic actions played a crucial role in undermining Korea's authoritarian regimes prior to 1988 and in the transition to democracy. Since then, Korea has unambiguously been ranked as a full democracy by all international indicators. Nonetheless, there is the continuing prevalence of large-scale social movements that engage in widespread and frequent popular demonstrations and other protest activities, often illegal. There was an annual average of 372 protests per year over the period 1988–2007, and throughout the Roh Moo-hyun period in particular street protests were almost ritualized (S.H. Kim 2009). The vast majority of protests are characterized as 'violent and disruptive', and mass public demonstrations such as the candlelight vigils from April to August in 2008 protesting against the resumption of United States beef imports have the potential virtually to paralyse Korean governments (S.H. Kim 2009).

Why would such a culture of mass civic demonstrations and protests have developed in Korea? Almond and Verba (1963: 338) stress that activity, involvement and rationality are required components of 'civic culture', referred to as a set of related political and social attitudes, in fostering democratic stability. Mass civic actions in Korea in the recent past are far from the norm of the rational activist model of democratic citizenship. A number of explanations for this prevalence of violent and disruptive demonstrations in Korea are put forward. The first is the large number of NGOs, as already examined, networked through the Internet, who can mobilize their members easily. Second, as examined above, because the party system is underdeveloped and does not aggregate and represent societal interests, people resort to mass movements. This cannot explain their violent and disruptive characteristics. Third, as S.H. Kim (2009) suggests, the politics of protest is a legacy of the democratic transition process from the military dictatorship prior to 1988. As a result, Koreans are generally sympathetic to social movements and mass mobilization. It should be noted, though, that it was largely students who staged mass protests against the military dictatorships. Many of those radical student leaders were eventually 'rewarded' with candidacies for the National Assembly elections by political parties and with high positions in the government, particularly by the Roh Moo-hyun administration.

Fourth, Almond and Verda (1963: 341) suggest that the gap between the actual governmental responsiveness to the demands of citizens and the standards set may sway citizens' political activities away from the rational activist norm. In this regard, presidential candidates in Korea with the single five-year term are likely to make impractical and unreasonably high policy promises. The marked gap between the political pledge and reality may generate violent and disruptive civic actions. Fifth, Almond and Verda (1963: 356) also point out that civic actions are tempered in intensity by the norms of social trust, cooperativeness and confidence. As discussed in Chapter 2, attitudes of interpersonal trust and cooperation have abated significantly in Korea in the recent past. In particular, the sense of trust in politicians has ebbed remarkably in Korea due to the prevalence of corruption scandals and uncivilized behaviours in public places. This in turn leads to a low compliance of the rule of law.

Finally, the large number of persistent and disruptive protests over time implies that there prevails a perception in Korean society that the government takes heed of such protests, and that illegal activities are condoned. Indeed there have been numerous cases in which the government gave in to the demands of protesters. It appears that enforcement of laws on illegal activities and their organizers has not been adequately implemented; the incumbent minister in charge of such protests, with his or her typically short tenure, seeks to settle the issues quickly with no adequate punishment of those illegal activities, nor with any serious concern with the long-term ramifications of the settlements. All this indicates that Korean democracy has yet to be consolidated for its stability.[12] Taking into account these salient characteristics, different political systems since 1962 are assessed against the success criteria identified above.

3.4 IMPACTS OF THE KOREAN POLITICAL SYSTEMS ON THE ECONOMY

3.4.1 Economic Development under the Authoritarian Regimes, 1962–87

The authoritarian regimes from the early 1960s, with a strong central authority, were quite successful in achieving a high annual average growth rate of 8.6 per cent over the 1962–87 period and have been regarded as the model of the authoritarian capitalist developmental state (Han 1995). Obviously the authoritarian regimes were quite successful in meeting those criteria that require the political system to be conducive to economic development. The Park and Chun regimes, which took a grip on political power by military means, maintained a vision and objectives consistent with the national interest of rapid economic development as a way of legitimizing their political power. A widely accepted objective of rapid economic growth prevailed in Korean society during the 1960s and 1970s. After prolonged poverty as a result of the Korean War, citizens assigned high priority to the economic growth of the nation. This burning desire for rapid growth was bolstered by public campaigns by the regimes to mobilize the nation toward this objective, which was also reinforced by strong nationalism. In this context, the predatory behaviour of state officials was not of serious concern in Korea. Similarly, special interest groups, either suppressed by the central authorities or non-existent, could not distract the encompassing national attention from the growth objective.

The military regimes established or maintained a proper institutional framework. Even though they led a state-directed economy with extensive intervention, the regimes maintained a free-market economy by maintaining private property rights, provided powerful incentives for business by allowing companies to utilize profits after taxes at their discretion, and gave subsidies and protection against foreign competition. The regimes also maintained competition within the domestic market by ensuring that at least two companies operated in one industrial sector, unless it was run as a state-owned monopoly. Transaction costs would remain low because of harsh enforcements of laws and regulations by the military regime. In addition, the Park government established an autonomous and effective state apparatus, the Economic Planning Board (EPB), which provided a high degree of autonomy to a bureaucracy staffed by talented technocrats, and it also established economic research institutes under government ministries. The government provided a proper educational infrastructure for human resource development and managed to maintain it reasonably efficiently in the sense of matching the demand and supply of labour in the market and maintaining real wage increments equal to the rapid rises of productivity until the end of the 1980s (S.K. Kim 2001). This high real wage growth served to dampen social discontent (Amsden 1989: 10).

Economic policies implemented by the authoritarian regimes were decisive, consistent over time and credible. From 1962 until the end of 1980s, the government was able to implement consistently its consecutive five-year economic plans with specific targets. The underlying thrust of economic policies was rapid economic growth, although their directives evolved as the economy developed. With the constitutional clauses that permitted President Park to be elected for an unlimited number of times and President Chun to serve for a seven-year term, their time horizons were long, reflected by consecutive five-year economic plans. In particular, the government utilized efficiently a limited number of *chaebols* as a policy conduit for economic control and economic growth. State discipline of large enterprises took the form of both rewarding good performers and penalizing poor performers. In exchange for meeting or exceeding targets given by the state, firms were rewarded with additional licenses to diversify and expand the scale of their businesses. On the other hand, firms which did poorly in achieving the targets or in complying with state directives were subject to rationalization, refusal of credits or tax scrutiny (Amsden 1989: 14).

The Roh Tae Woo regime over the period 1988–93 pursued political democratization, ending the authoritarianism of over four decades. All the merit of the authoritarian regimes with respect to economic development dissipated with them. The political transition imposed tremendous economic adjustment costs on the country. Labour disputes, which had remained suppressed under the authoritarian regimes for the sake of maximum economic growth and political stability, became rampant and violent, and wages rose far in excess of productivity. Real-estate speculation flared up, and economic injustice was exacerbated. Throughout this adjustment process, the Korean economy lost part of its economic growth vitality and international competitiveness.

3.4.2 Economic Development under the Democratic Regimes from 1993

The Kim Young Sam government was inaugurated in 1993 as the first civilian regime in three decades and made a remarkable transition in the Korean political terrain. The new political system comprised a larger number of political stakeholders, fostered a more diverse and activist civil society, and made the system of political decision-making more complex and difficult (S.H. Kim 1997). For example, the Kim Young Sam government ended up abandoning the labour reform bill that had passed through the National Assembly, due to militant labour activism. At the same time, rapid modernization following industrialization, urbanization and economic growth had profoundly transformed Korea's traditional social structures and created new social cleavages. This process, in turn, made it difficult to generate social consensus on national economic policy. Under the banner of 'New Korea through change and reform', the new regime embarked on a 'A Five-Year Plan for the New Economy' with a focus on globalization. However, as the new civilian democratic regime was relatively unstable because of the presence of strong interest groups and with the decline of central authority, the government lost its decisiveness and consistency in economic policy, as attested by its five-year economic plan being left unattended.

A number of political scientists argue that, although the Kim Young Sam government heralded a new era of a pluralistic democracy, democracy under his regime remained confined to a purely procedural process without any substantive or meaningful economic redistribution or mass participation beyond the act of voting in a free and fair election and the constitutional guarantee of political participation (S.H. Kim 1997; Han 1995; Lee and Lee 2008). Most of the Korean middle and working class remained reconciled to the conservative status quo, although some militant civil society groups continued their struggle against the regime. The fundamental tenets of economic policy of the Kim Young Sam government, although less successfully, remained the same as those of the preceding authoritarian regimes, that is, they were committed to a 'growth-first' strategy (Ha 1997).[13] As a result, the regime failed to undertake serious institutional reforms other than introducing the real-name deposit system, and it ended in financial crisis.

It was the Kim Dae-jung and Roh Moo-hyun governments that have differentiated their regimes from the conservative administrations of the early democratization era. These administrations promoted the idea of participatory democracy, which meant the active participation of citizens in the policy-making process, the democratization of industrial relations, and the monitoring of state and business actors by a proactive civil society (Y.H. Lee 2005). However, as Lee and Lee (2008) argue, the two regimes were still in the process of democratic consolidation which required not only procedural democracy, but also a democratic culture among the political leadership and civil society, whereby political leaders were expected to be equipped with the democratic leadership skills of political mediation, coordination and compromise, and civil society was required to accept the democratic rule of law and partake in the political process (Lee and Lee 2008). The consolidation process of Korean democracy has yet to be completed (Lee and Lee 2008; J.C. Lee 2001; J.W. Lee 2004).

The slow process of democratic consolidation is attributable to a number of factors. The political leadership has not cast off the authoritarian style of leadership. There is a lack of compromise among political stakeholders, thereby raising political confrontations and political instability. This would be attributable to paternalistic leadership with concentrated political power, as examined above. Under pluralistic democracy, a large number of new political stakeholders have emerged. Due to the nascent status of democracy, some stakeholders have occasionally applied tactics beyond the rule of law in asserting their political interests. Corruption is still high in Korea politics, which is in turn attributable to the distorted party politics as examined above and the high costs of participating in politics.

During the period of democratic consolidation, neither the Kim Dae-jung nor the Roh Moo-hyun government was regarded as a successful regime in terms of economic policy. In its early stages, Kim Dae-jung's government managed the financial crisis quite successfully and undertook various economic reforms, as examined in Chapter 1. This was attributable not only to the leader's decisiveness and resoluteness but also to the whole society being united for a drastic shift in the economic policy paradigm to overcome the devastating crisis. As pointed out in Chapter 1, President Kim's approach to economic reform was through coercion and intervention rather than relying on market principles. Once the emergency period of recovering from the crisis was over, President Kim Dae-jung could not accomplish much due to his lack of coordination skills (Lee and Lee 2008) and a high density of strong interest groups that applied militant and even illegal tactics for political gain. Furthermore, his presidential authority and credibility were weakened by corruption cases in which his son and close allies were involved.

The Roh Moo-hyun government over the period 2003–08 was a disreputable regime for its political instability which was in turn attributable to various factors such as his lack of democratic leadership and the immature democratic orientation of civil society. Roh was elected under the banner of political reform and, in particular, the elimination of ingrained political regionalism and corruption in politics. His 'participatory democracy' was aimed at social cohesion and voluntary cooperation with the state by fostering civil society organizations as a 'third sector'. Roh's stance raised expectations among various social groups and led to a prevalence of illegal strikes by unions and uncontrollable street demonstrations by interest groups or NGOs making 'an explosion of demands' throughout the five-year term (H.Y. Lee 2004). Corruption scandals tainted his regime during the first year, in which close associates were implicated. Roh's approval rating dipped with these developments and in less than a year's time his party (the MDP) was split into two factions supporting and opposing the President. Roh loyalists formed a new party, the Uri Party, with only 44 of the 299 National Assembly seats (Fukuyama et al. 2005). With such minority support in the National Assembly, Roh was unable to pursue his legislative agenda.

President Roh and the Uri Party were dedicated to broad and highly sensitive reform agendas such as the decentralization of administration to the regions as part of its regionally balanced development agenda; reconciliation and cooperation with North Korea; amelioration of the income gap between rich and poor; a reinterpretation of Korean history during the 1940s to the 1960s; and a stabilization in the speculative hikes in real-estate prices (Hahm and Kim 2005). Public opinion on his reform agenda was polarized into conservative and progressive positions, and the conflicts between the two blocs escalated over time. These political conflicts culminated in March 2004 in an impeachment resolution by the National Assembly for the first time in Korean history for Roh's speech in support of his party in the then forthcoming National Assembly election. In May 2004, the Constitutional Court ruled that Roh had indeed violated the electoral law but the violation was not enough to warrant removal of a directly elected president (Hahm and Kim 2005). In the meantime, because of public dissatisfaction with the disruptive impeachment process, the 2004 election results delivered a resounding victory to Roh's Uri Party, winning a majority of seats in the National Assembly (Cha 2005; Fukuyama et al. 2005).

The resolution of this constitutional crisis from the impeachment has demonstrated two important aspects of the Korean political system. First, the authority of the judiciary was enhanced in holding both the executive and the legislature accountable. Second, it demonstrated the viability of Korea's relatively new democratic institutions (Fukuyama et al. 2005). Despite the Uri Party's convincing win in the 2004 National Assembly elections, however, public dissatisfaction with the President's policy and reforms soared rapidly, and Roh's party dramatically lost a series of by-elections to the GNP, and the party eventually disappeared by the time of the 2007 presidential election, demonstrating again the volatility of Korean democracy (Lie and Park 2006).

The Roh Moo-hyun government was not able to make significant accomplishments for economic development because of its lack of democratic leadership and the lack of encompassing interest, decisiveness, consistency and credibility in its attempted policies. Added to this were uncooperative rent-seeking interest groups employing non-democratic tactics for their claims. In terms of economic policy, the Roh administration posited a 'free and fair' market order with equitable distribution of income as the strategic economic objective for the new government (Y.H. Lee 2005). When public opinion on his reform agendas was polarized into conservative and progressive positions, and the conflicts between the two blocs escalated, President Roh revealed his lack of democratic leadership and compromising political skills, as attested by his divisive rhetoric and promotion of the confrontation between the two blocs and the impeachment resolution. All these developments exacerbated political instability. With such political instability and with a socially fragmented and divisive society, introduction of new policies and institutional reforms became untenable, thereby contributing to the nation's sluggish economic performance from 2003 to 2007.

The year 2008 began with the inauguration of President Lee Myung-bak from the conservative GNP, marking the end of a ten-year period of progressive government. President Lee was elected on a platform of revitalizing the economy through business-friendly policies, job creation and tax reductions. The GNP also won a clear victory in the April 2008 National Assembly election, giving the governing party the largest majority in the legislature since democratization in 1987. President Lee's honeymoon period did not last long, however, as the new conservative government was quickly beset by a series of crises. His approval rating, which peaked at 51.1 per cent in March 2008, plummeted to less than 20 per cent in June (Hundt 2008; Moon 2009).

The first of President Lee's political problems revolved around his selection of cabinet ministers from his close associates based on his alma mater and church and from a wealthy area. Of the 15 candidates put to the National Assembly for approval, 13 were accused of a variety of improprieties including real-estate speculation, tax evasion and plagiarism. Three of the nominations were withdrawn and the President was forced to apologize (Moon 2009). This incident has alienated a large portion of the citizens from his government. Soon after this, on 15 April 2008, President

Lee announced that the government was rescinding Korea's ban on beef imports from the United States that had been imposed after a case of mad cow disease in 2003. This prompted massive public demonstrations across the country and developed into an anti-government movement with anti-American overtones (Hundt 2008; Moon 2009; Kirk 2008). Eventually, after four months of political paralysis, the Lee government settled on imposing more stringent regulations on United States beef imports, and the entire cabinet and various presidential aides offered their resignations (Moon 2009). In August, President Lee angered Korea's Buddhist community, which represents about a quarter of the population (KNSO 2009), for alleged discrimination. There were claims that because of Lee's strong Christian faith, senior public servants in government had been evangelizing for Christianity and disparaging Buddhism (Moon 2009).

Since September 2008, the Lee government's major political problems have revolved around Korea's rapidly deterioration economic position resulting from the global financial crisis started in the United States and the ensuing global economic recession. By the final quarter of 2008, the Korean economy clearly fell into a recession. President Lee was elected on the so-called '747' slogan: 7 per cent annual GDP growth over the next ten years, US$40 000 per capita income, and Korea becoming the 7th largest economy in the world within ten years.[14] Additionally, President Lee advocated further deregulation, privatization, greater tax incentives for R&D, a canal across the country, and a harder line on North Korea. The canal proposal was abandoned in June 2008 due to a lack of popular support (Hundt 2008). No significant initiatives have been undertaken for his own growth-oriented strategy either in institutional changes or in economic policy measures. President Lee has also been accused of a delayed response to the global financial crisis, and a lack of policy coordination among ministries and agencies. This has all contributed to the current lack of confidence in his government (Moon 2009).

The Lee administration has not received much support or cooperation from the legislative branch in the face of a sustained deadlock and occasional fist-fights in the National Assembly. The Lee government is seeking parliamentary approval for a number of bills including the free trade agreement (FTA) with the United States. Opposition legislators have threatened to oppose all of them. Although the GNP holds a majority in the National Assembly, it is apprehensive about passing laws without opposition support, as opposition parties and labour unions could easily provoke another wave of destabilizing protests given President Lee's low approval rate (Oliver 2009: 3).

It is too early to assess the effect of the political system of the Lee government on the economy. However, it appears that President Lee has so far failed to make a significant contribution to democratic consolidation and stability, which would in turn contribute to economic development. Perhaps because of his long career as a chief executive officer of Hyundai Construction and as Mayor of Seoul City for four years, he is lacking the leadership skills of political coordination and compromise. D.J. Kim (2009), a renowned columnist of the *Chosun Ilbo*, which is well known as a supporter of the conservative GNP, argues that President Lee lacks the political skills of compromising with National Assembly members and the opposing factions within his own party. Kang (2009), another columnist of the *Chosun Ilbo*, argues that President Lee has focused on economic growth and overlooked a number of other social issues, thereby losing the support of a large portion of the public. With his weakened presidential authority together with his low approval rate and with the lack of support from the National Assembly, it appears unlikely that the Lee government will be able to undertake significant institutional reforms and economic measures that meet the policy success criteria identified above.

3.5 CONCLUSION

Economic development is a complex phenomenon with a variety of contributing factors. Recognizing the complementarity of the multiple factors for economic development, this chapter has examined the impacts of political systems on economic development in Korea from the authoritarian military regimes of the 1960s and 1970s to the present liberal-democratic political system in 2009. To this end, a set of criteria against which to assess the impact of the political system on economic performance have been developed through a literature review. Under the assumption that the political system affects economic development through economic policies and institutional reforms, a set of evaluation criteria have been chosen which include: the establishment of proper institutions to minimize transaction costs, secure property rights and promote competition; and the implementation of national economic policy with a high degree of deliberation of the nation's aggregate social interests, decisiveness, consistency, credibility, flexibility and a long-term orientation.

The Korean political system has made remarkable progress over a short period of time and its democracy has matured substantially. It made a historic transition from authoritarian regimes to a democratic regime with corresponding constitutional reform in 1987. Since then, peaceful power transfers have occurred twice from the ruling party to an opposition party, and Korea has even experienced an impeachment trial of the President. The contents of Korea's existing Constitution follow closely the norms in Western democratic countries, and the formal structure of government is little different from those of politically advanced Western models. However, the Korean political system maintains some *sui generis* characteristics resulting from its idiosyncratic Confucian culture.

It is generally considered that the authoritarian regimes in Korea were quite successful in terms of economic development. The regimes were committed to economic development without serious predatory activities. They established proper institutions for secured property rights and market competition and established policy-making organizations staffed with efficient officials. The military regimes repressed or destroyed most special-interest organizations, including unions. Economic policies under these circumstances met the success criteria of encompassing interests, decisiveness, certainty, credibility and long-term orientation. However, the merits that authoritarian regimes had with respect to economic development all dissipated with the political transition which imposed tremendous economic adjustment costs.

The system of political decision-making under the Kim Young Sam government was much more complex and difficult with a large number of political stakeholders and a diverse and active civil society. The first civilian regime was not able to generate social consensus on its national economic policy and lost the decisiveness, consistency and flexibility in its policy. Democracy under this regime was transitional in nature, with the fundamental tenet of its economic policy remaining anchored by the growth-first strategy as under the authoritarian regimes. Thus, the Kim Young Sam regime failed to undertake serious institutional reforms, resulting in the 1997 financial crisis.

Korean democracy further progressed to its consolidation stage under the Kim Dae-jung and Roh Moo-hyun governments. For a completion of democratic consolidation, political leaders need to be equipped with the democratic leadership skills of political compromise, and civil society is required to accept the rule of law and partake responsibly in the political process. Neither the Kim Dae-jung nor Roh Moo-hyun governments succeeded in this step due to a lack of leadership and an immature civil society with a civic culture not conducive to democracy. As a result, neither was regarded as a successful regime in terms of economic policy. In particular, President Kim Dae-jung was quite successful at the beginning of his term in managing the financial crisis and implementing various economic reforms, largely because the whole society was united behind him to overcome the devastating crisis. Beyond this, though, he could not accomplish much due to his lack of coordination skills and to a high density of strong interest groups often using militant and illegal tactics. Further, his presidential authority was weakened by corruption cases, and this undermined the credibility of his policies.

The Roh Moo-hyun administration was not able to make significant accomplishments in economic development because of its lack of democratic leadership and the narrow encompassing interest and the lack of decisiveness, consistency and credibility in its attempted policies. Added to this was the immature democratic orientation of civil society as attested by the prevalence of illegal strikes and demonstrations. Roh started with a broad agenda of political reforms and economic policies. However, public opinion on his policy agenda soon became polarized and civil and political conflicts escalated. This led to a constitutional crisis of an impeachment resolution and to further political instability. Under such social fragmentation and political instability, the government failed to implement significant new policies and institutional reforms, thereby contributing to the sluggish economic performance over the 2003–07 period. While it is far too early in 2009 to make a clear assessment, the Lee Myung-bak presidency has started very badly. A series of political crises throughout 2008 were ineptly handled by the government. This was followed in the midst of legislative deadlock by a precipitous economic decline in late 2008 and early 2009 exacerbated by the global financial crisis.

The underlying weakness of the Korean political systems under the 1987 Constitution has been demonstrated by recent democratic governments. In addition to deficient democratic consolidation and a civic culture of disruptive protests, one of the major problems with the Korean political system under the existing Constitution is the system's inherent instability resulting from the instability and factionalism of its political parties and the single five-year term of the presidency. Korean political parties, built around the leaders' personality and regionalism, are poorly institutionalized. They are unable to develop a stable party politics and are vulnerable to corruption. Under the single five-year term, presidential candidates are likely to make impractical policy promises, and once elected, the President has strong incentives to pursue short-run economic programmes. Once disenchanted with the President, electorates are likely to elect opposition party members to the National Assembly and resort to mass civic protests, raising the prospect of minority government and political deadlock. Under such political instability, the government is less likely to meet the success policy criteria with institutional reforms and economic policy measures. Society perceives the lack of decisiveness, consistency, certainty, credibility and long-term orientation of development policy, which renders the task of reaching policy consensus more difficult.

Clearly, the political system is an important variable for economic development and is not a matter of *ceteris paribus*. Even if all else remains the same, the prospects for the Korean economy will be tainted because of the low level of democratic consolidation, the unstable political party system and inappropriate civic culture. All this is highly attributable to Korean culture, which changes only at a glacial pace. In order to improve its economic prospects and to attain the nation's long-cherished goal of the status of an advanced country, Korea needs to accelerate the democratic consolidation process, and improve its party political system as well as its overall political system.

NOTES

1. Political systems for this study are referred to in the political science literature as 'regime types'. The study of the effects of economic development on political systems is beyond of the scope of this chapter.
2. Probably because of this, most of the studies that argue for beneficial effects of authoritarianism on economic growth were done before the end of the Cold War.
3. For those specific studies, see Przeworski and Limongi (1993) and Sirowy and Inkeles (1990).
4. Not many studies have been done in the literature in Korean on the impact of the political system on economic development, nor in the Korean context in the English literature after democratization at the end of the 1980s. Mo (2000) applies three different political systems (parliamentary, power-concentrated presidential and power-decentralized presidential systems) over three different periods – 1970–80, 1980–90, 1970–90 – with a large number of countries. Differences in growth rates by political systems do not appear convincing. J.C. Lee (2001) examines the political system and its effects on economic liberalization reforms – not the effects on the economy. J.W. Lee (2004) argues that as there is no theoretical basis nor empirical evidence favouring either authoritarianism or democracy for economic development, democracy together with the market system should be chosen for the sake of more freedom.
5. Moberg (2000) argues that the impressive growth of the Swedish economy during the 1950s and 1960s was attributable to its unique encompassing interest-group structure.
6. In the only empirical study that investigates economic performance and presidential versus parliamentary democratic systems, Cheibub and Przeworski (1999) find that there was no statistically significant relationship between presidential democracy and economic performance, and only a very minor correlation between parliamentary democracy and growth of the labour force.
7. National Assembly elections were held throughout the period of authoritarian rule in Korea prior to 1987. Authoritarian rulers recognized the important legitimating function of a democratic electoral facade, both to the domestic polity and to their United States ally (Heo and Stockton 2005).
8. Elections in Korea until the Roh Tae Woo regimes were 'quasi-democratic' or 'pseudo-democratic' in nature in that the regime imposed biased electoral rules and manipulated boundaries and electoral seats to ensure that the ruling party could not be defeated (Heo and Stockton 2005).
9. This belief is supported by a national survey conducted in 1996 by the Institute of Social Sciences, Seoul National University, which found that 72 per cent of respondents reported that the political parties did not differ from one another (Shin 1995). Kwon (2000) also observed this at the April 2000 election of National Assembly members.
10. This was clearly witnessed during the so-called 'three Kim era' from the 1980s to the 1990s during which the four major political parties were: one led by President Roh Tae Woo based

in Kyeongsangbuk Province; one led by President Kim Young Sam based in Kyeongsangnam Province; one led by President Kim Dae-jung based in Jeolla Province; and one led by former Prime Minister Kim Jong Pil based in Chungcheong Province. After the 'three Kim era' was over, the power of personality-cult-based politics has been incrementally weakening, while regionalism is still strong in Korean politics.

11. During the authoritarian regimes from 1948 to the end of 1980s, the role of students was highly important in Korean politics. They were regarded as the group of 'social conscience' and stood up against social injustice, dictatorships and corruption under the banner of democracy, justice, and unification of the nation. From the 1990s, students' role in Korean politics has ebbed remarkably.
12. Almond and Verba (1963: 366–70) argue that proper civic culture, like culture in general, develops over time through transmission from generation to generation, and that formal education would be a vehicle in expediting the development of civic culture conducive to democratic stability.
13. Y.H. Lee (2005) argues that the Kim Young Sam government was strongly influenced by the 'New Right' movement of the international re-emergence of classical liberal political economy in the 1980s, exemplified by the Thatcher government in the UK. New Right ideology espoused a strong but minimal state, economic liberalization, privatization and free-market fundamentalism.
14. All this appears to be impractical and irresponsible, as he will no longer be President after his five-year term.

REFERENCES

Almeida, Heitor and Daniel Ferreira (2002), 'Democracy and the variability of economic performance', *Economics and Politics*, **14** (3), 225–57.

Almond, G.A. and S. Verba (1963), *The Civic Culture: political attitudes and democracy in five nations*, Boston, MA: Little, Brown & Company.

Amsden, Alice H. (1989), *Asia's Next Giant: South Korea and late industrialization*, New York: Oxford University Press.

Asiaweek (2000), 'The nations: South Korea: the power of the NGOs: civic groups are the new political force', 11 February.

Beaulier, Scott A. and J. Robert Subrick (2006), 'The political foundations of development: the case of Botswana', *Constitutional Political Economy*, **17**, 103–15.

Beeson, Mark (2002), 'Theorising institutional change in East Asia', in Mark Beeson (ed.), *Reconfiguring East Asia: regional institutions and organisations after the crisis*, London: RoutledgeCurzon, pp. 7–27.

Burkhart, Ross E. and Michael S. Lewis-Beck (1994), 'Comparative democracy: the economic development thesis', *American Political Science Review*, **88** (4), 903–10.

Cha, Victor D. (2005), 'South Korea in 2004: peninsular flux', *Asian Survey*, **45** (1), 33–40.

Chaudhry, Azam and Phillip Garner (2007), 'Do governments suppress growth? Institutions, rent-seeking, and innovation blocking in a model of Schumpeterian growth', *Economics and Politics*, **19** (1), 35–52.

Cheibub, José Antonio and Adam Przeworski (1999), 'Democracy, elections, and accountability for economic outcomes', in Adam Przeworski, Susan C. Stokes and Bernard Manin (eds), *Democracy, Accountability, and Representation*, Cambridge: Cambridge University Press, pp. 222–49.

Chosun Ilbo (2009), 'Reprehensible story from advanced peoples network, an NGO', *Chosun Ilbo Daily*, 12 April, Seoul, Korea.

Cohen, Youssef (1985), 'The impact of bureaucratic-authoritarian rule on economic growth', *Comparative Political Studies*, **18** (1), 123–36.

Cox, Gary W. and Mathew D. McCubbins (2001), 'The institutional determinants of economic policy outcomes', in Stephan Haggard and Mathew D. McCubbins (eds), *Presidents, Parliaments, and Policy*, Cambridge: Cambridge University Press, pp. 21–63.

Ersson, Svante and Jan-Erik Lane (1996), 'Democracy and development: a statistical exploration', in Adrian Leftwich (ed.), *Democracy and Development: theory and practice*, Cambridge: Polity, pp. 45–73.

Feng, Yi (1995), 'Regime, polity, and economic growth: the Latin American experience', *Growth and Change*, **26**, Winter, 77–104.

Fukuyama, Francis, Bjoern Dressel and Boo-Seung Chang (2005), 'Facing the perils of presidentialism', *Journal of Democracy*, **16** (2), 102–16.

Gerring, John, Philip Bond, William T. Barndt and Carola Moreno (2005), 'Democracy and economic growth: a historical perspective', *World Politics*, **57** (3), 323–64.

Ha, Yeon-Seob (1997), 'Public finance and budgeting in Korea under democracy: a critical appraisal', *Public Budgeting and Finance*, **17** (1), 56–73.

Haggard, Stephan (1990), *Pathways from the Periphery: the politics of growth in newly industrializing countries*, Ithaca, NY, USA and London, UK: Cornell University Press.

Hahm, Chaihark and Sung Ho Kim (2005), 'Constitutionalism on trial in South Korea', *Journal of Democracy*, **16** (2), 28–42.

Han, Sang-Jin (1995), 'Economic development and democracy: Korea as a new model?', *Korea Journal*, **35** (2), 5–17.

Harrison, Lawrence E. (1985), *Underdevelopment is a State of Mind*, Cambridge, MA: Harvard University Press.

Helgesen, Geir (1998), *Democracy and Authority in Korea: the cultural dimension in Korean politics*, London: Curzon.

Helliwell, John F. (1994), 'Empirical linkages between democracy and economic growth', *British Journal of Political Science*, **24**, 225–48.

Heo, Uk and Hans Stockton (2005), 'The impact of democratic transition on elections and parties in South Korea', *Party Politics*, **11** (6), 674–88.

Hundt, David (2008), 'Korea – squandering a mandate for change?', *Australian Journal of International Affairs*, **62** (4), 497–512.

Kang, Chan-seok (2009), 'The Lee government should get smarter', *Chosun Ilbo Daily*, 19 March, Seoul: Korea.

Kim, Dae-jung (2009), 'Lee Myung-bak's antipathy of politics', *Chosun Ilbo Daily*, 1 March, Seoul: Korea.

Kim, Kwang-ok (1988), 'A Study on the Political Manipulation of Elite Culture: Confucian culture in local-level politics', *Korean Journal*, **28** (11), 4–16.

Kim, Sookon (2001), 'Korea's industrial relations in transition', in O.Y. Kwon and W. Shepherd (eds), *Korea's Economic Prospects: from financial crisis to prosperity*, Cheltenham, UK and Northampton, MA, USA: Edward Elgar Publishing, pp. 207–24.

Kim, Sunhyuk (1997), 'State and civil society in South Korea's democratic consolidation: is the battle really over?', *Asian Survey*, **37** (12), 1135–44.

Kim, Sunhyuk (2009), 'Civic engagement and democracy in South Korea', *Korea Observer*, **41** (1), 1–26.

Kirk, Donald (2008), 'Korea's "bulldozer" leader hits the wall', *Far Eastern Economic Review*, **171** (6), July/August, 8–12.

Kohli, Atul, Michael F. Altfeld, Saideh Lotfian and Russell Mardon (1984), 'Inequality in the third world: an assessment of competing explanations', *Comparative Political Studies*, **17** (3), 283–319.

Korea National Statistical Office (KNSO) (2009), *Social Indicators in Korea*, Seoul: KNSO.

Kwon, O. Yul (2000), 'Weaknesses of Korean politics and their remedies', (in Korean), *Korea Economic Daily*, 24 April.

LeBlang, David A. (1997), 'Political democracy and economic growth: pooled cross-sectional and time-series evidence', *British Journal of Political Science*, **27**, 453–72.

Lee, Dong-Yoon and Jaeheon Lee (2008), 'Political crises after democratization in South Korea and Thailand: comparative perspectives of democratic consolidation', *Korea Observer*, **39** (1), 121–56.

Lee, Hong Yung (2004), 'South Korea in 2003: A question of leadership?' *Asian Survey*, **44** (1), 130–38.

Lee, Jong Chan (2001), 'Political system and economic liberalisation reform', in S.H. Jwa and D.R. Yoon (eds), *Korea's Institutional Reform: issues and direction*, Seoul: Korea Economic Research Institute, pp. 177–213.

Lee, Jung Woo (2004), 'Democracy and economic development', (in Korean), in H.Y. Byun (ed.), *Ways of Economic Reform: international comparison of economic reform policies*, Seoul: Seoul Social and Economic Research Institute, pp. 161–90.

Lee, Yeonho (2005), 'Participatory democracy and chaebol regulation in Korea', *Asian Survey*, **45** (2), 279–301.

Lie, John and M.K. Park (2006), 'South Korea in 2005: economic dynamism, generational conflicts, and social transformation', *Asian Survey*, **46** (1), 56–62.

McGuire, M. and M. Olson (1996), 'Economics of autocracy and majority rule', *Journal of Economic Literature*, **34**, March, 72–96.

Milner, Helen V. and Keiko Kubota (2005), 'Why the move to free trade? Democracy and trade policy in the developing countries', *International Organization*, **59**, Winter, 107–43.

Mo, Jong Lin (2000), 'Political system and economic growth', in S.H. Jwa and S.H. Lee (eds), *Institutions and Economic Development*, Seoul: Korea Economic Research Institute, pp. 155–78.

Moberg, Erik (2000), 'The Swedish model: a comment on Mancur Olson's analysis', in M. Olson and S. Kahkonen (eds), *A Not-So-Dismal Science: a broad view of economies and societies*, Oxford: Oxford University Press, pp. 168–81.

Moon, Chung-in (2009), 'South Korea in 2008: from crisis to crisis', *Asian Survey*, **49** (1), 120–28.

Oliver, Christian (2009), 'Reform bills pile up as battling Seoul legislators play to cameras', *Financial Times*, UK edn, 10 March, p. 3.

Olson, Mancur (2000), 'Big bills left on the sidewalk: why some nations are rich, and others poor', in M. Olson and S. Kahkonen (eds), *A Not-So-Dismal Science: a broad view of economies and societies*, Oxford: Oxford University Press, pp. 37–60.

Przeworski, Adam, Michael E. Alvarez, José Antonio Cheibub and Fernando Limongi (2000), *Democracy and Development*, Cambridge: Cambridge University Press.

Przeworski, Adam and Fernando Limongi (1993), 'Political regimes and economic growth', *Journal of Economic Perspectives*, **7** (3), 51–69.

Rao, Vaman (1985), 'Democracy and economic development', *Studies in Comparative International Development*, **19** (4), 67–81.

Rodrik, Dani (1992), 'Political economy and development policy', *European Economic Review*, **36**, 329–36.

Shin, Doh Chull (1995), 'Political parties and democratisation in South Korea: the mass public and the democratic consolidation of political parties', *Democratisation*, **2** (2), 20–55.

Sirowy, Larry and Alex Inkeles (1990), 'The effects of democracy on economic growth and equality: a review', *Studies in Comparative International Development*, **25** (1), 126–57.

Tiruneh, Gizachew (2006), 'Regime type and economic growth in Africa: a cross-national analysis', *Social Science Journal*, **43**, 3–18.

Weede, Erich (1996), 'Political regime type and variation in economic growth rates', *Constitutional Political Economy*, **7**, 167–76.

4. The Korean economy: transition to a knowledge-based economy

4.1 INTRODUCTION

Another facet of the transition of the Korean economy is its development toward a knowledge-based economy (KBE), which this chapter examines. Caught between rapidly developing, export-oriented neighbouring countries, and in particular China and the technologically advanced countries of the West, as well as Japan, Korea has been forced to replace the export-led industrialization strategy of its past and seek a new strategy for economic growth. Another important imperative for Korea's move to a KBE is its demographic decline and rapid population ageing, which will quickly erode Korea's traditional comparative advantage in high-quality, low-cost workers. Recognizing both the increasing importance of knowledge-based industries and the structural weaknesses of the Korean economy, the government released in January 2000 a proposal for a three-year plan to serve as a blueprint for Korea's transformation into a KBE (Pai et al. 2003). Since then, Korea has been active in promoting various aspects of the KBE, whilst not neglecting others (Dahlman and Andersson 2000: 31).

Yuen and Griffy-Brown (2001) argue that economic growth in advanced countries is now predicated on the success of a knowledge-based economic development strategy and point out that knowledge-based sectors have been attracting high resources in all leading OECD economies. The OECD (1996: 9) estimated that more than half of GDP in the advanced OECD economies is knowledge-based. In this, Korea is not an exception. For instance, Korea's R&D as a percentage of its GDP was 3 per cent in 2005, the fifth-highest among OECD countries, compared to an OECD average ratio of 2.25 per cent (OECD 2007: 25). Korea's investment in knowledge (R&D, software and education) amounted to 5.8 per cent of GDP in 2002, the fourth-highest among OECD countries (World Bank 2006: 8). Further, the contribution of knowledge-based industries to the Korean economy was 39.5 per cent in 2002, compared to the European Union (EU) average of 37.8 per cent (OECD 2005a: 204). However, Korea is still far behind numerous countries with its drive toward a KBE. Korea ranked 31st in 2008 out of 134 countries with the Knowledge Economy Index (KEI) estimated by the World Bank (2008a). Singapore, Taiwan and Hong Kong as well as Japan outranked Korea. Korea's score on the KEI was 7.68 in 2008, indicating its ranking of 76.8 percentile of the 134 countries surveyed. This is compared to its score of 7.56 in 1995 (Suh and Chen 2007: 12). Therefore, for its sustainable economic growth, Korea has faced a critical challenge of upgrading its KBE to the levels of newly industrialized countries in East Asia as well as advanced countries.

This chapter critically assesses and evaluates Korea's transition to a KBE, which has already advanced significantly. First, the analytical framework adopted for this study is outlined. This incorporates key determinants or elements of a KBE. In line with this framework, this chapter examines Korean government policy in facilitating the transition to a KBE and assesses the current status of Korea's KBE. By examining policy and assessing the current status, the chapter will identify and discuss measures that still need to be undertaken. Finally, the chapter concludes with an assessment of Korea's prospects as a KBE, and a set of policy suggestions.

4.2 ANALYTICAL FRAMEWORK

The term 'knowledge-based economy' refers essentially to an economy in which the production, distribution and application of knowledge are the bases of economic activities and the main drivers of economic growth (Tan and Hooy 2007; APEC 2002; Pai et al. 2003). Every business uses technology and knowledge in some form to transform its inputs into outputs. The difference in the knowledge-based economic era, particularly in conjunction with the increasingly competitive and globalizing market, is that the use of new technologies and communications is vital to a nation's competitiveness and continued economic growth. Therefore, as Yuen and Griffy-Brown (2001) argue, to maintain economic growth, the ability to create, distribute and exploit new knowledge will be critical not only in existing industries but also in newer high-technology fields.

Knowledge has a number of special features as compared to other factors of production. It is in general accepted that knowledge leads to increasing returns to scale, and the social return to knowledge creation exceeds the private return. Also, knowledge contains properties similar to public goods and has a social networking effect of raising the value by increasing the number of connected users. These characteristics require the government to set up special policies to promote the acquisition, dissemination and application of knowledge. Because of its nature as a public good and the higher social return over private return, societal support for the creation of knowledge is justified. Because of its intangible characteristics, knowledge requires special protection for its development and dissemination. Because of the long process from creation to application through multiple channels, the government should promote a collaborative R&D system interlocking pertinent organizations such as government, universities and industries.

The OECD, which has analysed the KBE extensively, has clearly elucidated these special characteristics of knowledge and corresponding strategic programmes required for the development of a KBE. It has provided a four-part analytical framework for examining the determinants or 'necessary conditions' for a KBE (Dahlman and Andersson 2000; Chen and Dahlman 2005). The four pillars of an KBE identified by Dahlman and Andersson (2000: 21) are:

1. appropriate institutions and incentives;
2. educated and skilled human resources;
3. a dynamic information and communication technology (ICT) infrastructure; and
4. an effective innovation system interlocking universities, research centres and other organizations.[1]

A successful transition to the KBE involves the coordinated and complementary development of all these four elements. Based on this framework, the transition of the Korean economy toward a KBE will be assessed. Each of these four pillars is further elaborated as follows.

4.2.1 Institutions and Policy Settings

To develop a country's KBE, it is critically important that an appropriate institutional structure and policy settings should be established that provide legal and regulatory underpinnings for secured intellectual property rights and a competition environment. It should also foster a creative society, suitable social attitudes, and transparent and accountable governance structures. Furthermore, appropriate policy settings, including economic incentives, must be in place that promote the value of knowledge and innovation, and encourage and reward risk-taking and entrepreneurship. Institutions should also induce people and companies to capitalize on the constant change in knowledge by providing a high level of flexibility in both the social and economic spheres of life. In this regard, labour markets, social safety nets and retraining programmes must be flexible and robust enough to manage the constant redeployment and periodical restructuring of human resource requirements. An appropriate financial system should be in place that provides funds to promising new opportunities and redirects assets from failed enterprises to productive ones. Institutions should improve the country's capacity to tap the global system that creates and transmits knowledge. At the same time, domestic legal and governance regimes must be compatible with those at the international level in order to harmonize the treatment of intellectual property protection, competition policy and taxation (Dahlman and Andersson 2000: 33).

4.2.2 Human Resources

To develop a KBE, educated and skilled human capital is an indispensable element, for which an appropriate education system is critically important. The population must be skilled and able to take advantage of the opportunities that new knowledge offers (Pai et al. 2003). Particularly important is assuring that educational resources are allocated in the most efficient way so that the entire population can develop the skills to participate in a KBE through lifelong learning. In particular, higher-level teaching with an emphasis on creative thinking and problem-solving is most important in the production of new knowledge and its adaptation to a particular economic setting. In addition, the domestic education system should constantly adapt to developing global knowledge environments (Dahlman and Andersson 2000: 34).

4.2.3 ICT Infrastructure

Information and communications technology is the backbone of the KBE (Dahlman and Andersson 2000: 34). Yet, the existence of ICT alone is not sufficient, and an appropriate information infrastructure is required to ensure knowledge creation, dissemination and use throughout the economy (H.G. Kim 2001). The information infrastructure of a country encompasses telecommunications networks, coordinated information systems, appropriate policy and legal frameworks, and skilled people that are capable of using and further developing this infrastructure. Therefore, many stakeholders throughout society, such as government, business, ICT service providers and individuals, must be mobilized to produce an effective national information infrastructure. Because the infrastructure has the nature of public goods, government has a critical role to play by assessing the available resources already in place, and then by developing the education and training systems necessary to bring the national information infrastructure to the required standard.

4.2.4 The Innovation System

The innovation system for a KBE consists of the network of institutions, rules and procedures that affect how a country acquires, creates, disseminates and uses knowledge (Dahlman and Andersson 2000: 35). The scope and intensity of networking between the various sectors and stakeholders in the KBE is extremely important for its success. The most important sites for knowledge creation are universities and public and private research centres. The role of government here is to promote the effectiveness of knowledge creation through universities and research centres and also to facilitate the dissemination of knowledge to firms, government and other organizations that put it to use. The innovation sector is critically affected by incentive and institutional regimes in the areas of technology imports and licensing, foreign direct investment (FDI) and strategic alliances.

4.2.5 Digital Divide

A potential negative impact of the transition to a KBE is the emergence of a 'digital divide', in which the divide between the technological haves and have-nots is clearly visible. Those less advantaged will, without adequate government intervention, find it increasingly difficult to access technology, and will be left behind as the country develops. Thus, government policies must ensure that those disadvantaged people are given access to information infrastructure (Dahlman and Andersson 2000: 41–50; H.G. Kim 2001). In recognition of the ineluctable transition to a KBE, the Korean government laid out its strategy, strategic goals and programmes to promote a KBE. These are critically examined in section 4.3.

4.3 KOREAN GOVERNMENT POLICY FOR A KBE

In 2000 the Korean government announced a grand 'three-year strategy' for development of a KBE, that had four basic goals:

1. transformation of Korea to a market-oriented economy;
2. establishment of a new economic infrastructure for the transition of Korea to a KBE;
3. acceleration of Korea's globalization; and
4. promotion of systematic economic reform (H.G. Kim 2001; Pai et al. 2003).

In the same year, the government announced five strategic programmes:

- promotion of the national informatization;
- improving R&D innovation capacity;
- fostering new knowledge-based industries and digitizing existing ones;
- developing human resources for a KBE; and
- addressing the digital divide (Dahlman and Andersson 2000: 133; H.G. Kim 2001).

These strategic goals and programmes are consistent with, and complementary to, the economic reforms outlined in the wake of the 1997 crisis, as examined in Chapter 1.[2]

4.3.1 Institutions and Policy Settings

With respect to institutions and policy measures for a KBE, the strategy consists of:

- promoting competition and entrepreneurship, deregulation and an efficient economic regulatory framework;
- securing the rule of law and fostering greater transparency and accountability in both market and government actors and functions;
- creating a modern legal and institutional infrastructure relevant to the KBE including laws for intellectual property rights protection and cyber laws covering privacy, security and digital transactions;
- addressing welfare and equity issues resulting from the deepening of market forces, continuous workforce restructuring and labour market flexibility;
- ensuring public goods such as quality education and research; and
- addressing gaps in KBE opportunities and markets through fostering market-led mechanisms in targeted areas (Dahlman and Andersson 2000: 41).

4.3.2 Human Resources

In terms of human resource development, a series of education reforms have been undertaken since the early 1990s. These were coordinated in 1995 by the Presidential Commission on Education Reform (PCER) and subsequently revised in conjunction with the 2002 'Vision for Education'. Broadly, these policies constitute a reform agenda seeking:

- greater university autonomy;
- the nurturing of leading regional universities;

- the establishment of international education and research networking; and
- fostering of a more open and equitable education system through an Education Credit Bank (Dahlman and Andersson 2000: 73; Pai et al. 2003).

In addition, the 'Brain Korea 21' programme and the 'New University for Regional Innovation' project have sought to establish a number of centres of excellence in higher education through substantial public investment (Pai et al. 2003).

4.3.3 ICT Infrastructure

Policy to develop Korea's national information infrastructure (NII) was set out in 1999 and promulgated as Cyber Korea 21. The reform agenda for developing Korea's NII includes:

- subsidization of telecommunications providers in establishing a national broadband network and measures to stimulate competition in the telecommunications market;
- nationwide computer literacy and informatization programmes;
- the establishment of Internet plazas for easy access;
- the subsidization of PCs; and
- the wiring of all schools to broadband Internet services (Yoon and Sonn 2003).

In addition, government policy in this area has also sought to increase productivity and transparency by informatizing and coordinating public sector administrative services via a multi-purpose single portal and by promoting e-government. In the private sector, government policy has sought to promote e-commerce by setting up the necessary facilities and establishing knowledge-management systems by coordinating computer network linkages among complementary industries and firms. Policy measures to promote investment and employment have also been put in place, with systems to support IT venture companies from start-up to product marketing, and government support for the transition from universities as IT 'venture incubators' to commercial markets (Yoon and Sonn 2003).[3]

4.3.4 The Innovation System

In 2004, the government announced a policy programme to restructure Korea's R&D innovation system from the traditional 'catch-up' model to a more creative approach.[4] The new policy programme consists of five major initiatives. The first one is intended to upgrade the innovation capacity of industry, universities and government research centres by raising R&D spending to 3 per cent of GDP by 2007. To this end, the government seeks to foster the creation of new innovation-driven SMEs, to provide employment subsidies to enhance labour mobility toward innovation industries, and to undertake further deregulations to encourage business innovation initiatives in high-tech sectors. The second major initiative involves measures to improve the efficiency of R&D investment and the supply of highly qualified human resources. This is to be achieved by focusing national-level public R&D spending on basic research, minimizing duplication between public and private spending initiatives, strengthening the monitoring of human resource supply required for a KBE, and promoting technical and vocational and S&T (science and technology) education.

The third initiative involves measures to develop technology and upgrade the diffusion mechanism. This is to be achieved by: identifying and fostering certain technologies to act as 'growth engines' (OECD 2005b: 108);[5] creating intermediaries between invention and diffusion; creating effective intellectual property rights systems; and developing regional R&D clusters such as Daedeok Science Town as a special R&D region.[6] The fourth initiative seeks to upgrade the performance of the innovation system. This is to be achieved through: strengthening the collaboration between universities, government and business; fostering greater international R&D collaboration; the construction of a national S&T information system by 2008; and enhancing policy coordination among relevant ministries. The fifth initiative involves measures to promote a national culture conducive to S&T and innovation. This is to be achieved by: creating job opportunities through a virtuous cycle of innovation, diffusion and employment; improving the 'social compensation' of highly skilled workers with higher monetary and non-monetary rewards; and ensuring social and ethical responsibility of S&T in Korea (OECD 2005b: 109). It appears that Korea's strategic goals and programmes are set up quite systemically and comprehensively for its transition to a KBE.[7] Korea's current KBE status is assessed in section 4.4 in terms of the four pillars.

4.4 ASSESSMENT OF THE CURRENT STATUS OF KOREA'S KBE

It has been shown earlier that Korea has already developed into a relatively mature KBE in terms of input in knowledge and the share of output in GDP (World Bank 2006: 8). It is, however, a recent phenomenon that the transition to a KBE has been seriously undertaken from the dawn of the twenty-first century after the recognition of structural weakness of the economy in conjunction with the 1997 crisis. The Bank of Korea (2007) shows that the proportion of GDP generated from the ICT sector accounted for 4.2 per cent in 1997 and increased to 14.4 per cent in 2006. It also shows that the share of ICT goods in total exports of goods and services in Korea increased from 29.6 per cent in 2000 to 42.5 per cent in 2006.[8]

There are a number of methods with which to evaluate Korea's current status as a KBE. The methodology proposed by Dahlman and Andersson (2000), which uses the analytical framework discussed above, is employed for the present purpose.[9] Although this method does not assess directly the effects of individual policy measures on specific policy goals, it evaluates Korea's comparative performance of the four pillars of the KBE as compared to other countries. Dahlman and Andersson (2000: 146) assign a number of indicators to each of the four elements of a KBE: institutions and incentives, human resources, innovation system and ICT infrastructure. The specific indicators are included in the following comparative tables.

The World Bank has recently developed two indices to measure the KBE. The first is the Knowledge Economy Index (KEI). The KEI measures whether the national environment 'is conducive for knowledge to be used effectively for economic development'. It is an aggregate index of normalized scores for the four pillars of the KBE. The second index is the Knowledge Index (KI). The KI assesses a nation's 'ability to generate, adopt and diffuse knowledge'. It is an indication of a country's overall potential for knowledge development. It is based on an average of normalized scores over the three pillars of education, innovation and ICT (World Bank 2008b).

The countries chosen for comparison consist of a group of world leaders in KBEs (listed in Table 4.1), which are all members of the OECD and are Korea's important trade and investment partners, and another group of the emerging economies in East Asia. Table 4.1 shows that Korea's ranking on the KEI was 31st in 2008, and its score was 7.68 indicating Korea's ranking of 76.8 percentile of the 134 countries surveyed. The 2008 score of 7.68 was somewhat higher than the 1995 score of 7.56. Korea's 2008 score is substantially lower than world leaders in the KBE such as Sweden (9.52) and Finland (9.37). It is also lower than scores for a number of Korea's East Asian competitors such as Taiwan, Japan, Singapore and Hong Kong. However, Korea did substantially outperform the less-developed Southeast Asian countries and China. Korea's score of 7.68 is compared to average scores of 8.31 and 6.59, respectively, of higher-income countries and East Asia. Korea performed much better on the KI of knowledge potential with a score of 8.38, demonstrating that institutions and policy settings remain Korea's weak link in developing a KBE. Korea was ranked 21st on the KI, almost at par with high-income countries (8.41); and comparable with, or a little behind, Germany, Japan and Taiwan; ahead of Hong Kong and Singapore; and substantially better than other Association of South East Asian Nations (ASEAN) countries and China.

Table 4.1 Knowledge Economy Index (KEI) and Knowledge Index (KI) 2008 by the World Bank: rankings and scores

Country	KEI ranking	KEI scores	KI rankings	KI scores
Australia	10	9.05	6	9.17
Canada	6	9.21	7	9.14
Finland	3	9.37	4	9.33
Germany	14	8.87	14	8.83
Japan	19	8.56	13	8.84
Netherlands	4	9.32	3	9.36
Sweden	2	9.52	1	9.63
UK	8	9.09	10	9.03
USA	9	9.08	8	9.05
Korea	**31**	**7.68**	**21**	**8.38**
China	77	4.35	77	4.46
Hong Kong	26	8.20	29	7.73
Singapore	24	8.24	28	7.75
Taiwan	17	8.69	16	8.80
High income	–	8.31	–	8.41
East Asia	–	6.59	–	6.88

Source: World Bank (2008a).

4.4.1 Institutions and Policy Settings

Table 4.2 shows a series of indicators to assess Korea's comparative performance in terms of its institutional structure. To measure the appropriateness of the institutional structure, five globally well-known indexes are used: the Index of Economic Freedom by the Heritage Foundation; the World Competitiveness Scoreboard by the International Institute of Management Development (IMD); the Intellectual Property Protection Index by the World Economic Forum (WEF); the Doing Business index by the World Bank, and the Economic Incentive Regime sub-index of the World Bank's KEI in Table 4.1.[10]

In terms of economic freedom, Korea has yet to improve institutions to develop a KBE. The Index of Economic Freedom aggregates ten sub-indices: business freedom, trade freedom, monetary freedom, freedom from state intervention, fiscal freedom, security of property rights, investment freedom, financial freedom, freedom from corruption and freedom of labour. In this index, Korea rates at the mid- to lower end of the spectrum on a score of 68.1

in 2009, comparable with Taiwan. There is some distance behind most world leaders in KBEs.

Table 4.2 Institutions and policy settings

Country	Index of economic freedom (2009) 0–100	IMD world competitiveness scoreboard (2008) 0–100	WEF intellectual property protection (2008) 1–7	WB doing business index (2009) rank	Economic incentive regime by WB (2008) 0–10
Australia	82.6	83.5	5.9	9	8.66
Canada	80.5	82.9	5.6	8	9.42
Finland	74.5	75.0	6.2	14	9.47
Germany	70.5	74.7	6.0	25	8.99
Japan	72.8	70.0	5.7	12	7.71
Netherlands	77.0	80.5	5.9	26	9.18
Sweden	70.5	82.5	6.0	17	9.18
UK	79.0	71.9	5.4	6	9.28
US	80.7	100.0	5.6	3	9.16
Korea	**68.1**	**58.9**	**5.0**	**23**	**5.57**
China	53.2	73.8	3.9	83	4.01
Hong Kong	90.0	94.9	5.4	4	9.60
Singapore	87.1	99.3	6.3	1	9.71
Taiwan	69.5	77.4	4.9	61	8.35

Sources: World Bank (2004, 2007, 2008a, 2009a, 2009b); Heritage Foundation (2009); IMD (2008); WEF (2008: 365).

Moving across Table 4.2, the next four indicators show that Korea's comparative institutional structure is the weak link in its movement towards a KBE. For these four indexes, Korea rates poorer than global KBE leaders and among the middle spectrum among East Asian countries, except for the Doing Business Index where Korea's rank of 23rd is comparable to the Netherlands (26th) and Germany (25th), and also much better than Taiwan (61st). However, Korea's 2008 IMD competitiveness score was much lower than those of East Asian emerging countries such as Taiwan, Hong Kong and Singapore, and also behind even China, let alone the recognized KBE leaders such as the United States and Japan.[11] In terms of intellectual property rights (IPR) protection, Korea rates relatively poorly, comparable with Taiwan, and substantially behind the global leaders of the KBE.[12] Even though Korea has improved its legal framework for IPR, bringing it in line with global standards such as those of the WTO (Jones 2007), Korea's practical protection appears to be lagging behind advanced countries and East Asian competitors. The final column of Table 4.2 shows Korea's comparative performance on the economic incentive regime index of the World Bank's

KEI. Korea's score in 2008 was 5.57, which was below those of newly industrialized countries in East Asia as well as all KBE leaders. Overall, Korea can be considered a relatively poor performer in the area of institutions. Hence, the establishment of appropriate institutions and policy settings is one of the most critical challenge for Korea's push to a KBE.[13]

4.4.2 Human Resources

Table 4.3 shows that Korea fares quite well with respect to quantitative aspects of human resources such as gross tertiary enrolment rates and public spending on education. In 2006, Korea's tertiary student enrolment rate of 91 per cent was second overall and only slightly lower than Finland (92 per cent). In terms of public spending on education, Korea is middle-ranked, comparable with Australia and Germany, but well behind the leaders Sweden and Finland. This would be balanced, however, by Korea's extremely high rates of private spending on education (Dahlman and Andersson 2000: 57; OECD 2004: 27). The private outlays do not include spending for students' private tutoring provided at institutes known as *hakwon*.[14] Thus, Korea's overall education expenditure as a percentage of GDP should be one of the highest among OECD countries.

Korea has been doing relatively well with supplying scientists and engineers, who are at centre stage for a KBE. On average over the period 2002–05 the number of graduates in engineering, manufacturing and construction as a percentage of total tertiary graduates was highest in Korea among OECD countries with 29.5 per cent, compared to an OECD average of 13.5 per cent. Over the same period, the proportion of graduates in science of total tertiary graduates in Korea was behind a number of KBE leaders (10 per cent, as compared to the OECD average of 10.2 per cent) (Laporte 2007). This may indicate a relative lack of interest in science in Korea, which is in a sense an ill omen for innovation.

Korea rates relatively highly in terms of the level of firms' technological readiness and technological absorption capacity. Table 4.3 shows that in 2008 Korea rated a score of 5.5 for technological readiness, comparable with all countries except for two recognized KBE world leaders, Sweden (6.0) and Netherlands (6.0). A similar trend is in evidence in the indicator for technological absorption capacity, where Korea ranks highly, comparable with Hong Kong, and is only slightly outperformed by Singapore, Taiwan and Japan in Asia. A consideration of these quantitative indicators suggests that, overall, Korea's human resource potential for development toward a KBE is close to the world's best. However, as will be examined later, the quality and direction of the Korean education system is a serious concern for the development of a KBE, particularly for its goal of restructuring the innovation system from a catch-up model to a creative one. This is reflected in the education pillar of the KEI by the World Bank, with a score of 7.97 in 2008 which is substantially below those of KBE leaders (Table 4.3).

Table 4.3 Human resources

Country	Gross tertiary enrolment rate (2006) % relevant age cohort	Public spending on education (2006) % GDP	Techno-logical readiness (2008) 1–7	Techno-logical absorption (2008) 1–7	Education WB KEI (2008) 0–10
Australia	73	4.6	5.2	5.8	9.64
Canada	62	5.2	5.6	5.6	9.26
Finland	92	6.5	5.5	6.1	9.78
Germany	n.a.	4.6	5.2	6.0	8.46
Japan	55	3.7	5.1	6.3	8.71
Netherlands	59	5.2	6.0	5.5	9.26
Sweden	82	7.3	6.0	6.2	9.40
UK	59	5.4	5.6	5.6	8.54
USA	82	5.6	5.6	6.3	8.77
Korea	**91**	**4.6**	**5.5**	**5.8**	**7.97**
China	22	n.a.	3.2	5.1	4.11
Hong Kong	33	3.9	5.6	5.8	5.30
Singapore	n.a.	n.a.	5.7	6.0	5.19
Taiwan	n.a.	n.a.	5.3	6.1	7.91

Sources: World Bank (2008a, 2008c); WEF (2008).

4.4.3 ICT Infrastructure

The ICT industry, which is an integral part of a KBE, has expanded rapidly in the recent past. It was shown earlier that both the proportion of GDP generated from ICT production and the share of ICT goods in exports of goods and services roughly doubled from 1997 to 2006. In addition, similar patterns are shown in ICT consumption and investment. As a percentage of GDP, ICT consumption increased from 4.9 per cent in 1997 to 9.5 per cent in 2006, and investment in ICT increased from 3.7 per cent in 1997 to 5.6 per cent in 2000 and remained at slightly less than the 2000 ratio until 2006. Investment in ICT as a percentage of total domestic investment jumped from 25 per cent in 1997 to 38.7 per cent in 2000, and remained more or less unchanged until 2006 (Bank of Korea 2007). Table 4.4 shows a series of indicators evaluating comparative progress in terms of ICT infrastructure. It has been shown earlier that the proportion of value-added by the ICT sector in the Korean economy was already the second-highest among OECD countries in 2003. In terms of ICT expenditure as a percentage of GDP,

Korea's figure of 7.1 per cent is at the upper end of the spectrum in 2007.[15] The next two indicators in Table 4.4 show Korea's ICT consumption pattern as compared to other countries. Korea is comparable with, or even better than, KBE world leaders in Internet users per hundred of population. With a figure of 30.4, Korea ranked third in the number of broadband subscribers per 100 persons in 2007 after the Netherlands (33.6) and Finland (33.3).

Table 4.4 ICT infrastructure

Country	ICT expend-iture (2007) % GDP	Internet users per 100 pop. (2007)	Broad-band sub-scribers per 100 pop. (2007)	Band-width bits per cap. (2006)	Internet afford. US$ price per month (2006)	ICT by WB (2008) 0–10
Australia	6.6	53.3	23.0	5 903 [a]	22.5	9.16
Canada	6.4	84.9	22.9[b]	6 800 [a]	9.5	8.74
Finland	5.1	68.1	33.3	4 326 [a]	22.5	8.56
Germany	6.2	51.7	24.1	6 860 [a]	7.5	9.04
Japan	7.2	73.6	22.1	1 038 [a]	13.1	8.66
Netherlands	6.7	91.6	33.6	20549 [a]	8.8	9.36
Sweden	6.5	76.5	25.8[b]	17 531 [a]	19.2	9.69
UK	6.9	65.9	25.4	13 062 [a]	27.6	9.38
USA	7.5	72.9	21.8	3 306 [a]	15.0	8.93
Korea	**7.1**	**71.7**	**30.4**	**1 029**	**34.6**	**8.71**
China	7.8	15.9	5.0	196	10.0	4.16
Hong Kong	4.7	57.2	27.1	13 439	3.9	9.26
Singapore	6.5	58.8	19.2	5 826	13.2	8.50
Taiwan	n.a.	n.a.	n.a.	n.a.	n.a.	9.26

Notes:
Taiwan is not included in WB World Development Indicators.
[a] 2005 data.
[b] 2006 data.

Source: World Bank (2008a, 2008c, 2009b).

Despite its high proportion of broadband subscribers, Korea falls behind others in broadband infrastructure. Korea's bandwidth (bit per capita), or speed, is a long way off that of the world leader, the Netherlands, and is also well behind all advanced OECD economies shown in Table 4.4, and Hong Kong and Singapore. In terms of Internet affordability, Korea is the most expensive country on the list. Because of relatively lower-quality service (in terms of broadband speed) and relatively high costs of the Internet, Korea ranks quite poorly in terms of quality and price (or the ratio of bandwidth to price per month), compared to all the global leaders as well as Hong Kong and Singapore.

On the ICT pillar of the KEI, as shown in the last column of Table 4.4, Korea rated quite well overall in 2008. Korea's score of 8.71 was ranked at 17th in the world, a little behind KBE leaders and Taiwan, but comparable with most advanced OECD countries. In sum, the ICT industry has rapidly grown in the recent past, thereby achieving a ranking of 87.1 percentile out of 134 countries surveyed by the World Bank. Such a rapid development is attributable to the government's systematic development strategy over time, of privatization, liberalization and encouragement of competition (Hong et al. 2007). In addition, in 2004 the government started the IT839 strategy with the objective of developing eight information technology (IT) services that are deployed on three new network infrastructures, which will in turn pave the way for the rapid growth of nine new sectors as new growth engines (Song 2006). It ultimately aims to realize a country where ICT connectivity is ubiquitous by forming a virtuous circle of developing new services, infrastructure and growth engines. The IT839 strategy is expected to transform the Korean IT industry from a 'catch-up' development model to a world market leader (Hong et al. 2007). Nonetheless, Korea's recent spending on the ICT sector is around the median level of advanced countries, with very high rates of information technology usage among the population, but with substantially lower quality than world leaders in 2006–07.

4.4.4 Korea's Innovation System

Table 4.5 seeks to evaluate Korea's innovation system comparatively. The R&D intensity in Korea was 3 per cent in 2005, the fourth-highest among the listed countries. The intensity increased by 3.6 per cent a year in Korea between 1991 and 2005, compared to an annual growth of 0.1 per cent of OECD countries over the same period (OECD 2005a: 190). The number of researchers and technicians in R&D may show another indicator of the R&D intensity for which Korea was around the median level of advanced countries over the period 2000–05. The number of filed patents may also reflect the R&D intensity. In 2006 Korea ranked a close second in the world to Japan in terms of United States patents filed by residents per million of population, demonstrating significant innovation capacity.[16]

With respect to receipts from royalty and license fees, Korea ranked in the lower-middle strata in 2006, well behind all the KBE world leaders, except Australia and Finland. This may reflect Korea's recent transition to a KBE, its nascent status and new patents not being adopted well for commercialization. This indicates in turn low R&D productivity which is attributable to the lack or inefficiency of collaboration among the major actors of innovation: universities, research centres and industries.

Table 4.5 Innovation system

Country	R&D intensity R&D gross exp./GDP (2000–05)	Researchers & technicians in R&D per mill. pop. (2000–05)	US patents filed (by residents) per mill. pop. (2006)	Royalty & license fees receipts US$ mill. (2006)	Research collaboration between universities & industry (2008) 1–7	Capacity for innovation (2008) 1–7	Innovation by WB (2008) 0–10
Australia	1.8	4 099	138.3	621	4.8	4.0	8.72
Canada	2.0	5 389	169.6	3 245	5.0	4.5	9.43
Finland	3.5	7 541	345.6	1 494	5.5	5.6	9.66
Germany	2.5	4 298	582.6	5 888	5.4	6.0	9.00
Japan	3.3	5 822	2 720.7	20 096	4.6	5.9	9.15
Netherlands	1.8	4 074	132.4	4 126	5.1	5.1	9.48
Sweden	3.9	5 977	270.4	3 964	5.6	5.8	9.79
UK	1.8	n.a.	289.7	13 588	5.1	4.9	9.18
USA	2.6	4 605	741.8	62 378	5.8	5.5	9.45
Korea	**3.0**	**4 327**	**2 591.5**	**2 011**	**5.1**	**5.3**	**8.47**
China	1.3	708	93.2	205	4.5	4.2	5.12
Hong Kong	0.7	2 513	24.5	245	4.5	3.8	8.64
Singapore	2.4	5 881	142.4	730	5.5	4.5	9.56
Taiwan	n.a.	n.a.	n.a.	n.a.	5.1	4.7	9.24

Sources: World Bank (2008a, 2008c); WEF (2008); World Intellectual Property Organization (WIPO) (2008); Bank of Korea (2006).

In terms of this research collaboration, Korea ranked in the middle of KBE leading economies, and slightly behind Singapore but equal with Taiwan in Asia.[17] In regard to capacity for innovation, Korea was equal to or not far behind most global leaders, and ahead of all East Asian countries. On the innovation pillar of the KEI, as shown in Table 4.5, Korea's overall position in 2008 is comparable to Hong Kong, sitting slightly behind world leaders, Taiwan and Singapore, but well ahead of China. Overall, for the innovation system, Korea is nearly comparable to the advanced KBE economies, although there is room for improvement, particularly in the areas of commercialization of innovations and R&D collaboration.

From the above assessment, it could be concluded that Korea has been certainly in transition to a KBE, which has been taking place from the beginning of the 2000s. Korea has been well on the way to developing a KBE in terms of quantitative provision and usage of ICT infrastructure, some quantitative indicators of human resource development, and R&D intensity. However, there are still deficiencies in the less-tangible or qualitative aspects of institutions, human resources, ICT infrastructure and the national innovation system. Consequently Korea is placed somewhat behind world leaders in overall terms.[18] As a result of these weaknesses, Korea's KBE share of value-added in gross value-added was 39.5 per cent in 2002, compared with Ireland (47.8 per cent), Luxembourg (45.5 per cent), United States. (43.1 per cent), Germany (42.8 per cent), Switzerland (42.5 per cent), Sweden (42.1 per cent), Belgium (41.6 per cent) and the United Kingdom (40.7 per cent) (OECD 2005a: 204). The KEI and KI by the World Bank indicate that the development level of Korea's KBE is substantially below those of KBE world leaders and that institutions and policy settings remain Korea's weak link in developing a KBE.

4.4.5 Digital Divide

In recognition of the risk of a digital divide as an attendant social issue of a KBE, the government has introduced a variety of programmes related to ICT facilities and infrastructure, particularly for schools. It has also provided a nationwide education campaign on computer and information programmes, and subsidized purchases of PCs by households. As a result, Korea has ranked comparably with the KBE global leaders in terms of information usage among the population, including the number of Internet users and broadband subscribers (Table 4.4). As shown in Table 4.6, income inequality among households in Korea has somewhat worsened in the recent past as measured by the Gini coefficient, which increased in general from 0.296 in 2000 to 0.306 in 2007. However, it should be noted that there is no information available in the literature with which to isolate the effect of digital divide on the Gini coefficient.[19]

Table 4.6 Income distribution of all Korean families (Gini coefficient)

	1991–96	1997	1999	2000	2003	2004	2005	2006	2007
Gini	0.279	0.276	0.315	0.296	0.298	0.304	0.304	0.303	0.306

Sources: For the period 1991–99: Bank of Korea (2006); for the period 2000–07: KIHASA (2008).

It is extremely difficult to compare the extent of the digital divide in Korea with those of other countries; no study has been found in the literature about an international comparison of digital divides. The Gini coefficients are not readily available to be compared across countries and those available in the literature are estimated for different years. Given these limitations, it appears that Korea is around the median level of advanced countries and well ahead of all countries in Asia. In 2000, Korea's Gini coefficient (0.296) was higher than those of Finland (0.269), Germany (0.283) and Sweden (0.250), while lower than those of Canada (0.326) and the USA (0.408).[20]

4.5 WHAT NEEDS TO BE DONE FURTHER IN DEVELOPING KOREA'S KBE

4.5.1 Institutions and Policy Settings

The weakest pillar of Korea's transition to a KBE is its institutions and policy settings. Despite Korea's comprehensive regulatory reform agenda since the 1997 financial crisis, which was in part reinforced by the 2000 strategy for a KBE, significant and complicated administrative barriers still remain to market entry and exit. Although central government regulations have been substantially phased out, significant obstacles remain at the local government level to the establishment of new businesses (OECD 2005b: 114–18). In support of this observation, Kwon (2008: 114–37) points out the perception held by foreign business people in Korea that there is inadequate protection of intellectual property; complex administrative procedures; inconsistency in policy, regulations and administrative procedures between the central and local governments; and opacity and variability in interpreting and applying regulations at the local level.[21]

In particular, the OECD (2005b: 118) stresses the continuous existence of significant entry and exit barriers in the service sector and particularly in professional sectors such as law and accounting.[22] In its 2006 Country Report on Korea, the IMF emphasized deregulation of the service sector, greater labour market flexibility and improved access to financing for SMEs as the crucial future tasks for enhancing Korea's competition and innovation and in achieving its long-standing goal of catching up to the world's richest nations (IMF 2006: 12–15). Regulatory restrictions remaining in the service sector may be reflected in low productivity, compared with both the manufacturing sector and OECD standards (Jones 2007).[23]

4.5.2 Human Resources

Korea has been moderately successful in developing human resources for a KBE in terms of the tertiary enrolment rate and education spending. However, Korea has a long way to go to develop the quality of learning required by the KBE. Dahlman and Andersson (2000: 60) have advanced a number of proposals to reform Korea's education system under the headings of:

- deregulation and decentralization;
- diversification;
- gender, relevance and quality; and
- lifelong learning.

Deregulation and decentralization involves the devolution from central government control of both the secondary and tertiary education systems with clearly defined autonomy and accountability at the institutional level in terms of curriculum, admissions systems, tuition fees, staff administration, teaching loads and enrolment quotas. This would introduce a market-oriented and stakeholder-driven governing system of education, and encourage flexibility and competition. However, the government still maintains rigid control over all these aspects of the secondary and tertiary education system. This has led to the lack of transparency of university operations and competition among them (Ahn 2002; Yoo 2001; Jones 2007).[24] This has in turn led to the lack of competitiveness of the education system. In 2008, for instance, the IMD ranked Korea 39th out of 55 countries in the overall competitiveness of the education sector. Korea took 53rd place in the extent to which university education meets the needs of a competitive economy, clearly indicating that the nation's highest educational institutions have failed to provide the quality education required for its KBE (IMD 2008: 466–7).

To improve the quality of tertiary education in line with a KBE, Korea's education service market should be liberalized and internationalized. Maintaining tight control over the education system hinders any transition from rote learning to the development of critical thinking and problem-solving skills. One option Korea should take is to open the education service market for foreign competitors.[25] Even though legal institutions allow FDI in private tutoring institutions and graduate schools, no foreign university has landed in Korea (Kang et al. 2006: 216–53; KIEP 2006: 231–3). Due to the poor quality of the Korean tertiary education system, a large number of Korean students go abroad for their education, raising the danger of brain drains. This is reflected in a large educational service trade deficit of $3.4 billion in 2005 (KIEP 2006: 227).[26]

Diversification refers to institutional and curricular diversity in promoting interdisciplinary studies, dual degrees, and coordination between academic and vocational education by means of flexible and supportive administrative regulations. School educational pathways need to be dualized with the flexibility to lead students to either tertiary education or vocational training. Vocational colleges should be able to teach degree courses with recognition in the university system. This will enhance competition among universities. The flexible duality between four-year university programmes and two-year vocational colleges does not exist in Korea. Vocational colleges are still disdained by society and courses at vocational colleges are not recognized by four-year universities. Institutions should also diversify by focusing on their disciplinary strengths and not necessarily providing a full spectrum of university programmes. This is not the case in Korea; most four-year universities, except for a few, are the so-called general universities, providing full university programmes.

In terms of relevance and quality, the curriculum should be more consistent with the requirements of a KBE, such as a greater emphasis on new technologies and communication skills, the use of ICTs, problem-solving capabilities and group social skills. Relevance should also be enhanced by expanded industry–university partnerships and international exchange of staff and students with foreign universities. In this respect, the OECD (2005b: 124) notes that, while Korea is the second-largest source for international student flows into the OECD, its role as a destination is among the lowest in the OECD. According to a survey by the Korea Chamber of Commerce and Industry, Korean companies are quite unhappy with their newly employed workers from universities, particularly with respect to their professional knowledge, adaptability and challenging attitudes (Kang et al. 2006: 226).

Knowledge quickly becomes obsolete and replaced by new knowledge which emerges incessantly. Hence, knowledge workers have to keep up with the development of new knowledge. This requires lifelong learning (Dahlman and Andersson 2000: 71). Korea needs to integrate its formal education system with the adult, informal, vocational and distance education systems, which must all receive adequate investment in building their information economy infrastructures. Ultimately, lifelong learning should mean that every citizen should be able to learn in the most convenient way possible at low cost. A facet of the salient characteristics of Korean culture is a high emphasis on face-saving. This hinders older generations from undertaking education together with younger generations, making it difficult to promote lifelong learning. Suh and Chen (2007) point out that only 19 per cent of Korean adults participated in lifelong education in 2001, compared to the 35 per cent OECD average.

The core cause underlying Korea's education challenges is its culture. Korean culture places a high value on education and embraces hierarchical collectivism. Hence, Korean society retains a subtle social stratification by education, alma maters, income and other social status. Social stratification together with educational zeal leads to fierce competition to enter particularly prestigious universities. Under these circumstances, government control of university admission through its common national aptitude test has resulted in an explicit ranking structure of universities with a concentration of prestigious universities in Seoul.[27] All this leads to cut-throat competition to get admission to those prestigious universities, thereby making all students from elementary to high school completely preoccupied with preparing for entrance examinations for universities. This in turn leads to rote learning instead of nurturing independent creative thinking and problem-solving. Under the strong familism of Korean tradition, parents and even siblings are willing to sacrifice financially for the education of their children, thereby sending students to private tutoring institutes and raising education spending for private institutions to be the highest in the OECD in 2003 (Jones 2007).[28] Education at these private tutoring institutes consists of further rote memorization, as they are established specifically for the purpose of preparing for university entrance. Because of cultural rigidity and inertia, education reform is one of the most daunting tasks faced by Korea for its transition to a KBE.

4.5.3 ICT Infrastructure

As section 4.4 has demonstrated, Korea is among the world leaders in the national provision of physical ICT infrastructure and usage. Consequently, Korea's shortcomings and required improvements in the ICT industry relate more to its efficiency. To this end, the government needs to keep the regulatory framework up to date in rapidly changing ICT market environments. Competition in the ICT industry is fierce and its risk is high due to the short life cycle of ICT products and winner-takes-all characteristics of its industry. As indicated by rapidly rising interindustry international trade and outsourcing in the recent past, production processes of high-tech products are typically fragmented. Hence, to sustain the current momentum of Korea's ICT industry, international collaboration is critically important. This requires further opening of the ICT sector to wider domestic and international competition, attracting FDI to the sector, and reducing micro-regulation and controls.

One serious weakness of the Korean ICT industry is its heavy dependence on imports, mainly from Japan, for its components and materials, as attested by the import-inducing coefficient of the key ICT components ranging from 0.45 to 0.55 (Hong et al. 2007). Hence, Korea's ICT industry which is anchored on ICT final goods is vulnerable to external shocks such as fluctuations of exchange rates and trade disputes. Without developing an intermediate goods industry (components and materials) along with final goods, the long-run prospects for the ICT industry does not look favourable. SMEs have failed to play significant roles in the development of intermediate goods. Due to its being capital-intensive in nature, Korea's ICT industry is concentrated in a limited number of *chaebols*, more so than the manufacturing sector (Hong et al. 2007). Private sector R&D is also concentrated in those *chaebols*. It follows that productivity of large firms is bound to be higher than that of SMEs. In the ensuing oligopsony market, SMEs could not deal with *chaebols* on a level playing field, thereby prohibiting SMEs from playing a proper role in the components and materials industries of ICT. Therefore, for the long-term health of the ICT industry, it is important to strengthen the innovative capabilities of SMEs and improve their relations with *chaebols*.[29]

Another important improvement that needs to be made is a more rigorous regulatory framework for e-commerce in Korea. To this end, the government needs to minimize the overlap between responsible ministries and to simplify administration. In addition, the government needs to encourage the foundation of a digital economy by mapping emerging clusters of e-commerce particularly among SMEs through assistance with electronic signatures, payment and certification systems. Particularly important to the long-term sustainability of the e-commerce sector is the enhancement of trust through the provision of secure infrastructure, filters and encryption, and the vigorous prosecution of electronic crimes and fraud (Kwon 2008: 103–7).

4.5.4 The National Innovation System

Although Korea's R&D innovation system has improved particularly in tangible and quantitative aspects, there are a number of major shortfalls that need to be addressed by government. Kim et al. (2006) find from their empirical study that increases in basic research expenditure – not the overall R&D expenditure – raise economic growth of developing economies such as Korea, Japan and Taiwan. They point out that although Korea's R&D expenditure is relatively high, the proportion for basic research is relatively quite low. This is one of the fundamental problems Korea has faced for its long-term development of a KBE, as scientific research and capability determine a nation's technological potential.

The weakness in the scientific base has resulted from a small share of R&D conducted by the public sector. While Korea dedicates high aggregate levels of investment to R&D, about three-quarters of it was undertaken by the private sector as of 2004 (Suh and Chen 2007: 15). Private sector R&D was in turn concentrated in a small number of firms and industries. For example, in 2004, three-quarters of business sector R&D in Korea was concentrated in high-technology and medium to high-technology manufacturing, while R&D investment dedicated to the services sector was almost negligible (OECD 2005b: 103; Jones 2007). This makes the innovation system vulnerable in a few respects. Not only does private sector R&D pay little emphasis to basic science, but it is volatile and vulnerable to cyclical economic movements. A high concentration of R&D implies low interfirm and interindustry interaction, a key element of the innovation system, and the weakness of SMEs in R&D. The lack of R&D by SMEs could be a bottleneck in maintaining technological competitiveness, as discussed in conjunction with the ICT infrastructure. Also as examined above, R&D by *chaebols* has been focused on ICT outputs, not on components and materials, a serious weakness for the long-term health of the ICT industry. The lack of R&D investment in the service sector slows down dissemination and utilization of knowledge. Korea's R&D basis should be broad enough to maintain the flexibility and adaptability of its innovation system comparable to those of the most advanced OECD countries.

Technology transfer, diffusion and commercialization in Korea have remained weak. Despite the numbers of United States patents filed, as shown in Table 4.5, the OECD (2005b: 103–4) points out that in 2004, for instance, 61 per cent of patents filed had not been used in 2004. This would be attributable to the relatively weak linkage between business, university and government research institutes in Korea. In addition, Korea's international collaboration of R&D is also weak. Jones (2007) argues that Korea's R&D systems in general are relatively isolated internationally, with only 0.4 per cent of R&D financed by foreign sources, the lowest share among OECD countries. Over the 1998–2002 period, R&D expenditure funded by foreign affiliates accounted for only 1.4 per cent of Korea's total R&D, while the ratios were 20.5 per cent and 3.2 per cent, respectively, in China and Japan (Kwon 2008: 119).

There are some cultural hindrances to undertaking venturesome business such as R&D. Koreans are risk-averse by culture, as attested by the strong predilection of job-seekers for more secure positions in the civil service, teaching or large *chaebols*, and the still prevalent lifetime employment and seniority practices of human resource management (Kwon 2008: 203–30).

This will hinder Koreans from undertaking innovations which are by nature risky. Therefore, Korea needs relatively more aggressive incentive structures, particularly for SMEs. Strongly influenced by Confucian tradition, Korea is a group society whereby Koreans discriminate between in-groups and out-groups. The culture of group society lacks the attitudes that support knowledge-sharing and networking among stakeholders including universities, industry and government, let alone with foreign counterparts.

4.5.5 Digital Divide

Income distribution in Korea fares quite well in comparison with the KBE global leaders and is remarkably more equitable than in countries in East Asia, as shown in Table 12.2 in Chapter 12. Over the recent past, Korea's income inequity has somewhat worsened in spite of improvements in social security programmes after the 1997 crisis (Table 4.6). This indicates that the Korean welfare system still suffers from serious deficiencies and does not provide an adequate safety net for the entire population, as further examined in Chapter 12. In particular, the low-income class has been worse off since 1997. The proportion of national income held by the low-income class declined, and that of low-income households of total households increased (Bank of Korea 2006). This may reflect the inevitable digital divide arising from the transition to a KBE and indicates the need to further support low-income families by means of the provision of ICT facilities and education.

4.6 CONCLUSION

This chapter has critically assessed Korea's transition to a KBE, which has been embarked on at the dawn of the twenty-first century as its main economic strategy. In doing so, the chapter has adopted the analytical framework proposed by Dahlman and Andersson (2000). This framework is built on the four pillars of a KBE: institutions, human resources, ICT infrastructure and innovation system. A successful transition to the KBE involves the coordinated and complementary development of all four of these elements. In recognition of the ineluctable transition to a KBE, the Korean government laid out its strategy and programmes to promote a KBE more or less in line with the above analytical framework in 2000. They included the development of national information infrastructure, the fostering of a KBE-responsive human resources system, improving innovation capacity in S&T, development of new knowledge-based industries and digitization of existing industries, and programmes to address the digital divide. Based on the above analytical framework, this chapter has assessed and evaluated Korea's progress across these four pillars in comparison with a group of world leaders in KBEs and the emerging economies in East Asia.

It has been demonstrated that Korea is performing well in its transition to a KBE in terms of the quantitative provision and usage of ICT infrastructure, some quantitative indicators of human resource development, and investment in R&D. Korea also performs well in its R&D outputs in terms of United States patents filed. A variety of deficiencies have been identified in Korea's transition to a KBE. It has been pointed out that the establishment of appropriate institutions and policy settings is the weakest pillar in Korea's push to a KBE, thereby rendering Korea relatively weak in comparison to world leaders. In spite of some quantitatively successful indicators of Korea's education system, its quality in terms of creativity and innovation is questionable. Although Korea's investment in and usage of ICT infrastructure are comparable to global leaders, Korea is relatively weak in terms of its components and materials, and with the quality of services of Internet. Similarly, in spite of relatively high R&D expenditure, Korea is relatively poor in commercialization of innovation and in international and domestic collaboration of R&D. In recognition of the risk of a digital divide as an attendant social issue of a KBE, the government has introduced a variety of social safety net programmes. However, income distribution in Korea, measured by the Gini coefficient, has slightly worsened in the recent past.

In terms of the four pillars, this chapter has identified a number of remaining tasks still required to be addressed in order to develop Korea's KBE to the comparable level of global leaders in this area:

- further deregulation in the services and professional sectors;
- effective, transparent, and consistent regulatory frameworks in the areas of e-commerce and intellectual property rights;
- adequate financial and other supports for SMEs;
- liberalization and internationalization of the education system by undertaking serious deregulation, decentralization and diversification;
- broadening the R&D bases toward SMEs and the service sector and by emphasizing basic science;
- diffusion and commercialization of innovation by improving domestic and international research collaboration; and
- programmes to prevent further aggravation of the digital divide.

In conclusion, the transition of the Korean economy to a KBE has already progressed substantially, and Korea is poised soon to be on a par with KBE global leaders. Korea has made remarkable achievements in its transition to a KBE particularly in the quantitative and tangible elements of a KBE. Yet,

Korea has faced a variety of challenges, particularly in the qualitative and intangible areas. Korea is efficient in the application of knowledge but less so in its creation and diffusion. The shortfalls are to a large extent politico-cultural in nature. Burdened with an inefficient political system and cultural inertia, a concerted effort of the government and society is required to undertake further reform and address those issues identified here.

NOTES

1. A similar framework is advanced by Pai et al. (2003).
2. It should be noted that some of these goals and programmes include policies and programmes that had already been in place. For a further detailed target tasks for the three-year plan for the KBE, see Woo and Suh (2007).
3. As part of the government plan to promote ICT, the government established the Ministry of Information and Communications in 1994, and a research centre, the Korea Information Society Development Institute, in 1999.
4. The remainder of this section is drawn from OECD (2005b: 108–9) unless otherwise noted; see also Park and Lee (2006) for Korea's performance under the catch-up model.
5. These were: biomedical; next-generation computer displays, semiconductors, batteries and mobile telecommunications; future automobiles; intelligent robots; digital TV and broadcasting; intelligent home networks; digital content; and software solutions.
6. See Poon et al. (2006) for history and information on Daedeok Science Town.
7. Consistent with the transition to a KBE already well under way, the Lee Myung-bak government's strategic vision is to turn Korea 'into a first-class, advanced nation' (Jwa 2008). In pursuing this, the Lee government has set five strategic policy agendas: a small government serving the people; a dynamic market economy; proactive welfare; a country rich in talent; and a global Korea (Korea.net 2009; Jwa 2008). Within these agendas, a number of specific policy tasks intended to make contributions to Korea's transition to a KBE have been announced (Korea.net 2009). It appears though that they include all those strategic programmes explained previously, with a few new initiatives such as infrastructure for new eco-friendly industries and the building of an open, global society.
8. Assessment of the effects of the five strategic programmes directly on the four strategic goals and on the extent of Korea's KBE development is beyond the scope of this chapter. There is a paucity of information to undertake that task.
9. Tan and Hooy (2007) compare the progress of Korea and East Asian emerging countries (Singapore, China, Malaysia, the Philippines and Thailand) against the benchmarking countries of the United States, Finland and Japan. Their study is based on a statistical analysis of the relationships between knowledge inputs and knowledge outputs. They find that Korea devotes the most resources as knowledge inputs among the similar-sized East Asian economies and is relatively efficient in generating knowledge outputs. They conclude that Korea is already one of the world's most efficient countries in its development toward a KBE.
10. For the methodology and variables included in each of these indexes, see the sources in Table 4.2.
11. Korea ranked 31st in 2008 out of 55 countries studied (IMD 2008).
12. In terms of the WEF intellectual property protection, Korea was ranked 26th out of 134 countries in 2008 (WEF 2008: 365).
13. Chapter 1 demonstrated that the shift in the policy paradigm and attendant reforms in Korea after the 1997 crisis are incomplete and inadequate and suggested a further across-the-board reform. This conclusion is applicable to Korea's transition to a KBE.
14. According to the *Hankyoreh* (2008), total expenditure for education at these *hakwons* amounted to 2.2 per cent of GDP in 2007.

15. It appears that ICT 'expenditure' in Table 4.4 differs from ICT 'investment' in Korea's National Accounts, the latter being 4.6 per cent of GDP, as compared to 7.1 per cent in Table 4.4.
16. Although in terms of the number of US patents filed in 2006, Korea surpassed the world leaders of the KBE, Korean numbers had been quite low prior to 2006, compared to those of world leaders (Chung and Suh 2007). Jones (2007) points out that despite its relatively high level of R&D intensity, Korea's output of knowledge, as measured by patents and publications, is relatively small.
17. According to the WEF executive opinion survey, Korea was comparable to world leaders in collaboration between the university sector and industry as of 2008. Korea ranked 12th out of 134 countries with a score of 5.1 out of 7. This is compared to the US which ranked first with a score of 5.8 out of 7 (WEF 2008).
18. According to Chataway and Wield (2000), many countries emphasize quantitative and tangible aspects over qualitative and intangible elements in developing KBEs. Jones (2007) points out a different type of weakness, that Korea is still in the midst of the transition from a catch-up model of innovation, which has emphasized imports of technology and reverse engineering, to a more creative approach.
19. For a further comprehensive analysis of recent developments in income distribution in Korea, see Chapter 12.
20. For an international comparison of the Gini coefficients over years, see Table 12.2 in Chapter 12.
21. For a further comprehensive examination of regulatory reforms and the current status of regulations, see Chapter 10.
22. For a detailed study on Korea's service sector in the context of a KBE, see Goo (2003).
23. Liberalization of the service sector and the lack thereof are further examined in Chapter 5.
24. Ahn (2002) argues that all of the sources of weaknesses and shortcomings in the Korean education system originate from government control. It remains to be seen how the new Lee Myung-bak government will develop its own education policy.
25. KIEP (2006) strongly argues for an opening of the education market to global competition.
26. Korea ranked second in terms of brain drain among the OECD countries in 2000. Two-thirds of those Korean students who have obtained PhDs from overseas universities are not willing to go back to Korea (*Overseas Korean Newspaper* 2008).
27. Out of the top 3.5 per cent from the national aptitude test in 1997, 72 per cent applied for Seoul National University and 88 per cent applied for the top three universities: Seoul National University, Korea University and Yonsei University. In 1996, 67 per cent of all cabinet members and equivalents in government, 77 per cent of the editors-in-chief of prestigious national daily newspapers and TV stations, and 81 per cent of all senior judges (equivalent to Deputy Minister and higher) were from Seoul National University (Yoo 2001).
28. In 1997, 73.8 per cent of families sent their children to private tutoring institutes, as compared to 36.3 per cent in 1982. Costs for private tutoring institutions amounted to 7.8 per cent of household consumption expenditure in 1997, compared to 2.7 per cent in 1992 (Yoo 2001).
29. Relations between *chaebols* and SMEs are further explored in Chapter 8.

REFERENCES

Ahn, Jae Wook (2002), 'Transformation of educational perceptions', (in Korean), in S.R. Park, S.K. Bae and Y.M. Kwon (eds), *Ways of Developing Korea for Every One's Economic Prosperity (IV)*, Seoul: Korea Economic Research Institute, pp. 237–66.

Asia-Pacific Economic Cooperation (APEC) (2002), *The New Economy in APEC: innovations, digital divide and policy*, Singapore: APEC Secretariat.

Bank of Korea (2006), 'Effects of changes in income distribution on consumption', (in Korean), *Monthly Bulletin*, April, 23–56.

Bank of Korea (2007), *Quarterly National Accounts*, No. 4, Seoul: Bank of Korea.

Chataway, Joanna and D. Wield (2000), 'Industrialization, innovation and development: What does knowledge management change?', *Journal of International Development*, **12**, 803–24.

Chen, Derek H.C. and C.J. Dahlman (2005), 'The knowledge economy, the KAM methodology and World Bank operations', http://siteresources.worldbank.org/KFDLP/Resources/KAM_Paper_WP.pdf.

Chung, S.C. and J.H. Suh (2007), 'Harnessing the potential of science and technology', in J.H. Suh and D.H.C. Chen (eds), *Korea as a Knowledge Economy: evolutionary process and lessons learned*, Seoul: Korea Development Institute, pp. 135–65.

Dahlman, Carl and Thomas Andersson (2000), *Korea and the Knowledge-Based Economy: making the transition*, Paris, France and Washington, DC, USA: OECD/World Bank Institute.

Goo, Moon Mo (2003), 'Knowledge-based service industry as a new growth engine', *Korea Focus*, **11** (6), 106–23.

Hankyoreh (2008), 'Private education costs, 20 billion won, surpassing the nation's education budget', Seoul, Korea, 22 February, www.hani.co.kr/arti/economy/economy_general/271404.html.

Heritage Foundation (HF) (2009), '2009 index of economic freedom', http://www.heritage.org/index/Ranking.aspx.

Hong, D.P., S.W. Ko and A. Volynets (2007), 'Information and communication technologies for a knowledge-based economy', in J.H. Suh and D.H.C. Chen (eds), *Korea as a Knowledge Economy: evolutionary process and lessons learned*, Seoul: Korea Development Institute, pp. 79–105.

International Institute for Management Development (IMD) (2008), *World Competitiveness Yearbook 2008*, Lausanne: IMD.

IMF (2006), *Republic of Korea: selected issues*, IMF Country Report No. 06/381, Washington, DC.

Jones, Randall (2007), 'Sustaining rapid growth in Korea through innovation', *Korea's Economy 2007*, **23**, 35–43.

Jwa, Sung-Hee (2008), '"MBnomics": a review and the road ahead', *International Journal of Korean Studies*, **12** (1), 83–100.

Kang, I.S., K.-H. Kim and H.Y. Han (2006), *Mid and Long-Term Strategies towards an Advanced Trading Economy: open and globalised economy*, Seoul: Korea Institute for International Economic Policy.

Kim, Ho-Gyun (2001), 'Developing Korea's knowledge-based economy', *Korea Focus*, **9** (3), 135–48.

Kim, Y.J., J.H. Lee and J.K. Ha (2006), 'Optimal combination of basic research and applied development expenditures', (in Korean), *Quarterly Economic Analysis*, Bank of Korea, **12** (3), 1–27.

Korea Institute for Health and Social Affairs (KIHASA) (2008), *2008 Poverty Statistics Yearbook*, Seoul: KIHASA.

Korea Institute for International Economic Policy (KIEP) (2006), *Mid & Long-Term Strategies Towards an Advanced Trading Economy: open and globalized economy*, Research Series: 06-02, Seoul: KIEP.

Korea.net (2009), 'Lee Myung-Bak administration', http://www.korea.net/.

Kwon, O.Y. (2008), *International Business in Korea: an evolution of the market in the globalization era*, Cheltenham, UK and Northampton, MA, USA: Edward Elgar Publishing.

Laporte, Bruno (2007), 'Building knowledge economies: education in a global and competitive world', presented at the IFEES Global Engineering Education Summit, Istanbul, 30 September, www.ifees.net/dosuments/2007_ifess_presentation/laporte_presentation.ppt.

OECD (1996), *The Knowledge-Based Economy*, Paris: OECD.

OECD (2004), *OECD Economic Surveys: Korea*, Paris: OECD.

OECD (2005a), *OECD Science, Technology and Industry Scoreboard 2005*, Paris: OECD.

OECD (2005b), *OECD Economic Surveys: Korea*, Paris: OECD.

OECD (2007), *OECD Science, Technology and Industry Scoreboard 2007*, Paris: OECD.

Overseas Korean Newspaper (2008), 'Two-thirds of PhDs from abroad decline to go back to Korea', 23 April.

Pai, Kwan Sun, Ki-Hong Park and Suk-In Chang (2003), 'Korea's drive for a knowledge-based economy', in O. Yul Kwon, Sung-Hee Jwa and Kyung-Tae Lee (eds), *Korea's New Economic Strategy in the Globalization Era*, Cheltenham, UK and Northampton, MA, USA: Edward Elgar Publishing, pp. 215–30.

Poon, Jessie P.H., Jinn-Yuh Hsu and Jeongwook Suh (2006), 'The geography of learning and knowledge acquisition among Asian latecomers', *Journal of Economic Geography*, **6**, 541–59.

Song, Jung-Hee (2006), 'IT839 policy leading to u-Korea', Ministry of Information and Communication, http://delivery.acm.org/10.1145/1170000/1164222/p1103-song.pdf?key1=1164222&key2=9815101621&coll=GUIDE&dl=GUIDE&CFID=67026047&CFTOKEN=67758638.

Suh, Joonghae and Derek H.C. Chen (2007), *Korea as a Knowledge Economy: evolutionary process and lessons learned*, Washington, DC: World Bank.

Tan, Hui Boon and Chee Wooi Hooy (2007), 'The development of East Asian countries towards a knowledge-based economy: a DEA analysis', *Journal of the Asia-Pacific Economy*, **12** (1), 17–33.

Woo, C.S. and J.H. Suh (2007), 'The challenges for Korea's development strategy', in J.H. Suh and D.H.C. Chen (eds), *Korea as a Knowledge Economy: evolutionary process and lessons learned*, Seoul: Korea Development Institute, pp. 47–52.

World Bank (2004), *2004 World Development Indicators*, Washington, DC: World Bank.

World Bank (2006), *Korea as a Knowledge Economy: evolutionary process and lessons learned*, Washington, DC: World Bank.

World Bank (2007), *2007 World Development Indicators*, Washington, DC: World Bank.

World Bank (2008a), 'KEI and KI indexes (KAM 2008)', http://info.worldbank.org/etools/kam2/KAM_page5.asp.

World Bank (2008b), 'KI and KEI indexes', http://web.worldbank.org/BSITE/XTERNAL/WBI/WBIPROGRAMS/KFDLP/EXTUNIKAM/0,,contentMDK:20584278~menuPK:1433216~pagePK:64168445~piPK:64168309~theSitePK:1414721,00.html.

World Bank (2008c), *2008 World Development Indicators*, Washington, DC: World Bank.

World Bank (2009a), 'Doing business: measuring business regulations', http://www.doingbusiness.org.

World Bank (2009b), 'WDI online', www.worldbank.org.

World Economic Forum (WEF) (2008), *The Global Competitiveness Report 2008–2009*, Geneva: WEF.

World Intellectual Property Organization (WIPO) (2008), *World Patent Report: a statistical review*, Geneva: WIPO, http://www.wipo.int/export/sites/www/ipstats/en/statistics/patents/pdf/wipo_pub_931.pdf.

Yoo, Jung-sik (2001), 'Institutional failure in the area of education and educational reform', (in Korean), in S.H. Jwa and D.R. Yoon (eds) *Issues and Directions of Institutional Reform in Korea*, Institutional Research Series 2, Seoul: Korea Economic Research Institute, pp. 95–175.

Yoon, Chang-Bun and Sang-Young Sonn (2003), 'A development strategy for Korea's information society', in O. Yul Kwon, Sung-Hee Jwa and Kyung-Tae Lee (eds), *Korea's New Economic Strategy in the Globalization Era*, Cheltenham, UK and Northampton, MA, USA: Edward Elgar Publishing, pp. 231–9.

Yuen, Ng Chee and Charla Griffy-Brown (2001), 'Introduction: knowledge-based economic growth and socio-political implications in East Asia', in Ng Chee Yuen and Charla Griffy-Brown (eds), *Trends and Issues in East Asia 2001*, Tokyo: Foundation for Advanced Studies on International Development, pp. 3–21.

Zin, Ragayah H.M. (2005), 'Income distribution in East Asian developing countries: recent trends', *Asian-Pacific Economic Literature*, **19** (2), 36–54.

PART II

External economic relations

5. Korea's trade policy in transition

5.1 INTRODUCTION

Korea's remarkable economic growth in the second half of the twentieth century has been well documented in the extensive literature. Government policy, especially the targeting of export-led industrialization, paved the way for Korea's economic success. Trade policy during the rapid economic growth period, which played an important role in achieving this economic success, included promotion of exports and restraining imports. This type of trade policy was justified in light of the narrow domestic market, the lack of natural resources, and the infant stage of domestic industries. It worked well under the cooperative international environments which were attributable to Korea's unique strategic position during the Cold War period, and to the open, liberal and rules-based multilateral trading system of the GATT and WTO.

As a result of its export-driven development strategy, the Korean economy has come to be heavily reliant on trade, and Korea has been transformed into one of the globe's leading trading nations. Between 1970 and 2007, the trade reliance of the economy, as expressed by the ratio of trade (exports plus imports) to GDP, increased from 34.6 per cent to 75.1 per cent, one of the highest in the world.[1] Korea's exports in US dollars increased 413-fold, or an annual average of 17.7 per cent growth, while world exports increased by 42.5-fold, or an annual growth of 10.7 per cent (KNSO 2008; WTO 2008). In 2007, Korea's exports accounted for 2.8 per cent of world exports, maintaining its ranking as the 11th-largest exporting country in the world (WTO 2008).

Trade policy is part of a nation's economic policy, which is in turn predicated on the nation's economic objectives and policy environments. As explained in Chapter 1, sustainable and equitable economic development will be regarded as Korea's main economic objective. The world economy has been accelerating toward globalization and a knowledge-based economy. The East Asian economies together with their intra-regional economic relations have been expanding most rapidly, and the importance of the Chinese economy continues to rise. Domestically, the Korean economy, society and politics have changed remarkably in recent years. Under these evolving national and international trade policy environments, the challenge faced by Korea is to establish its external economic policy, including trade policy, consistent with the emerging policy environments.

The purpose of this chapter is therefore to examine Korea's international trade policy in the recent past and to assess the future directions of its trade prospects and policy. Other types of external economic policy, and in particular those related to inward and outward foreign direct investment (FDI), will be dealt with in the following chapter. Trade policy instruments, including the tariff system, opening of the economy (or its particular sectors) for trade, and free trade agreements, which have been implemented by Korea in the recent past are assessed in light of policy objectives and domestic and international policy environments.

5.2 KOREA'S TRADE RELATIONS WITH THE WORLD AND EAST ASIA

5.2.1 Merchandise Trade: Trade Destination and Partners

Table 5.1 shows Korea's exports to the world, OECD, East Asian countries, and selected trading partners between 1990 and 2008. During this period, Korea's total exports increased from US$65 billion to $422 billion, an average annual growth rate of 11 per cent over the period. As Korea's export destination, the importance of the OECD has declined over time, while the East Asia region became increasingly important surpassing the OECD. Exports to the East Asian region, comprising Northeast Asia (Japan, China, Hong Kong and Taiwan) and Association of South East Asian Nations (ASEAN), increased from $23.4 billion in 1990 to $200.3 billion in 2008. Exports to East Asia accounted for 36 per cent of Korea's total exports in 1990. This had increased to 47.5 per cent in 2008.

The importance of selected individual countries as Korea's export destinations has changed remarkably over the recent past. While Korea's exports to the United States and Japan have increased, their relative importance has declined significantly. Outside the OECD, exports to India and to Taiwan, Singapore and Thailand increased rapidly. These trends in exports are dwarfed, however, by the exponential growth in export trade with China. Korean exports to China increased from only $0.6 billion in 1990 to $91.4 billion in 2008, an average growth rate of 32.5 per cent per annum. From 2003, China has become Korea's largest export market, surpassing the US. In 2008, exports to China accounted for 21.7 per cent of Korea's total exports, compared with 11 per cent and 6.7 per cent for the United States and Japan respectively.

Table 5.1 Korea exports – rest of the world, 1990–2008 (US$ billion)

	1990	1995	2000	2004	2005	2006	2007	2008
World	65.0	125.1	172.3	253.8	284.4	325.5	371.5	422.0
OECD	46.4	64.2	92.3	114.1	112.4	136.1	146.3	153.2
(% total)	(71.4)	(51.3)	(53.6)	(45.0)	(43.0)	(41.8)	(39.4)	(36.3)
East Asia	23.4	58.7	77.8	123.1	139.8	160.2	178.8	200.3
(% total)	(36.0)	(47.0)	(45.2)	(48.5)	(49.1)	(49.2)	(48.1)	(47.5)
China	0.6	9.1	18.5	49.8	62.0	69.6	82.0	91.4
Japan	12.6	17.0	20.5	21.7	24.0	26.5	26.4	28.3
Hong Kong	3.8	10.7	10.7	18.1	15.5	19.0	18.7	19.8
Taiwan	1.2	3.9	8.0	9.8	10.9	13.0	13.0	11.5
Singapore	1.8	6.7	5.6	5.6	7.4	9.5	11.9	16.3
USA	19.4	24.1	37.6	42.8	41.3	43.2	45.8	46.4

Source: KITA (2009).

Table 5.2 shows Korea's imports from the world, OECD, the East Asia region and selected non-OECD trading partners between 1990 and 2008. This table also shows changes in import sources in the recent past. It shows that Korea's total imports increased at an annual average rate of 10.8 per cent between 1990 and 2008, from $69.8 billion to $435.3 billion. The share of OECD countries in Korea's total imports declined from 72.1 per cent in 1990 to only 38.5 per cent by 2008, while that for the East Asian region increased from 40.3 per cent to 44 per cent.

Between 1990 and 2008 Korea's three main sources of imports were Japan, China and the US, and their relative importance changed remarkably. Over this period, imports from Japan increased from $18.6 billion to $61 billion, although Japan's share in the Korean market declined significantly. Similarly, the US market share in Korea declined from 24.2 per cent to 8.8 per cent. Imports from China increased most rapidly from $2.3 billion to $76.9 billion between 1990 and 2008, raising the Chinese market share from 3.3 per cent to 17.7 per cent. In 2007 for the first time, China overtook Japan as the leading source of Korea's imports.

As indicated by Tables 5.1 and 5.2, Korea, which had chronic trade deficits since the 1960s except for three years at the end of the 1980s, has consistently enjoyed merchandise trade surpluses since 1998, amounting to $14.6 billion in 2007. Korea's trade balance returned to negative territory in 2008, with a deficit of $13.3 billion. Korea's trade balance with the OECD has been variable over the period and it has maintained a trade surplus with the East Asian region and the United States throughout most of the period after the crisis. By contrast, Korea has maintained large and increasing trade deficits with Japan over the 18-year period 1990–2008. This is indicative of Korea's heavy reliance on high-technology industrial inputs from Japan.

Table 5.2 Korea imports – rest of the world, 1990–2008 (US$ billion)

	1990	1995	2000	2004	2005	2006	2007	2008
World	69.8	135.1	160.5	224.5	261.2	309.4	356.8	435.3
OECD	50.3	91.8	87.7	111.7	121.9	134.1	152.3	167.8
(% total)	(72.1)	(67.9)	(54.6)	(49.8)	(46.7)	(43.3)	(42.7)	(38.5)
East Asia	28.1	53.5	68.7	109.1	123.2	141.6	164.5	191.6
(% total)	(40.3)	(39.6)	(42.8)	(48.6)	(47.2)	(45.8)	(46.1)	(44.0)
China	2.3	7.4	12.8	30.0	38.6	48.6	63.0	76.9
Japan	18.6	32.6	31.8	46.1	48.4	51.9	56.3	61.0
Hong Kong	0.6	0.8	1.3	3.3	2.0	2.1	2.1	2.2
Taiwan	1.5	2.6	4.7	7.3	8.1	9.3	10.0	10.6
Singapore	0.9	2.2	3.7	4.5	5.3	5.9	6.9	8.4
Malaysia	1.6	2.5	4.9	5.7	6.0	7.2	8.4	9.9
Thailand	0.4	0.9	1.6	2.4	2.7	3.3	3.8	4.3
Indonesia	1.6	3.3	5.3	6.4	8.2	8.8	9.1	11.3
India	0.3	0.8	1.0	1.8	2.1	3.6	4.6	6.6
USA	16.9	30.4	29.2	28.8	30.6	33.7	37.2	38.4

Source: KITA (2009).

By industry, Korea's exports are mainly heavy industry products which accounted for 83.7 per cent of total exports in 2007 (Bank of Korea 2008). This is attributable to the heavy and chemical industrial policy of the 1970s and to the transition of the economy toward a knowledge-based economy. Korea's exports are limited to a few product classifications such as machinery and transport, manufactured goods, fuels and lubricants and chemical products (Table 5.3). These classifications have become increasingly important over time and accounted for 97.7 per cent of total exports in 2008. Of these items, exports of electrical and electronic products – including cellular phones, computers, household electrical and electronic products, and semiconductors – amounted to $126.9 billion in 2007, or 34.2 per cent of total exports (KITA 2009). As Korean exports are limited to a few items, they are subject to the vulnerability of international market developments in price, terms of trade and cyclical movements of developed countries.

Table 5.4 shows Korea's imports by commodity. As of 2008, main import items were fuels and lubricants, machinery and transport equipment, manufactured goods, chemical products, and crude materials. These items accounted for 95.5 per cent of imports in 2008, and their shares of the Korean import market all increased significantly over the period 1991–2008. As Korea relies on imports for all its fuel demands, fuel imports have risen rapidly and accounted for 32.7 per cent of total imports in 2008. Although Korea exports electrical and electronic products and machinery and precision equipment, it also imports these products to a large extent. This indicates the weakness in the industrial structure of the major export items.

Table 5.3 Korea's exports by commodity, 1991–2008 (US$ billion)

Commodity	1991	1995	2000	2004	2005	2006	2007	2008
Total	71.9	125.1	172.3	253.8	284.4	325.5	371.5	422.0
Fuels & lubricants	1.5	2.5	9.4	10.5	15.7	20.9	24.6	38.5
Machinery & transport	30.0	65.6	100.3	160.0	173.5	192.4	216.7	233.7
Manufactures	33.7	41.0	42.8	51.8	61.3	73.1	84.2	97.2
Chemical products	3.2	8.9	13.8	23.1	27.7	31.8	37.5	42.7
Crude materials (excluding fuels)	0.1	1.8	1.8	2.5	2.8	3.3	4.2	5.1
Food and live animals	2.2	2.7	2.4	2.4	2.5	2.4	2.6	3.0
Beverages & tobacco	0.1	0.1	0.2	0.5	0.5	0.6	0.7	0.8
Oils, fats, waxes	–	0.2	0.0	0.0	0.0	0.0	0.0	0.1
Other	0.2	2.4	1.6	3.0	0.3	0.9	0.8	1.4

Source: KITA (2009).

Table 5.4 Korea's imports by commodity, 1991–2008 (US$ billion)

Commodity	1991	1995	2000	2004	2005	2006	2007	2008
Total	81.5	135.1	160.5	224.5	261.2	309.4	356.8	435.3
Fuels & lubricants	12.7	19.0	38.0	50.3	67.5	86.7	96.5	142.5
Machinery & transport	28.2	49.4	59.0	75.4	82.5	92.7	107.5	114.5
Manufactures	18.6	32.1	30.3	50.7	59.2	69.0	79.5	93.6
Chemical products	8.3	13.2	13.5	20.7	24.5	27.6	32.4	36.7
Crude materials (excluding fuels)	8.9	11.7	9.9	13.5	15.4	19.7	24.1	28.3
Food and live animals	3.9	5.9	6.5	9.3	10.0	11.4	13.6	16.4
Beverages & tobacco	0.2	0.5	0.5	0.6	0.5	0.6	0.8	0.9
Oils, fats, waxes	0.2	0.4	0.3	0.5	0.6	0.6	0.8	1.1
Other	0.4	2.9	2.3	3.6	0.9	1.1	1.7	1.3

Source: KITA (2009).

5.2.2 Service Trade

Another important sphere of Korea's trade relations with the rest of the world is service trade. As examined in Chapter 1, the service sector of the Korean economy has been rising, as the economy matures and moves toward advanced status. Thus, international trade in services is expected to increase. Although this process has been accelerated in the wake of trade liberalization since the financial crisis, service trade is the weakest link in Korea's trade relations. Table 5.5 shows that Korea's exports of services increased from

$22.8 billion in 1995 to $63 billion in 2007, or an annual average growth rate of 8.8 per cent. However, the share of services exports in total exports only increased from 13.1 per cent to 14.5 per cent over the same period.[2] The main service export item is transport services, which accounted for 53.7 per cent of total service exports in 2007. In the same year, exports of travel services and business services accounted for 9.2 per cent and 22.4 per cent respectively. Services of financing, insurance, education, and computing and information, which include knowledge-based types of services, have performed poorly in export.

Table 5.6 shows that imports of services increased from $25.8 billion to $83.6 billion between 1995 and 2007, or a 10.3 per cent annual growth rate – significantly higher than the growth of service exports. Korea's balance of service trade has been in deficit in the 1990–2007 period, increasing at an annual rate of 22 per cent, and thus demonstrating the serious weakness of Korea's international trade in services. Out of the 12 service trade items in Tables 5.5 and 5.6, only transport, financing and government services had a surplus in 2006. Rapid increases in service imports and increasing service trade deficits would be attributable to the liberalization of the Korean economy, its accession to the WTO in 1995 and to the OECD in 1996. In this respect, Yeo et al. (2004) argue that Korea has liberalized the service sector beyond WTO commitments after the crisis.

Table 5.5 Korea's exports of services, 1990–2007 (US$ billion and %)

Services sector	1990	1995	2000	2002	2004	2005	2006	2007
Total	9.6	22.8	30.5	28.4	41.9	45.1	51.9	63.0
(% of total exports)	(13.1)	(15.5)	(14.8)	(14.8)	(14.0)	(13.5)	(13.5)	(14.5)
Transport	3.2	9.3	13.7	13.2	22.5	23.9	25.8	33.8
Travel	3.2	5.2	6.8	5.9	6.1	5.8	5.8	5.8
Education*	–	0.0	0.0	0.0	0.0	0.0	0.0	0.0
Communication	0.4	0.5	0.4	0.4	0.4	0.4	0.6	0.6
Construction	–	–	0.0	0.0	0.1	0.1	0.1	n.a.
Insurance	0.0	0.0	0.1	0.0	0.1	0.2	0.3	0.3
Financial	0.0	0.1	0.7	0.7	1.1	1.7	2.6	n.a.
Computing & information	0.0	0.0	0.0	0.0	0.0	0.1	0.2	n.a.
Royalties & licenses	0.0	0.3	0.7	1.0	1.9	1.9	2.0	1.9
Other business services	2.4	6.8	7.2	6.0	8.1	9.4	10.5	14.1
Cultural & recreational	–	–	0.1	0.2	0.1	0.3	0.4	n.a.
Government	0.5	0.7	0.8	1.0	1.4	1.4	1.5	1.5

Note: * Education is listed as a subcategory of travel.

Sources: Bank of Korea (2008); OECD (2008).

Table 5.6 Korea's imports of services, 1990–2007 (US$ billion and %)

	1990	1995	2000	2002	2004	2005	2006	2007
Total	10.3	25.8	33.4	36.6	49.9	58.8	68.9	83.6
(% of total imports)	(13.4)	(16.7)	(17.3)	(19.8)	(18.5)	(18.7)	(18.9)	(19.0)
Service trade balance (X–M)*	–0.7	–3.0	–2.8	–8.2	–8.0	–13.7	–18.9	–20.6
Transport	4.0	9.6	11.0	11.3	17.7	20.1	23.1	29.9
Travel	2.8	6.3	7.1	10.5	12.4	15.4	18.9	20.9
Education	–	1.0	1.0	1.4	2.5	3.4	4.5	5.0
Communication	0.2	0.6	0.6	0.7	0.6	0.8	1.0	0.9
Construction	–	–	0.0	0.0	0.0	0.0	0.0	n.a.
Insurance	–	0.3	0.1	0.6	0.5	0.7	0.9	1.1
Financial	0.0	0.1	0.2	0.1	0.1	0.2	0.6	n.a.
Computing & information	0.0	0.1	0.1	0.1	0.1	0.2	0.8	n.a.
Royalties & licenses	1.4	2.4	3.2	3.0	4.4	4.6	4.7	5.1
Other business services	1.7	5.8	10.3	9.6	13.2	15.5	17.7	22.5
Cultural & recreational	0.0	0.1	0.2	0.3	0.4	0.5	0.7	n.a.
Government	0.2	0.4	0.4	0.5	0.6	0.7	0.8	1.1

Note: * Exports (X) minus imports (M) of services.

Sources: Bank of Korea (2008); OECD (2008).

5.3 RECENT CHANGES IN KOREA'S TRADE POLICY ENVIRONMENTS

5.3.1 Changes in Global Economic and Trade Environments

Trade policy is predicated on the nation's policy environment, and the Korean policy environment has changed remarkably in the recent past. A new geopolitical situation has emerged after the Cold War and a sympathetic strategic view of Korea by the Western allies has dissipated. The world economy has been accelerating toward the globalization, information and knowledge-based era, integrating nation-state economies into an interdependent yet more competitive global system. To thrive in it, national economies are opening their doors to the global economy and are transforming further to market-based economies.

The rising importance of the Chinese economy is another important environment variable for Korean trade policy. China has achieved extremely rapid economic growth over the last few decades, largely through industrialization in low-value-creation areas using cheap labour and FDI. However, it is likely that China will move toward an economy of high-value creation. China's accession to the WTO in 2001 has helped liberalize and promote its economy. If the Chinese economy continues its recent rapid growth, it will become equivalent in size to the US economy in terms of purchasing power by 2015 (J.H. Kim 2002). Regardless of the relative size of the Chinese economy, it has become the paramount economic player in Asia and at the same time a formidable competitor with Korea.

The WTO, which came into effect in 1995, extended its rules to services and intellectual property, and has promoted global free trade by lowering barriers to cross-border trade and investment. The WTO and its multilateral trading system have faced a serious challenge after it launched a new round of trade talks with a broader programme at Doha in 2001, referred to as the Doha Development Agenda (DDA). The Doha round was an 'ambitious' effort to make globalization more inclusive and able to help the world's poorest by slashing trade barriers and subsidies for farming in rich countries. It includes a broad range of negotiations on a host of issues, including non-agricultural tariffs, trade, environment, anti-dumping, subsidies, investment, competition policy, transparency in government procurement, intellectual property, and a number of issues raised by developing countries (WTO 2007). The decision-making rule by consensus of the entire membership of 151 member countries as of May 2008 does not augur well for the future of the WTO. The Doha trade talks collapsed on 24 July 2006.

In the absence of progress in the multilateral trading system, as an alternative, regional and bilateral trade agreements have flourished in the recent past. Regionalism or free trade agreements (FTAs) among a limited number of countries has the negative aspect of trade diversion as well as the positive aspect of trade creation in the short run. However, in the long run regionalism provides participating countries with economic benefits arising from economies of scale, enhanced competition and efficiency, and expansion of investment. It is argued, therefore, that multilateralism under the WTO and regionalism are complementary. As of March 2006, 193 FTAs had been established, and of them 94 (48.7 per cent) had been established since 2001 (KIEP 2006a: 76). In recent years, 55 per cent of world trade has taken place through FTAs (Stangarone 2008).

Regionalism has been buoyant in East Asia. The East Asian region is distinct from other geographical regions of the world in its absence of a formal multilateral institution for regional economic cooperation (Yu 2003). Yet, regional economic interdependence in East Asia, and more particularly in Northeast Asia, has deepened at an accelerating pace, as demonstrated by increasing mutual trade in goods and services and mutual direct investment in recent years. This is attributed to a number of facilitating factors in the region, such as differential growth rates, ongoing structural changes in the wake of the 1997 Asian financial crisis, and China's entry into the WTO in 2001 (Mansourov 2005).

5.3.2 Changes in Domestic Economic and Institutional Environments

Domestic trade policy environments have also changed. As examined in Chapters 1 to 4, the Korean economy has been in transition toward a market-based and knowledge-based economy. The political system has transformed, whereby a large number of political stakeholders with diverse interests have emerged and political governance has changed remarkably. Korean society and culture relevant to trade policy have changed in recent years. Industrialization of the Korean economy and urbanization since the 1960s have transformed traditional Korean society into a more industrial society, whereby social stratification, patriarchal familism and patriotism have been eclipsed. Industrialization has also shifted emphasis in the value system from morality and humaneness to materialism. Continuous economic prosperity has further changed the focus of the value system from materialism to a quality-of-life concept.[3]

An epoch-making transformation of Korean culture occurred in conjunction with its 1997 financial crisis. The crisis made the general public appreciate the inevitability of emerging globalization and provided an opportunity to review value systems. As a result, Koreans have come to value foreign business and culture, and extreme patriotism has faded significantly. They support, in general, the government in introducing international economic policy, including trade policy, consistent with the globalization and information era.

It is therefore incumbent upon the Korean government to set up trade policy for further globalization of the economy, improvement of national competitiveness and advancement of the industrial structure toward a knowledge-based economy so as to meet societal values. Added to this is the amelioration of social conflicts among trade policy stakeholders and income inequality. Korea's trade policy is geared towards influencing trade relations – bilateral or multilateral – with its trade partners. To achieve this, the government applies policy instruments that include, for this chapter, liberalization of the domestic market to foreign goods, the tariff system and free trade agreements.[4] As trade policy is bound to create conflicts among different domestic interest groups or political stakeholders, the government should make efforts to obtain the support of domestic stakeholders for trade negotiations and policy. In light of its trade policy objectives, Korea's trade policy instruments are assessed in section 5.4.

5.4 ASSESSMENT OF KOREA'S RECENT TRADE POLICY

5.4.1 Trade Liberalization, Tariff and Informal Non-Tariff Barriers

In the first decade after the Korean War, the government followed an import substitution policy and tightly restricted imports in order to control foreign exchange reserves. Korea laid the foundation for its export-driven development in the 1960s with the establishment of labour-intensive light industries. In the 1970s, the government used an infant industry protection policy to establish and foster the heavy and chemical industries, such as steel, automobiles, shipbuilding, chemicals and electronics. The shift in trade and industrial policy is reflected in Korea's export structure which has changed markedly since 1970. From 1970 to 2007, the percentage of light industrial products exported fell from nearly 70 per cent to 6.9 per cent, whilst exports of heavy and chemical products rose from approximately 13 per cent to 91.5 per cent (KNSO 2008).

Korea has strongly supported the concept of the open multilateral trading system, since its entry into the GATT in 1967. Korea has been an active participant in GATT and WTO trade negotiations. After consultations with the GATT in the late 1980s, the Korean government began to liberalize some of its markets to accept foreign imports. Yet serious liberalization of the Korean trade regime has been undertaken only through a series of developments since the mid-1990s. First, since its accession to the WTO in 1995, Korea has comprehensively implemented WTO agreements and undertaken unilateral measures to liberalize the nation's trade and investment regime. Second, Korea has complied with OECD trade guidelines required as the condition of its accession to the membership in 1996. Third, the financial crisis in 1997 prompted the government to move quickly with further liberalization of trade. Fourth, since 1998, Korea has accelerated the liberalization of the service sector beyond its commitments to the OECD and the WTO as a way of attracting more foreign investment and enhancing overall economic efficiency (Kim and Kim 2003; Yeo et al. 2004).

As a result of this series of policy measures, Korea's import system has been remarkably liberalized, with a merchandize import liberalization rate of 99.9 per cent for the economy as a whole and 99 per cent for agricultural imports as of 2001 (Yoo 2003; Yeo et al. 2004).[5] Most import restrictions have been eliminated, and import procedures have been streamlined. Most goods can now be imported freely into Korea without import licenses, and only some selected items require approval (EIU 2003). Goods that are prohibited or restricted, except for rice, are normally associated with national security, public health and safety.[6]

It should be noted that although import quantitative restrictions have been eliminated, tariffs, tariff quotas and other informal non-tariff barriers are still imposed. In accordance with Korea's Uruguay Round commitments, the tariff system has improved. The number of bound tariff lines has been increased to 91.7 per cent of total tariff lines, including 92.6 per cent of industrial products. Tariffs on all agricultural products are bound with the exception of forestry and fisheries products. After a number of downward adjustments of the tariff rates as a policy instrument since 1983, the government set the 'general' rate at 8 per cent for final manufactured goods, 5 per cent for intermediate products, 1–3 per cent for raw materials, and 16.6 per cent for agricultural products in 1994 (Korea Customs and Trade Institute 2001). Each category has a range of tariff rates centred on the given general rate. For instance, for manufactured final products, there are 12 different rates ranging from zero to 30 per cent, although a majority of such products are subject to the general rate of 8 per cent.[7] The effective tariff rate, the ratio of tariff paid to import value, has declined from 23.7 per cent in 1983 to 7.7 per cent in 2003.[8] The 2003 rate of 7.7 per cent in Korea is compared to 3.9 per cent, 3.7 per cent and 10.5 per cent, respectively, for the United States, Japan and China (Bank of Korea 2007).[9]

The tariff rate structure as an industrial policy appears to be tenuous, and Korea's tariff rate should be lowered further. As the Bank of Korea (2007) points out, given the common general tariff rate, the government has applied differentiated rates to protect certain industries, not necessarily based on economic rationale but because of the influence of strong interest groups. Differential tariff rates distort resource allocation in the economy, and may end up supporting declining industries without comparative advantages or international competitiveness. Once introduced for political reasons, such policy measures may not be easily removed and create moral hazard in those protected industries. They may also raise retaliatory responses from trade partners. If the government intends to utilize tariff rates to protect certain industries, it should aim at supporting knowledge-based industries within a certain limited time period. Otherwise, a desirable tariff rate policy should be a neutral one without affecting resource allocation.

Korea's tariff rates are in general relatively high. The common general rate of 8 per cent for manufactured final products corresponds to a 3–4 per cent rate in other developed countries (KIEP 2006b: 58). This runs counter to the fundamental principle of Korean economic policy of opening and enhancing competitiveness and efficiency through competition. The DDA, if it resumes, and FTAs with other countries will demand a reduction of tariff rates. It appears therefore that Korea should gradually reduce the general rates toward those of other developed countries.

Although non-tariff or informal barriers to trade have been substantially eliminated, some are still in place, thus causing trade disputes or irritations with trade partners. These barriers include a variety of opaque and inconsistent import-related regulations, customs clearance procedures such as testing requirements, and licensing requirements (KIEP 2007: 93).[10] Technical barriers have also largely been eliminated, and the domestic regulatory framework has been made more transparent in line with international standards. Implementation of an immediate release system, an electronic data interchange (EDI) system for both imports and exports, and electronic publication of customs information in English have significantly enhanced and streamlined customs procedures. The Korean government is also committed to phasing out export subsidy programmes that fail to conform to the WTO Agreement on Subsidies and Countervailing Measures (Yeo et al. 2004). Nonetheless, although Korea's non-tariff barriers are lower than most East Asian countries, except for Japan (Bank of Korea 2007), they are still substantially (about 50 per cent) higher than Oceanian and North American countries and somewhat higher than the EU average (KIEP 2007: 92).

5.4.2 Agricultural Trade Policy

The Korean agricultural sector has declined over time in terms of GDP and employment shares, and Korea has increasingly relied on imported agricultural products. In addition, the income gap within the agricultural sector has increased over time (KIEP 2006a: 131). Table 5.7 shows import trends in agricultural products and food self-sufficiency ratios between 1990 and 2007. Over this period, the value of Korea's agricultural imports increased from $3.6 billion in 1990 to $15.1 billion in 2007, with an average growth rate of 8.8 per cent. As a percentage of Korea's overall imports, agricultural products comprise only a small share of around 4–5 per cent, although the opening of the sector has been a serious political issue. Korea's need to import agricultural products is reflected in its low food self-sufficiency ratio. The overall food self-sufficiency ratio has decreased from 53.6 per cent in 1990 to 36.3 per cent in 2007. Korea has very low self-sufficiency ratios in cereals, pulses, oil crops and oils and fats, and so has become a major world importer of oilseeds and coarse grains (Beghin et al. 2003).

For the agricultural sector, the Korean government has long sought protection from international competition through high tariff and non-tariff barriers. However, since the Uruguay Round (UR) the government has eliminated most non-tariff import restrictions, thereby raising the import liberalization rate of agriculture to 99 per cent. Korea has also lowered the level of tariffs in this sector. Yet, Korea's average effective tariff rate for agricultural products was 49 per cent in 2007, one of the highest in the OECD, and compared to a 21.8 per cent and 15.8 per cent rate, respectively, in Japan and China (WTO 2008). Rice is regarded as a 'special product' or an exception as a food security measure and remains a restricted item by the UR agreement. Under the agreement, tariffication of the import restrictions on rice has been postponed until 2014, and the minimum market access amount was set at 4 per cent of domestic rice consumption in 2005 and is scheduled to increase to 7.96 per cent by 2014.

Table 5.7 Trends in Korean agricultural imports and food self-sufficiency ratio, 1990–2007 (US$ billion and %)

Agriculture	1990	1995	2000	2002	2004	2005	2006	2007
Imports (US$ billion)[a]	3.62	6.85	7.31	8.65	10.38	11.11	12.58	15.14
(% of total imports)	(5.2)	(5.1)	(4.6)	(5.7)	(4.6)	(4.2)	(4.1)	(4.2)
Food self-sufficiency ratio (%):								
Total[b]	53.6	44.9	41.6	40.1	37.4	36.8	36.3	36.3
Cereals	43.8	30.0	30.8	31.0	27.6	29.3	27.8	27.4
(Rice)	108.3	91.1	102.9	99.2	94.3	95.7	95.3	92.5
Starch	100.0	98.7	98.9	99.0	96.6	98.3	98.5	98.3
Pulses	24.5	11.7	8.2	8.8	8.0	10.7	14.2	11.6
Oil crops	86.3	44.7	34.2	37.5	23.9	29.5	30.0	30.4
Vegetables	98.9	99.2	97.7	97.7	95.0	94.5	92.2	90.4
Fruit	102.5	93.2	88.7	89.1	85.2	85.6	82.7	83.5
Meat	92.9	89.2	83.9	82.0	83.5	81.6	78.4	78.2
Eggs	100.0	99.9	100.0	100.0	100.0	100.0	99.4	99.4
Milk	92.8	93.3	81.2	81.0	74.2	72.8	72.4	70.8
Seafood	121.7	100.4	87.7	63.8	55.4	64.3	64.0	110.7
Oils & fats	8.0	4.8	3.2	3.5	2.5	2.8	1.9	1.9

Note:
[a] Calculated from the sum of national accounts classifications: food and live animals; beverages and tobacco; animal and vegetable oils, fats and waxes.
[b] Arithmetic average of self-sufficiency rate of energy, protein and fat supplies.

Sources: KNSO (2008); KREI (2008).

Korea's agricultural trade policy should transform in line with changes in the policy environment and its national policy goal. Policy goals of the agricultural sector consistent with the nation's economic goal of sustainable and equitable growth would be a further liberalization of the sector and structural change to enhance its efficiency and production of high-value-added items.[11] The Uruguay Round agreement required developing countries (including Korea in terms of agriculture) to reduce tariffs on agricultural products by an annual average of 24 per cent over a period of ten years, reduce domestic subsidies by 13.3 per cent over ten years, and reduce export subsidy outlays by 24 per cent in ten years (Choi 2002: 35). The future DDA and Korea's FTA negotiations will certainly require significant reductions of tariff rates and non-tariff barriers.

Tariffication of import restrictions should be advanced. The Korea Institute for International Economic Policy (KIEP) (2006a: 205; 2006b: 93) argues that Korea's high tariff system has failed in providing adequate protection to the agricultural sector and that a lowering of tariff rates would not have serious impacts. As the tariff rate on rice has been decreasing and the minimum market access amount has been rising regularly over time by the UR agreement, the impact of the eventual tariffication on domestic rice will be higher by postponing its implementation. By implementing the tariffication of rice restrictions, the agricultural sector becomes more market-oriented and will be directed to high-value and special products.[12] As the international price of rice has increased greatly in the last few years, it would be an opportune time to implement the tariffication to minimize its impact on domestic rice.

In addition, acknowledging the inevitability of the further liberalization of the agricultural sector, the government should introduce a principle-based, consistent, comprehensive and transparent policy in support of the agricultural sector, or for farmers adversely affected by changes in trade policy with specific sunset causes. The government has provided ad hoc financial support to farmers after the opening of the agricultural sector by the UR agreement and has taken over farmers' accumulated debt (KIEP 2006a: 132). In order to raise farmers' support for the Korea–Chile free trade agreement, the government introduced an FTA-agricultural support Act with a specific amount of budget for this particular agreement. This has raised serious implications in relation to moral hazard for farmers, leading them to maintain traditional farming, slowing down adoption of new technology and structural reform, distorting a balanced support among different sectors, and requiring budgetary assistance for future FTA agreements.

5.4.3 Policy toward Service Trade

One of the major challenges faced by Korea for its economic policy objective is the development of its service sector. With the limited prospects of developing its manufacturing sector due to rising competition from China and other emerging economies, Korea may not be able to accomplish its economic policy goal without accelerating its service sector. Many types of services such as financing, communication, legal and accounting services generate externalities beneficial to the manufacturing sector. As examined in

Chapter 1, the service sector has been sluggish and its productivity stagnant. The relative size of the service sector in the Korean economy has remained more or less unchanged in the recent past. In 2003, the service sector in Korea was 56.3 per cent of GDP, compared to an OECD average of 67.6 per cent (KIEP 2006b: 67).[13] The growth rate of labour productivity in the service sector declined from 2.7 per cent per year during the 1980s to 1.6 per cent during the 1990s, while that in the manufacturing sector increased from 5.9 per cent to 9.8 per cent over the same period (KIEP 2006a: 67).[14] The levels of labour productivity in the service sectors of the United States and Japan were, respectively, 2.4 and 1.8 times higher than in Korea in 2005 (KIEP 2006b: 68).

Service trade could contribute to the development of the service sector, just as exports of manufactured goods did in relation to the growth of the manufacturing sector during Korea's rapid growth period by cultivating economies of scale and attracting foreign capital and technology. As shown earlier, however, service trade has been the weakest link in Korea's trade relations, and has failed to contribute to developing the service sector. In 2003 service exports accounted for 14.3 per cent of total exports, compared to an average of 22.1 per cent and 29.1 per cent respectively for the OECD and the United States (KIEP 2006b: 72).[15] The poor performance of exports is attributable to low productivity in the service sector.

There are a number of causes for this low productivity and the resulting sluggish exports. The lack of specialization, the weak domestic supply capacity of services, and the small scale of operations are the major causes of low productivity in the service sector (H.J. Kim 2007; KIEP 2006b: 64–87). To a large extent, this is a result of limited market opening and the ensuing lack of competition. Recognizing this, and under pressure from trade partners, Korea has implemented the specific market opening commitments made under WTO agreements, with particular focus on the telecommunications and financial sectors. By 2000, 471 service sectors had been opened to foreign investment, with only 24 remaining restricted in areas with a strong public interest and cultural component, such as popular media (Yeo et al. 2004). Liberalization of sector-specific restrictions has also extended beyond the Uruguay Round commitments. For instance, Korea has eliminated the restriction on the foreign acquisition of land and the ceilings imposed on foreign portfolio investment in stocks.

Nonetheless, Korea has yet to improve its service sector by undertaking further deregulation and market opening. Even though liberalization has improved for some subsectors after the WTO agreement, trade barriers on service sector activities are still high. Construction, retail, real estate, food and accommodation services are more or less fully opened to foreign markets. However, a plethora of domestic regulations and a variety of barriers still exist which hinder entry not only of foreign competitors but also of domestic companies to the service sector, thereby causing the lack of competition, small-scale operations and inefficiency (KIEP 2006a: 200). In 2001, the entry restriction ratio (the number of industries subject to entry restrictions compared to the total number of industries) was 20.1 per cent in the manufacturing sector, while it was on average 58.2 per cent in the service sector (KIEP 2006b: 81). Trade barrier indices were still high, with more than 60 per cent for public utilities (electrical power, natural gas and water), transportation and warehousing, communication and broadcasting, education, and culture and recreation. In particular, the restriction ratios were 60.4 per cent, 76.5 per cent and 91.3 per cent, respectively, for transportation, finance and insurance, and education. Out of 23 education industries, 21 are subject to entry restrictions. This supports the argument in Chapter 4 that the education system is one of the most inefficient services in Korea.

A comprehensive and consistent government strategy to promote service exports is required to enhance international competitiveness of the sector by means of market opening, deregulation and competition, rather than supporting certain industries as an industrial policy. The strategy may focus on high-value-adding sectors and 'producer services' including communications, finance, insurance, real estate, renting of machinery and equipment, advertising, business services and broadcasting. Producer services have direct impacts on the manufacturing sector, which are, according to H.J. Kim (2007), underdeveloped with low productivity. It appears that the government has not seriously sought to promote service exports; in many respects, the service sector is treated unfavourably compared to the manufacturing sector, which has benefited from economic development policy over a long period of time. Industries in the service sector are subject to different ministerial jurisdictions, so that it is difficult to develop a comprehensive and coordinated policy for service exports.

5.4.4 Comparative Assessment of the Korean Trade Regime

The Korean trade regime should be assessed in comparison with other countries. A number of international organizations provide comparative indicators for trade policy. According to the Heritage Foundation's Index of Economic Freedom (IEF), Korea's performance has shown a marked decline, from 26th position in 2000 to 34th in 2008, although it has fluctuated somewhat over time (Table 5.8). Of the Asian countries, Hong Kong (1st), Singapore (2nd), Japan (17th) and Taiwan (28th) outranked Korea in 2008. One of the ten sub-indices of economic freedom used by the Heritage Foundation is 'trade freedom', which is a composite measure of the relative absence of tariff and non-tariff barriers to trade. Korea's performance in relation to trade freedom is significantly worse than overall economic freedom; its rank decreased from 58th in 2000 to 113th in 2008 (out of 157 countries). By comparison, the trade freedom rankings of Hong Kong, Singapore, Japan and Taiwan were, respectively, 1st, 2nd, 56th and 9th in 2008.

Table 5.8 Comparative indicators of Korea's trade regime, 2000–08

	2000	2001	2002	2004	2005	2006	2007	2008
HF	26	30	27	31	40	36	37	34
Trade freedom (HF)	58	70	72	75	62	101	101	113
Prevalence of trade barriers (WEF)	n.a.	n.a.	n.a.	n.a.	42	56	32	39
Trade-weighted tariff rate (WEF)	n.a.	51*	51*	n.a.	78	n.a.	99	n.a.
Customs' authorities (IMD)	n.a.	n.a.	34	40	38	41	36	33
Protectionism (IMD)	45	43	37	53	35	55	43	41
International transaction (IMD)	n.a.	n.a.	n.a.	n.a.	38	54	51	47

Note: * Average tariff rate.

Sources: HF (2009); WEF (various years); IMD (various years).

Table 5.8 shows World Economic Forum (WEF) indicators of Korea's trade barriers. Korea's rank for the overall prevalence of trade barriers improved marginally from 42nd position in 2005 to a rank of 39th in 2008. In 2008, Hong Kong (1st) and Singapore (2nd) outperformed Korea, which in turn fared better than Taiwan (54th) and Japan (85th). In terms of trade-weighted tariff rate calculated by the WEF, Korea ranked 99th in 2007, with an average tariff rate of 9.9 per cent. Both Hong Kong and Singapore had a tariff rate of zero per cent, and Japan and Taiwan had respectively 3.3 per cent and 5.4 per cent in 2007. As shown in Table 5.8, similar messages were put forward by the IMD on the Korean trade regime. In 2008, Korea ranked 33rd out of 55 countries in terms of customs' authorities, indicating a relatively cumbersome customs clearance process, which has remained more or less unchanged in recent times. In 2008 Korea ranked 41st and 47th out of 55 countries surveyed, respectively, in terms of protectionism and international transactions. There is no clear sign of improvement in these areas of trade policy. This indicates that Korea still is a relatively difficult country in which to conduct business and international trade. All this indicates that Korea's practical trade liberalization still has room for improvement.

5.4.5 Policy toward Free Trade Agreements

Korea has traditionally maintained a policy preference for a multilateral trading system supported by the GATT and WTO rather than bilateral or regional FTAs. However, in view of the difficulties and uncertainties encountered by the DDA round of the WTO, mushrooming FTAs around the world, and establishments of FTAs by its major trading partners, Korea could not help but change its trade policy and engage in establishing FTAs. As a result, after a few years of negotiation, Korea and Chile consummated an FTA that took effect in 2004. Since then, Korea has established FTAs with Singapore, EFTA (the four-member European Free Trade Association), and ASEAN (WTO 2006). Korea signed an FTA with the United States in 2007, although it was not ratified by either of the countries as of May 2009. In addition, Korea has been negotiating FTAs with 29 countries including Canada, the European Union and Australia. Joint studies for FTAs are also under way with eight countries including China (Stangarone 2008; KIEP 2007: 99).

Although Korea established its first FTA with Chile and has been negotiating with a number of countries, it has been most active in promoting regional partnerships within East Asia in order to take advantage of the region's economic dynamism. Participation in regional economic interdependence through the mechanism of FTAs is expected to provide the Korean economy with trade and investment creation effects, in addition to increased market access. The ASEAN+3 grouping (China, Japan and South Korea) was established in December 1997. In recent years this group, under the acronym of EAFTA (East Asia Free Trade Agreement), embarked on a feasibility study in 2004 and submitted its report to Economic Ministers in 2006 (C.J. Lee et al. 2006: 19). The EAFTA has become subject to greater institutionalization through regular summit and ministerial meetings, and is taking root as the central axis for regional cooperation in East Asia, yet no formal treaty status has been established. With individual countries in the region, an agreement has been reached between Korea and China to establish an FTA within a decade by the mid-2010s. Korea and Japan also undertook negotiations for a Japan–Korea FTA, although that measure has since stalled (Mansourov 2005; C.G. Park 2006).

Korea has obviously recognized that FTAs are ineluctable and urgently required policy tools to achieve the nation's economic objectives. As examined in Chapter 1, Korea's potential growth rate for the ten-year period (2005–14) was estimated to be quite low (about 4–5 per cent) because of, among other variables, low total factor productivity. To increase total factor productivity, the economy has to improve its overall efficiency through further trade liberalization and competition, and adoption of international standards, and attraction of foreign technology. By establishing FTAs, not only can the Korean economy, particularly the inefficient service sector, gain access to stable international markets, but it can also utilize FTAs expediently for political purposes to open the service sector, minimize non-trade barriers and pursue domestic economic reforms.

Those countries with which Korea has already established FTAs, or is undertaking negotiations, represent more than 90 per cent of the world's GDP (Stangarone 2008). If Korea successfully concludes FTAs with them, they will provide an immense opportunity for Korean products. Yet in order to take advantage of such opportunities, a few strategic directions are identified for Korea's FTA policy. First, it should aim at opening foreign markets for Korean high-technology products to be consistent with Korea's drive for a knowledge-based economy (Chapter 4). Second, it should spur greater competition and international competitiveness by pursuing economic reforms and opening the closed and inefficient sectors of the economy. For these strategic directions, the agenda for FTA negotiations should include non-liberalized areas of the economy such as the service sector, non-tariff barriers and intellectual property rights. However, the service sector and intellectual property rights issues have been excluded from Korea's FTAs with Chile, Singapore and EFTA (KIEP 2007: 102). For the Korea–ASEAN FTA, important issues such as non-tariff barriers, quotas, anti-dumping and countervailing duties were not included. Korea should be willing to lift its own non-tariff barriers to leverage the lifting of those of FTA partners. Korea should attempt to renegotiate existing FTAs to deepen the extent of liberalization. Through a series of negotiations for overlapping FTA agreements, attempts should be made to harmonize them so as to contribute to eventual multilateral trade liberalization.

As examined in Chapter 3, the number of political stakeholders has expanded in Korea and achieving national consensus on any policy has become an increasingly daunting task. Market-opening trade policy would be more so, as it identifies those sectors that would be unfavourably affected by it. Unless social consensus is achieved, multitrack negotiations for a number of FTAs would be futile exercises. Hence, the policy-making mechanism has to improve. To achieve political consensus, domestic negotiations among political stakeholders should be conducted simultaneously with FTA negotiations with foreign partners. An example of this lack of a coordinated campaign to promote social consensus was the candlelight vigils against a resumption of beef imports from the United States, which was intended to be part of the US Congress ratification of the Korea–US FTA that was in turn supported by two-thirds of Koreans (*Korea Times* 2008). The vigil was undertaken over more than three months during the middle of 2008, paralysing the country's politics and administration. Any type of trade policy as well as FTAs will affect various industries such as agriculture, manufacturing and services that are under different ministerial jurisdictions. Hence, an institution may be required that will coordinate structural reforms and compensation for industries adversely affected by trade policy. In particular, Korea should introduce a comprehensive trade adjustment assistance programme consistent across all affected sectors that would not encourage moral hazard of the recipients, rather than ad hoc arrangements such as those for farmers after the Korea–Chile FTA.

One of main features of the new Lee Myung-bak government's economic policies is a strong drive for FTAs (Jwa 2008). It has planned to pursue FTAs with a number of partners, including China, Japan, India, Canada, Australia and the European Union (MOSF 2009). There is little detail, however, in the government's 100 policy tasks on taking office that refers to trade, except for the simple undertaking to conclude as many FTAs as possible (Korea.net 2009). As of mid-2009, FTA negotiations were not progressing quickly and the Korea–US FTA, signed in June 2007, was still not ratified. No significant measures have been undertaken by the new government.

5.5 CONCLUSION

The Korean economic miracle of the last half of the twentieth century was achieved by an export-led economic strategy. Foreign trade is a critical component of the economy, amounting to about 70 per cent of GDP in the recent past. Korea has also established itself as one of the globe's leading trading nations with its exports accounting for 2.8 per cent of world exports, ranking it the 11th-largest exporting country in the world as of 2007. In the recent past, however, major concerns with the economy have been its sluggish development from 2001 and a substantial decline in growth potential. They are attributable mainly to the sluggish development of the service sector and low total factor productivity (Chapter 1). In this context, an intriguing question arises as to the role of Korea's trade policy, which this chapter has attempted to address. To this end, specific trade policy such as trade liberalization, the tariff system and free trade agreements have been assessed in light of the policy objective of sustainable and equitable economic development under the emerging domestic and trade policy environments.

Trade policy environments have changed in the recent past. The world economy has been accelerating toward globalization and a knowledge-based economy. The multilateral global trading system has been in an uncertain and apprehensive state as a result of the collapse of the Doha round in 2006. This has led regionalism to flourish and Korea to engage in establishing FTAs.

Korean society has changed significantly in recent times, and societal values of quality-of-life need to be upheld. Korean politics has also changed remarkably and the number of political stakeholders has increased, making the achievement of national consensus on policy an increasingly daunting task. Finally, the Korean economy is transforming into a knowledge-based one and is developing a twenty-first century strategy of economic growth based on knowledge and information.

Recent trends of Korea's trade show remarkable changes in its nature. Korea's trade has continuously expanded faster than total world trade in recent years. Korea's major export destination and import source have both moved from the OECD to East Asia. China has become Korea's largest export market since 2004, surpassing the United States, and has become the largest import source since 2007, surpassing Japan. This suggests that Korea has to emphasize the East Asian region as its main trading region.

Challenging issues facing Korea's trade have been identified. Growth of Korea's trade has slowed substantially to about 10 per cent a year in the recent past, compared to about 20 per cent annual growth during the 1970s and 1980s. As the economy relies heavily on imported fuel, industrial inputs and agricultural products, continuous growth of exports is an inevitable demand for the future development of the economy. Korea's main exports are focused on a few items, rendering Korean exports vulnerable to international developments of price and cyclical changes. This indicates the necessity to broaden the export base.

In light of the changes in policy environments, the necessary strategic direction of Korea's trade policy should be set so as to contribute to total factor productivity and national economic competitiveness by trade liberalization and adoption of international standards. Korea's import system has been remarkably liberalized, the average tariff rate has declined substantially, and most import restrictions have been eliminated. Despite these improvements, Korea's tariff rates are still relatively high, and its non-tariff import restrictions are also substantially higher that those of developed countries. Another area where improvement is required is Korea's policy toward agriculture. Korea has long sought protection of agriculture from international competition through high tariff and non-tariff barriers. Because of its political sensitivity, liberalization of agricultural trade has been slow and controversial. Under the Uruguay Round agreements, Korea opened the agricultural sector and lowered tariff rates, although its tariff rates are still among the highest of OECD member countries. The most controversial agricultural product is rice, which is still a restricted item as a food security measure. The tariffication of the rice restriction was postponed until 2014, although the government should seriously consider earlier implementation.

Trade policy for the service sector has to improve urgently. Korea's service sector has been relatively underdeveloped and has low productivity and exports. This is attributable to the lack of specialization, the weak supply capacity, and small-scale operation of service industries. These are, in turn, caused largely by the low extent of market opening and ensuing lack of competition. Although the liberalization of the service sector has improved after the WTO agreement, a plethora of domestic regulations and a variety of barriers, which hinder entry of domestic companies as well as foreign companies, still exist. This suggests strongly the need for further deregulations to open up the market. Because of Korea's export promotion of manufactured products in place over a long period, the government has failed to implement a comprehensive and coordinated strategy for service exports.

All these weaknesses and limitations with the Korean trade regime are clearly revealed in its assessment in comparison with other countries. Although it may be argued that formal trade liberalization has advanced to an extent comparable to developed countries, Korea's trade liberalization in operation is not regarded highly by a number of international organizations. Korea's 'trade freedom' index measured by the Heritage Foundation is much lower than those of other developed countries. The WEF points out that trade barriers and effective tariff rates are still relatively high. A similar assessment was put forward by the IMD, saying that protectionism is relatively high in Korea and its trade procedure is relatively burdensome.

There is room for improvement in Korea's strategy in establishing FTAs, which has been recognized as an ineluctable and urgently required trade policy tool for the twenty-first century. Korea has established FTAs with a number of countries and has been negotiating with many other countries and regions. FTA policy needs to focus on opening foreign markets for Korean high-technology products and spurring greater competition and international competitiveness by opening the closed and inefficient sectors of the economy. For these strategic directions to realize their true potential, the agenda for FTA negotiations should include non-liberalized areas of the economy, such as the service sector, non-tariff barriers and intellectual property rights. Notably, the service sector and intellectual property rights issues have been excluded from Korea's existing FTAs, and important non-tariff barriers are not included in ongoing negotiations. Korea should be willing to lift its own non-tariff barriers to influence its FTA partners. Another area of required improvement is the policy-making mechanism so as to achieve social consensus on FTAs among political stakeholders and to provide coordinated and consistent trade adjustment assistance.

In conclusion, under the evolving domestic and international policy environments, Korea has quite successfully implemented trade policy in terms of trade liberalization, the tariff and non-tariff systems, agricultural trade, service trade and FTAs, thereby making a significant contribution to the achievement of Korea's economic objective of sustainable and equitable development. However, further improvements are required for each of these trade policy instruments in order for trade to play an adequate role in future economic development, and for Korea to enhance its role in the global and regional economy.

NOTES

1. In 2004, smaller economies such as Hong Kong, Singapore, Belgium, Luxembourg, the Netherlands, Portugal, Taiwan, Ireland and Austria had a higher trade reliance than Korea (KIEP 2006b: 34).
2. According to the KIEP (2006b: 72), the ratio of service exports to total exports in 2003 was 14.2 per cent in Korea, compared to 29.1 per cent in the United States and 22.1 per cent as an OECD average.
3. For a detailed analysis of the recent developments of Korean culture, see Kwon (2008: 64–85).
4. KIEP (2006a) argues that Korea should implement its trade policy in three strategic directions: open and globalized economy, strategically cooperative economy, and efficient trade policy governance.
5. The import liberalization rate is measured as the percentage of items in Korea's ten-digit industrial classification that face no quantitative restriction on imports (DFAT 1999: 55).
6. Applications can be made to import restricted goods, and these require a case-by-case screening and approval process (KOTRA 2006).
7. It should be noted that the tariff rate structure includes up to seven different rates for each product such as the anti-dumping rate, WTO concession rate, adjustment rate, general preferential rate, temporary rate and the general rate, in this order of precedence in application (Korea Customs and Trade Institute 2001).
8. The 1983 average tariff rate is sourced from KIEP (2006b: 48) and the 2003 rate from the Bank of Korea (2007). In Korea, there is also a value-added tax of 10 per cent imposed on all imports and domestically manufactured goods. Luxury items attract a further 10 to 20 per cent special excise tax (KOTRA 2006).
9. In fostering trade with the world's least-developed countries, Korea has extended its duty-free, quota-free treatment to 80 products as of 2000 (Yeo et al. 2004).
10. It should be noted that certain categories of goods are subject to lengthy and costly testing requirements, including cosmetics, pharmaceuticals, medical devices and food products (Singapore Abroad 2006).
11. Korea has a highly inefficient agricultural sector compared with most OECD countries (Stangarone 2008).
12. Japan and Taiwan implemented the tariffication of rice restrictions earlier than the negotiated date with the WTO (KIEP 2006b: 93).
13. Korea has the least-developed service sector of the OECD countries (Stangarone 2008).
14. The growth rate of total factor productivity in the service sector declined from an annual average of 1.7 per cent in the 1980s to 0.4 per cent in the 1990s, while that in the manufacturing sector increased from 3.5 per cent to 5 per cent over the same period (H.J. Kim 2007).
15. In terms of exports of commercial services as a percentage of GDP, Korea ranked 37th and 34th, respectively, in 2006 and 2007, and ranked 32nd and 34th, respectively, in terms of productivity in services (IMD various years).

REFERENCES

Bank of Korea (2007), 'An analysis of determining factors of Korea's trade policy', (in Korean), *Monthly Bulletin*, Bank of Korea, April, 23–69.

Bank of Korea (2008), *Economic Statistics Yearbook 2008*, Seoul: Bank of Korea.

Beghin, John C., Jean-Christophe Bureau and Sung Joon Park (2003), 'Food security and agricultural protection in South Korea', *American Journal of Agricultural Economics*, **85** (3), August, 618–32.

Choi, Nakgyoon (2002), *Korea's Trade Policy Regime in the Development Process*, Seoul: Korea Institute for International Economic Policy.

Department of Foreign Affairs and Trade (DFAT) (1999), *Korea Rebuilds: from crisis to opportunity*, Canberra: DFAT.

Economist Intelligence Unit (EIU) (2003), *Country Commerce Report – South Korea*, London: EIU.

Heritage Foundation (HF) (2009), 'Index of Economic Freedom rankings', http://www.heritage.org.

International Institute for Management Development (IMD) (various years), *World Competitiveness Yearbook*, Lausanne: IMD.

Jwa, Sung-Hee (2008), '"MBnomics": a review and the road ahead', *International Journal of Korean Studies*, **12** (1), 83–100.

Kim, Hyunb-Jeong (2007), 'The shift toward the service economy', *Economic Papers*, Bank of Korea, **10** (1), 169–211.

Kim, Joo Hoon (2002), 'New vision and strategy required for another takeoff', *Korea Focus*, **10** (4), 130–43.

Kim, June-Dong and Jong-Il Kim (2003), 'Korea's liberalization of trade in services and its impacts on productivity', in O.Y. Kwon, S.H. Jwa and K.T. Lee (eds), *Korea's New Economic Strategy in the Globalization Era*, Cheltenham, UK and Northampton, MA, USA: Edward Elgar Publishing, pp. 63–79.

Korea Customs and Trade Institute (2001), *Tariff Schedules of Korea 2001*, Seoul: Korea Customs and Trade Institute.

Korea Institute for International Economic Policy (KIEP) (2006a), *Mid & Long-Term Strategies Towards an Advanced Trading Economy*, (in Korean), Research Series: 06-01, Seoul: KIEP.

Korea Institute for International Economic Policy (KIEP) (2006b), *Mid & Long-Term Strategies Towards an Advanced Trading Economy: open and globalized economy*, (in Korean), Research Series: 06-02, Seoul: KIEP.

Korea Institute for International Economic Policy (KIEP) (2007), *Korea's Mid- to Long-Term Economic Strategy for the World*, (in Korean), Seoul: KIEP.

Korea International Trade Association (KITA) (2009), 'Korea trade statistics', http://global.kita.net.

Korea National Statistical Office (KNSO) (2008), *Korea Statistical Yearbook 2008*, Seoul: KNSO.

Korea Rural Economic Institute (KREI) (2008), *2007 Food Balance Sheet*, Seoul, KREI.

Korea Times (2008), 'Two-thirds of Koreans back FTA with US', *Korea Times*, 8 June, http://www.koreatimes.co.kr/www/news/nation/2008/06/116_25487.html.

Korea.net (2009), 'Lee Myung-Bak administration', http://www.korea.net/.

Korea Trade-Investment Promotion Agency (KOTRA) (2006), 'General trade information, current status of exports and imports', http://www.kotra.or.kr/eng/file/sub2_1.jsp.

Kwon, O. Yul (2008), *International Business in Korea: the evolution of the market in the globalization era*, Cheltenham, UK and Northampton, MA, USA: Edward Elgar Publishing.

Lee, C.J., H.G. Jeong, H.S. Kim and H.K Bang (2006), *From East Asian FTAS to an EAFTA: typology of East Asian FTAs and implications for an EAFTA*, Seoul: Korea Institute for International Economic Policy.

Mansourov, Alexandre Y. (2005), 'Northeast Asian vortex: regional change, global implications', *Korea Observer*, **36** (3), 511–41.

Ministry of Strategy and Finance (MOSF) (2009), 'Comprehensive policies to overcome the current economic difficulties', http://english.mofe.go.kr/public/direction_view.php?sect=laws_policies&pmode=&cat=&sn=6276&page=1&SK=ALL&SW.

OECD (2008), 'Services statistics', http://stats.oecd.org/wbos/default.aspx?datasetcode=TIS.

Park, Chang-Gun (2006), 'Japan's emerging role in promoting regional integration in East Asia: towards an East Asian Integration Regime (EAIR)', *Journal of International and Area Studies*, **13** (1), June, 53–72.

Singapore Abroad (2006), 'Korea-setting up business', www.singaporeabroad.org.sg/html/knowmkt.asp?cid=39&topic=228.

Stangarone, Troy (2008), 'Peering into the future: Korea's response to the new trading landscape', *Korea's Economy*, **24**, 74–81.

World Economic Forum (WEF) (various years), *The Global Competitiveness Report*, New York: Oxford University Press and Geneva: WEF.

World Trade Organization (WTO) (2006), 'Regional trade agreements: facts and figures', http://www.wto.org/english/tratop_e/region_e/summary_e.xls and http://www.wto.org/english/res_e/statis_e/statis_e.htm.

World Trade Organization (WTO) (2007), 'The World Trade Organization in brief', http://www.wto.org.

World Trade Organization (WTO) (2008), 'Statistics database', http://stat.wto.org//Home/WSDBHome.aspx.

Yeo, Taekdong, Y.M. Yoon and K.Y. Wong (2004), 'Post-crisis foreign trade and foreign investment in Korea: Korea's recovery and challenges ahead', in Charles Harvey, Hyun-Hoon Lee and Junggun Oh (eds), *The Korean Economy: post-crisis policies, issues and prospects*, Cheltenham, UK and Northampton, MA, USA: Edward Elgar Publishing, pp. 191–220.

Yoo, Chul Ho (2003), 'Korea's agricultural strategy in the globalization era', in O.Y. Kwon, S.H. Jwa and K.T. Lee (eds), *Korea's New Economic Strategy in the Globalization Era*, Cheltenham, UK and Northampton, MA, USA: Edward Elgar Publishing, pp. 133–54.

Yu, Hyun Seog (2003), 'The role of Korea in East Asian regional economic cooperation', *East Asia*, **20** (4), Winter, 77–98.

6. Korea's inward and outward foreign direct investment

6.1 INTRODUCTION

Korea now plays an important role in the global economy both as a destination and as a source country for foreign direct investment (FDI). The economic benefits of FDI for the host economy are well explored in the literature. The Korean economy is in need of inward FDI not only to attract technology, capital and the managerial know-how of advanced countries, but also to spur domestic investment through creating supplier linkages and to improve its international competitiveness. Nevertheless, inward FDI in Korea has been waning in the recent past while outward FDI has been robust. As the Korean economy matures, some Korean companies have become multinational enterprises (MNEs) equipped with ownership of the competitive advantages necessary for successful foreign ventures.

The chapter will critically examine and evaluate the system and institutions related to both inward and outward FDI. It will focus on inward FDI, something Korea is keener to attract than it is to promote outward FDI. It should be noted, however, that the systems of inward and outward FDI are related, because if the inward FDI system is not conducive to investment, outward FDI will expand.

6.2 RECENT DEVELOPMENTS IN INWARD FDI IN KOREA

Inflows of FDI to Korea have increased remarkably since the 1997 crisis in response to the liberalization of the FDI regime and improvements in the business environment. FDI in Korea leaped from US$2.8 billion in 1997 to $5.1 billion in 1998, and further to $9.0 billion in 2000. However, this is still small when compared to other countries, indicating a low contribution of FDI to the Korean economy. In 2000, FDI in Korea accounted for 5.4 per cent of gross fixed capital formation, while the corresponding figures for the world and East Asia were 19.8 per cent and 15.2 per cent, respectively (Table 6.1).

In the same year, the ratio of FDI stock to GDP was 7.4 per cent in Korea, compared with 18.3 per cent and 30.3 per cent respectively for the world and East Asia (Table 6.2).

Table 6.1 FDI inflows in Korea and East Asian countries, 2000–07 (US$ billion and %)

	2000	2001	2002	2003	2004	2005	2006	2007
FDI in Korea ($bill.)	9.0	4.1	3.4	4.4	9.0	7.1	4.9	2.6
World	1411.3	832.6	622.0	564.1	742.1	958.7	1411.0	1833.3
East Asia[a]	144.8	106.2	92.7	102.6	149.2	167.4	208.9	247.8
FDI/GI[b], Korea (%)	5.4	2.6	1.9	2.1	4.2	3.0	1.9	0.9
FDI/GI, World	19.8	12.0	10.6	7.3	8.5	9.7	12.9	14.8
FDI/GI, East Asia	15.2	10.8	8.2	7.7	10.2	9.0	9.5	9.3

Notes:
[a] East Asia includes South, East and Southeast Asia.
[b] GI denotes gross fixed capital formation.

Source: UNCTAD (various years).

Table 6.2 Inward FDI stocks as a percentage of GDP, 1995–2007 (%)

	1990	1995	2000	2001	2002	2004	2005	2006	2007
Korea	2.0	1.9	7.4	9.5	9.2	8.1	8.0	8.0	12.3
World	8.4	10.3	18.3	21.2	22.3	21.7	22.7	24.8	27.9
East Asia	20.9	21.1	30.3	37.2	37.9	26.2	25.8	26.8	30.1

Source: UNCTAD (various years).

Furthermore, as shown in Table 6.1, FDI in Korea fell sharply in 2001 and remained sluggish until 2003. During this three-year period (2001–03), the FDI ratio to gross fixed capital formation also declined and was markedly lower than those for the world and East Asia. Similarly, the ratio of FDI stock to GDP was also markedly lower than the corresponding ratios for the world and East Asia (Tables 6.1 and 6.2). In 2007, FDI in Korea amounted to only 0.9 per cent of gross fixed capital formation, while the corresponding figures for the world and East Asia were, respectively, 14.8 per cent and 9.3 per cent. The ratio of FDI stock to GDP was 12.3 per cent in Korea as of 2007, compared to 27.9 per cent and 30.1 per cent for the world and East Asia.

FDI in Korea has played only a minor role in increasing value-added levels and employment in the economy. In 1999, the value-added level by foreign affiliates as a percentage of GDP was 3.1 per cent in Korea compared to an average of 18.4 per cent in 33 developing countries. In the same year, employment by foreign affiliates accounted for only 2.2 per cent of total employment in Korea, while the ratio was 4.8 per cent for the average of 33 developing countries (UNCTAD 2002).[1] The number of workers employed by FDI companies in the Korean manufacturing sector accounted for 8.3 per cent of the total number of workers in the sector in 2001, which was the lowest among OECD countries except Japan (KIEP 2006b: 161).

Korea has attracted less FDI than could be expected given the size of its national economy. In recent years the United Nations Conference on Trade and Development (UNCTAD) has put forward a global ranking of inward FDI performance, denoting the ratio of a country's share in global FDI flows to its share in global GDP. Korea's relative performance was quite poor, with its rank of 130th out of 140 countries studied in 2007, and was the second-worst-ranked performer in East Asia, above only Japan, in 2006. Furthermore, Korea's ranking has shown a steady decline since 1990 (Table 6.3).

Table 6.3 FDI performance and potential index rankings, 1990–2007

	1990	2000	2001	2002	2004	2005	2006	2007
Korea's performance	83	98	98	110	116	115	126	130
Korea's potential	21	18	19	18	17	19	19	n.a.

Source: UNCTAD (various years).

Korea has clearly failed to attract FDI to its full potential. According to the UNCTAD inward FDI potential rankings, Korea has fared reasonably well. As Table 6.3 shows, Korea's ranking on the FDI potential index has improved from 21st in 1990 to 19th in 2006 out of 140 countries.[2] By comparing the rankings on the performance and potential indices of inward FDI, UNCTAD designates Korea as one of the 'below-potential economies', with a weak FDI performance because of government policy, a tradition of low reliance on FDI, unpropitious political and social factors, and weak international competitiveness (UNCTAD 2002).

Another aspect of FDI in Korea is that foreign affiliates do not undertake significant R&D activities in Korea as compared to its total business R&D expenditure. As shown in Table 6.4, over the five-year period from 1998 to 2002, foreign affiliates contributed only 1.4 per cent of total business R&D expenditures in Korea. Over the same period the corresponding figure for China was 20.5 per cent (UNCTAD 2005).[3] In this respect, Korea also fares poorly compared with Japan – 1.3 per cent, compared to 3.2 per cent in the 1998–2001 period (UNCTAD 2005). Part of the benefit of FDI to the host economy is the diffusion of advanced technology through the R&D activities of foreign MNEs (Cherry 2006). In this respect, the contribution of FDI to the Korean economy is relatively small.

Table 6.4 R&D expenditure by foreign affiliates to total business R&D expenditure, 1997–2003: Korea, China and Japan (%)

	1997	1998	1999	2000	2001	2002	2003
Korea	0.4	0.5	1.5	1.6	1.7	1.6	–
China	–	18.0	19.2	21.6	21.7	22.0	23.7
Japan	1.3	1.7	3.9	3.6	3.4	–	–

Source: UNCTAD (2005).

In summary, on the basis of the World Investment Reports by UNCTAD, Korea has performed quite poorly in attracting FDI, compared to East Asia and the world. FDI inflows to Korea have remained sluggish in the recent past. As compared to domestic gross investment and GDP, inflows of FDI to Korea have been significantly less than for neighbouring countries in East Asia and the world total. Korea has clearly failed to attract FDI to its full potential. Contributions of FDI to domestic value-added and employment were relatively low in Korea. Similarly, contributions of FDI to R&D are relatively less in Korea than in China and Japan.

Table 6.5 FDI by industry on a notification basis, 2000–07 (US$ billion and %)

	2000	2001	2002	2003	2004	2005	2006	2007
Manufact-	6.8	2.9	2.3	1.7	6.2	3.1	4.2	2.7
uring	(45.0)	(25.8)	(25.6)	(26.2)	(48.6)	(26.6)	(37.8)	(25.6)
Services	8.1	7.2	5.1	4.1	6.1	8.3	6.6	7.6
	(53.3)	(64.1)	(56.4)	(63.9)	(48.0)	(71.8)	(58.9)	(72.4)
Others	0.3	1.1	1.6	0.6	0.4	0.2	0.4	0.2
	(1.7)	(10.1)	(17.9)	(9.9)	(3.4)	(1.6)	(3.3)	(2.0)
Total	15.2	11.3	9.1	6.5	12.8	11.6	11.2	10.5
	(100.0)	(100.0)	(100.0)	(100.0)	(100.0)	(100.0)	(100.0)	(100.0)

Note: ( ) indicate %.

Source: Ministry of Knowledge Economy (MKE, formerly MOCIE) (2008).

FDI shares by industry have changed in the recent past. Table 6.5 shows FDI data on a notification (or approval) basis from the Ministry of Knowledge Economy (formerly Ministry of Commerce, Industry and Energy). The trend of FDI inflows in Table 6.5 is consistent with the trend of FDI inflows on an arrival basis shown in Table 6.1. In the past, more than 50 per cent of FDI in Korea had been undertaken in the manufacturing sector. However, from 2001, the FDI share in the manufacturing sector has declined, while that in the services sector has increased. Over the eight-year period 2001–07, the FDI share of the service sector amounted on average to 61.1 per cent, and reached 72.4 per cent in 2007, while that for the manufacturing sector had declined to 25.6 per cent by 2007. Lately, FDI has been mainly concentrated in the finance and insurance, electronics, wholesale and retail sales, industrial services, telecommunications and automobiles sectors (MOFE 2006). This may reflect structural change in the Korean economy and the opening of the service sector after the financial crisis. At the same time, the decline in FDI in the manufacturing sector may also indicate the loss of international competitiveness of the sector in the recent past.

Table 6.6 FDI in Korea by investment type on a notification basis, 2000–07(US$ billion and %)

	2000	2001	2002	2003	2004	2005	2006	2007
Greenfield	13.6	8.8	8.2	4.6	7.1	6.5	6.7	7.6
	(89.3)	(77.7)	(90.0)	(71.6)	(55.7)	(56.3)	(59.3)	(72.7)
M&As	1.3	1.9	0.7	1.8	4.6	5.0	4.2	2.3
	(8.4)	(16.8)	(7.8)	(27.2)	(36.1)	(42.9)	(37.3)	(22.2)
Long-term loans	0.3	0.6	0.2	0.1	1.0	0.1	0.4	0.5
	(2.3)	(5.5)	(2.2)	(1.2)	(8.0)	(0.8)	(3.5)	(5.1)
Total	15.2	11.3	9.1	6.5	12.8	11.6	11.2	10.5
	(100.0)	(100.0)	(100.0)	(100.0)	(100.0)	(100.0)	(100.0)	(100.0)

Note: ( ) indicate %.

Source: Ministry of Knowledge Economy (MKE) (2008).

Table 6.6 shows recent trends in FDI by investment type. The share of M&As type of FDI has increased more or less steadily over the period 2000–05 at the expense of greenfield FDI, and declined thereafter. In particular, over the four-year period 2004–07, M&As accounted for about 35 per cent of total FDI, although declining to 22.2 per cent in 2007 (Table 6.6). Most M&As were in the form of purchasing existing shares (KIEP 2006a), indicating that about 30 to 40 per cent of FDI in Korea has been in the form of purchasing shares in existing firms with the intention of gaining managerial control. The increasing share of M&As at the expense of greenfield FDI raises concern about rising levels of business concentration which may lead ultimately to streamlining, plant closures and job losses. Probably due to social concern about the takeover of Korean companies by foreigners, 2007 marked a rebound in greenfield FDI, with a 72.7 per cent share of total FDI (Table 6.6). Over the period 1999–2005, most greenfield investment was in operational facilities rather than for new factories (KIEP 2006b). This shows that Korea is no longer a target country for FDI in factories for manufacturing purposes.

In summary, Tables 6.5 and 6.6 show that recent FDI in Korea is concentrated in the services and high-technology sectors. Thus, the countries which undertake FDI in Korea are limited mainly to advanced countries (MKE 2008), and their recent types of FDI are in the form of greenfield FDI. In the recent past, FDI decreased annually at a remarkable rate to become a serious issue in Korean society. At the same time, the support of the general public for FDI has faded, and social concern has arisen about foreign control of domestic industries. In this regard, the evolution of the FDI regime in conjunction with the crisis will be examined in section 6.3.

6.3 THE INWARD FDI REGIME BEFORE AND AFTER THE FINANCIAL CRISIS

6.3.1 FDI Policy before the 1997 Financial Crisis

Unlike trade, for which international rules exist under the GATT and WTO, there has been no significant progress made on investment-related multilateral rules for FDI. In the absence of international guidelines, until the mid-1980s Korea pursued a singular FDI policy that restricted and discouraged FDI by laws and regulations to protect domestic industries. From the mid-1980s, however, Korea began to liberalize the FDI regime under increasing pressure from trade partners, thereby opening more business categories for FDI and relaxing restrictive regulations. Also, the FDI permission system was changed from a 'positive system' to a 'negative system', where FDI could enter any industry except those with specific prohibitions.

Over the period 1990–97, Korea further liberalized its FDI regime with the launch of the WTO in 1995 and its admission to the OECD in 1996. The approval system for FDI was replaced by a reporting system. Non-hostile M&As were allowed, and long-term offshore borrowings with terms of five years or longer were liberalized. However, the basic position of the government towards FDI was passive and restrictive, except for high-technology areas. Under anti-FDI policy, a number of sectors were closed to FDI by law until the mid-1990s. These included most service industries (distribution including wholesale and retail industries, communications, transport, banking and financing, insurance, trust, real estate, investment consulting and business services), the agricultural sector, and heavy and chemical industries. Even in those areas where FDI was permitted, the administrative regulations and procedures were complex and lacked transparency.

The Korean economic structure and socio-culture were not conducive to incoming FDI either. The Korean economy was heavily concentrated in a handful of large *chaebols* that enjoyed various types of institutionalized advantages over foreign firms (Kwon 2001). The Korean labour market was not flexible and unions were renowned for their militant tactics. Restrictive zoning laws raised real-estate prices extraordinarily high and foreigners were prohibited from purchasing real estate. Korean society was xenophobic, failing to appreciate the economic benefits of FDI. Korean business culture had not been congruous with foreign investors, and Koreans in general preferred to work for domestic firms rather than foreign firms. As a result, Korea was regarded as the worst place to invest among Asian countries until 1997 (*Far Eastern Economic Review* 1998).

The consequences of Korea's restrictive policy toward FDI and the business environment have been enormous. The sudden economic crippling borne out of the 1997 financial crisis was an inescapable watershed, signalling unmistakably that both the structure and the principles that had supported Korean economic policy could not be sustained. As a consequence, Korea had to make a shift in policy principles not only for FDI but also for other areas.

6.3.2 Liberalization of the Inward FDI Regime after 1997

As a result of the 1997 financial crisis, Korea has realized the value of FDI in its recovery from the crisis, in preventing future crises, in undertaking economic structural reform, and in developing its economy toward an advanced economy in a globalizing world. Hence, Korea has switched its policy emphasis on FDI from 'restriction and control' to 'promotion and assistance', and has undertaken a series of policy measures with the highest priority to improve the business environment to attract FDI (MOFE 2006).

The new Foreign Investment Promotion Act (FIPA) was enacted in 1998, replacing the Foreign Capital Inducement Act of 1966. It provides the legal foundation for FDI procedure, financial support, administration of FDI projects, and FDI sites.[4] Under this Act, Korea has liberalized its FDI regime to OECD standards and its institutional system has advanced to be on a par with those of advanced countries (Bishop 2001). The new Act has opened more business sectors (including the service and real-estate sectors) to FDI, and the liberalization rate rose to 99.8 per cent by 2002 in terms of the number of business sectors opened (Bishop 2001; Sohn et al. 2002). That is, out of 1058 business lines, only two remain closed to FDI (KIEP 2006b: 167).

The new Act in essence provides for 'national treatment' of FDI, eliminating discriminatory laws and regulations against foreign investors.

The process of establishing a company with FDI is treated as domestic investment except for requiring advance notification and its registration (KIEP 2006b: 169). The Act also permits hostile M&As of domestic companies, and has eased complicated administrative procedures by dismantling or relaxing more than 50 per cent of extant restrictions, as discussed in detail in Chapter 10. In addition, it has also introduced the so-called 'one-stop' service system for FDI, and the government provides a variety of tax and other incentives for FDI such as provision of investment sites and cash grants for high technology and R&D. Some restrictions on FDI remain in the agricultural, media and telecommunications, transport and power generation sectors (Kwon 2004).

A set of organizations have been established to implement FDI policy. The Foreign Investment Committee is the highest organizational level for FDI policy and its deliberation and coordination. This is not a permanent organization but an ad hoc body chaired by the Minister of Finance and Economy and convened to deal with specific issues. It coordinates central and local government activities related to the implementation of improvements in the FDI environment, including tax and other subsidies for FDI. In charge of the administration of FDI policy is the Ministry of Knowledge Economy (formerly the Ministry of Commerce, Industry and Energy). A supporting organization for incoming FDI is the Korea Trade-Investment Promotion Agency (KOTRA), under which Investment Korea provides all administrative services for FDI. Local governments are also involved in attracting FDI (KIEP 2006b: 210–12).

The business environment has also improved remarkably since 1997. Most of the institutionalized privileges that had been enjoyed by *chaebols*, and collusive government–*chaebol* relations, have been eliminated, as discussed in detail in Chapter 8. The corporate governance and management transparency and accountability of Korean firms have also improved. The penetration of foreign capital into the Korean business sector has reduced government intervention in business operations. Reform of the Korean labour market has substantially improved its flexibility. Management practices have substantially changed toward the Western style.

In the wider and less tangible arena of Korean society and culture, perceptions of FDI have undergone significant change since 1997. Once suspicious of perceived foreign control through capital inflows, Korean society has come to appreciate the value of FDI in aiding the recovery of the crisis-stricken economy and in sustaining economic prosperity. In conjunction with changes in Korean society toward FDI, preferences for domestic companies and products, and discrimination against foreign firms have declined among ordinary Koreans. This makes it easier for foreign firms to recruit and retain competent local staff.[5] In sum, liberalization and the institutional system for FDI are on a par with those of advanced countries and FDI environments have improved significantly. How, then, can the relatively low magnitude of FDI in Korea be explained? What further should Korea do to attract FDI to a level comparable to that of neighbouring countries and commensurate with its economic size? Section 6.4 attempts to address these vexing questions.

6.4 CAUSES FOR SLUGGISH INWARD FDI IN KOREA

6.4.1 Macro and Global Effects

FDI inflows in Korea surged over the three-year period (1998–2000) following the crisis. This was largely attributable to hasty sales of assets by a number of financially troubled or bankrupt companies. The drastic change in the FDI regime, buoyant global economic conditions, rapid increases in world FDI flows, and a steep decline in the value of Korean currency also contributed to the surge in FDI. This initial surge has waned, partly due to the recovery of the Korean economy, but also to decreases in the number of troubled companies available for sale. As a result, FDI in Korea fell sharply in 2001 and remained sluggish for three consecutive years from 2001 to 2003 (Table 6.1). From the perspective of foreign investors, the sharp fall in FDI to Korea during this period was also attributable to global events such as the slowdown in the world economy, marked decreases in world FDI flows, the 11 September 2001 terrorist attacks, and the emergence of China as an attractive destination for global capital (Cherry 2006).

In the recent past, FDI in Korea has been in continuous decline, except for a positive increment in 2004–05 (Table 6.1), even though the world economy has performed remarkably well. This indicates that the causes for sluggish FDI in Korea should be found internally. Kwon (2004) has found from a comprehensive survey of foreign businesspeople in Korea that foreign firms chose to pursue FDI to capitalize on the emerging business opportunities in Korea by means of their firm-specific advantages. The Korean economy and its prospects, the market size, technology and quality of factors of production are relatively quite robust. Causes for the fall in FDI must be found in areas other than economic performance.

6.4.2 Loss of Korea's Location Advantages

It appears that Korea has been losing its indigenous competitiveness in attracting FDI. According to Dunning (1980, 1998, 2000), who is widely employed in analysing FDI, three key determinants for FDI are location advantages, ownership advantages and internalization advantages. Ha (2002) has found empirically that location advantage is one of the key determinants for FDI in Korea. Emerging business opportunities are regarded by foreign investors as one of Korea's most important location advantages, and they remain relatively sanguine. This is supported by a survey of foreign investors by the Korea Development Institute in 2004 (cited in KIEP 2006b: 173) on the relative strengths of FDI environments of four countries: Korea, Hong Kong, Singapore and China. The survey shows that Korea has competitive strengths over the other three countries in geographical and strategic location, market size, social overhead infrastructure, manufacturing facilities and technology, and professional human resources. Hence, as Kwon (2004) argues, the causes for the loss of Korea's location advantages should be found in areas other than economic performance, as explored in the following.

Public support for FDI has faded (MOFE 2006; Cherry 2006). As the Korean economy began to recover from the financial crisis, the social consensus on the necessity and benefits of FDI and globalization for the economy has weakened. Negative views of FDI, such as foreign control of domestic industries, have revived after remaining dormant soon after the crisis. Furthermore, public support for the sales of assets of Korean companies has fallen, as many of the early deals were criticized as 'fire sales'. This negative view is reflected in the relentless resistance of unions to FDI, and in Koreans' prejudice against foreign companies and products (Kwon 2006). As public support for FDI has faded, the government began putting the brakes on its liberalization programme for FDI. New regulations and guidelines were introduced to restrain foreigners' takeovers of Korean banks and companies and to prevent the wholesale outflow of profits from the Korean economy (Thurbon and Weiss 2006).[6]

As examined in Chapter 10, Korea's regulatory reform undertaken soon after the 1997 crisis was incomplete and deficient. Although the number of regulations decreased almost by half, domestic and foreign businesspeople remained critical of perceived excessive and poor-quality regulations. The lack of transparency in regulations, varying interpretations, discrimination against foreign competitors, slow implementation and cumbersome administrative procedures are the most common criticisms of the Korean regulatory regime. Conway et al. (2005) point out that Korea's barriers to trade and investments are substantially higher than the OECD average, and its barriers to entrepreneurship, including heavy administrative burdens on business start-ups, are also substantially higher than the OECD average. The KIEP (2006b: 173) shows a survey result that Korea is rated quite poorly relative to Hong Kong and Singapore and equivalent to China in terms of regulations on economic activities.

Even though laws and regulations were liberalized on a par with the OECD average, implementation of the liberalization policy has been lukewarm. Stoever (2005) argues that the Korean government drew back from the liberalization of FDI as soon as the financial crisis eased slightly. According to Thurbon and Weiss (2006), Korea's post-crisis FDI policies represent the government's streamlining efforts to attract FDI and do not indicate any profound shift in national orientation from its erstwhile strategic approach to governing FDI flows. They argue that the Korean authorities still systematically link the promotion of FDI with the goal of the nation's industrial policy by means of incentives geared to the promotion of preferred domestic industries, technology transfers and particular regions. They also point out the new FDI guidelines introduced to restrain foreigners' takeover of domestic banks and outflows of profits, and conclude that the fall in FDI is attributable to still excessive regulations.

The lack of labour market flexibility and poor labour relations are another reason for sluggish FDI. It is common knowledge that unions employ militant tactics and an unyielding posture. Although the labour law allows lay-off for management reasons, it is, in effect, impractical to lay-off unionized employees because of stringent restrictions and unions' combative attitudes. According to a World Bank study of labour market flexibility, Korea ranked 51st out of 133 countries (cited in Bank of Korea 2004). The International Institute for Management Development (IMD) has also estimated Korea's labour market flexibility based on its labour regulations and labour relations (IMD 2008). In 2008, the IMD ranked Korea 54th out of 55 countries surveyed in its labour regulations (hiring and firing practices, minimum wages), and the worst (55th out of 55) in its labour relations.[7]

The relative high wage rate is another reason for the low level of FDI in Korea. Labour costs have risen rapidly in recent years, surpassing productivity increments. Over the seven-year period from 2000 to 2007, the real wage rate increased annually on average by 4.3 per cent, while labour productivity per hour increased by only 3.9 per cent (KLI 2008). This raised labour costs in Korea per unit of output in the manufacturing sector faster than those of neighbouring countries. Over the six-year period 2000–05, the labour unit cost in the manufacturing sector in US$ increased by 20.2 per cent in Korea, while it decreased by 19.9 per cent, 13.6 per cent and 12 per cent respectively in Taiwan, Japan and the United States (KLI 2007).

Table 6.4 shows that foreign affiliates do not undertake much R&D activity in Korea.[8] This is attributable to a variety of challenges. As Chapter 4 points out, they include inappropriate institutions (including protection of intellectual property rights) and incentives, the shortage of innovative and creative human resources for R&D, the lack of an educational emphasis on basic science, and the lack of international research collaboration. These problems are also identified by Invest Korea through its own survey of foreign businesspeople in Korea (KIEP 2006b: 195). The KIEP (2006b: 198) points out that Korea's lack of international research collaboration is reflected in the small portion (6 per cent) of Korean patents filed jointly with foreigners, which is the lowest among OECD countries.

6.4.3 Perceptions of Foreign Businesspeople

Certainly foreign businesspeople who would undertake FDI in Korea are an important group of stakeholders. Any viable strategy, either by governments or by private firms, to attract or undertake FDI must be based on relevant, accurate market information. One of the most effective sources of information is companies with first-hand experience of undertaking FDI and operating overseas businesses. These companies influence foreign stakeholders for FDI in Korea. To this end, a comprehensive survey was undertaken from May to July 2002 of foreign companies that had undertaken FDI and were operating businesses in Korea.[9] In order to supplement the survey and garner additional information, personal interviews were conducted with a number of the responding company representatives and some foreign business expatriates. As mentioned earlier, the survey found that the predominant motive of foreign companies to invest in Korea was to capitalize on emerging business opportunities by means of their firm-specific advantages. Foreign businesspeople had a negative view, though moderate, on the importance of the other location-specific variables. They include: 'advanced related industries', 'easy access to information and technology', 'abundant skilled workers', 'investment incentives by Korea', 'easy access to parts and materials', 'low production costs' and 'overcoming tariff and other import barriers'. It also appears that foreign investors did not consider Korea as a stepping stone to other Asian markets.

Foreign businesspeople pointed out difficulties in setting up investment projects in Korea such as the onerous procedure for investment, the complex, inconsistent and opaque policies, regulations and administrative procedures, inadequate protection of intellectual properties, inadequate corporate governance of Korean companies and their opaque financial statements, and militant unions. Some of them were also aggrieved by interauthority turf wars between fire, police, construction and environmental authorities at both local and regional levels, since these battles delay approval requirements. These survey and interview results vindicate the earlier arguments that Korea's liberalization is incomplete and deficient, and that the regulatory regime remains excessive, complex and opaque.

Contrary to a number of arguments that the business environment in Korea had improved (Kim and Choo 2002; Kim 2003; Kim and Kim 2003), foreign businesspeople had, in general, a moderately negative view of the improvement except for political stability and economic prospects. They did not feel that foreign firms engaged in level playing-field competition with Korean counterparts. Foreign businesspeople remained negative in their views on whether Koreans had improved in terms of their discrimination against foreigners and foreign products, and their nationalistic mindsets. Instead, they also pointed to the fading social consensus on the benefits of FDI and globalization, the reviving negative view on inward FDI, and the discriminatory regulations against foreign companies.

The survey attempted to identify difficulties encountered by foreign businesspeople in on-site management of businesses in Korea. They pointed out many types of difficulties in the area of government–business relations such as 'lack of transparency and consistency in regulations', 'prevailing cronyism and corruption', 'excessive discretionary power of bureaucrats' and 'excessive government regulations'. These survey findings are also consistent with the above argument. On their business operations and relations with Korean companies, respondents rated 'importance of personal relationships in business' and 'unfair advantages held by Korean firms, especially *chaebols*' as the most difficult areas.

The survey appears to confirm the reputable nature of Korean workers. Foreign businesspeople agreed strongly with positive aspects of Korean workers such as being hard-working, and their high loyalty to companies and supervisors, willingness to work for foreign companies, collaborative team spirit and willingness to train for new jobs. However, foreigners did not consider Korean workers as being highly skilled and efficient, nor were they thought of as possessing high reliability and stability. Poor English language skills were rated as one of the most serious issues relating to Korean workers.

Foreign businesspeople considered that coping with Korean society was difficult for them because of cultural and communication differences, and the closure of society to foreigners. Finally, many respondents regarded poor social amenities for expatriates' families as a serious concern.[10] The findings of the survey may indicate that, while the Korean government provides various types of support, incentives and assistance in attracting FDI and streamlining the FDI procedure, it does not perform as well in supporting the on-site operations of FDI projects.

6.4.4 Assessment of Comparative FDI Environments in Korea

So far Korea's FDI policy and environments have been examined and assessed in isolation. They should also be assessed in comparison with other countries, as foreign investors choose their FDI host countries based on comparative analysis. Korea is still regarded as a difficult place to acquire control of domestic companies and the capital market is not adequately liberalized. On freedom of acquiring control of domestic companies, the IMD (2007, 2008) ranked Korea 49th and 47th, respectively, in 2007 and 2008 out of 55 countries. On capital market liberalization, Korea ranked 43rd and 47th, respectively, in 2007 and 2008. Koreans' reluctance to open their mindsets and the country's relatively poor FDI environments are shown by a low extent of globalization. As shown in Table 6.7, Korea ranked 35th out of 72 countries in 2007 on the A.T. Kearney globalization index. What is worse, Korea ranked 61st in 2007 for economic integration with FDI. Dreher (2006) has also developed a globalization index covering three main dimensions: economic integration, social integration and political integration. As shown in Table 6.8, Korea ranked 29th overall in 2006 out of 123 countries. This was an improvement from 40th in 2000. Of the dimensions of globalization most relevant to the present chapter, Korea ranked 63rd in 2006 on the sub-index of economic integration.[11] These two indexes clearly indicate that the extent of Korea's globalization has to improve to attract FDI.

Table 6.7 Korea's ranks in globalization, economic freedom and transparency, 2000–08

	2000	2001	2002	2004	2005	2006	2007	2008
WEF	29	23	21	29	17	24	11	13
IMD	29	29	29	31	27	32	29	31
Kearney	n.a.	31	31	32	30	29	35	n.a.
HF	24	25	30	35	38	38	36	41
TI	48	42	40	47	40	42	43	40

Sources: World Economic Forum (WEF) (various years); International Institute for Management Development (IMD) (2007, 2008); A.T. Kearney/*Foreign Policy* (various years); Heritage Foundation (HF) (2009); Transparency International (TI) (2009).

Table 6.8 Dreher's globalization index and ranking for Korea (rating index and ranking)

	Globalization summary rating	Economic integration	Social integration	Political integration
2000	3.37 (40th)	3.86 (62nd)	2.72 (29th)	3.65 (42nd)
2006	3.15 (29th)	3.64 (63rd)	2.45 (27th)	3.50 (21st)

Notes:
Values range between 0 (not globalized) to 10 (globalization).
Ranking is out of 123 countries.

Source: Dreher (2006).

Levels of economic freedom and corruption also have important effects on FDI. As shown in Table 6.7, Korea's ranking on the Heritage Foundation's Index of Economic Freedom has significantly worsened in the recent past. Korea's ranking deteriorated from 24th in 2000 to 41st in 2008. Korea was outperformed by East Asian neighbours Hong Kong, Singapore, Japan and Taiwan in 2008 (Heritage Foundation 2009). Similarly, Korea performed quite poorly on the Transparency International Corruption Perceptions Index. Between 2000 and 2007, Korea's ranking has ranged between 40th and 50th position on the index without significant improvement (Table 6.7).

National competitiveness as measured by the WEF and the IMD is also indicative of relative location advantages.[12] According to the WEF Global Competitiveness Index (GCI), Korea's performance has fluctuated markedly, ranking 24th in 2006 and 13th in 2008 (Table 6.7). In 2008, only Singapore, Japan and Hong Kong outperformed Korea in East Asia. The WEF indices show that Korea's relatively high rankings are due to its technological prowess. The IMD index is based on economic performance, government efficiency, business efficiency and infrastructure. Korea's relative position on the IMD scoreboard has fluctuated with a ranking of 31st in 2008, down from 27th in 2005. Most countries in East Asia such as Hong Kong, Singapore, China, Taiwan, Malaysia, Thailand and Japan outperformed Korea in 2008 (IMD 2008).

It should be noted that the above assessment of FDI environments in Korea is applicable not only to FDI but also to investment in Korea by domestic firms. The OECD (2006) argues that coherence and transparency of policy formulation and implementation, accountability of government agencies, property protection and non-discrimination among types of investment are key determinants not only for international but also for domestic investment. Korea's poor indicators in these key determinants of investment are reflected not only in the low level of FDI but also in sagging domestic investment, as shown in Table 1.1 of Chapter 1. As the domestic environment is not conducive to investment, domestic investors move to foreign countries to undertake overseas investment. This is reflected in the rapid rise of Korean overseas investment, as examined in section 6.5.

6.5 EVOLUTION OF OUTWARD FDI REGULATION

There were no regulations on Korean outward FDI prior to 1968.[13] Korea's overseas direct investment was then subject to heavy regulation until the mid-1980s predominantly through the use of an extensive system of foreign exchange controls. Outward FDI proposals were subject to approval by the Bank of Korea on a case-by-case basis. Firms approved from the 'positive list system' were required to fund overseas investment projects from domestic sources rather than foreign borrowing. Firms' overseas operations also remained subject to supervision from Korean diplomatic representation in the host country. This regulated approach was due to Korea's chronic balance-of-payments deficits and large foreign debt burden in the early decades of its rapid growth period. During this time, the government only permitted overseas investment projects that would make a contribution to Korea's national development strategy (Kim and Mah 2006).

From 1986, Korea maintained consistent current account surpluses and the government began to liberalize its outward FDI policies. The first steps taken over the 1986 to 1990 period were the streamlining of the regulatory process and the encouragement of outward FDI in certain economic sectors. The Bank of Korea approval system was substituted with a notification system for permitted industries. The restrictions on foreign borrowing to fund overseas investment projects were also lifted to finance overseas expansion including M&As. In addition, the government also provided support for outward FDI with the provision of loans, insurance and preferential tax treatment. The Overseas Investment Insurance Plan included coverage for up to 90 per cent of losses resulting from political or commercial risk factors and a major tax subsidy allowed companies to claim up to 20 per cent of their total investment as losses for tax purposes. The list of permitted sectors was also increased to include real-estate developments (Kim and Mah 2006).

Outward FDI was further liberalized during the 1990s through the simplification of application procedures, easing of investor qualifications and the expanding of loan facilities available through the Export–Import Bank of Korea. Finally, overseas investment from Korea was fully liberalized in 1997. Projects were no longer subject to government approval and the foreign exchange control system was abolished in 1999. The positive list system for outward FDI was replaced with a negative list system whereby overseas investment could be undertaken freely except in 14 restricted areas. By the end of the 1990s, Korean businesses had covered the globe – from Southeast Asia, China and the United States to Eastern Europe – with automobile and electronics factories and construction operations (Kim and Mah 2006). As a result, the amount of Korea's outward FDI surpassed that of inward FDI in 2001 for the first time, and has remained so (Tables 6.1 and 6.9).

Currently, any resident Korean individual or institution wishing to undertake overseas investment must firstly submit an investment plan and project proposal to a major foreign exchange bank. The bank then evaluates the institution or individual concerned and their investment plan. Certain overseas investments, particularly in real estate and finance and insurance, must be notified to the Ministry of Finance and Economy (MOFE). In the post-1997 financial crisis period, firms have also been required to include their overseas investment structure as part of their overall financial position. Quarterly reports and annual consolidated financial statements must now include a firm's foreign operations. The evolution of Korea's FDI policy is mirrored by the actual pattern of outward FDI growth by Korean firms. Between 1968 and the early 1990s, overseas investments increased very slowly until a rapid expansion from the mid-1990s (Kimura and Lee 1998; Kim and Mah 2006).

Table 6.9 Korea FDI outflows on an arrivals basis, 1990–2007 (US$ billion)

	1990	2000	2001	2002	2004	2005	2006	2007	Total*
World	1.1	5.1	5.2	3.8	6.1	6.8	11.0	20.4	97.7
China	0.0	0.7	0.7	1.1	2.3	2.8	3.3	5.2	23.4
US	0.4	1.4	1.5	0.6	1.4	1.3	1.8	3.4	22.4
Hong Kong	0.1	0.3	0.1	0.2	0.2	0.3	0.8	1.2	5.5
Vietnam	–	0.1	0.1	0.2	0.2	0.3	0.6	1.3	3.8
Indonesia	0.2	0.1	0.2	0.1	0.1	0.1	0.1	0.2	2.8
Netherlands	0.4	0.0	1.6	0.3	0.0	0.0	0.1	0.3	2.8
Bermuda	–	1.4	0.0	0.0	0.0	0.1	0.3	0.3	2.4
UK	0.0	0.0	0.3	0.1	0.3	0.1	0.1	0.1	2.3
Singapore	0.0	0.1	0.0	0.1	0.2	0.1	0.3	0.5	2.2
Japan	0.0	0.1	0.1	0.1	0.3	0.2	0.2	0.5	2.1

Note: * 1968–2007.

Source: Export–Import Bank of Korea (2008).

6.5.1 Outward FDI by Major Recipient Countries

Table 6.9 shows the major trend in Korea's outward FDI flows on an arrivals basis. Total outward flows increased from \$1.1 billion in 1990 to \$20.4 billion in 2007, an average annual growth rate of 19 per cent. Total outward FDI of \$20.4 billion in 2007 is compared to \$2.6 billion of inward FDI in the same year, indicating the seriousness of the inward FDI policy issue (Table 6.1). The composition of major recipients has changed in the recent past. China and the United States remain the largest recipients of outward flows by a large margin over all other countries, with totals of \$23.4 billion and \$22.4 billion respectively. In 2007, flows to China accounted for 25.7 per cent of Korea's total by arrival, while flows to the United States accounted for 16.7 per cent. In 2002, China surpassed the United States as the leading recipient of outward FDI flows, recording an annual average growth rate of 40.7 per cent between 1990 and 2007. Another country to which Korea's overseas investment has risen most rapidly is Vietnam, recording 17.5 per cent annual growth over the period 1995–2007, reaching \$1.3 billion in 2007. Vietnam became the third-largest recipient of Korean overseas investment in 2007, replacing Hong Kong. China, the United States, Vietnam and Hong Kong received 54.4 per cent of total Korean outward FDI in 2007. Although Korea's outward FDI flows to Singapore and Japan have grown steadily in the recent past, the total amounts the two countries received in 2007 were just over 5 per cent of Korea's overall outward FDI.

Table 6.10 Korea FDI outflows by sector (arrivals), 1990–2007 (US$ billion)

	1990	2000	2001	2002	2004	2005	2006	2007	Total[a]
Total	1.1	5.1	5.2	3.8	6.1	6.8	11.0	20.4	97.7
Mining	0.2	0.1	0.1	0.2	0.3	0.5	1.4	2.0	8.9
Manufacturing	0.5	1.6	3.8	1.8	3.5	3.7	5.6	7.6	46.9
Construction	0.0	0.1	0.0	0.1	0.1	0.2	0.5	0.8	2.6
Wholesale & retail trade	0.2	0.8	0.9	1.2	1.1	1.0	1.2	2.0	16.3
Hotel & restaurant	0.0	0.2	0.0	0.0	0.1	0.2	0.2	0.3	2.1
Finance & insurance	0.1	0.0	0.0	0.1	0.1	0.1	0.2	1.2	3.0
Real estate	0.0	0.5	0.2	0.2	0.6	0.4	0.8	1.5	5.7
Business services	0.0	1.4	0.0	0.0	0.1	0.2	0.4	3.4	6.0
Others[b]	0.0	0.0	0.1	0.1	0.2	0.5	0.7	3.7	5.8

Notes:
[a] For period 1968–2007.
[b] Others include agriculture & forestry, fishing, utilities (electricity, gas and water), transport, post & communications, public administration and defence, education, health and social work, recreation, culture and sport, other community and personal services, private household services, and extra-territorial organizations.

Source: Export–Import Bank of Korea (2008).

6.5.2 Outward FDI by Economic Sector

Table 6.10 shows Korea's outward FDI flows on an arrivals basis by world total and by economic sector. The manufacturing sector is the largest destination for Korea's FDI outflows by a large margin, with 48 per cent of the world total (1968–2007). As regulations on overseas FDI were relaxed and other sectors were opened, the share of the manufacturing sector declined to 37.1 per cent of total outflows of FDI in 2007. The next largest destination for FDI outflows is the wholesale and retail trade sector, which comprised 16.7 per cent of Korea's world total. These are for establishing sales affiliates of Korean *chaebols*. The third-largest destination for Korea's outward FDI flows was the mining sector, accounting for 9.1 per cent of Korea's world total (1968–2007). As Korea relies heavily on foreign minerals, it has attempted to develop and import overseas mineral resources and lately has increased its investment in overseas oil and gas exploration. The real-estate, business services, and finance and insurance sectors are the other significant destination sectors for Korea's FDI outflows. These sectors also recorded much higher growth rates than the three leading sectors over the period in question. In particular, the real-estate sector has grown most rapidly for the last few years after regulations were relaxed. The business services sector increased by an average annual rate of 62 per cent over the period, accounting for 16.6 per cent of Korea's 2007 total.

Korea's outward FDI, as examined above, suggests a few implications. Since outward FDI was fully liberalized, domestic investors have searched for the best location for their businesses. As Korea's investment environments became relatively less conducive to investment, and its manufacturing sector lost its comparative advantages, Korean investors expanded their investment into the overseas manufacturing sector, particularly in China and Vietnam. The series of recent developments in Korea's inward and outward FDI shows clearly that the country is fully open in terms of investment, and hence its FDI policy should aim at comprehensive improvement in its domestic investment environments.

6.6 EXPLORATION OF THE WAYS TO ATTRACT MORE FDI

Korea's FDI policy has to improve, not only to attract FDI but also to increase sagging domestic investment. In this respect, some suggestions are explored from institutional perspectives. First, to attract further inward FDI, Korea should not only undertake an across-the-board liberalization of the FDI regime, but also further regulatory reforms, and an enhancement of public awareness and understanding of the benefits of FDI and globalization. Although the FDI regime has been liberalized and the entry procedure streamlined, clearly there is substantial room for improvement at both the central and local levels of government. To improve the poor quality of the domestic business environment, not only should excessive government regulations and bureaucratic power be removed, but so should unfair advantages bestowed on domestic firms and continued rigidities in the labour market. The living conditions of foreign expatriates should also be improved. Korean society and Koreans in general need to become more open and amicable to foreigners and foreign business operations in Korea.

Second, there are a number of organizations involved in Korea's FDI policy and implementation: the Foreign Investment Committee, the Ministry of Knowledge Economy, the Korea Trade-Investment Promotion Agency (KOTRA) and Invest Korea, all under the central government. Local governments also play important roles. With a large number of organizations involved in various aspects of FDI, it is difficult to maintain policy consistency, coherency and transparency. The Foreign Investment Committee is the peak organization for FDI policy and coordination. However, it is chaired by the Minister of Strategy and Finance (MOSF) and is not a permanent organization. It has been demonstrated that the task of attracting FDI is not limited to establishing an FDI regime similar to the OECD standards. The task involves a broad scope of policy measures to improve the investment environments, regulations, R&D activities, English language skills, management environment and even expatriate living conditions. Under its current form and mandate, the Foreign Investment Committee is certainly not capable of undertaking the entire task, while also maintaining the policy consistency, coherency and transparency that are essential for investment promotion.

It is suggested therefore that the Foreign Investment Committee should be replaced by a Presidential Committee on Investment directly under presidential authority, and should be a permanent organization dealing with both FDI and domestic investment.[14] Without having presidential authority and commitment, coordination of all issues involved in promoting national and international investment is not possible under the Korean political system. The committee may be co-chaired by the President and a civilian expert, and should include as members not only domestic experts but also some representatives of foreign chambers of commerce and industry as well as some experts from central and local government. FDI promotional activities by individual local governments should be coordinated, and interauthority turf wars between agencies under local governments should be prohibited.

Third, in conjunction with the proposed Presidential Committee on Investment, the task of attracting FDI should be part of a comprehensive promotional policy. As Korea has already liberalized the FDI regime to the extent of 'national treatment', further measures to attract FDI may result in discrimination against domestic investment, which in turn creates negative societal attitudes to FDI. Hence, the comprehensive investment policy should aim at improving overall policy consistency and transparency, creating business environments conducive to both FDI and domestic investment, and enhancing overall national competitiveness.

Fourth, FDI policy includes a number of disparate political stakeholders: not only foreign investors but also domestic businesspeople and the general public. Hence, achieving a social consensus on FDI policy among these stakeholders is an arduous but essential task. Unless social consensus is achieved, public support for FDI will fade, as happened soon after the 1997 reforms, thereby weakening the policy drive to attract FDI. To help achieve social consensus, a variety of stakeholders should be informed and invited to take part in the policy-making and implementation process that is transparent and accountable. A public campaign for FDI should be undertaken based on objective regular evaluation of FDI and other investment policy. Through this process, Koreans' mindset can be further opened.

One of the main features of the new Lee Myung-bak government's economic policies is an aggressive attitude to attracting FDI (Jwa 2008). The government's first policy objective under its strategic goal of a dynamic market economy is 'to drastically improve the investment climate'. For FDI, this includes the policy tasks of cutting taxes 'to revitalize investment and consumption' and making the country 'more attractive to foreign investors' (Korea.net 2009). Lee's economic policies on entering office have been overtaken to a large degree by the global financial crisis (GFC) that commenced in September 2008. Even prior to the GFC, however, the Lee government was in trouble with its economic policies. After one year in office, the proposed tax reductions to stimulate investment had not passed the National Assembly. In early 2009, the Lee government put a number of specific measures into place to combat the effects of the GFC. A number of these are dedicated to promoting investment through regulatory reform, although FDI is not specifically mentioned (MOSF 2009).

6.7 CONCLUSION

The Korean government restricted and controlled inward FDI up to the 1997 financial crisis, largely because of its historical obsession with protecting domestic industries. Neither were the Korean economic structure and socio-culture conducive to incoming FDI. As a result, Korea was regarded as the worst place to invest among Asian nations until 1997, as reflected in the flagging level of FDI. After the 1997 financial crisis, the Korean government has recognized the value of inward FDI and undertaken a paradigm shift in its FDI policy from one of 'restriction and control' to 'promotion and assistance'. Accordingly, it has undertaken a series of policy measures and all-out efforts to improve the business environment and attract FDI. As a result, FDI in Korea increased remarkably over the three-year period, 1998–2000. Despite this spurt, the attraction of FDI to Korea is still low by international comparison. FDI in Korea decreased markedly in 2001, and remained sluggish until 2004 when it finally increased substantially, although declining again in the two consecutive years, 2006–07.

This chapter has identified a variety of causes for the sluggish rate of FDI in Korea and the worsening of location advantages in the recent past. No sooner had economic difficulties from the financial crisis eased, than social consensus on the benefit of FDI and globalization weakened, and societal suspicion of FDI came to the fore. In response to these changes in the social mood, the government has begun to put the brakes on its liberalization programmes, rendering the institutional and structural reforms incomplete and deficient. Consequently, the Korean regulatory regime is still excessive, incoherent and opaque. The lack of policy transparency and coherence begets the lack of accountability of civil servants, which is in turn reflected in high corruption. The labour market lacks flexibility and labour relations are turbulent and wage rates have increased rapidly, exceeding those of East Asian competitors. This series of recent developments in Korea has been borne out in well-known global indicators. Korea ranks relatively poorly in the indices of globalization, economic freedom, corruption perception and national competitiveness as compared to East Asian countries with similar economic development stages.

Another important determinant of FDI in Korea is the perception of the Korean FDI environment held by foreign investors. Survey results indicate that foreign investors encountered various types of difficulties in establishing FDI projects in Korea. Although formal entry barriers have been reduced to OECD standards, there remain difficulties in setting up investment projects and on-site management. These difficulties arise not only from excessive, complex and opaque government regulations and bureaucratic discretion, but also from unique Korean business cultures, unfair advantages held by domestic firms, and cultural and social differences.

Since outward FDI has been fully liberalized and domestic investment environments have not improved, Korea's overseas direct investment has increased rapidly. Korean investors have been expanding their investment in China and Vietnam to capitalize on the location advantages of these countries, particularly in their manufacturing sectors. Korea has also expanded its overseas investment in advanced countries to acquire advanced technology and human resources. Since 2001, Korea's outward FDI has been larger than its inward FDI.

To attract further inward FDI, Korea should not only undertake an across-the-board liberalization of the FDI regime, but also further its regulatory reforms and enhancement of public awareness and understanding of the benefits of FDI and globalization. This chapter emphasizes a comprehensive approach in tackling the challenge faced by sagging FDI. To this end, it is pointed out that policy consistency, coherency, transparency and coordination are key factors for international and domestic investment. To achieve this, an institution in charge of promoting overall investment should be established.

A Presidential Committee on Investment has been proposed as a permanent coordination, implementation and promotional organization dealing with both FDI and domestic investment.

A comprehensive investment policy should aim at improving overall policy consistency and transparency, creating globalized business environments conducive both to FDI and domestic investment, and enhancing overall national competitiveness. A social consensus on FDI policy among stakeholders is another important key to success. Unless social consensus is achieved, public support for FDI will fade as happened soon after the 1997 reforms, thereby weakening the policy drive to attract FDI. To help achieve social consensus, transparency and accountability in the policy process are necessary. A public campaign for FDI should be undertaken based on an objective regular evaluation of FDI and other investment policies, from which Korean society would become more open and amicable to foreigners and foreign business operations.

NOTES

1. Subsequent issues of the *World Investment Report* do not include data on the levels of value-added and employment by foreign affiliates.
2. The factors used in estimating the UNCTAD inward FDI potential index include: the rate of growth of GDP; per capita GDP; share of exports in GDP; telephone lines per 1000 inhabitants; commercial energy use per capita; share of R&D expenditures in gross national income; share of tertiary students in population; country risk; exports of natural resources as a percentage of world total; imports of parts and components of electronics and automobiles as a percentage of world total; exports in services as a percentage of world total; and inward FDI stock as a percentage of world total. The index is an unweighted average of the normalized values of these variables (UNCTAD 2005).
3. The relatively high ratio of R&D expenditure by foreign affiliates in China may be attributable to its relatively low level of domestic business R&D expenditure.
4. Other than the Foreign Investment Promotion Act, there are a number of laws related to FDI, including those related to foreign exchange, taxes, securities transaction, and fair competition. They are supplementary to the Foreign Investment Promotion Act.
5. For further details of the change in the Korea FDI regime soon after the 1997 crisis, see Kwon (2001), Kim and Choo (2002), J.D. Kim (2003), Kwon (2004) and Cherry (2006).
6. In 2003 the Bank of Korea halted the privatization of domestic banks until local buyers are found. In 2005 the Financial Supervisory Commission (FSC) suspended the voting rights of investors purchasing 5 per cent or more of stocks in Korean companies for five days to allow the target company time to deal with the threat of takeover. The FSC also introduced in 2005 a guideline requiring that Korean nationals comprise at least 50 per cent of the boards of all local banks. In the same year, there was also a spate of surprise tax audits on foreign investment funds (Thurbon and Weiss 2006).
7. KIEP (2006b: 173) also points out labour relations as one of the main causes of Korea's loss of international competitiveness as compared to Hong Kong, Singapore and China.
8. KIEP (2006b: 192) estimates that R&D expenditures in Korea by foreign affiliates amounted to about 4 per cent of total domestic R&D expenditure in 2003, compared to 10–30 per cent in OECD countries.
9. For details of the survey, its procedure and findings, see Kwon (2004).

10. KIEP (2006b: 173) cited a survey result indicating that the living conditions for expatriates are worse in Korea than in Hong Kong and Singapore, and similar to those in China.
11. This index is calculated by the weighted average of actual flows (such as trade volume, FDI, portfolio investment, income payments to foreign nationals) to GDP and restrictions (such as hidden import barriers, mean tariff rate, taxes on international trade, capital account restrictions).
12. National competitiveness refers to, in short, 'a well-functioning market economy' which in turn determines a country's ability to maintain and expand its economic prosperity (ADB 2003).
13. Unless otherwise cited, the material in this section is drawn from Kwon and Oh (2001).
14. A similar idea has been proposed by KIEP (2006b: 210–11).

REFERENCES

Asian Development Bank (ADB) (2003), *Asian Development Outlook 2003*, Manila: ADB.

A.T. Kearney/*Foreign Policy* (various years), 'Globalisation index rankings', *Foreign Policy*.

Bank of Korea (2004), 'Korean labour market inflexibility and future agenda', (in Korean), *Monthly Bulletin*, August, 23–53.

Bishop, Bernie (2001), 'Barriers to foreign direct investment in Korea and Australia', in O.Y. Kwon and W. Shepherd (eds), *Korea's Economic Prospects: from financial crisis to prosperity*, Cheltenham, UK and Northampton, MA, USA: Edward Elgar Publishing, pp. 266–80.

Cherry, Judith (2006), 'Killing five birds with one stone: inward foreign direct investment in post-crisis Korea', *Pacific Affairs*, **79** (1), 9–27.

Conway, P., V. Janod and G. Nicoletti (2005), 'Product market regulation in OECD countries: 1998–2003', OECD Economics Department Working Papers No. 419, Paris: OECD.

Dreher, Axel (2006), 'Does globalization affect growth? Evidence from a new index of globalisation', *Applied Economics*, **38** (10), 1091–110.

Dunning, John H. (1980), 'Toward an eclectic theory of international production: some empirical tests', *Journal of International Business Studies*, **11** (1), 9–31.

Dunning, John H. (1998), 'Location and multinational enterprises: a neglected factor?', *Journal of International Business Studies*, **29** (1), 45–66.

Dunning, John H. (2000), 'The eclectic paradigm as an envelope for economic and business theories of MNE activity', *International Business Review*, **9**, 163–90.

Export–Import Bank of Korea (2008), 'Foreign investment statistics', http://www.koreaexim.go.kr/en/.

Far Eastern Economic Review (1998), 'Asian executives poll', 18 June, p. 36.

Ha, Jong-Wook (2002), 'A study of the patterns of FDI in Korea', (in Korean), *Review of International Management*, **6** (1), 1–22.

Heritage Foundation (HF) (2009), '2009 Index of economic freedom', http://www.heritage.org.

International Institute for Management Development (IMD) (2007), *World Competitiveness Yearbook*, Lausanne, Switzerland: IMD.

International Institute for Management Development (IMD) (2008), *World Competitiveness Yearbook*, Lausanne, Switzerland: IMD.

Jwa, Sung-Hee (2008), '"MBnomics": a review and the road ahead', *International Journal of Korean Studies*, **12** (1), 83–100.

Kim, Eun Mee and Jai S. Mah (2006), 'Patterns of South Korea's foreign direct investment flows into China', *Asian Survey*, **46** (6), 881–97.

Kim, June-Dong (2003), 'Inward foreign direct investment into Korea: recent performance and future agenda', Discussion Paper 03-01, Seoul: Korea Institute for International Economic Policy.

Kim, June-Dong and Yong-Il Kim (2003), 'Korea's liberalisation of trade in services and implications for Australia', in O.Y. Kwon, S.H. Jwa and K.T. Lee (eds), *Korea's New Economic Strategy in the Globalization Era*, Cheltenham, UK and Northampton, MA, USA: Edward Elgar Publishing, pp. 63–81.

Kim, Wan-Soon and M.J. Choo (2002), *Managing the Road to Globalization: the Korean experience*, Seoul: Korea Trade & Investment Promotion Agency (KOTRA).

Kimura, Yiu and Hae Kyoung Lee (1998), 'Korean direct investment in manufacturing: its patterns and determinants – an empirical analysis', *Journal of International Management*, **4** (2), 109–27.

Korea Institute for International Economic Policy (KIEP) (2006a), *Global Economic Review*, **9** (8), September/October, 135–8.

Korea Institute for International Economic Policy (KIEP) (2006b), *Mid & Long-Term Strategies Towards an Advanced Trading Economy: open and globalized economy*, (in Korean), Research Series: 06-02, Seoul: KIEP.

Korea Labor Institute (KLI) (2007), *2007 Labor Statistics*, Seoul: KLI.

Korea Labor Institute (KLI) (2008), *2008 Labor Statistics*, Seoul: KLI.

Korea.net (2009), 'Lee Myung-Bak administration', http://www.korea.net/.

Kwon, O. Yul (2001), 'Korea's international business environment before and after the financial crisis', in O.Y. Kwon and W. Shepherd (eds), *Korea's Economic Prospects: from financial crisis to prosperity*, Cheltenham, UK and Northampton, MA, USA: Edward Elgar Publishing, pp. 245–65.

Kwon, O. Yul (2004), 'Causes for sluggish foreign direct investment in Korea: a foreign perspective', *Journal of the Korean Economy*, **5** (1), Spring, 69–96.

Kwon, O. Yul (2006), 'Recent changes in Korea's business environment: views of foreign business people in Korea', *Asia Pacific Business Review*, **12** (1), 77–94.

Kwon, O. Yul and Inshik Oh (2001), 'Korean direct investment in Australia: issues and prospects', Australia–Korea Paper No. 5, Brisbane: Australian Centre for Korea Studies.

Ministry of Finance and Economy (MOFE) (2006), 'FDI vision 2015 and implementation strategy', *Economic Bulletin*, **28** (1), November, 40–47.

Ministry of Knowledge Economy (MKE, formerly MOCIE) (2008), 'Key figures: foreign direct investment', http://www.mke.go.kr/language/eng/glance/news_list.jsp.

Ministry of Strategy and Finance (MOSF) (2009), 'Comprehensive policies to overcome the current economic difficulties', http://english.mofe.go.kr/public/direction_view.php?sect=laws_policies&pmode=&cat=&sn=6276&page=1&SK=ALL&SW.

OECD (2006), *Policy Framework for Investment: a review of good practices*, Paris: OECD.

Sohn, C.H., J.S. Yang and S.B. Kim (2002), 'Liberalization measures in the process of Korea's corporate restructuring: trade, investment and capital account market opening', Discussion Paper 02-11, Korea Institute for International Economic Policy (KIEP), Seoul, Korea.

Stoever, William A. (2005), 'Restructuring FDI policy in emerging economies: the Republic of Korea case', *Thunderbird International Business Review*, **47** (5), September–October, 555–74.

Thurbon, Elizabeth and Linda Weiss (2006), 'Investing in openness: the evolution of FDI strategy in South Korea and Taiwan', *New Political Economy*, **11** (1), March, 1–22.

Transparency International (TI) (2009), 'Corruption Perceptions Index 2008', www.transparency.org.

United Nations Conference on Trade and Development (UNCTAD) (various years), *World Investment Report*, New York, USA and Geneva, Switzerland: UN.

World Economic Forum (WEF) (various years), *The Global Competitiveness Report*, New York: Oxford University Press and Geneva: WEF.

7. North Korea's economic reform and inter-Korean economic relations

7.1 INTRODUCTION

A critical issue for the Korean Peninsula is how to maintain peace and prosperity. Together with a host of geopolitical variables such as the six-party talks on nuclear non-proliferation, the North Korean economy is critically important not only for peace and prosperity on the Korean Peninsula but also for the South Korean economy. The North Korean economy also vindicates the importance of formal institutions in economic development; its economic difficulties are largely due to its institutional failure. The North Korean economy experienced consecutive negative growth over the 1990–98 period followed by minimal annual growth until 2005, and again substantial shrinkages over the 2006–07 period. To revitalize its stagnant economy, North Korea undertook its most ambitious economic reform policy in July 2002. A number of questions arise as to the nature of the economic reform, its prospects and its impact on inter-Korean economic relations.

Inter-Korean economic relations commenced in 1988 and expanded throughout the 1990s, predominantly at the initiative of South Korea. The impetus for inter-Korean economic relations intensified in the late 1990s with the election of the Kim Dae-jung administration in the South. Inaugurated in 1998, President Kim's 'Sunshine Policy' was predicated on the view that mutual economic interests could provide the basis for a minimization of political and military provocations, for reconciliation and cooperation, and for the ultimate unification of the two Koreas (Lee and Yoon 2004). The Roh Moo-hyun government carried on its own Peace and Prosperity Policy toward North Korea consistent with the Sunshine Policy. The Lee Myung-bak government repudiated its two predecessors' policies toward North Korea, and announced pragmatic engagements on a reciprocation basis (H.J. Kim 2008). Observers have argued that Lee's stance marks a return to a traditional South Korean strategy of closely cooperating with the United States and maintaining a cautious and defensive approach to North Korea (Snyder 2009: 85).

This chapter seeks to analyse critically recent economic developments in North Korea, and in particular its 2002 economic reform, and assesses inter-Korean economic relations as of 2009. The chapter is divided into two parts. The first part focuses on the North Korean economic reform in 2002. The second part examines inter-Korean economic relations with trade, foreign direct investment (FDI) and tourism.

7.2 NORTH KOREAN ECONOMY

7.2.1 Geopolitical Developments in North Korea

Upon becoming independent from Japanese colonial occupation in 1945, Korea was divided into South and North Korea. In 1948, North Korea established the Democratic People's Republic of Korea (DPRK) under Kim Il-sung, embracing socialism. In 1950, the Korean War occurred, which ended in 1953 with an armistice agreement. In 1971, US President Nixon's visit to China terrified North Korea and led it to adopt its *juche* ideology, or self-reliance, and to seek to be able to defend itself by its own means, including the development of nuclear power. In 1994, Kim Il-sung died and his son Kim Jong-il took over the regime. In the same year, North Korea and the United States signed an agreement by which North Korea made a commitment not to develop nuclear weapons in exchange for two light water nuclear power reactors and other economic aid. In June 2000, an inter-Korean summit meeting was held for the first time in history. In 2002, North Korea restarted its nuclear facilities, withdrawing from the Nuclear Non-Proliferation Treaty (NPT). In May 2003, the international community launched the Proliferation Security Initiative (PSI), aimed primarily at North Korea, with the objective of interdicting the transport of WMD (weapons of mass destruction) materials (Congressional Research Service 2006). In August 2003, the six-party talks, including South and North Korea, China, the United States, Japan and Russia, started. At the fourth round on 19 September 2005, North Korea committed to abandoning all nuclear weapons and existing nuclear programmes and returning to the NPT.

In 2005, the United States imposed a banking sanction on North Korea in retaliation for the counterfeiting of US dollars and money-laundering incidents. On 4 July 2006, North Korea conducted six long-range ballistic missile tests followed by an underground nuclear test on 9 October, obfuscating the prospects of the six-party talks. In response to these tests, the UN Security Council applied the toughest sanctions on North Korea since the Korean War, and China drastically reduced its food and fuel aid. South Korea had already suspended aid subsequent to the July missile tests. With severe economic consequences looming, North Korea agreed to return to the six-party talks in December 2006 (J.H. Lee 2008).

In February 2007, the sixth round of the talks resumed and a deal was hammered out. This is known as the 2.13 Agreement, whereby North Korea would freeze its nuclear programmes within 60 days in return for a resumption of food and fuel aid, the lifting of banking sanctions, and the instigation of bilateral talks with the United States aimed at normalizing its diplomatic status by removing North Korea from the list of state sponsors of terrorism (J.H. Lee 2008). On 3 October, the DPRK agreed on a framework to permanently disable its three core nuclear programmes and promised, only orally, to provide for international verification. On 8 May 2008, North Korea provided 18 000 pages of documentation on its nuclear programmes in a first step toward verification (US Department of State 2008). In early September 2008, however, North Korea announced it would restart its nuclear programme due to the failure of the United States to remove Pyongyang from the list of state sponsors of terrorism (*New York Times* 2008a). After a further deal was reached to resume dismantling of the nuclear programme, the Bush administration removed North Korea from the list on 11 October (*New York Times* 2008b).

The situation stagnated through the remainder of 2008 with new administrations due to take office in both Washington and Seoul in early 2009. The six-party talks had again stalled over the issue of concluding a verification protocol for North Korea's denuclearization (ICG 2009: 1). A series of tit-for-tat provocative events have occurred. In March 2009, US–South Korea military exercises were held, and in April North Korea launched a three-stage rocket into the East Sea. In May, North Korea conducted another nuclear test, followed by a number of missile tests. In response, in June 2009 the United Nations Security Council unanimously passed a resolution that imposes new sanctions on North Korea. It remains to be seen how the UN implements its new sanction against North Korea and how the latter responds to UN actions.

North Korea has remained since the 1950s a highly centralized and militarized totalitarian regime organized around an all-powerful leader (Scobell 2006). Even after his death, Kim Il-sung remains as the Deity of North Korea.[1] Hence, criticism and reappraisal of Kim Il-sung is unthinkable. North Korea is the world's most militarized and politicized society (Noland 2004). Internally, all aspects of society are suffused with politics, and externally, politics thoroughly permeates not only the country's diplomatic relationships but also its economic relations. To maintain such power and authority, the regime maintains an ever-vigilant coercive apparatus and a large national defence organization with the 'military-first strategy' slogan. Although the country is still under the absolute authoritative control of Kim

Jong-il, it appears lately that North Korea's ideology has shifted from that of the socialist state to the instrumental goals of economic recovery and development, thereby firming up regime power (Scobell 2006). This shift in ideology is reflected in the economic reform in 2002.

7.2.2 Recent Trend of the North Korean Economy

North Korea has maintained a conventional centrally planned socialist economy since 1945. In the decade immediately following the armistice in 1953, North Korea was able to achieve rapid economic development through utilizing its substantial natural resources, mobilizing its labour force and concentrating heavy industries and mining. It also relied on assistance from the former Soviet Union. By the 1970s, however, the North Korean economy was experiencing serious problems when its ability to grow through labour force mobilization began to reach its limits. In response to these difficulties, North Korea began a large-scale modernization programme. The programme was financed by loans from OECD countries, which by 1975 totalled some US$1.2 billion (Winder 2000). A combination of operational and quality control problems and reduced Soviet assistance rendered the programme a failure. Consequently, North Korea was forced (or chose) to default on its foreign loans, a decision that effectively isolated it from international capital markets. The North Korean economy continued to experience difficulties throughout the 1980s.

During the 1990s the economic decline deepened considerably, as other command economies in Europe collapsed, trade relations deteriorated, and foreign aid from socialist countries was drastically reduced. Over the nine-year period 1990–98, the North Korean economy contracted by an annual average of 3.8 per cent (Table 7.1).[2] The nation experienced food shortages from the beginning of the 1990s and a serious famine over the 1995–98 period, in which starvation was estimated to claim somewhere between 1 million and 2.4 million lives (Kirk 1998). In August 2007, North Korea was again beset by natural disaster, with floods destroying 11 per cent of agricultural land (Rembrandt 2008).

As shown in Table 7.1, the North Korean economy recorded minimal positive growth between 1999 and 2005, and negative growth over the 2006–07 period. The positive growth is attributed to China's aid, increased economic cooperation between South and North Korea and rising domestic demand resulting from the economic reform in 2002 (Park 2002). As shown in Table 7.2, the size of the North Korean economy is much smaller than that of South Korea with gross national income (GNI) of $26.7 billion in 2007, as compared to $971.3 billion for the South Korean economy. Per capita GNI was $1152 in the North, while it was $20 045 in the South in 2007.

Table 7.1 Economic growth of South and North Korea, 1990–2007 (%)

	1990–98	1999	2000	2001	2002	2003	2004	2005	2006	2007
N. Korea	–3.8/yr	6.2	1.3	3.7	1.2	1.8	2.2	3.8	–1.1	–2.3
S. Korea	+5.7/yr	10.7	8.5	3.8	7.0	3.1	4.6	4.2	5.1	5.0

Source: Up to 2006, Bank of Korea (2007); for 2007, Ministry of Unification (2008b).

Table 7.2 Comparison of economic size between South and North Korea, 2006–07

	South Korea (A)	North Korea (B)	A/B
Population (2007)	48.5 mill.	23.2 mill.	2.1
GNI (2007)	US$971.3 bill.	US$26.7 bill.	36.4
GNI/capita (2006)	US$20 045	US$1 152	17.4

Source: Ministry of Unification (2008b).

7.2.3 Structure of the North Korean Economy

Table 7.3 shows the shares of GDP by industrial sector in the DPRK between 2004 and 2006. It also shows the differences in industrial structure between North and South Korea as of 2006. The North Korean economy is built on its agricultural sector, which is critically important to it in many respects. Not only did it contribute 23.3 per cent to the economy in 2006 (Table 7.3), but self-sufficiency in food is directly related to North Korea's ideology of *juche*, and probably to its political survival. Thus, one of the biggest challenges North Korea has faced in the recent past is to develop its agriculture to mitigate persistent food shortages.

Table 7.3 Industrial structure of North Korea, 2004–06 (% of GDP)

Industry	North Korea			South Korea
	2004	2005	2006	2006
Agriculture	26.7	25.0	23.3	3.2
Mining	8.7	9.9	10.2	0.4
Manufacturing	18.5	19.0	19.5	27.8
Services	46.0	46.1	47.1	68.6

Source: Bank of Korea (2007).

North Korea has undertaken a variety of measures to achieve self-sufficiency in food production. Nonetheless, productivity actually diminished in the decade of the 1990s. There are a number of reasons for this, such as the lack of incentives in collective farming, and outdated agricultural infrastructure and shortages of farming resources including fertilizer, pesticides, machinery and equipment, fuel and spare parts, and electricity for irrigation systems (KIEP 2004: 34). The system of cooperative farming has changed over time, and under the latest system, a unit of farmers is assigned a production target and the cooperative is allowed to dispose of the excess for their own purposes. This system has not been successful because farmers have had difficulties in achieving the set target level, because of shortages of fertilizer and pesticides (KIEP 2004: 107).

North Korea's agricultural problems are structural in nature. Its arable land comprises just 15 per cent of the total land area. To solve food shortages, farmers have long been cultivating on hillsides illegally but with government acquiescence. Cultivation on hillsides damages forests and causes erosion of the hillsides. This in turn creates landsides and accumulates silt in rivers, making rivers flood frequently. Most farmland in North Korea is either polluted or acidified because of excessive use of fertilizers and pesticides. Thus chronic food shortages, which amount annually to about a 30 per cent shortfall, cannot be solved easily (Table 7.4). If the likely downward trend in international food aid continues, North Korea's food security can only deteriorate further.

Table 7.4 North Korea's agricultural status, 2001–07 (1000 tons)

Year	Estimated consumption (A)	Total production (B)	Self-sufficient demand (B/A) %
2001	6130	3590	58.6
2002	6260	3950	63.1
2003	6320	4130	65.3
2004	6390	4250	66.5
2005	6450	4310	66.8
2006	6510	4540	69.7
2007	6500	4480	68.9

Source: KIEP (2004: 111); Ministry of Unification (2008b).

Another feature of the North Korean economic structure is a planned economy. Economic activity is structurally divided into the official, military and private economies (Lee and Yoon 2004). The three are not closely integrated, and the relative weight of each has shifted dramatically since the 1990s crisis. The 'official economy' denotes the socialist central planning system in which the state, rather than market forces, dictates resource allocation.[3] North Korea's military, or 'second economy' is administered independently of the state budget and enjoys priority over the official and private economies in the distribution of materials and resources. The military economy comprises the production, distribution and trade of all military goods in North Korea's extensive defence manufacturing industry. In the wake of the collapse of the Soviet bloc and the North's deteriorating economic situation throughout the 1990s, Kim Jong-il introduced the 'military-first strategy' in 1998 to reinforce the regime's hold on power (Lee and Yoon 2004: 54).

The private economy exists outside the central planning system and operates according to market mechanisms. Informal markets for agricultural produce have operated for decades in North Korea. Since the economic crises of the 1990s, however, the 'farmers' markets' have expanded dramatically, both in size and number, with the acquiescence of authorities. Goods and services in the markets flow from a number of sources, including cooperative and household agricultural surpluses, 'leakages' from international aid shipments, cross-border trade from China, items 'diverted' or 'recycled' from state-owned enterprises (SOEs), and goods and services offered by small household enterprises (Chung 2004). Private sector production has expanded at the expense of the official economy and has become an essential survival strategy for a majority of ordinary North Koreans (Lee and Yoon 2004).

7.3 THE 2002 REFORM OF THE NORTH KOREAN ECONOMY

7.3.1 Background of the Reform

After serious economic contractions over nine consecutive years from 1990 to 1998, and stagnant economic development thereafter, North Korea implemented its Economic Management Improvement Policy from 1 July 2002. The reform is regarded as the most extraordinary institutional change ever undertaken by North Korea, and may serve as an important milestone in deciding the future direction of its economic system. Under the tightly controlled socialist planned economy in North Korea, all property rights belong to the state, resources are allocated in line with its policy objectives, and consumer goods are distributed by the Public Distribution System (PDS). Prices, wages and the exchange rate are all determined and controlled by the central policy authority. Under this institutional setting, economic contraction and stagnation have occurred. This is attributed to a combination of factors.

First, the gross misallocation of resources is one of the most serious causes of the North Korean economic malaise. This was reflected in a high military spending, accounting for somewhere between 20–40 per cent of GDP

(Noland 2000: 72–3). It was further heightened by the excessive diversification of the economy under the ideological principles of *juche*, justifying its isolation and propagating self-reliance. The autarkic orientation of the economy meant that production difficulties in a particular industry also adversely affect other areas of the economy, creating a bottleneck effect on economic operations. The tightly controlled economic system with state ownership of property rights and the misallocation of scarce resources has deprived workers and companies of economic incentives, resulting in low productivity.

A second factor is its inability to access external capital for economic development (KIEP 2004: 308). North Korea could not receive financial support from the outside due to its default on foreign loans in the mid-1970s. It desperately requires development assistance and concessional loans from international financial institution such as the World Bank, Asian Development Bank (ADB) and Japan as reparations for its colonial occupation (KIEP 2004: 183). However, until the nuclear crisis is resolved, the United States and Japan will continue to block access to these funds. Without foreign capital, North Korea cannot replace outdated and deteriorating infrastructure, let alone make new investment for development.[4] For the same geopolitical reasons, North Korea has failed to attract FDI (KIEP 2004: 200).

Third, the crisis in output has been further exacerbated by a shortage of energy (KIEP 2004: 96). North Korea relies heavily on imported oil, and as the economy has deteriorated, it has been unable to import oil. As a consequence, the amount of generated electrical power has decreased remarkably in the recent past (KIEP 2004: 45). Energy shortages were further heightened by the reduction in subsidized energy supplies from Russia and China, although China still provides a significant amount of oil to North Korea.

Fourth, the North Korean government was under severe budgetary pressure. During the 1990s crisis, revenues and expenditures declined by 50 per cent due to the collapse of North Korea's industrial sector (Chung 2004). The source of government revenue was management income from state-owned organizations, firms and cooperative farms. Because of the continuous difficulties of these economic units, government revenues declined. Furthermore, because of crippled production ability and the rationing system, the supplied liquidity currency could not be retrieved into official channels. Rather, currencies were accumulated on the black market and the farmers' markets, as products manufactured by the state or its enterprises were leaked out and sold at these markets. This aggravated the government budgetary situation in the absence of taxation. The gap between high government purchasing prices of rationing commodities and lower prices charged to consumers under the public rationing system has become increasingly burdensome to the government budget.

Fifth, perhaps because of its *juche* ideology, North Korea has not paid adequate attention to foreign economic relations. Historically, the Soviet Union was North Korea's most important trading partner and the primary source of both military and oil assistance (Noland 2000: 96–8). However, with the implosion of the Soviet Union, North Korean–Soviet Union trade declined drastically, as did the flow of aid. Although China and South Korea partially filled the void, the North Korean economy was never able to recover fully from this external shock, and its total trade volume in 2002 amounted only to 54.2 per cent of the 1990 volume (KIEP 2004: 199).

Sixth, the North Korean authorities had obviously lost confidence in the economic planning mechanism in overcoming further deteriorating economic difficulties. The regime had attempted to tackle economic problems through the implementation of seven-year economic plans from the early 1970s, but failed to announce any more proposals or plans after the completion of the third Seven-Year Plan in 1993, implicitly admitting the absence of economic power or socialist policy strategies to overcome economic difficulties (KIEP 2004: 304). The North Korean government could no longer provide people with essential household necessities as well as raw materials needed for production. As a result, the PDS was paralysed and shelves of the rationing stores remained empty. The government, on the other hand, began actively to encourage citizens and enterprises to provide the necessary items and commodities for themselves. This led to the development of unofficial markets similar in concept to free markets.

Seventh, North Korea had also implemented a number of non-economic measures to mobilize people and promote economic recovery before 2002. These included the 'arduous march', 'socialist hardship march', 'powerful state' through 'military-first strategy', '*chollima* movement' and so on (KIEP 2004: 314). However, none of these had sustainable effects on the economy. Under the exacerbating economic hardship, the general public were fatigued with those slogans, rendering them ineffectual.

Finally, one of the principal reasons that caused North Korea to initiate reform is the growing deterioration of social and political order resulting from the prolonged economic difficulties. Citizens had lost trust in the government, including its ideology, as it could not provide their necessities. Wages that were set in line with the rationing system were not enough to cover the costs of goods in the unofficial markets. Continuous economic difficulties led to increased crime rates for fraud, embezzlement, corruption and larceny of government property, committed by ordinary workers, civil servants and soldiers (KIEP 2004: 306). Although the North Korean government was able to maintain its political power through the idolization of its leader, Kim Jong-il, together with ruthless oppression, the regime would obviously have realized that social and political problems resulting from economic difficulties would only get worse without economic recovery. Hence, in the absence of viable socialist policy measures, North Korea could not help but implement a radical economic reform in July 2002.

All these economic problems and the ensuing deterioration of social and political order are attributable to the failure of formal socialist institutions. This has also been witnessed in the collapse of the former Soviet bloc, and from the success of the Chinese economy in the wake of abandoning its socialist economic doctrine. In the absence of institutions which secure property rights, provide incentives for workers and enterprises and promote market competition, economic policy and resource allocation without reflecting encompassing public interests cannot be successful in the long run. The reform is an attempt to ameliorate the institutional failure of the socialist system.

7.3.2 Main Contents of the Reform

In conjunction with Kim Jong-il's consolidation of political power, North Korea amended its Constitution in 1998. This amendment provided the legal foundation for the economic reform, such as individual ownership of the proceeds of private economic activity, more autonomy for SOEs including the right to directly conduct foreign trade, and the establishment of Special Economic Zones to attract FDI. These provisions were followed by a raft of new legislation enacted between 1999 and 2001, such as the Law on Foreign Investment, the Joint Venture Law, the Foreign Currency Law, the Law on Processing Trade, Copyright Law, and the Law on Technology Transfer from Foreign Enterprises (J.W. Lee 2004). This series of laws and events culminated with the 1 July 2002 Economic Management Improvement Policy. The main contents of the reform are as follows.

First, a new price system was introduced. The previous price system was based on the Marxist foundation of 'the value of labour'. For certain scarce commodities such as rice, however, prices were intentionally lowered below the estimated value of labour input as part of socio-economic policy. As a result, for instance, the selling price to consumers of rice was one-tenth the purchasing price from farmers. Under the new price concept of the reform, prices of a number of household necessities including food, fuel, electricity and public transport were adjusted to an unprecedented extent. For instance, the government's purchase price of rice from farmers was increased by 50 times, while the selling price to the public increased by 550 times to the level at the farmers' markets (KIEP 2004: 290).[5] These price adjustments were made by taking into account three elements: the initial cost of production, the going rate in the international market and the domestic supply–demand condition in the markets (KIEP 2004: 289). In essence, it appears that North Korea attempted to eliminate the gap between the state-set price and the price set at private markets by adjusting the former to the latter. Farmers were allowed to determine production and sell their excess produce over quotas to farmers' markets from 2001 (DFAT 2005). Trading of non-farm goods in farmers' markets, formerly only tolerated, was officially legalized as part of the reform. Even the prices of production goods such as machinery, raw materials and fuel were adjusted so that SOEs could support themselves through their own sales income (KIEP 2004: 331).

The new price system does not mean that the government has rescinded its price control authority nor does it signify a complete transformation into a free-market price system. The state still sets standard prices, based on which producers and consumers set prices independently according to demand and supply conditions, within a range of 5 to 10 per cent of state-set prices. In other words, the regime continues to regulate the function of the market price.[6] In setting prices for other commodities, the state uses the price of food as the standard, while in the past the prices of principal industrial goods such as coal and electricity were used as the standard (KIEP 2004: 293). The foreign exchange rate was also adjusted to market signals, whereby the North Korean won was devalued from 2 won to US$1 to 150:1, close to the prevailing black market rate of 200:1, in an effort to bolster exports (KIEP 2004: 72).

Second, a new wage system was introduced. In the past wages were determined in line with the egalitarian principle of socialism, and standardized wages were paid based on the basic need circumstances of individual workers, such as the minimum amount of money needed to sustain a basic living. This type of wage system creates disincentive to work as it does not take into account individual workers' merit such as skills, knowledge and efficiency. The new system had to boost wages in line with the upward adjustment of prices to maintain workers' livelihoods. In doing so, the new wage system has attempted to introduce some incentives by means of wage differentials based on skill levels, quality of work and occupational demands. Thus, a higher increase in wages was given to more efficient workers and to those in more important sectors such as field workers, technicians and scientists. Under this system, wages increased in the range of 17 to 25 times depending on occupation (KIEP 2004: 294).

It appears that the new wage system seeks to achieve two purposes: enhancing workers' incentives and decreasing government expenditure. The new level of wage is a 'standard wage' and does not have to be paid in full; rather the actual amount of wage paid depends on 'the amount of work' and net income of the enterprise (KIEP 2004: 335). Under the new system, net income is composed of the remaining revenue from gross sales revenue after deducting production cost, excluding wages. Thus, no wage will be paid to workers if they do not work or their factories do not earn net income. On the other hand, more wages will be paid than the standard wage for extra work or more net income.[7] Under the new system, workers became responsible for food, rent, public transit and water, thereby drastically decreasing state subsidies. The new wage system even introduced cash incentives for people and institutes that contribute to the development of scientific technology to stimulate productivity. In particular, to increase agricultural products, cooperative agricultural workers are to be remunerated for productivity rather than number of hours worked.

Third, remarkable changes were introduced in the principles and implementation of North Korea's planning system. The State Planning Committee had controlled both distribution based on the egalitarian principle and production of goods. The distribution system had been used as a welfare system guaranteeing workers' living conditions. This system had bred people's perceptions of entitlement and generated moral hazard, waste and economic inefficiency. Normalization of prices and wages toward market levels was intended not only to introduce private economic operation but also to eliminate people's perception of entitlement. Thus, the state-run system of basic goods rationing was cancelled, and the informal private sector including farmers' markets became a formal sector. In March 2003, farmers' markets were transformed into general consumers' markets where not only agricultural products but also other goods could be traded (J.W. Lee 2004: 107; KIEP 2004: 330). By the end of 2005, there were around 300 private markets in operation throughout the country (Ming 2007) although they could by no means be described as a unified market system (Seliger 2007). The prices of most commodities and production costs are now determined by supply and demand. Even raw materials are traded in exchange markets where market mechanisms are applied in trading input materials (Lim and Chung 2004).

Another part of the change in the planning system is the decentralization of the central planning mechanism. In the past not only the strategic management of the overall economy but also the most trivial production activities at factory levels were guided and controlled by the central planning authority. The reform reduced such micro-control by central government and increased the independence of regional governments, factories, enterprises and farms in establishing and executing production plans. For farming, working units on cooperative farms were reduced to ten persons and up to 40 per cent of farm products are allowed to be sold autonomously (MOU 2005a). SOEs that produce various daily commodities and retail goods can determine specific prices subject to approval under the standard prices given by the state.

They are also permitted to make production decisions, to purchase intermediate inputs, to make autonomous investment decisions out of retained earnings, and engage in international trade under the guiding principles of the central planning authority. With the increased autonomy of local government, enterprises and farms, subsidies by the central government have been drastically decreased. At the same time, enterprises are to be evaluated not by the fulfilment of production quotas set by the planning authority, as in the past, but by profitability or 'collective net earned income'. The reform has therefore made each enterprise independently responsible for the sale and purchase of materials so that enterprises have to operate with profit as the highest priority.[8]

Finally, the economic reform included North Korea's open-door policy. Following the July 2002 economic reforms, Pyongyang has established three Special Economic Zones (SEZs) to attract FDI and expand foreign trade, including the Sinuiju Special Administrative Region (SAR), the Gaesong Industrial Complex and Mt Kumgang Tourism District (KIEP 2004: 302). Each of these Special Economic Zones was granted strong economic autonomy under the guidance of market economy principles. For the Mt Kumgang Tourism District and the Gaesong Industrial Complex, North Korea granted South Korea easy land-route access and set minimum labour wages, thereby creating hospitable environments for South Korean companies and tourists.

7.3.3 Nature of the Reform: Market Socialism?

The economic reform measures were undertaken with an eye to rebuilding the debilitated economy. Some North Korean observers and scholars have argued that the reforms indicate a movement toward some form of market economy (Lee and Yoon 2004). Some have maintained it as a set of economic recovery measures, as the North Korea authority claimed (Hong 2002). Socialism as an economic system is associated with state ownership of property rights and the central planning of production and distribution of outputs – in contrast, respectively, to private ownership and the market mechanism under capitalism. As a hybrid of socialism and capitalism, the idea of market socialism has been introduced after the collapse of the Soviet bloc. Market socialism refers to a form of an economic organization where the state owns capital (the means of production) and operates those areas deemed critical to the implementation of socialist principles such as heavy industry, energy and infrastructure, while for the rest of the economy prices are used to allocate resources as under a market economy (Stiglitz 1994; Lane and Ersson 1997). Under market socialism, managers are instructed to maximize profits, and prices are determined not by the market mechanism alone but are coordinated, or controlled, by the state to equate supply and demand. Stiglitz (1994: 9) argues that the principal differences between market economies and market socialism are the method of setting prices and the ownership of capital.

Judged by its content, the 2002 North Korean reform appears to be a transitionary move toward a currency and market-functioning economy, while maintaining the guiding principles of a planned economy. This assessment is contrary to North Korea's claim that the reform is not an abandonment of socialist economic principles. The 2002 reform measures include decentralization of the planned economy, normalization of prices in line with the market mechanism, establishment of private marketplaces, elimination of the rationing system, wage rationalization based on merit, autonomous enterprise management based on profitability, and an open-door policy. However, North Korea is obviously reluctant to transform its system fully into a market system, and holds on to its so-called 'central guidance' as an overarching control instrument behind the decentralization of economic management. Nor did the state relinquish its ownership of capital. Thus the 2002 reform fits well into market socialism as delineated by Stiglitz (1994). It should be noted though that North Korea is now in the initial phase of a partial transition toward a market economy and that it has yet to take steps comparable to China's decision in 1987 to accept market mechanisms fully.

7.3.4 Prospects of the Reform

Regardless of whether the reforms fit into market socialism or not, a more critical question is whether North Korea will continue with the transition or revert to the previous system. Although North Korea has claimed success with the reform, the success has so far been limited at best. It is highly likely that North Korea will encounter difficulties in implementing the 2002 reform and bolstering its moribund economy.[9] Judged by economic growth, the reform has not been quite as successful as claimed. As shown in Table 7.1, North Korea recorded minimal positive growth rates over the period 2003–05, while in the following two consecutive years, 2006–07, it recorded negative growth rates. As an indication of difficulties in implementing the reform, North Korea has introduced, since 2002, further measures to reinforce and extend the reforms. These are: an enlargement of the role of markets; enhanced autonomy for factories and enterprises; introduction of competition for some household necessities; and the introduction of an experimental one-family farming unit (Lee and Yoon 2004: 57; KIEP 2004).

Inflation problems resulting from upward adjustments of prices and wages have been serious. North Korea has suffered from hyperinflation with increases in the price of rice by 270 per cent per year from June 2002 to May

2005. Over the same period the North Korean won was depreciated by 550 per cent against the euro (Seliger 2006). Ming (2007) reported that the US dollar rate of exchange in 2007 was 6000 won to the dollar, compared with 200 won when the reform commenced in 2002. Although the prices of most commodities increased rapidly after the reform, the supply of commodities could not increase through price signals because of a low price elasticity of supply. This happens because, even though private trading has increased, production is still largely carried out under state control, thereby rendering prompt adjustments of resource allocation to market signals difficult. Because of shortages of energy and material inputs, most factories still remain moribund with a capacity utilization of 20 per cent (Seliger 2006). This supply shortage is the major factor hampering the economic reform as well as fanning inflationary pressures.

As a way of controlling inflation, North Korea reintroduced the rationing system in the late 2005 (Scobell 2006). The Public Distribution System (PDS) once again became the sole legal source for staple foods, especially cereals and rice, preventing farmers from selling their products other than to the PDS. The role of the state in food distribution has been further strengthened since 2005, with Chinese and South Korean food aid now channelled through the PDS (Seliger 2007).[10] Agricultural products have increased as a result of allowing excess products to be sold in the markets, but this has been partially or completely reversed by the reintroduction of the PDS.

The 2002 reform has not contributed to the attraction of FDI or trade. Because of geopolitical factors, foreign capital has not flowed into North Korea, with the exception of Chinese investment. China has undertaken investment since 2002 in a variety of sectors in North Korea, ranging from small-scale informal investments to large-scale mining projects involving major Chinese SOEs (Haggard and Noland 2007). Attraction of FDI in SEZs has been minimal, other than some investments by South Korean companies. As shown in Table 7.5, North Korea's external trade, including trade with the South, increased substantially in 2007 over the 2002 level. The increments are largely accounted for by trade with China and South Korea due to their special geopolitical relations. China's role in DPRK external trade has rapidly increased from 25.4 per cent in 2002 to 41.7 per cent in 2007, while intra-Korean trade has expanded from 22.1 per cent in 2002 to 37.9 per cent in 2007. As compared to the national economic size, the ratio of external trade to GNI remained more or less unchanged at around 17 per cent over the 2001–07 period, compared to South Korea's ratio of 87 per cent in 2007 (Bank of Korea 2008).

It is difficult at this time to predict whether and when North Korea will follow China's lead and move toward a genuine market socialism. Toloraya

(2007) argues that comprehensive external security guarantees will have to be in place for the leadership to widen and deepen the market reforms. However, it is inconceivable that North Korea will reverse its economic system and return to pre-2002 times, even in the absence of external security guarantees.[11] None of the economic difficulties that forced North Korea to undertake the reform have been ameliorated since 2002. North Korea would have undertaken the institutional changes certainly within a range judged tolerable by the regime. However, as was the case in the Soviet Union, the initial change generates a dynamic process for further changes toward a market system, and the private economy has been growing more rapidly than the official economy (Lee and Yoon 2004). As the private economy grows, the general public's understanding and acceptance of the market system will increase, and as they experience economic benefits from it, their individualism will likely rise at the expense of collectivism. Under this trend of social change, economic *dirigisme* becomes more difficult and the regime cannot help but embrace an economic system that is, in essence, a market system.

Table 7.5 Trade of North Korea, 1998–2007 (US$ million)

Type/year	1998	1999	2000	2001	2003	2004	2005	2006	2007
External trade*	1663	1813	2394	2672	3115	3554	4057	4345	4738
Nominal GNI (US$bill.)	12.6	15.8	16.8	15.7	18.4	20.8	24.2	25.6	26.7
Trade/GNI	13.2	11.5	14.3	17.0	16.9	17.1	16.8	17.0	17.7
Trade with China	413 (24.8)	370 (20.4)	488 (20.4)	737 (27.6)	1022 (32.2)	1385 (39.0)	1580 (38.9)	1699 (38.4)	1974 (41.7)
Trade with South Korea	221 (13.3)	333 (18.4)	425 (17.8)	402 (15.0)	724 (23.2)	697 (19.6)	1055 (26.0)	1349 (31.0)	1798 (37.9)

Note: * External trade includes trade with South Korea.

Source: Ministry of Unification (MOU) (2008b).

As the world witnessed from the transition of the old Soviet bloc economies, it is highly likely that North Korea will encounter serious difficulties in pursuing the reform, such as high inflation, the widening gap between rich and poor, and dwindling socialist collectivism. Nevertheless, it is inconceivable that the North Korean regime will reverse to the centrally planned system of pre-2002. Nor has there been any indication that it will abandon the reform and reverse policy direction, other than the reintroduction of the rationing of staple foods as a way of stemming hyperinflation. It is therefore highly likely that North Korea will carry on further economic and institutional reforms toward market socialism.

7.4 INTER-KOREAN ECONOMIC RELATIONS

7.4.1 Political Initiatives and Institutional Arrangements

After a division of more than 40 years, the two Koreas commenced their economic relations in 1988 under the Special Declaration in the Interest of National Self-Esteem, Unification and Prosperity. Since then, inter-Korean trade volume has more or less steadily increased. Political impetus for the expansion of inter-Korean economic relations was intensified by President Kim Dae-jung's Sunshine Policy of reconciliation and cooperation with the North in 1998. The Sunshine Policy was predicated on a separation of economic relations from political and security issues. Under the Sunshine Policy, unification by military takeover and absorption is explicitly ruled out, as are any activities that either overtly or covertly encourage a North Korean state collapse (MOU 2002a). It ultimately aims at expediting the process of peaceful unification and minimizing the unification costs by building a balanced 'national' economy on both sides of the Demilitarized Zone (DMZ) (MOU 2002b). The Sunshine Policy came to be symbolized by the historic 2000 summit meeting between Kim Dae-jung and Kim Jong-il in Pyongyang.

Soon after the summit, the two Koreas signed the Four-Point Agreement for Inter-Korean Economic Cooperation on 16 December 2000 (J.W. Lee 2004). Like any international agreement for trade and investment, the Four-Point Agreement contains the Agreement on Investment Protection, the Agreement on Prevention of Double Taxation, the Agreement on Procedures for Resolution of Commercial Disputes and the Agreement on Clearing Settlement (MOU 2002a). The investment protection agreement provides for asset protection by both governments, free transfer of funds and free movement across the border. Most importantly for South Korean investors, it also guarantees against state expropriation. Dispute resolution provides for the establishment of a South–North Commercial Dispute Arbitration Committee. The clearing settlement agreement seeks to establish a direct account settlement arrangement between the two Koreas to replace the existing cumbersome method of indirect settlement through a third-country bank.

The Sunshine Policy was renamed the Peace and Prosperity Policy by President Roh Moo-hyun in December 2002. Although Roh's policies were subtly different from those of the Kim government in terms of emphasis on commercial viability in inter-Korean investment and trade, and on rationalizing and improving the transparency of South Korea's aid, there was little overall change in the direction of inter-Korean relations (Babson 2005). The Roh administration has focused on the institutionalization of economic cooperation based on the four-point inter-Korean agreement in 2000, and has also emphasized developing the major projects inaugurated at the June 2000 summit such as the Gaesong Industrial Complex, Seoul–Shinuiju railway connection, and Munsan–Gaesong Highway (MOU 2002a). A second inter-Korean summit was held in 2007, and the Joint Declaration of October 4 essentially reiterated the same commitments as those at the 2000 summit (Hong 2008).

The conservative Lee Myung-bak administration dismissed the engagement policy and unconditional economic assistance of the Kim and Roh governments as a failure and reiterated inter-Korean policy based on a more pragmatic, reciprocal footing. The Lee government refused to commit to further implementation of the previous inter-Korean agreements reached at the two summit meetings (Moon 2009: 127). Lee proposed that if the DPRK genuinely complied with its agreements to dismantle its nuclear programmes and did not engage in provocations, South Korea would assist the North in increasing its per capita income to $3000 (Moon 2009: 127; Snyder 2009: 86).

The North immediately rejected Lee's proposals as attempts to damage regime security, and became unremittingly hostile to the Lee Myung-bak government; both political and economic relations between the two Koreas have deteriorated sharply. Soon after the inception of the Lee government, Pyongyang suspended official exchanges with Seoul, expelled Republic of Korea (ROK) officials from the Gaesong Industrial Complex, and kept up a steady flow of invective against the Lee government. The North has restricted inter-Korean land travel and threatened to close the border completely. Inter-Korean economic activity related to the Gaesong complex has reportedly been reduced significantly (Snyder 2009: 94–5). It remains to be seen how the Lee Myung-bak's policy toward the North and the North's response to it will transpire under these deteriorating conditions. The prospects in early 2009, after one year of the Lee administration, do not look favourable. However, given the importance and delicacy of North–South relations, it is likely over the longer term that the Lee government will follow the established pattern of reconciliation and engagement with the North, at least in the commercial sphere. Under these political and institutional backgrounds, inter-Korean trade, FDI and tourism are examined.

7.4.2 Inter-Korean Trade

Trade has been the main sector driving inter-Korean economic relations since their commencement in 1988. As shown in Table 7.6, inter-Korean trade expanded from $333 million in 1999 to $1798 million 2007, recording a 23.4 per cent annual growth rate over the period. Rapid increases in inter-Korean trade since 2005 were attributable to the easing of tension over the nuclear issue. In the recent past South Korea has been consistently the North's second-largest trading partner after China, although China's share of North Korean trade has been on the rise (Table 7.5). South Korea's exports to the North have increased more than South Korea's imports from the North, the former amounting to $1033 million in 2007, and the latter to $765, indicating South Korea's financial assistance to the North.

Table 7.6 Inter-Korean trade, 1999–2007 (US$ million)

Direction	1999	2000	2001	2002	2003	2004	2005	2006	2007
South to north	212	273	227	370	435	439	715	830	1033
North to south	122	152	176	272	289	258	340	520	765
Total	333	425	403	642	724	697	1056	1350	1798

Sources: Bank of Korea (2005, 2007); for 2007, MOU (2008b).

Inter-Korean trade consists of two components: commercial and non-commercial trade. The non-commercial trade component flows almost exclusively from South to North Korea. Non-commercial trade has increased steadily from $287 million in 2002 to $368 million in 2007, as large-scale projects such as the Gaesong Industrial Complex have gradually come on-stream. Trade that is not based on commercial motivations is highly susceptible to the volatile international political climate that surrounds the North. There has been serious political criticism about unilateral economic aid to the North without mutual benefits. However, supporters of greater engagement argue that the success of inter-Korean relations are important to the South Korean economy, and assisting in the rehabilitation and development of North Korea will produce significant economic benefits for South Korea in the longer term (Hong 2008).

The volume of commercial trade increased faster than that of non-commercial trade, and in 2007 the former was almost four times as large as the latter (Table 7.7). This can be attributed to the Roh administration's emphasis on the development of commercial over non-commercial trade. Certainly commercial trade is based on comparative advantages. South Korea's commercial exports to the North are comprised of textile, electronic, agricultural and chemical products, while North Korea's exports to the South are predominantly made up of agricultural, forestry and fishing products, textiles, steel and mineral-based commodities. As shown in Table 7.8, a significant portion of commercial trade is in the form of commission-based processing trade, whereby South Korean firms supply labour-intensive machinery and raw materials to the North for low-cost processing. Goods are then 'exported' back to the South as finished products. Commission-based processing trade is mutually beneficial. North Korea is provided with the means to earn desperately needed foreign currency by utilizing its idle industrial capacity and labour force, and also gains the opportunity to acquire technical knowledge by engaging with South Korean firms. South Korean companies gain access to cheap labour without having to make significant foreign investments. Commodities produced in the inter-Korean processing trade are limited mainly to labour-intensive products such as textiles, footwear and bags, and more recently some electronic goods (MOU 2005b). Other commercial trades are mainly those through South Korean companies located in Gaesong which are similar in nature to commission-based processing trade. In 2007, commission-based processing trade and trade through Gaesong accounted for 68.3 per cent of total inter-Korean commercial trade (Table 7.8). As long as geopolitical stability maintains in the peninsula, commercial trade will expand as it is mutually beneficial.

Table 7.7 Inter-Korean trade by type, 2002–07 (US$ million)

Type	2002	2003	2004	2005	2006	2007
Commercial	355	425	437	690	928	1430
Non-commercial	287	299	260	366	422	368
Total	642	724	697	1056	1350	1798

Source: Lim (2007); MOU (2008b).

Table 7.8 Inter-Korean commercial trade, 2002–07 (US$ million)

Type	2002	2003	2004	2005	2006	2007
Commercial trade (total)	355	425	437	690	928	1430
Processing-on-commission trade	182	193	176	210	253	330
General commercial trade	173	227	172	210	304	462
Others (Gaesong)	13	17	90	270	371	567

Source: calculated from MOU (2008a).

7.4.3 Inter-Korean Foreign Direct Investment

Foreign direct investment, which flows exclusively from South to North Korea, has not expanded as quickly as inter-Korean trade, because the former is more contingent on geopolitical uncertainty. A number of South Korean companies have ownership and internalization advantages *vis-à-vis* North Korea, and the North has location advantages except for its political and institutional uncertainty. South Korean companies have technology, management skill and marketing ability, and the North has a low-wage labour force with a common language and culture. However, because of geopolitical uncertainties, only a limited number of FDI projects have been undertaken with explicit sanctions from both governments.

From the commencement of inter-Korean economic relations in 1988, both governments have maintained restrictions on direct investment in North Korea. Through the 1998 Sunshine Policy, the South Korean government has removed many of its restrictions on inter-Korean FDI. Then, in October 1998, Hyundai created a subsidiary, Hyundai-Asan, to manage the Mt Kumgang Tourism District in the North for South Korean visitors (Lee and Yoon 2004). Beyond this there was little development in FDI until 2000 when the Four-Point Agreement on investment was signed. Since then, large-scale investment projects such as the Mt Kumgang Tourism District, Gaesong Industrial Complex and associated inter-Korean transport infrastructure were established (Lee and Yoon 2004). These projects had earned Pyongyang approximately US$1 billion in hard currency by 2006 (Lim 2007). North Korea has also recently implemented a number of general measures to encourage the growth of FDI such as lowering minimum wages and prices for utilities, and establishing a number of foreign exchange centres. In addition, foreign companies operating at Mt Kumgang and Gaesong are permitted to negotiate labour contracts directly with North Korean workers (MOU 2005a). As a result, as shown in Table 7.9, a rising number of FDI projects were approved, from 2 in 2003 to 26 in 2004 and 176 in 2007.

Table 7.9 Number of cooperative FDI projects approved, 1991–2007

	1991–2001	2002	2003	2004	2005	2006	2007	Total
FDI projects	23	2	2	26	39	23	176	291

Source: MOU (2008b).

The Gaesong Industrial Complex Project is a particularly important test case for future developments of not only FDI but also other inter-Korean relations. The site encompasses 66 km^2 of land at Gaesong, located 69 km north of South Korea's largest market, Seoul. By February 2005, 300 South Korean managers at the Gaesong Complex employed a total of 1800 North Korean workers (Lim 2007). From an economic perspective, the project has good prospects for success as it combines North Korea's low-wage workers with the technology, management skill and marketing ability of South Korean companies. The success of the project hinges only on the political cooperation of the two Koreas. Pyongyang enacted the Gaesong Industrial Complex Law in November 2002. The North Korean government has mandated a minimum monthly wage of $57.50, and a maximum 48-hour working week. These wages are about a third of Chinese wages and about one-tenth of the South Korean wage level in 2004 (Lim 2007). For the first time since the partition of the Korean Peninsula, the electricity supply was connected from the South to a number of firms operating at Gaesong on 16 March 2005 (Korea.net 2005a). In recent years, the Gaesong Industrial Complex has come to symbolize and showcase inter-Korean cooperation. For South Korea, 'visible success is necessary' as this may lead to a dramatic expansion of North Korea's reforms and openings. From Pyongyang's perspective, the failure of Gaesong would mean the disastrous loss of the last development option available through the SEZ promotion policy (J.W. Lee 2004).

7.4.4 Inter-Korean Tourism

Inter-Korean tourism has good prospects, as the North has a number of scenic and historical sites which South Koreans are eager to visit, and it will provide a good source of foreign currency to the North. So far, inter-Korean tourism has been centred on two sites: Mt Kumgang and Gaesong City. The scenic Mt Kumgang in North Korea's southeast was opened to South Korean tourists as a showcase of the Sunshine Policy. Pyongyang granted Hyundai-Asan exclusive rights to develop the Mt Kumgang Tourism District in 1999. Hyundai-Asan developed hotel accommodation and infrastructure and operated a number of vessels to provide exclusive transport to Mt Kumgang until 2002 when the east coast road to the mountain opened. Transport via the sea route was ceased in January 2004 after the carriage of 557 681 passengers (Korea.net 2005b). As shown in Table 7.10, the number of tourists jumped after the east coast road was opened in 2002. By July 2008, 1.9 million tourists had visited Mt Kumgang. The second tourism project was developed by Hyundai-Asan at Gaesong City, endorsed by North Korea, and began operations in 2004. Table 7.10 shows that 1500 South Korean tourists made the trip to Gaesong City in 2005, the first year after the opening, rising to 7400 in 2007. Over the first seven months of 2008, 76 000 people visited Gaesong City.

Table 7.10 Number of tourists to Kumgang and Gaesong, 2002–08 (000)

Location/year	2002	2003	2004	2005	2006	2007	2008*	Total (1998–2008)
Kumgang	84.7	74.3	268.4	298.2	234.4	345.0	200.0	1934
Gaesong				1.5	–	7.4	76.2	85
Total	84.7	74.3	268.4	299.7	234.4	352.4	276.2	2020

Note: * Over the first seven-month period in 2008.

Source: MOU (2008a).

Inter-Korean projects have provided a large sum of foreign currency to North Korea. Over the period from 1998 to October 2008 South Korean companies paid $1176 million to the North Korean authorities. Of this, $565 million was paid directly related to the Mt Kumgang Tourism Project, and $73.1 million for the Gaesong Tourism Project (*DongA News* 2008). The remaining $450 million has been paid for the authorization of seven projects. These exclude expenses incurred by South Korean companies in undertaking FDI in the North.[12]

7.5 CONCLUSION

After the bitter experience of a series of severe economic and social predicaments resulting from institutional failure, the North Korean regime realized that it could not secure people's living, and introduced a market mechanism and opened the economy in 2002. The 2002 reform measures amount to institutional reforms including decentralization of the planned economy, normalization of price and wages in line with the market mechanism, establishment of private market places, elimination of the rationing system, autonomous enterprise management based on profitability, and an open-door policy. Under the reform, prices are not set by market forces alone but are anchored on the standard prices set by the government, and the state does not relinquish its ownership of capital. Although the North Korean regime has disclaimed the reform as market socialism, it is very significant because it is the first systemized measure to approve market functions, and it is a movement toward the co-existence of a planned and a free-market economy. It appears that the 2002 reform fits well into market socialism.

It is highly likely that North Korea will encounter serious difficulties in pursuing the reform. Nevertheless, it is inconceivable that the North Korean regime will reverse the economic system to the pre-2002 system. The reform will work as a catalyst for further reforms. Over time, with the reform measures that encourage market coordination, the private economy will grow more rapidly than the overall economy, and people's individualism will rise. Therefore, it is highly likely that North Korea will carry on further economic reforms. Prospects of the North Korean economy must, of course, be constrained by the volatile international relations climate that surrounds Pyongyang. Until the nuclear issue is resolved, North Korea's economy may remain fragile and dysfunctional, and the chances of a successful transition to a market economy as in the Chinese case will be limited. Yet the North Korean regime has proven since 2002 that a gradual movement toward the coexistence of a planned and a free-market economy has taken place.

Future developments of North Korea's economic reform in 2002 and inter-Korean economic relations are mutually intertwined. The assessment for inter-Korean economic relations was much more positive, notwithstanding the 2006 nuclear test, until the nuclear and missile tests of 2009. The volumes of trade, FDI and tourist numbers have all been steadily increasing in recent years. This suggests that South Korea's policy of separating economic from political issues has been successful, and that commercial motivations rather than political considerations are increasingly becoming the determinant for inter-Korean economic relations. Ongoing and expanding inter-Korean economic relations have an important bearing on both economies, geopolitical developments in North Korea and peace on the Korean Peninsula. Active inter-Korean economic relations will lower country risk, as they will discourage the North from engaging in political and military provocation for fear of damaging its economy.

All these inter-Korean economic relations are mutually beneficial. The two economies are certainly complementary, based on their different comparative advantages. For South Korean industries, the North offers a pool of low-cost labour that enhances global competitiveness, a consumer market of 22 million people and, potentially, the benefits of the economy of scale of the entire Korean Peninsula. From the North Korean perspective, the strengthening of inter-Korean economic relations has the greatest potential to provide desperately needed foreign currency and to lift the North from its current poverty trap by means of South Korea's capital, technology, and managerial and marketing know-how. Once an appropriate regulatory environment is established, private investment could be facilitated relatively smoothly due to the cultural homogeneity between the two Koreas. Success in trade and FDI projects will help North Korea's reforms and opening, and enhance its reputation in the world. The increasing number of visitors between the two Koreas and South Korean tourists to the North will help the North open its society. Given the high political and economic stakes involved for both North and South Korea, it is likely that inter-Korean economic cooperation will further expand.

NOTES

1. The author visited North Korea in October 2005, and observed there a kind of an ongoing religious cult with Kim Il-sung as the Deity.
2. It is important to note that economic data on North Korea are extremely limited and prone to error, and should generally be considered as 'indicative' rather than 'authoritative'.
3. A predominant allocation of resources by the state is reflected in a high proportion of government expenditure for production and public distribution. The state share of national expenditure is generally around 70 per cent and reached 90 per cent in 1993–94 (Lee and Yoon 2004).

4. When the author was visiting Pyongyang in October 2005, a European businessperson confided that the most serious problem faced by North Korea was the lack of foreign capital and credit lines.
5. For price adjustments for individual items of consumer goods, see KIEP (2004: 292).
6. Compared to North Korea's new pricing system, China started initially to leave prices to be determined by markets alone for a certain number of products in the beginning of the 1980s, and gradually let the prices of all commodities be determined by markets by 1992 (KIEP 2004: 332).
7. China carried out wage reform under its economic reform, consisting of two parts. First, the Chinese government introduced a wage apportionment system whereby it controlled the total sum of wages, allowing the local authorities and enterprises to determine wages within the total sum. Second, the sum total of wages was linked to productivity. Although the North Korean wage reform is similar to the Chinese one, government intervention in the wage determination is likely to be much higher in North Korea than in China.
8. KIEP (2004) argues that the North Korean reform with regard to enterprise autonomy is similar to the Chinese reform before 1984. In 1984, China gave full responsibility to enterprise managers, separating politics and enterprise management.
9. It should be pointed out that market reform processes in both China and Vietnam have taken place over many years since the late 1970s, remain ongoing, and have suffered from many setbacks and unevenness in implementation (Stradiotto and Guo 2007).
10. In order to enhance state control, the World Food Programme (WFP) and other independent humanitarian non-governmental organizations (NGOs) involved in food distribution were required to withdraw from the country in 2005 (Ming 2007).
11. Lim and Chung (2004) argue that North Korea's current status can be well compared to that of the regulated markets that existed during the early stages of socialist reform in Eastern Europe, and that 'North Korea is now in a position from which it cannot turn back the clock'.
12. The number of mutual visits made by South and North Koreans, other than those tourists to Mt Kumgang and Gaesong, has also increased steadily over time, demonstrating the rapid gains made in inter-Korean relations in recent years. According to the Ministry of Unification (MOU 2008a), there were 541 405 visits by South Koreans to the North, and 7380 visits by North Koreans to the South, excluding travel associated with Mt Kumgang and Gaesong, over the period from 1989 to July 2008.

REFERENCES

Babson, Bradley, O. (2005), 'The North Korean economy and the new Asian economic order', *Joint US–Korea Academic Studies*, **15**, 117–36.

Bank of Korea (2005), 'Gross domestic product of North Korea in 2004', http://www.bok.or.kr/contents_admin/info_admin/eng/home/press/pressre/info/NKGDP20042.doc.

Bank of Korea (2007), 'Gross domestic product of North Korea in 2006', http://www.bok.or.kr/index.jsp.

Bank of Korea (2008), *Economic Statistics Yearbook 2008*, Seoul: Bank of Korea.

Chung, Young Chul (2004), 'North Korean reform and opening: dual strategy and "*silli* (practical) socialism"', *Pacific Affairs*, **77** (2), 283–304.

Congressional Research Service (CRS) (2006), 'Proliferation security initiative', http://fpc.state.gov/documents/organization/74917.pdf.

Department of Foreign Affairs and Trade (DFAT) (Australia) (2005), 'Country brief: Democratic People's Republic of Korea', http://www.dfat.gov.au/geo/dprk/dprk_brief.html.

DongA News (2008), 'South Korean companies paid $1.2 billion of cash to North Korea since 1998', *DongA News Daily*, 2 October, http://www.donga.com/news/print_web.php?n=200810020134.

Haggard, Stephan and Marcus Noland (2007), 'North Korea's external economic relations', Working Paper Series WP 07-7, August, Peterson Institute for International Economics.

Hong, Ihk-pyo (2002), 'A shift toward capitalism? Recent economic reforms in North Korea', *East Asian Review*, **14** (4), 93–106.

Hong, Soon-jick (2008), 'Inter-Korean economic cooperation: prospects for 2008', *Korea Focus*, **16** (1), 98–106.

International Crisis Group (ICG) (2009), 'North Korea's missile launch: the risks of overreaction', Asia Briefing No. 91, Seoul, Korea and Brussels, Belgium: ICG.

Kim, Ho-jin (2008), 'Unification leadership of South Korean presidents', *Korea Focus*, **16** (3), 110–20.

Kirk, Mark (1998), *Mission to North Korea and China*, 11–23 August 1998, International Relations Committee, Washington, DC: US House of Representatives.

Korea Institute for International Economic Policy (KIEP) (2004), *North Korea Development Report 2003/04*, Seoul: KIEP.

Korea.net (2005a), 'Gaeseong industrial complex', http://www.korea.net/News/News/NewsView.asp?serial_no=20050616007.

Korea.net (2005b), 'Mt Geumgang tourists exceed 1 million', http://www.korea.net/News/News/NewsView.asp?serial_no=20050616020.

Lane, Jan-Erik and S. Ersson (1997), *Comparative Political Economy: a developmental approach*, 2nd edn, London: Redwood Books.

Lee, Jong-woon (2004), 'North Korea's economic reforms under an international framework', Working Paper 04-09, Seoul: Korea Institute for International Economic Policy.

Lee, Jung-hoon (2008), 'A real deal or a political masquerade? The North Korean nuclear question revisited', *Joint US–Korea Academic Studies*, **18**, 137–48.

Lee, Young-sun and Deok-ryong Yoon (2004), 'The structure of North Korea's political economy: changes and effects', in Choong-yong Ahn, Nicholas Eberstadt and Young-sun Lee (eds), *A New International Engagement Framework for North Korea? Contending Perspectives*, Washington, DC: Korea Economic Institute of America, pp. 45–61.

Lim, Hyun-chin and Young Chul Chung (2004), 'Is North Korea moving toward a market economy', *Korea Focus*, **12** (4), 47–79.

Lim, Wonhyuk (2007), 'Inter-Korean economic cooperation at a crossroads', *Joint US–Korea Academic Studies*, **17**, 139–64.

Ming, Lui (2007), 'North Korean economic reform: an uncertain future for a third-way exploration', *Joint US–Korea Academic Studies*, **17**, 83–110.

Ministry of Unification (MOU) (2002a), 'Institutionalization of inter-Korean cooperation', http://www.unikorea.go.kr/en/library/library.php?page_code=ue0503&mode=view&cpb_num=39.

Ministry of Unification (MOU) (2002b), 'Main points in the June 15 joint declaration', http://www.unikorea.go.kr/en/library/library.php?page_code=ue0503&mode=view&cpb_num=11.

Ministry of Unification (MOU) (2005a), 'Recent changes in North Korea, March 2005', http://www.unikorea.go.kr/data/eng0303/000158/attach/eng0303_158A.doc.

Ministry of Unification (MOU) (2005b), 'Overview of inter-Korean exchanges & cooperation for May 2005', http://www.unikorea.go.kr/en/presspublic/presspublic.php?page_code=ue0304&mode=view&fdate=2005-05.
Ministry of Unification (MOU) (2008a), 'Inter-Korean affairs, exchanges and cooperation: monthly statistics', http://www.unikorea.go.kr/eng/default.jsp?pgname=ENGhome.
Ministry of Unification (MOU) (2008b), 'North Korea, tables & charts', http://www.unikorea.go.kr/eng/default.jsp?pgname=NORtables.
Moon, Chung-in (2009), 'South Korea in 2008: from crisis to crisis', *Asian Survey*, **49** (1), 120–28.
New York Times (2008a), 'N. Korea is closer to restart of nuclear program', 22 September, http://www.nytimes.com/2008/09/23/world/asia/23nuke.html.
New York Times (2008b), 'The latest North Korea deal', 14 October, http://www.nytimes.com/2008/10/14/opinion/14tue2.html.
Noland, Marcus (2000), *Avoiding the Apocalypse: economic turmoil on the Korean Peninsula*, Washington, DC: Petersen Institute for International Economics.
Noland, Marcus (2004), 'Political economy of North Korea: historical background and present situation', in Choong-yong Ahn, Nicholas Eberstadt and Young-sun Lee (eds), *A New International Engagement Framework for North Korea? Contending Perspectives*, Washington, DC: Korea Economic Institute of America, pp. 17–44.
Park, Suhk-sam (2002), 'Measuring and assessing economic activities in North Korea', *Korea's Economy 2002*, Korea Economic Institute, **18**, 76–82.
Rembrandt, Scott (2008), '"Peace in our time" at what cost? Possible financial and legal implications of denuclearizing North Korea', *Joint US–Korea Academic Studies*, **18**, 115–36.
Scobell, Andrew (2006), *Demystifying North Korea*, Carlisle, PA: Strategic Studies Institute.
Seliger, Bernhard (2006), 'North Korea's economy at a crossroads', *Korea's Economy 2006*, Korea Economic Institute, **22**, 62–71.
Seliger, Bernhard (2007), 'Monetary and exchange rate policy in declining centrally planned economies and in early transition economies: some observations of North Korea', *Joint US–Korea Academic Studies*, **17**, 111–38.
Snyder, Scott (2009), 'Lee Myung-bak's foreign policy: a 250-day assessment', *Korean Journal of Defence Analysis*, **21** (1), 85–102.
Stiglitz, Joseph E. (1994), *Whither Socialism?*, Cambridge, MA: MIT Press.
Stradiotto, Gary and Sujian Guo (2007), 'Market socialism in North Korea: a comparative perspective', *Journal of the Asia Pacific Economy*, **12** (2), 188–214.
Toloraya, Georgy (2007), 'The economic future of North Korea – will the market rule?', *Academic Paper Series on Korea*, Korea Economic Institute, **1**, 22–39.
US Department of State (2008), 'Update on the six-party talks', http://www.state.gov/r/pa/prs/ps/2008/may/104558.htm.
Winder, A.B. (2000), 'The economic dynamics of the Korea Peninsula peace process', paper presented at the Conference on the Korean Peninsula, Northwestern University, 26 May 2000.

PART III

Transition of individual sectors

8. Recent evolution of the business sector: *chaebols* and SMEs

8.1 INTRODUCTION

The Korean business sector has undergone a metamorphosis in its configuration in parallel with its economic transformation. In the wake of the Korean War (1950–53), there were few incorporated companies with business activity largely undertaken by small enterprises. By 2008, the number had increased rapidly to more than 3 million, of which 99.9 per cent were SMEs (SMBA 2009). The most distinctive feature of the Korean business sector is the dominance of large conglomerates, or *chaebols*, although it has always consisted predominantly of SMEs in terms of numbers.[1] Before the crisis in 1997, the largest 30 *chaebols* had extensively diversified their operations into 821 subsidiaries, and their economic concentration increased steadily (Jwa 2002: 45). By 1995, the top 30 *chaebols* accounted for 16.2 per cent of total value-added in the economy, 45.8 per cent of total sales, and 44.6 per cent of total assets in the economy (Jwa 2002: 33).

After the post-crisis restructuring, the number of subsidiaries was reduced to 544 in 2000 (Choe and Pattnaik 2007). In 2002, the 30 largest *chaebols* accounted for 17.7 per cent of total value-added, 36 per cent of total sales and 34 per cent of total assets in the economy (J.G. Kim 2006). That is, *chaebols*' economic concentration in terms of their shares of total sales and assets decreased substantially, while their share of value-added actually increased. A question naturally arises as to why such a concentration of economic power in *chaebols* has occurred and been maintained. This chapter concentrates on the evolution, nature, scale and scope of *chaebols* as a way to analyse the Korean business sector. Added to this is an examination of recent developments in the SME sector and its relationship to *chaebols*.

Two broad models explicate the Korean business system and, in particular, the concentration of economic power in a limited number of *chaebols*. One is based on Korean culture and the special privileges provided to large companies as part of that policy. Companies sought to adapt to the prevailing formal and informal institutions. The other is based on the transaction cost theory of the firm. Companies sought to minimize high transaction costs by internalizing market transactions, with the expansion and diversification of *chaebols* (Rhee 2002). In the absence of a name in the literature, the first model will be referred to as the 'institutionalized privilege model'.

8.2 TWO MODELS FOR THE EVOLUTION OF KOREAN BUSINESS

8.2.1 Cultural Influences on Korean Business

A country's culture will influence the structure of its economic organizations, and the idiosyncratic traits of Korean culture have influenced the structure of business in a distinctive way. As examined in Chapter 2, Korea has developed a unique hierarchically structured group society under Confucian influences. Relative social rankings were determined by family background, age, gender, education level and occupation. Within this hierarchical society, loyalty, filial piety, obedience and trust were the primary codes of conduct. At the same time, Confucianism emphasized the concept of reciprocity; individuals, regardless of their social rank, have a duty to reciprocate the virtuous and pious deeds of others. Korean society is family-centred and male-dominated. As a result, traditional Korean society placed the utmost importance on family, kinship and filial piety. Individuals in collectivist societies tend to discriminate against outsiders, and naturally invest greater levels of trust in fellow group members.

In such a society, Korean firms have developed and been run along familial lines. The owner has acted as a paternalistic leader with obligations to look after the employees, with the reciprocal expectation of employee loyalty to the owner. Consensus and harmony in business dealings are privileged over conflict and litigation (Miles 2006). Company ownership structures have typically been 'insider-controlled', with majority shareholdings held by the founding family. Koreans are renowned as hardworking, well-educated, diligent, disciplined people, loyal to authority. Taking advantage of such human resources, Korean companies have flourished and expanded in parallel with the country's rapid economic development from the 1960s. Because of the low level of trust assigned to non-family members, family-oriented firms have consequently flourished in Korea.

An intriguing question naturally arises as to why only a relatively limited number of *chaebols* have flourished and expanded since the 1960s. Clearly, human resources alone are not sufficient for the success of an enterprise. A host of other factors and formal institutions have contributed to the development of the Korean business sector to its current status. Korea's unique economic policy since the 1960s and the resulting institutions have been the most critical factors.

8.2.2 Institutionalized Privileges for *Chaebols*

The formal institutions, developed through government intervention, have greatly influenced the structure of Korean firms, particularly benefiting *chaebols*. As examined in Chapter 1, because of the lack of natural resources and a small domestic market, export-led industrialization has been adopted as Korea's fundamental development strategy from the early 1960s, although targeted industries have changed over time. During the 1960s, the government promoted the export of labour-intensive manufactured goods, for which Korea had surplus labour. All possible policy tools were mobilized to support export-led industrialization, including tax benefits, credit and foreign exchange allowances, and export loans as well as a plethora of regulations. To facilitate foreign capital import by exporting firms, the government provided the latter with official repayment guarantees of foreign loans.

Out of these incentives, credit rationing or control played the most crucial role in Korea's export-led development. In the early 1960s, the government nationalized a number of commercial banks and prohibited private firms, including *chaebols*, from owning or controlling banks. Thus, the government could control and ration credit at will and for its own purposes. The government also established a variety of institutions as an integral part of export promotion, such as an export award system and the Korea Traders' Association. Finally, to take advantage of economies of scale and scope in international trade, the government promoted general trading companies, the progenitors of the *chaebols*, with incentives for exports. Simultaneously, the government utilized *chaebols* and the Korea Traders' Associations in controlling the business sector and in extracting support from the private sector for its policies.

Under the Park regime in the 1970s, Korea promoted a heavy and chemical industry policy, the beneficiaries of which were mainly *chaebols*. All policy tools were geared to six targeted industries: steel, petrochemicals, metals, shipbuilding, electronics and machinery (Harvie 2004). The government favoured small numbers of large firms to implement its industrial policy, due to the large amounts of capital and significant risks involved. Firms were designated, encouraged or exhorted to undertake specific projects in the heavy and chemical industries. Funds were then provided at preferential interest rates together with numerous other incentives. Protection from international competition was provided through restrictions on inward FDI and imports. Selected businesses were also protected from domestic competition through licensing processes and by the banning of hostile takeovers of *chaebols*.

Another type of institutionalized privilege was the cross-debt guarantee system, which was available only for large companies with a number of subsidiaries. While the system increased the availability of external capital, it also created the potential for the simultaneous failure of a series of firms, triggered by the failure of one firm of the same *chaebol*. The cross-debt guarantee system thus limited the freedom of the government to exercise its power in forcing any large firm to be declared bankrupt because of adverse effects on the economy. The government became insurer and underwriter, implicitly guaranteeing their investment, creating the perception that *chaebols* were 'too big to fail'. Governments did, in fact, bail out a number of subsidiaries in order to minimize the huge potential social cost of *chaebol* bankruptcies until 1997 (Joh 2001).

Another institutional factor contributing to *chaebol* expansion was the system of cross-shareholding among affiliates of the same *chaebol*. This system enabled a *chaebol* to have managerial control over a number of affiliates with relatively small amounts of investment. In the case of the 30 largest *chaebols*, an owner (or his family) typically invested, on average, in only 2 per cent of the total assets of the *chaebol* while exercising, almost unchallenged, overall managerial discretion (Jwa 2002: 47). This made it easy to conduct cross-subsidization, mutual forbearance, and intra-group trading and capital flows among affiliates, providing further unfair advantages to *chaebols*. Through cross-shareholding and cross-debt guarantees, the capital of *chaebols* and their subsidiaries increased fictitiously. Given the prevailing perception of their infallibility and their zeal to maintain control over their enterprises, *chaebols* were expected to rely on debt capital; if risk is low, debt capital is a sounder way of business financing. This was reflected in a markedly high debt–equity ratio of 519 per cent on average for the top 30 *chaebols* in 1997 (Joh 2001).

Although Korean companies relied heavily on commercial loans up until the 1997 crisis, financial institutions did not provide adequate monitoring of *chaebols* because of state intervention in the financial sector. Through its control of the financial sector, the government allocated funds for its policy purposes until the early 1990s. Under tight state control, banks could not build the capacity to monitor corporate borrowing because the government decided who would get bank loans and bailed out banks when in financial difficulties. It was therefore unnecessary for their survival for banks to monitor the firms that had borrowed from them. The moral hazard problem for both firms and banks was intensified under these arrangements. Furthermore, as examined in Chapter 9, banking regulation and supervision were also fragmented, and as a result, a close hierarchical relationship did not exist among commercial banks and non-bank financial intermediaries. Without such a relationship, firms were able to diversify their debt-financing methods, switching from banks to non-bank financial intermediaries. These characteristics of the banking system led large companies to rely on loans, rather than equity, for their expansion.

Under the influence of state intervention and its accompanying institutions, Korea developed a unique type of government–business relationship in which the government controlled business. Government supremacy is also ingrained in Korean culture and tradition. In Confucian cultures, the bureaucracy has historically been selected through fiercely competitive civil service examinations, and bureaucrats are respected by society as an elite group. The hierarchical government–business relationship in Korea was reinforced under the military regimes. In 1962 the Park regime arrested a number of prominent heads of *chaebols* for illegal profiteering and tax evasion, and ordered them to repay unfair profits. The Chun military regime took similar coercive actions against *chaebols* in the 1980s. As a result, the superior position of the political elite relative to businessmen was firmly established (Jung 1989).

8.2.3 Corporate Governance of *Chaebols*

Largely because of the influences of informal and formal institutions, corporate governance of *chaebols* has evolved in a unique and inefficient way. The OECD (1999) defines corporate governance as

> the system by which business corporations are directed and controlled. The corporate governance structure specifies the distribution of rights and responsibilities among different participants in the corporation, such as the board, managers, shareholders and stakeholders and spells out the rules and procedures for making decisions on corporate affairs. By doing this, it also provides the structure through which the company objectives are set, and the means of attaining those objectives and monitoring performance.

Under this definition, the OECD (1999) principles of corporate governance spell out five specific components:

1. protection of shareholders' rights;
2. equitable treatment of all shareholders, including minority and foreign shareholders;
3. recognition of the rights of stakeholders as established by law;
4. disclosure and transparency with all material matters, including the financial situation, performance, ownership and governance of the company; and

5. responsibility of the board to ensure the strategic guidance of the company and the effective monitoring of management, and the board's accountability to the company and the shareholders.

Based on these OECD principles, the corporate governance of *chaebols* will be evaluated with a focus on protection of minority shareholders, transparency and accountability, and ownership structure of *chaebols*.

All the institutions set up by the Korean government in its industrial and development policy are reflected in the inadequate corporate governance of *chaebols*. The owner or the controlling family of a *chaebol* could control management of all of its affiliates because of the pyramid ownership structure through cross-ownership and inadequate governance (Hwang 2002). The board has the critical role of monitoring management. However, before the 1997 crisis, appointments of board members were almost entirely in the hands of those families in control of *chaebols*. In the absence of internal monitoring and disciplining of management by the board and external disciplining by the banning of hostile takeovers, the controlling shareholders enjoyed almost full discretion without any challenge from outside shareholders. This generated an agency problem, whereby the interests of controlling shareholders rested in conglomerate expansion through diversification, while the interests of minority shareholders lay in the value of the company on capital markets (Lee and McCalman 2007; Chang et al. 2007). A study showed that only 27 per cent of 570 non-financial firms created shareholder value during the five years before the 1997 crisis, and the remaining firms did not generate earnings to cover capital costs (Lim 2002; Joh 2001).[2]

Shareholders were not treated equitably by *chaebols* in line with OECD principles. Minority shareholders had few legal rights or protections. Shareholders without at least 5 per cent of issued shares could not remove a director, file an injunction, demand convocation, inspect account books, inspect records of company affairs and company property, or remove liquidation. By 1997, over 98 per cent of shareholders were small investors who held less than 1 per cent of shares (Joh 2001). With no legal right in effect, minority shareholders had to absorb intolerable risks, as *chaebols* made loan guarantees to other firms controlled by the controlling shareholder and participated in new equity shares of a connected affiliate near insolvency. This amounted to an outright transfer of wealth from the participating firm to the firm issuing new equities.

There was a lack of disclosure and transparency related to company operations and Korean accounting standards were lower than international standards. Consequently, the market lacked accurate and reliable information on *chaebols*' performance and management. Furthermore, since *chaebols* relied on debt-financing, they did not need to attract equity investors through financial transparency. In addition, *chaebols* were not required to provide a consolidated financial report for the whole conglomerate. Without such a financial report, it was impossible to evaluate the overall performance of the *chaebol*. As a result, both domestic and foreign investors considered that Korean firms fell far short of adequate transparency and accountability in their governance structures. In sum, the corporate governance of *chaebols* was seriously deficient across each of the OECD principles. This inadequacy contributed to the 1997 financial crisis.

8.2.4 The Role of Entrepreneurs: the Transaction Cost Model

Although the Korean government indeed played a critical role for the growth of *chaebols*, the entrepreneurial flair of *chaebol* founders in expanding their companies should not be overlooked. The transaction cost model argues that *chaebol* expansion and diversification was generated as a way of internalizing market transactions in order to minimize transaction costs (Jwa 2002; Chang et al. 2007). Transaction costs were bound to be high in Korea because of weak property rights protection arising from a collusive politico-economic structure, widespread corruption, obscure law enforcement practices, difficulties in making and enforcing contracts, and a distorted banking system. It is also argued that *chaebols* expanded and diversified not only as a way of taking advantage of institutionalized privileges, but also as a way of pooling and reducing business risk. Under the prevailing perception of 'too big to fail', expansion and diversification were effective means of survival. Under their entrepreneurial leadership, *chaebols* expanded and broadened their business operations internationally to take advantage of economies of scale and scope in production and marketing. Because of similarities to Japan in business culture, and competition against Japanese firms in international markets, Korean firms emulated their Japanese counterparts by expanding their business scale comparable to that of Japanese firms.

As *chaebols* were formed and developed during the period from the 1960s to the 1980s, the manufacturing sector, in which *chaebols* had their roots, increased rapidly, and the sector fluctuated widely due to the rapid pace of industrialization and heavy dependency on exports. Comparative advantages in industries shifted quickly, impelling rapid changes in industrial structures. Such rapidly changing industrial structures forced companies constantly to look for new business opportunities. If they did not develop new business in time, they would be forced to lose their relative standing in the economy. *Chaebols* competed intensely with each other within the same industries, both domestically and internationally, not only for profit but also for the prestige attached to expansion and diversification. All this made *chaebols* diversify themselves into unrelated business areas.

It is difficult to discern which model, out of the institutionalized privilege model and the transaction cost model, better explains the development of the Korean business system and the concentration of economic power in *chaebols*. However, the transaction cost model begs a serious question as to why only a limited number of *chaebols* have expanded and diversified, given that property rights protection was weak for both large and small companies. It appears that both models are required to explain adequately the development of the Korean business system. The two models also provide a similar policy guideline toward *chaebols*. In view of the nation's challenge of mitigating the economic concentration in *chaebols* and improving their competitiveness, policy implications of the two models are similar; they suggest that institutionalized privileges as well as government interference with business operation ought be reduced and at the same time property rights protection ought to be enhanced.

8.3 REFORM OF THE BUSINESS SECTOR AFTER THE 1997 CRISIS

8.3.1 *Chaebols* as a Cause of the 1997 Crisis

Korea's financial crisis in 1997 has been extensively discussed from a variety of perspectives (Cha 2001; Jwa and Yi 2001; Kwon 1998). One particularly important cause of the crisis can be attributed to the nature of the *chaebols*. The unhealthy structure and financial weaknesses of *chaebols*, as examined above, rendered them vulnerable to a financial crisis. With high debt–equity ratios, *chaebols* were expected to yield high profitability on their equity. This was not the case. A paradox of domestic market protection against international competition materialized in Korea. Government protection generated excessive economic power concentration in a limited number of *chaebols*, which practised monopolistic business operations domestically. This, in turn, meant *chaebols* missed the opportunity to acquire the skills needed to improve their productivity and international competitiveness. Consequently, *chaebols* had slow growth in productivity and low rates of return on their equity capital, lower than the prevailing interest rates for loans, leading eventually to the loss of national competitiveness, a key cause of the financial crisis (Joh 2001).

In 1997, a number of the major *chaebols* became insolvent because of their excessive expansion and diversification with debt capital, together with their operational inefficiency. By allowing a number of *chaebols* to go bankrupt, the government signalled that it would no longer bail out large companies, a signal that caused their creditworthiness to crumble. These bankrupt companies eventually dumped their non-performing debt on domestic financial institutions, thereby further damaging the already weak financial system. This was the genesis of the financial crisis and required a drastic reform of *chaebols*.

8.3.2 Nature and Types of the Reform

Korea was rescued from its 1997 financial crisis by a $US57 billion stand-by loan from the IMF, which was conditional on multiple reforms across the economy (Harvie 2004). One condition was reform of the corporate sector with the aim of improving corporate governance, financial structure, efficiency and international competitiveness, while limiting the concentration of economic power in *chaebols*. In reforming the corporate sector, the government utilized financial institutions in distinguishing viable and non-viable firms. Non-viable firms were forced to exit, and for viable companies, workout programmes were introduced under agreements between the firms and creditors' financial institutions.

For *chaebols*, in particular, the first target of the reform was the improvement of their financial structure. They were required to reduce their debt–equity ratio to 200 per cent by the end of 1999. They were also required to phase out existing cross-debt guarantees among the groups' subsidiaries (Choe and Pattnaik 2007). The second targeted area for reform was business efficiency and international competitiveness. To this end, the government attempted to enhance competition and streamline the exit process for non-viable firms. The ban on any form of M&As, including hostile M&As, was eliminated. In addition, the ceiling on foreign shareholdings in individual companies was abolished, and restrictions on incoming FDI were largely eliminated (Choe and Pattnaik 2007). To facilitate the exit of insolvent firms, bankruptcy and corporate reorganization laws were revised. To prevent overinvestment and enhance efficiency, the top five *chaebols* were coerced to swap businesses (referred to as 'big deals') in such key industries as semiconductors, petrochemicals, aerospace, rolling stock, power plant equipment, vessel engines and oil refining.[3] This was to make the top five *chaebols* focus on their core competencies, and to reduce overcapacity in key industrial sectors.

8.3.3 Reform of Corporate Governance

The third targeted area for reform was the system of corporate governance. As Y.K. Kim (2007) and Miles (2006) argue, corporate governance reforms have attempted to transform the Korean system towards the Anglo–American corporate governance model, which has special features such as dispersed share ownership, corporate control by professional managers, boards of directors composed of a majority of outside appointees and an overarching first priority of shareholder interest.

To protect minority shareholders: the shareholding threshold for various initiatives was lowered to strengthen the voting rights of minority shareholders, and institutional investors were allowed to vote freely by the abolition of 'shadow voting'. In 2003 shareholders became able to undertake class actions for the first time (Choe and Pattnaik 2007). The reform also fortified the rules governing the board of directors and audit committee. The appointment of outside directors was made compulsory for up to 50 per cent of board members for listed companies with assets of 2 trillion won or more. To strengthen the independence of auditors, an external audit committee was to be established, with outside directors comprising of at least two-thirds of its membership (Cho and Youn 2008; Choe and Pattnaik 2007).

To improve managerial transparency and accountability: *chaebol* owners were forced to register as the directors of their leading affiliates, so that they would no longer be free from the consequences of management misconduct. *Chaebols* were required to prepare annually consolidated financial statements as well as audited financial statements of member companies in accordance with international standards. *Chaebols* were also required to disclose intra-group transactions, detailing cross-shareholdings amongst affiliates, intra-group guarantees and credit trading (Choe and Pattnaik 2007).

To limit the concentration and expansion of economic power in chaebols: the 'mutual shareholdings restriction rule' and 'equity investment sum caption rule' were introduced in 1986, both implemented by the Korea Fair Trade Commission (KFTC). By the former rule, an affiliate of a *chaebol* with total assets over 2 trillion won cannot buy the shares issued by a sister company of the same business group, if the sister company has owned the former's shares. This is to prevent cross-shareholdings of intra-group companies of a *chaebol*. The latter restricts the total sum of intra-corporate investment of a *chaebol* with total assets of 10 trillion won to no greater than 40 per cent (that is, 2.5 trillion won) of the *chaebol*'s assets, regardless of the number of affiliates (S.J. Lee 2008; KERI 2007).[4] The government prohibited cross-debt guaranteeing between affiliate firms in 1998. In 1999, the government amended the fair trade law to allow *chaebols* to adopt a holding company structure. The holding company must own at least 30 per cent of the group's affiliates, which are in turn prohibited from cross-investing in each other (Choe and Pattnaik 2007).

8.4 ASSESSMENT OF THE REFORM OF *CHAEBOLS*

Financial structure: The reform process has made substantial progress but is far from complete. In the area of financial structure, the debt–equity ratio of Korean firms on average has reduced drastically from 396 per cent at the end of 1997 to 135 per cent at the end of 2002. This contrasts with 167 per cent in the United States in 2002 and 163 per cent in Japan in 2001 (J. Lee 2003). The debt–equity ratio for the 43 *chaebols* further declined to 96.7 in 2006 (W. Lim 2008). Without the perception of 'too big to fail', *chaebols* are more cautious in investment and borrowing. In 2001, cross-debt guarantees were eliminated. In the absence of the cross-debt guaranteeing system, banks are reluctant to lend money to highly indebted companies. However, a number of Korea observers have expressed sceptical views on the validity of the quantitative debt–equity ratio of *chaebols*. Choe and Pattnaik (2007) point out that decreases in the debt–equity ratios were achieved in part through cross-shareholding among affiliates. Jang (2002) claims that, although cross-debt guarantees were eliminated, off-sheet agreements among subsidiaries and indirect debt payment guarantees have not been fully eliminated. Even though the average debt–equity ratio is low, there were still a number of financially distressed companies that did not earn enough operating income to cover interest payments for a number of years after the crisis. This is reflected in the low interest coverage ratio. Korean manufacturing firms had a ratio of 132.6 in 2001, compared to 354 in the United States in 2001 and 367.5 in Japan in 2000 (Ahn and Yang 2003). The interest coverage ratio since improved significantly to reach 469.8 in 2007 (Bank of Korea 2008).

Business efficiency: In the areas of business efficiency, reforms have made some progress. By allowing the exit of non-viable firms and rehabilitating viable firms with short-term financial difficulties, the reform programme restored confidence in both the financial and corporate sectors (Jwa 2001: 227–31). *Chaebols* have substantially changed their business strategy and focused on their core businesses following the crisis. This is reflected in the substantial decreases in the average number of subsidiaries of the top 30 *chaebols* from 27.3 in 1997 to 22.9 in 1999, and further to 18.1 in 2000 (Jang 2002).[5]

8.4.1 Assessment of the Reforms of Corporate Governance

In the area of corporate governance, significant improvements have been made, thereby improving corporate transparency and disciplining group owners to act more responsibly. However, because of Korean corporate governance rooted in the tradition of family management, institutional inertia and path-dependency, it is not likely that the corporate governance of *chaebols* has met the OECD criteria. It is still difficult for minority shareholders to check the moral hazard of managers. Because their shares are widely distributed, it is almost impossible for the individual shareholders of large corporations to mobilize the threshold amount of shares to do anything against controlling shareholders or management. The Act that was introduced for class action suits was whittled down to be almost meaningless (J. Lee 2003). Institutional investors do not influence the corporate governance of listed *chaebols*, because many of these institutional investors such as non-bank financial institutions are owned by *chaebols*.[6] Even public funds in Korea do not play significant roles in improving corporate governance or in the securities market, as there is no clear mandate of upholding the interests of public fund members and public funds are often utilized for policy purposes.

The outside director system has been embraced by *chaebol* groups. Choe and Pattnaik (2007) show that the average ratio of outside directors of *chaebol* groups was 39.3 per cent over the 2003–04 period. Foreign investors who have purchased a significant portion of shares in *chaebols* play an active role in monitoring directors and companies. However, a number of Korea observers have expressed sceptical views. J. Lee (2003) points out that most outside directors are appointed by heads of *chaebols* and are therefore more or less toothless. More specifically, Jang (2002) shows that 85 per cent of elected outside directors were still recommended by the controlling families and managers in 2000. This ratio declined to 76 per cent in 2003 (Cho and Youn 2008). Finally, Chang and Shin (2006) point out that although the chairman offices were dissolved after the crisis, the *chaebol* group headquarters continues to play the role of the board of directors, monitoring and disciplining the top management of group affiliated firms. All this indicates that neither the board nor outside investors can carry out the important duties of monitoring and disciplining management, and group owners continue to wield managerial control.

Choe and Pattnaik (2007) argue that corporate transparency has improved both in quantity and quality of information disclosed through the various reform measures. Thus *chaebol* owners have become more accountable for their management, and can no longer manage affiliated firms without due attention to minority shareholders. However, foreign investors still view the *chaebol* system as lacking transparency, in that owners still try to minimize outside interference. De Nicole et al. (2006) show that over the period 2000–03 Korea's disclosure and transparency score was the second-lowest among ten East Asian emerging economies.

To limit the concentration and expansion of chaebols: an Act limiting intra-group shareholding to 40 per cent of net capital has been in place. However, expansion of cross-shareholdings among intra-group companies has not abated. Jang (2002) argues that the proportion of internally held shares in *chaebols* has increased, strengthening controlling shareholders at the expense of minority shareholders. In this regard, S.J. Lee (2008) points out that in 2005–06, the average level of cross-shareholding by those 38 *chaebols* subject to the mutual-shareholding restrictions remained at approximately 51.2 per cent of affiliated companies' total shares. For those nine *chaebols* subject to the total intra-group investment limit, cross-shareholdings among member companies stood at around 47.7 per cent over the same period, compared to about 4.6 per cent of equity held by owning families. This transgression could happen because *chaebols* could effectively bypass the regulation on intra-group investments in the form of a circular pattern of investments using in-house financial institutions which are not subject to the same Act (S.J. Lee 2008).[7] Through this process, *chaebols* have obviously expanded, and in particular the market power of the top five *chaebols* has been further strengthened, as attested by a much higher average growth rate in asset accumulation for the top five than that for the top 6 to 30 *chaebols* (Jang 2002).

Through the circulatory shareholding, principal shareholders and families of *chaebols* have secured voting rights among affiliates without requiring any cash outlays, thereby wielding much higher managerial control over their groups than their ownership. Min (2007) points out that in 2006, among the top 41 *chaebols*, the voting rights of the chairman and family members was 6.71 times their share ownership. For 28 *chaebols* with chairmen and subject to the mutual-shareholding restrictions, the voting rights to share ownership by the chairmen and their families increased to 6.68 in 2007 and further to 7.39 in 2008, while their share ownership decreased from 4.9 per cent in 2007 to 4.23 per cent in 2008 (*Hankyoreh* 2008). The ratio of the voting rights to shares held by chairmen and their families in Korea is 5 to 8.2 times the ratios of business groups of advanced countries in Europe (Park 2008). The United States and United Kingdom have not developed business groups. Even in Japan, member companies of *keiretzu* operate independently, and the concentration of individual families is quite low, comparable to those of the United States and United Kingdom (Choi and Patterson 2007). Maybe because of the loopholes with the cross-shareholding regulations, the holding company ownership structure has not proven popular thus far. Of the 51 largest groups covered by the amended fair trade law, only four *chaebols* (LG, Dongwon, Seia and Nongshim) had moved to the new holding company structure by 2006 (Choe and Pattnaik 2007).

The securities market can play an important role in monitoring corporate management. As pointed out in Chapter 9, Korea seeks to transform its financial system from the bank-based system to the market-based one. To this end, securities and capital markets have been liberalized and most of the regulations preventing M&A, including hostile ones, have been removed. In the face of such a liberalized securities market, it is expected that management be efficient and maximize shareholder value. A market for corporate control has not worked well in Korea because *chaebol* owners have large voting rights, and *chaebols* do not rely much on the securities market for financing.

*Table 8.1 IMD business efficiency and corporate governance rankings 2008**

	Business efficiency (0–100)	Shareholder's rights (1–10)	Credibility of managers (1–10)	Supervision of corporate boards (1–10)	Auditing and accounting practices (1–10)	Share-holder value (1–10)
HK	1 (86.29)	30 (6.36)	3 (7.33)	3 (6.90)	5 (8.12)	9 (7.04)
Singapore	2 (77.33)	3 (7.81)	1 (8.11)	1 (7.28)	2 (8.23)	2 (7.49)
USA	3 (71.58)	16 (7.06)	25 (6.22)	27 (5.80)	21 (7.37)	15 (6.96)
Australia	6 (68.63)	4 (7.75)	12 (6.73)	7 (6.54)	8 (7.91)	1 (7.63)
Taiwan	10 (64.15)	34 (6.13)	21 (6.42)	19 (6.06)	33 (6.71)	34 (5.90)
Canada	11 (63.36)	7 (7.43)	5 (7.13)	22 (5.26)	15 (7.58)	8 (7.06)
Finland	17 (55.51)	6 (7.52)	19 (6.44)	17 (6.20)	11 (7.68)	9 (7.04)
UK	19 (54.29)	17 (7.02)	32 (5.70)	21 (6.02)	20 (7.40)	22 (6.55)
Japan	24 (48.10)	47 (5.26)	14 (6.52)	26 (5.80)	42 (6.13)	43 (5.47)
German	28 (45.48)	14 (7.17)	53 (4.19)	49 (4.73)	24 (7.15)	20 (6.60)
China	33 (39.00)	53 (4.42)	47 (4.77)	42 (5.09)	55 (4.81)	53 (4.81)
Korea	**36** (37.42)	**49** (4.58)	**46** (4.90)	**54** (4.14)	**51** (5.64)	**51** (4.91)

Note: * Ranking out of 55 countries.

Source: IMD (2008).

This lack of a disciplinary role of the market for corporate control is reflected in the so-called 'Korean Discount' phenomenon and low Tobin's Q due to the opportunistic behaviour of controlling shareholders. At the end of

2005, Tobin's Q for Korean firms was 1.02 which was significantly lower than for most other OECD and East Asian countries (Claessens 2008). Also, as shown in Table 8.1, Korea ranked 51st out of 55 countries for 'shareholder value', as estimated by the International Institute for Management Development (IMD 2008).

The Lee Myung-bak government has announced its intention to eliminate the restrictions on *chaebols*' equity investment ceilings (Lee & Ko 2008). In addition, his government plans to allow *chaebols* to own commercial banks. Although the details of the new government's policy have yet to be announced at the time of writing in mid-2009 and their evaluation remains to be done, it appears that the tenet of the announced policies runs counter to the progress of corporate governance. It therefore looks highly likely that once the Lee government policy is implemented, the impetus of corporate governance reform will dissipate, and Korea's corporate governance standards will fall further behind the levels of advanced and East Asian emerging countries.

8.4.2 Comparative Assessment of the Overall Corporate Reform

As Korea seeks to achieve the economic status of advanced countries, it is imperative to evaluate its corporate governance system comparatively from a global perspective. Incompleteness of Korea's corporate reform and in particular corporate governance reform is reflected in relatively poor international rankings. A few global organizations measure corporate governance-related indexes across countries. According to the 'business efficiency' index by the IMD (2008), Korea ranked 36th out of 55 countries in 2008, as shown in Table 8.1. A number of East Asian competitor countries such as Hong Kong, Singapore, Taiwan, Japan and even China performed better than Korea. Korea's ranking of 36th on the business efficiency index is compared to its rank of 31st with the IMD's national competitiveness index, indicating that the Korean business sector drags down its overall national competitiveness.

The IMD's business efficiency index has a number of components directly related to corporate governance such as shareholders' rights, credibility of managers, supervision of corporate boards, auditing and accounting practices, and shareholder value. Korea's rankings in these five corporate governance-related components ranged from 46th to 54th out of 55 countries in 2008 (Table 8.1). All East Asian competitors, except China, performed better than Korea with these components. GovernanceMetrics International (GMI) ranked Korea 40th out of 50 countries studied in 2007, and 34th out of 39 countries in 2008 with its global ratings of corporate governance practices (GMI 2008). The GMI rankings of corporate governance appear to be quite consistent with the IMD's rankings. All the above-mentioned East Asian countries, except China, let alone advanced countries, outperformed Korea in the GMI ranking.

De Nicole et al. (2006) estimate a corporate governance quality (CGQ) index for major emerging markets and developed economies during the period 1994–2003. The CGQ is a measurement of actual outcomes, not necessarily legal, of two dimensions of corporate governance: accounting disclosure and transparency. Korea fared quite poorly with the CGQ as compared to other emerging countries as well as advanced countries. Over the period 2000–03, Korea ranked 9th out of ten emerging East Asian markets. Korea's average CGQ index was 0.583, compared to an average of 0.609 and 0.647, respectively, for ten emerging markets in East Asia and 22 developed economies (the index ranging from 0 to 1). Korea's average score of 0.583 is compared to an average of 0.647 for Japan. Although the CGQ index narrowly focuses on outcomes of corporate governance, its results for Korea appear to be consistent with the other two indexes discussed above.

8.4.3 Causes of the Failure of Corporate Governance Reform

A question arises then as to why Korea has failed in improving its corporate governance to the level of advanced countries and even to the level of emerging neighbouring countries. First, from the cultural perspective, Korean corporate governance is fundamentally rooted in the tradition of family management. Hence, *chaebols* are reluctant to rescind their family management system and the public are tolerant to the skewed corporate governance. Second, as examined above, formal institutions contain some loopholes whereby *chaebols* could bypass the regulations of intra-group investment. Third, as S.J. Lee (2008) argues, the enforcement of formal institutions has not been effective because of path-dependency and institutional inertia. Cho and Youn (2008) estimate indexes for institutional arrangements and enforcement for Korea, with the former 0.80 as an average across 11 corporate governance elements and the latter 0.45, indicating relatively poor enforcement of institutions. Claessens (2008) also shows that investors' perception of corporate governance practices is significantly lower than corporate governance rules and regulations. This begs another question about the reasons for ineffective enforcement, which are not addressed by Cho and Youn (2008) or Claessens (2008).

The implementer of the corporate governance rules and regulations is the KFTC which was established in 1980 under the authority of the Prime Minister. The Commission consists of nine commissioners. The Chairman and Vice-Chairman are recommended by the Prime Minister and appointed by the President, while remaining commissioners are recommended by the

Chairman and appointed by the President for three-year terms. The KFTC is assigned four main mandates: promoting competition, strengthening consumers' rights, creating a competitive environment for SMEs and restraining concentration of economic power. To fulfil the mandates, the KFTC formulates and administers competition policies, and deliberates, decides and handles antitrust cases. The KFTC annually deals with a large number of cases of cartels such as price-fixing, business mergers, anticompetitive conduct and unfair trade practices of *chaebols* (Hur and Rhee 2008).

It appears that the KFTC lacks independence from government to serve as an effective competition advocate. The chairmen have changed 14 times in the 17-year history of the Commission, even though they are appointed for three-year terms. It is likely that as a Chairman changes, other commission members he or she recommends follow suit. In promoting a fair and competitive market system, the KFTC is bound to face challenges from politicians seeking to boost their own popularity, and politically strong lobby groups including the *chaebol* groups. Without strong independence from government, the KFTC will lose its compelling power.

The operations of the KFTC are regarded as inefficient. It lacks transparency and predictability in its examination and deliberation processes (OECD 2004: 143). There is also a reported lack of thorough economic analysis of the cases in which the KFTC is involved (Yun 2002; Shin 2002). Cooperation of citizens and employees is an important element for the KFTC's operation. With its operational inefficiencies, lack of political independence, and the overt persistence of economic power concentration in *chaebols*, it is difficult for the KFTC to garner support among general citizens and other stakeholders including the business community. Korean hierarchical family-based group society has an important bearing on the enforcement of corporate governance laws and regulations. Because of high loyalty toward their organizations, employees are reluctant to act as inside watchdogs or whistle-blowers against illegal and improper activities.

A question arises as to whether it is worth the effort to improve Korea's corporate governance to international levels and reduce economic power concentration in *chaebols*. Insofar as Korea seeks to improve corporate value, it is necessary to improve corporate governance and stem the economic power concentration. Kang (2004) postulates a trade-off relationship between ownership concentration and decision-making costs. As ownership concentration increases, quicker managerial decision-making becomes possible, which in turn lowers decision-making costs, while entailing costs arising from arbitrary and hasty decisions and commitments. The minimum point of summing up the decision-making costs and commitment costs is the optimal ownership concentration (or dispersion). Kang's model could be extended to a relationship between concentration and corporate value such that concentration and corporate value increase together to a certain extent of concentration; but beyond that extent, corporate value decreases. Indeed, an empirical study by Cho and Byun (2008), although it is not a testing of Kang's (2004) model, shows that ownership concentration in Korea and corporate value (measured by the rate of return to assets) increase together until the concentration ratio reaches about 50 per cent, and beyond that corporate value declines.[8] It appears that the ownership concentration in Korea has already reached or surpassed the optimal level. As mentioned earlier, the average level of cross-shareholdings of *chaebols* subject to the cross-shareholding restriction was 51.2 per cent over the period 2005–06, and that of *chaebols* subject to the total investment limit was 47.7. Aggregate concentration of the top 30 *chaebols* in terms of the proportion of assets held by them in relation to total assets in Korea increased more or less steadily from 1985 to 1998, reaching 46.3 per cent in 1998. The concentration rate in Korea was 43.6 per cent in 1993, compared to 22.4 per cent, 22.7 per cent, 22.7 per cent and 29.5 per cent, respectively, in the United States, Japan, Germany and the United Kingdom for their 30 top firms (Choi and Patterson 2007).

KERI (2007) argues that restrictions of cross-shareholdings should be eliminated because they are infringements on private property rights, impediments to investment and an arbitrary system found only in Korea that runs counter to the global trend of deregulation on business. The argument for the inhibitive effects of cross-shareholding restrictions on *chaebols*' investment appears tenuous, as there are a number of exceptions for investments in innovative industries and core-related industries, and for FDI where the cross-shareholding restrictions are not applied. Also, when the cross-shareholding restrictions were abolished in 1998, *chaebols* did nothing but expand their intra-shareholding, leading to the reintroduction of the regulation a year later. Further concentration of economic power in a limited number of *chaebols* will have serious implications. De Nicole et al. (2006) point out a positive relationship between improvements in corporate governance practices and GDP growth and total factor productivity (TFP). In Korea, economic power concentration in *chaebol* owners is already quite high, thereby enabling the owners to maximize private benefits at the expense of other stakeholders. The relaxation of bank ownership rules together with the elimination of cross-shareholding restrictions, both of which *chaebols* argue for, will surely lead *chaebols* to expand and penetrate the financial sector. As examined in Chapter 9, the Korean financial sector has become further open to global competition and susceptible to financial crisis with the introduction of the Financial Investment Services and Capital Market Act (FSCMA). *Chaebols*' further expansion may engender moral hazard arising from the perception of 'too important to fail'. Their extensions into the financial sector render them vulnerable to systemic risks. Cho (2009) points out that the influences of *chaebols* on Korean politics, society, the justice system and media are so great as to put policy-makers in danger of losing their perspective of neutrality and aggregate societal interest.

To improve social capital, *chaebol* expansion should be restrained. As mentioned earlier, the voting rights of *chaebol* owners are six to seven times as high as their share ownership. This indicates that *chaebol* owners can transfer their managerial control to family members without inheritance tax implications. This runs counter to social justice in terms of equal opportunity. Further expansion of *chaebols* will certainly exacerbate social bipolarization between big and small business and between rich and poor. This will in turn reduce social capital which, as discussed in Chapter 2, is an important element for economic development. Discriminatory intra-group trading and cross-shareholding provides *chaebols* with unfair competitive advantage against SMEs. Member companies of *chaebols* will be able to undertake predatory pricing against competitor SMEs or to impose entry barriers into industries on SMEs. SMEs play a critical role for Korea, and the evolution of SMEs and their relationship with *chaebols* are discussed in section 8.5.

8.5 SMALL AND MEDIUM-SIZED ENTERPRISES

The Korean business sector consists of not only *chaebols* but also a great number of SMEs. They are generally regarded as enterprises having less than 300 employees.[9] There were 3 million SMEs in all industries hiring 10.8 million workers in 2008. SMEs accounted for 99.9 per cent of all Korean firms, 87.5 per cent of total employment and 49.4 per cent of Korea's total production in 2008 (SMBA 2009). The SME share of Korean commodity exports gradually increased to reach 45.5 per cent in 1990, though it declined to 39.1 per cent in 2004 (Nugent and Yhee 2002; Nam 2005). Since SMEs are in general more agile and flexible than large companies in undertaking innovative activities, in adopting new technologies and in internationalization of production, they are highly important to the growth of a knowledge-based advanced economy.

Despite the importance of SMEs, the basic thrust of economic policy during the early stage of economic development in Korea was to achieve growth and export targets through the support of *chaebols*, with SMEs being relegated to a position of disadvantage (Kienzle and Shadur 1997). The government sought to assist and promote SMEs in limited ways in the 1960s. In the mid-1970s, the government introduced a credit guarantee system to support SMEs, as they were disadvantaged in getting loans due to their poor collateral and creditworthiness. In the mid-1980s, the government began to pay serious attention to the imbalance between large and small businesses. The government established 'sanctuaries' for SMEs in 1989, designating 237 business lines that neither large corporations nor their subsidiaries could enter. It also instructed commercial banks to allocate 35 per cent or more of their loans to SMEs, and more than 80 per cent for regional banks. A number of goods provided only by SMEs were also designated for government procurement. The government also started to promote SMEs as a way of fostering technology development, and established SME-related R&D centres and the Technology Credit Guarantee Fund (Kim and Seong 1997). The relative status of SMEs improved significantly until the 1997 crisis. In the manufacturing sector, the proportions of establishments, employment, value-added and production of SMEs all increased gradually from 1970 to 1997 (Nugent and Yhee 2002).

SMEs were especially hard hit by the 1998 recession in the wake of the crisis. They were seriously affected by the credit crunch as banks reduced their lending to SMEs and gave an increased share to larger firms, and by skyrocketing interest rates. Added to this were delayed payments by large firms to subcontracting SMEs. As a result, SMEs accounted for a large proportion of the sharp rise in the bankruptcy rate. The government responded with a variety of support measures such as making commercial banks roll over loans to SMEs, and providing loan guarantees and tax benefits (Harvie 2004). Yet, as pointed out by Nugent and Yhee (2002), the future prospect of Korean SMEs is not sanguine. SMEs have faced the challenge of increasing technological sophistication and international competitiveness, especially from China. It is questionable that SME entrepreneurs have the required marketing experience to accommodate rapid changes within the SME sector. SMEs have also reportedly been particularly hard hit by the 2008 global financial crisis, with around 70 per cent facing difficulties (SERI 2008).

In line with the liberalization of the economy and with the emerging globalization and information era, the government in 2000 significantly shifted its policy toward SMEs to a more market-oriented and technology-promoting policy (OECD 2001). It was assumed that the old-fashioned, excessive support measures that SMEs enjoyed could lower their competitiveness and weaken their viability by making them dependent on the government and subject to moral hazard. Thus, the number of business and government procurement lines reserved for SMEs have been reduced. At the same time, the government has sought to reduce restrictions on enterprise activities and to make SMEs develop their own capabilities on the basis of the flexibility and creativity unique to them. Currently, government policy on SMEs emphasizes assistance, with SME start-ups and financing; training and building capacity in human resources; building and strengthening technological innovation capacities; fostering venture businesses; and providing special services to micro-enterprises of less than ten employees (SMBA 2009).[10]

In spite of the large number of policies implemented for SMEs, their economic prosperity has been falling behind that of large companies in the recent past (SMBA 2009). As measured by profitability and productivity, the gap between large corporations and SMEs has been rising, creating bipolarization in Korea. Ju and Cho (2006) show that the gap in profitability (operating income to sales ratio) between large corporations and SMEs has widened recently in favour of the former. Over the period 1991–2001, the profitability of large corporations was on average 7.8 per cent, compared to 4.9 per cent for SMEs. Over the 2002–05 period the profitability of large corporations was 8.1 per cent, while that for SMEs was 3.5 per cent, the gap amounting to 4.6 percentage points (Ju and Cho 2006).[11] Another aspect of the relative declining prosperity of SMEs is shown in their lagging productivity. The ratio of the labour productivity of SMEs in the manufacturing sector to that of large corporations has declined more or less steadily from 48.6 per cent in 1991 to 33.1 per cent in 2005.[12] The relative falling labour productivity of SMEs may reflect not only the comparatively poor quality of workers and managerial know-how at SMEs, but also lesser R&D activities. The proportions of R&D expenditure and the number of researchers accounted for by SMEs fell significantly over the period 2002–05 (Ju and Cho 2006). Even SMEs' share of exports declined, from 42 per cent in 2002 to 39.1 per cent 2004 (Nam 2005).

The frail condition of SMEs appears more serious when it is viewed in terms of per capita indicators. SMEs' per capita wages and salaries amounted to 55.7 per cent of those of large corporations in the manufacturing sector in 2002. In the same sector and year, SMEs' per capita gross output and value-added were about 31.1 per cent and 32.2 per cent, respectively, of those of large enterprises. Furthermore, SMEs' per capita tangible assets in 2002 were estimated only at about 25.8 per cent of those of large corporations in the manufacturing sector (Nam 2005). The bipolarization between large corporations and SMEs appears to be structural in nature and shows no sign of ameliorating. The low profitability and productivity at SMEs leads to a relatively low wage level, which in turn, together with cultural preference of working for large enterprises, renders it difficult for SMEs to attract efficient workers. However, as the benchmark wage rates increase in capital-intensive *chaebol* industries, wage rates cannot help but increase in labour-intensive SMEs, causing them to suffer from higher costs of production, thus losing international competitiveness against China and other East Asian countries. This may lead SMEs to shift their operations to other countries, hollowing out part of the domestic job market. SMEs undertook about 1500 overseas investment projects annually over the 2001–04 period, and their share of overseas investment project numbers increased from 16.8 per cent in 2001 to 37.8 per cent in 2004.

As discussed in Chapter 2, the worsening bipolarization has serious implications for Korean society and the economy by lowering social capital. To mitigate or prevent polarization, various suggestions can be made. Ju and Cho (2006) propose an improvement in the innovative competence of SMEs. K.W. Lee (2006) suggests institutional and technical assistance as well as financial assistance for human resource development at SMEs. It is suggested that policy coordination be addressed, as a large number of ministries are involved in supporting SMEs. In 2004, for example, there were 76 different government programmes in support of SMEs supervised by 12 ministries (OECD 2005: 168–9). Clearly, one of the most serious tasks is to review the relationship between SMEs and large corporations, in particular *chaebols*.

8.6 RELATIONSHIP BETWEEN *CHAEBOLS* AND SMES

Chaebols are generally characterized by family ownership through cross-shareholdings, vertical integration, diverse business activities and hierarchical central control. One of the main differences in the roles of *chaebols* and Japanese *keiretsu* is their relationships with SMEs. *Keiretsu* always include and tightly control the activities of many SMEs under their corporate umbrella. The vertical integration of *chaebols*, however, has encouraged self-sufficiency in production, rather than integrating SMEs into the business group. By taking advantage of their privileges and relative strengths, *chaebols* have 'crowded-out' SMEs from both capital and labour markets. With their lack of capital and human resources, SMEs are constrained in developing their own R&D and in sourcing foreign technology. Hence, few SMEs have entered Korean business networks as independent operators; and the majority of them serve as subcontractors and suppliers to *chaebols* (Kienzle and Shadur 1997). According to Song (2004), 81.6 per cent of SMEs are subcontractors to large companies. An asymmetrical bargaining relationship with respect to price and contract arrangements exists when SMEs subcontract to *chaebols*. It is a monopsonistic relationship, whereby *chaebols* as a limited number of demanders have a superior hand over SMEs which represent a large number of input suppliers.

In view of the recent trends in global competition based on vertically networked business groups rather than individual business entities, it is imperative for Korea to develop a win–win cooperative strategy between *chaebols* and SMEs for their mutual growth as well as for overall economic growth. To this end, both *chaebols* and SMEs should recognize the necessity for cooperation in developing new technologies and parts, in penetrating overseas markets, in global sourcing of materials, in developing information networking and in human resource development. The government should provide both carrot and stick for win–win cooperation. In this respect the most challenging task for greater cooperation is to enforce fair trade practices between the two entities. The KFTC introduced in 2007 'the fair trade agreement system' and 'subcontract fairness assessment system' (KFTC 2008). Also, Korea established in 2004 the Cooperative Foundation for Large and Small Business. The effectiveness of these public and private institutions is yet to be evaluated at the time of writing in 2009. However, a large number of breaches of fair trade practices and abuses of asymmetric power by *chaebols* are reported annually (KFTC 2008). Typical cases include *chaebols*' refusal to increase the delivery unit costs arising from rising raw materials prices, undue price reduction on subcontractors, abusing SMEs' core technology, and negotiating with individual subcontractors instead of engaging an open tendering system.[13] Attending to these issues should help address bipolarization concerns and enhance national competitiveness.

8.7 CONCLUSION

This chapter has examined recent developments in the Korean business sector, particularly the expansion of *chaebols*, their contribution to the crisis and their reform in the wake of the crisis. Added to this was a critical investigation of recent developments of SMEs and their relationship with *chaebols*. In implementing export-led industrialization, and in particular its heavy and chemical industrial policy, the government utilized *chaebols* as a conduit and provided them with support and protection through a variety of incentives and regulations. The government allowed practices of cross-debt guaranteeing and cross-shareholding among affiliates of *chaebols* without enforcing proper corporate governance. Under these circumstances, the business operations of *chaebols* lacked transparency, and collusive relations developed between government and business. To take advantage of these institutionalized privileges, *chaebols* expanded and diversified with debt capital, leading them to be subject to moral hazard. From an alternative perspective, *chaebols* expanded and diversified as a way of minimizing transaction costs which were high over the developmental stage. Influenced by moral hazard arising from the perception of 'too big to fail', expansion was a way of minimizing survival risk.

Because of the incentives and inducements for expansion, *chaebols* developed unhealthy financial and organizational structures, thereby contributing to the 1997 crisis. The painful experience of the financial crisis forced a paradigm shift in Korean economic policy from a state-led to a market economy that has eliminated many of the institutionalized privileges previously given to *chaebols*. The government has implemented considerable economic liberalization, making the Korean market widely open to international competition. The capital market as well as the banking sector has been reformed and liberalized, whereby foreign investors have penetrated the financial and corporate sectors. The government has also undertaken dramatic reforms aimed at improving corporate governance, financial structure, and efficiency and international competitiveness. Each of the three reform areas has achieved significant progress. By allowing some *chaebols* to go bankrupt, the 'too big to fail' perception and moral hazard have been significantly reduced.

This chapter has demonstrated, however, that there is still a long way to go before the reforms are completed. This was vindicated by a comparative evaluation of the Korean business sector. Korea's business efficiency is relatively low, and the status of its corporate governance is far behind that of not only advanced countries but also neighbouring countries. In particular, policy attempts to reduce the concentration of economic power in *chaebols* and to restrain the concentration of managerial power in *chaebol* owners have not been successful. The main reason for this is the ineffective enforcement of the formal institutional arrangements of corporate governance. For this, the KFTC's lack of political independence and its operational transparency are pointed out as difficulties in corporate reform and enforcement. Added to this are Korea's traditional business culture, path-dependence in regulatory reform and waning political will to pursue reforms.

The Lee Myung-bak government appears to have reversed the direction of the post-1997 crisis corporate reforms. It should be pointed out that improvements in corporate governance contribute to economic and productivity growth. If concentration of economic power in *chaebols* and their managerial control are left unchecked, *chaebols* may wield too much influence in public decision-making, and be exposed to systemic risks and moral hazard. Such a power concentration will further exacerbate the bipolarization between *chaebols* and SMEs.

This chapter has also shown that SMEs, by utilizing their advantages in flexibility and creativity, could play an important role for Korea's economic development particularly for its drive for a knowledge-based economy. From the beginning of Korea's industrialization, however, SMEs have been treated less favourably than *chaebols*, creating a structural imbalance in the economy. In the wake of the 1997 crisis, SMEs were hit harder than *chaebols*, and large numbers went bankrupt. The relative economic prosperity of SMEs has been declining. The gap in profitability and productivity between *chaebols* and SMEs has been rising in the recent past. The low profitability and productivity of SMEs leads to a relatively low wage level, which is about half the level of large corporations. The wage gap, together with the cultural preference of working for large enterprises, renders it difficult for SMEs to attract efficient workers. Yet, with relatively high wages in Korea, SMEs have been losing international competitiveness and have shifted their operations abroad, leaving a hollowed-out domestic job market. The worsening bipolarization between large enterprises and SMEs has serious implications for Korean society and economy.

An important part of the solution of the bipolarization exists in the relationship between SMEs and large corporations. *Chaebols* by nature have attempted to minimize the role of SMEs and have been reluctant to include SMEs as strategic partners. Most SMEs serve as subcontractors and suppliers to *chaebols*. In the monopsonistic business relations between *chaebols* and SMEs, an asymmetrical bargaining relationship has developed with the superior power being held by *chaebols*. A large number of breaches of fair trade practices and abuses of asymmetric power by *chaebols* are reported. The government should seek to minimize *chaebols*' asymmetric power abuses and improve the business relationship between large and small businesses to create a more level playing field to maintain sustainable and balanced growth in the business sector and its international competitiveness.

NOTES

1. A *chaebol* is a multi-product business entity – not a legal entity – with a large number of subsidiaries controlled by a single founding family with a certain amount of assets. In 1989 there were 43 *chaebols* (Kwon 1997). The Korea Fair Trade Commission (FTC) designated the top 30 *chaebols* as a special group for policy purposes, and announces the list of 30 largest *chaebols* and their affiliates every year.
2. Another indication of the agency problem is that in 1995 the total amount of donations by *chaebols* was greater than that of dividends (Jang 2002).
3. See Harvie (2004) for a summary table of the 'big deals'.
4. Since cross-shareholdings among affiliates are prohibited by the mutual-shareholdings restriction rule, intra-corporate investment subject to the equity investment sum caption rule is a type of circular or pyramid investment. The scales of both *chaebol* total assets and the cap sum have changed a number of times since 1986.
5. For the extent and nature of consolidation of the top 30 *chaebols* after the crisis, see Choe and Pattnaik (2007).
6. Claessens (2008) points out that *chaebols* control more than half of Korea's insurance and securities companies.
7. As of April 2008, 17 *chaebols*, which were subject to the mutual shareholding restrictions, owned 56 insurance companies, of which 24 invested in 68 affiliate firms (KFTC 2008).
8. Cho and Byun (2008) also cite two studies that show a negative relationship between the ownership concentration and corporate value.

9. The definition of SMEs has changed over time. In 2009, SMEs in the manufacturing, mining, construction and transportation sectors were defined as firms with less than 300 employees, or less than US$8 million of paid-in capital. SMEs in the service sector are defined in terms of the number of employees or sales values depending on the type of service, with the maximum employee numbers ranging from less than 50 to 300, and the maximum sales values ranging from less than US$5 million to $30 million (SMBA 2009). To be classified as an SME, a company should not be a subsidiary of one of the nation's 30 *chaebols*. In 2000, the average number of employees per SME was 3.3, indicating that Korean SMEs are small businesses (Hall and Harvie 2003).
10. Assessment of these policy measures for SMEs is beyond the scope of this chapter. Kang (2007) assesses that financial assistance for venture capital investment has been positive, while credit guarantees and policy loans have been either ineffective or dubious.
11. In Japan, the profitability difference between large corporations and SMEs has remained steady at about one percentage point throughout the period 1991–2005 (Ju and Cho 2006).
12. In Japan, the labour productivity of SMEs remained more or less stable at about 50 per cent of that of large corporations over the period 1991–2003 (Ju and Cho 2006)
13. In this respect, Nugent and Yhee (2002) point out that the costs and lost time associated with enforcing contracts, which are often subcontracting relationships with *chaebol* firms, are prohibitive for SMEs.

REFERENCES

Ahn, Choong Yong and D.Y. Yang (2003), *Corporate Restructuring in Korea: empirical evaluation*, Seoul: Korea Institute for International Economic Policy.

Bank of Korea (2008), *Economic Statistics Yearbook 2008*, Seoul: Bank of Korea.

Cha, Dong-Se (2001), 'The Korean economy in the New Millennium: reform and revival', in O.Y. Kwon and W. Shepherd (eds), *Korea's Economic Prospects: from financial crisis to prosperity*, Cheltenham, UK and Northampton, MA, USA: Edward Elgar Publishing, pp. 39–59.

Chang, James J. and Hyun-Han Shin (2006), 'Governance system effectiveness following the crisis: the case of Korean business group headquarters', *Corporate Governance*, **14** (2), 85–97.

Chang, Jinho, Young Jun Cho and Hyun-Han Shin (2007), 'The change in corporate transparency of Korean firms after the Asian financial crisis: an analysis using analysts' forecast data', *Corporate Governance*, **15** (6), 1144–67.

Cho, Dong-keun and Min-sik Byun (2008), 'Relationship between ownership concentration of corporate ownership/control and corporate value in Korea after 1997', Working Paper, 08-07, Korea Economic Research Institute.

Cho, Sungbin and Taehoon Youn (2008), 'Changes in corporate governance of Korean enterprises after the financial crisis', in Dongsoo Kang (ed.), *Government Policies and Corporate Strategies under Structural Changes and Dynamism: the cases of Korea and China*, Seoul: Korea Development Institute, pp. 15–38.

Cho, Yoon-Je (2009), 'Korea's power structure and economic policy', (in Korean), mimeo.

Choe, Soonkyoo and Chinmay Pattnaik (2007), 'The transformation of Korean business groups after the Asian crisis', *Journal of Contemporary Asia*, **37** (2), 232–55.

Choi, J.P. and D. Patterson (2007), 'Conglomerate regulation and aggregate concentration in Korea: an empirical analysis', *Journal of the Asia Pacific Economy*, **12** (2), 250–71.

Claessens, S. (2008), 'Progress in corporate governance', *Korea's Economy 2008*, **24**, 45–53.
De Nicole, Gianni, L. Leaven and K. Ueda (2006), 'Corporate governance quality: trends and real effects', IMF Working Paper, WP/06/293, IMF.
GovernanceMetrics International (GMI) (2008), 'GMI country rankings: average overall rating by country', www.gmiratings.com.
Hall, Chris and Charles Harvie (2003), 'A comparison of the performance of SMEs in Korea and Taiwan: policy implications for turbulent times', University of Wollongong Economics Working Paper Series, WP 03-05.
Hankyoreh (2008), 'Chaebols' ownership/control structure worsened in 2008', 6 November, Seoul: Korea.
Harvie, Charles (2004), 'Corporate restructuring in the wake of the Financial Crisis', in Charles Harvie, Hyun-Hoon Lee and Junggun Oh (eds), *The Korean Economy: post-crisis policies, issues and prospects*, Cheltenham, UK and Northampton, MA, USA: Edward Elgar Publishing, pp. 38–78.
Hur, J.S. and P.S. Rhee (2008), 'Korean antitrust regulations', *International Financial Law Review*, October, 65–7.
Hwang, Inhak (2002), 'Chaebol structure, diversification and performance', in Z. Rhee and E. Chang (eds), *Korean Business and Management: the reality and the vision*, Elizabeth, NJ, USA and Seoul, Korea: Hollym, pp. 171–203.
International Institute for Management Development (IMD) (2008), *World Competitiveness Yearbook 2008*, Lausanne: IMD.
Jang, Hasung (2002), 'After the economic crisis: an analysis of the effects of corporate restructuring', in Z. Rhee and E. Chang (eds), *Korean Business and Management: the reality and the vision*, Elizabeth, NJ, USA and Seoul, Korea: Hollym, pp. 79–131.
Joh, Sung Wook (2001), 'The Korean corporate sector: crisis and reform', in O.Y. Kwon and W. Shepherd (eds), *Korea's Economic Prospects: from financial crisis to prosperity*, Cheltenham, UK and Northampton, MA, USA: Edward Elgar Publishing, pp. 116–32.
Ju, Hyeon and D.H. Cho (2006), *An Analysis of Polarization between Large Corporation and SMEs*, (in Korean), Policy Studies 2006-41, Seoul: Korea Institute for Industrial Economics and Trade (KIET).
Jung, K.H. (1989), 'Business–government relations in Korea', in K.H. Chung and H.C. Lee (eds), *Korea Managerial Dynamics*, New York: Praeger, pp. 11–26.
Jwa, Sung Hee (2001), *A New Paradigm for Korea's Economic Development*, New York: Palgrave.
Jwa, Sung Hee (2002), *The Evolution of Large Corporations in Korea*, Cheltenham, UK and Northampton, MA, USA: Edward Elgar Publishing.
Jwa, Sung Hee and Insill Yi (2001), 'The Korean financial crisis; evaluation and lessons', in O.Y. Kwon and W. Shepherd (eds), *Korea's Economic Prospects: from financial crisis to prosperity*, Cheltenham, UK and Northampton, MA, USA: Edward Elgar Publishing, pp. 73–98.
Kang, Dongsoo (2007), 'Empirical evaluations on the government financial assistances toward SMEs', (in Korean), in Dongsoo Kang (ed.), *Financial Innovation-Oriented Business to Promote Entrepreneurship: experiences of advanced countries and lessons to Korea*, Seoul, Korea Development Institute, pp. 87–119.
Kang, Shin Il (2004), 'Determinants of corporate ownership structure and their effects on corporate governance in South Korea', in S.R. Park, P. Drysdale, S.I. Kang and

I.K. Hong (eds), *Ownership Structure of Northeast Asian Countries*, Seoul: Korea Economic Research Institute, pp. 17–59.

Kienzle, René and Mark Shadur (1997), 'Developments in business networks in East Asia', *Management Decision*, **35** (1), 23–32.

Kim, Joongi (2006), 'The next stage of reforms: Korean corporate governance in the post-Asian financial crisis era', *Asian Journal of Comparative Law*, **1** (1), 1–23.

Kim, Linsu and S.M. Seong (1997), 'Science and technology: public policy and private strategy', in D.S. Cha, K.S. Kim and D.H. Perkins (eds), *The Korea Economy 1945–1995: performance and vision for the 21st century*, Seoul: Korea Development Institute, pp. 383–425.

Kim, Yong-Ki (2007), 'Last 10 years' corporate governance reform in retrospect', *Policy Issues*, Samsung Economic Research Institute, http://www.seriworld.org/05/wldColumnL.html?mn=F&mncd=0103.

Korea Economic Research Institute (KERI) (2007), *Comprehensive Analysis of Regulatory Reform: Issue 3: regulatory reform tasks to the market-oriented economy*, (in Korean), Seoul: Korea Economic Research Foundation.

Korea Fair Trade Commission (KFTC) (2008), '2008 Annual Report', www.ftc.go.kr.

Kwon, O.Y. (1997), 'Korean economic developments and prospects', *Asian-Pacific Economic Literature*, **11** (2), 15–39.

Kwon, O.Y. (1998), 'The Korean financial crisis: diagnosis, remedies and prospects', *Journal of the Asia Pacific Economy*, **3** (3), 331–57.

Lee & Ko (2008), 'South Korea: Fair Trade Commission', www.iflr.com.

Lee, Jaymin (2003), 'Economic crisis and structural reform in Korea', in C.H. Sohn (ed.), *Structural Reforms and Economic Development: experiences of the Northeast Asia*, Seoul: Korea Institute for International Economic Policy, pp. 35–64.

Lee, Jonathon and D.G. McCalman (2007), 'Changes in Korean governance since the Asian financial crisis', *Business Review*, **9** (1), 224–9.

Lee, Kye Woo (2006), 'Effectiveness of government's occupational skills development strategies for small- and medium-scale enterprises: a case study of Korea', *International Journal of Educational Development*, **26**, 278–94.

Lee, Sook Jong (2008), 'The politics of chaebol reform in Korea: social cleavage and new financial rules', *Journal of Contemporary Asia*, **38** (3), 439–52.

Lim, Gill-Chin (2002), 'Korean financial crisis in the global political-economic system', in Z. Rhee and E. Chang (eds), *Korean Business and Management: the reality and the vision*, Elizabeth, NJ, USA and Seoul, Korea: Hollym, pp. 23–47.

Lim, Wonhyuk (2008), 'Corporate governance reform and privatization of state-owned enterprises in Korea', in Dongsoo Kang (ed.), *Government Policies and Corporate Strategies under Structural Changes and Dynamism: the cases of Korea and China*, Seoul: Korea Development Institute, pp. 39–65.

Miles, Lilian (2006), 'The application of Anglo-American corporate practices in societies influenced by Confucian values', *Business and Society Review*, **111** (3), 305–21.

Min, Byung S. (2007), 'Changing pattern of corporate governance and financing in the Korean chaebols', *Economic Papers*, **26** (3), 211–30.

Nam, Sang-yirl (2005), *Innovation and SME Development – Korea's Perspective and APEC Cooperation*, Korea Institute for International Economic Policy (KIEP), http://www.apec.org.au/docs/koreapapers2/SVII-SN-Paper.pdf.

Nugent, Jeffrey B. and Seung-Jae Yhee (2002), 'Small and medium enterprises in Korea: achievements, constraints and policy issues', *Small Business Economics*, **18**, February–May, 85–119.

OECD (1999), *OECD Principles of Corporate Governance*, Paris: OECD.

OECD (2001), *OECD Economic Surveys: Korea*, Paris: OECD.

OECD (2004), *OECD Economic Surveys: Korea*, Paris: OECD.

OECD (2005), *OECD Economic Surveys: Korea*, Paris: OECD.

Park, Asarang (2008), 'Chaebols: bolstering their controlling power with clients' and affiliates' monies', (in Korean), http://cafe240.daum.net.

Rhee, Zusun (2002), 'Were regulations of economic concentration in the Korean Fair Trade Act effective?' in Z. Rhee and E. Chang (eds), *Korean Business and Management: the reality and the vision*, Elizabeth, NJ, USA and Seoul, Korea: Hollym, pp. 51–78.

Samsung Economic Research Institute (SERI) (2008), 'SMEs bear brunt of economic crisis', http://www.koreaeconomy.org.

Shin, Kwangshik (2002), 'The treatment of market power in Korea', *Review of Industrial Organization*, **21**, 113–28.

Small and Medium Business Administration (SMBA) (2009), 'Korean SMEs: statistics', www.smba.go.kr.

Song, Jang Jun (2004), 'Large-SMEs cooperation: from the perspectives of SMEs', (in Korean), Seoul: Korea Small Business Institute (KOSBI).

Yun, Sai-Ree (2002), 'Regulation of business combination under the Antimonopoly Regulation and Fair Trade Act with emphasis on the case law', *Journal of Korean Law*, **2** (1), 1–43.

9. The Korean financial sector: its transition and future agenda

9.1 INTRODUCTION

Financial systems play a critical role in economic development. They comprise financial intermediaries such as banks, securities companies and insurance companies that pool funds and allocate them to appropriate projects, monitor firms and facilitate financial transactions.[1] Each nation has a distinctive financial system shaped by traditions, regulations, institutions and stage of economic development. The literature on financial systems generally categorizes two types: the US financial system based on the securities market and the German financial system based on banks (Jwa and Hahn 2003). The former is referred to as the 'market-based' system and the latter as the 'bank-based' system. Korea has adopted the latter system.

The foundations of a modern financial system in Korea were laid in the early 1950s on the new institutional bases provided by the Bank of Korea Act and the General Banking Act. Since then, with several structural reforms, Korea's financial system has improved, strengthened and expanded over time. Yet by 1997 it became one of the main culprits of the financial crisis that rocked the Korean economy. Hence, the financial system, in particular the banking sector, has undergone drastic reforms in the wake of the crisis, and it has emerged as more efficient, transparent, stable and internationally competitive.

As the current global credit crisis has deepened, the Korean financial system has once again been destabilized. The 2008 US financial crisis, which was at first regarded as a parochial financial event, has spread quickly across the world, attesting to the advanced state of financial globalization. No country, whether advanced or emerging, has been immune to the crisis. Korea is no exception. Its financial industry has been engulfed in the typical patterns of the global financial crisis: liquidity in the money market has plummeted, stock prices have plunged and the confidence underpinning the financial system has evaporated. Commercial banks at the centre of the financial rout are set to be rescued by the government. In addition, the value of the Korean currency has been battered down to a dangerous level.

All this has raised apprehension in Korea about the soundness of its financial system, a repetition of the 1997 crisis and the ensuing economic hardship that Koreans experienced. It is a defining moment for Korean policy-makers who must seriously assess the present and future needs of the country's financial system in order to contrive an appropriate financial system that takes advantage of the benefits of financial globalization, while warding off the contagious effects of future global financial crises. This chapter attempts to make some contribution to this task by conducting the following: a critical examination of the recent developments and reforms undertaken by the Korean banking sector since 1997; an examination of Korea's securities market and its reform after the crisis; an evaluation of the Financial Investment Services and Capital Markets Act (FSCMA) implemented in February 2009; a comparative assessment of Korea's financial sector in comparison with those of advanced countries; and an assessment of the financial regulatory and supervisory systems.[2]

9.2 THE BANKING SECTOR

9.2.1 The Banking Sector as a Principal Cause of the 1997 Financial Crisis

The banking sector, comprising the Bank of Korea (the central bank), commercial banks and non-bank depository institutions, played a vital role in Korea's rapid economic growth over three decades from the early 1960s until the mid-1990s.[3] From the early 1960s, the Korean government embarked on consecutive five-year economic development plans that used banking institutions as the primary conduit for financing economic development projects. Under tight government control, specialized banks either provided funds for policy projects raised through overseas borrowings, or guaranteed the repayment of foreign borrowings by private firms. Commercial banks mobilized increasing domestic savings for policy projects during the 1960s and the 1970s.

Government controlled the banking sector through a variety of regulations, institutions and partial ownership of commercial banks. Its control was extensive, including credit allocation, assignment of bank officers, control over interest rates for loans and deposits, and control over new entries into the banking sector and ownership of banks. In particular, the government prohibited *chaebols* from owning more than 4 per cent of bank shares. The government also protected the sector from international competition by preventing entry of foreign banks. Such tight government control and protection disabled the banking sector from performing its principal functions of financial risk assessment, credit allocation and monitoring of debtor companies (Jwa and Yi 2001).

Under government control and protection together with a number of cases of bailing out financially troubled banks, a perception has been developed that the government would never allow the banks to fail, generating moral hazard within the banking sector. The fragmented framework of supervisory institutions failed to provide proper prudential supervision or restraint on the risk-taking behaviour of banks influenced by moral hazard. The Bank of Korea undertook supervision of commercial banks, while the remainder of institutions were under the direct supervision of the Ministry of Finance and Economy (MOFE). Fragmented and inefficient supervision led to a lack of transparency and accountability in bank management.

Korea's banking sector also lacked prudence in monitoring its main debtors. *Chaebols* took the lion's share of bank credit as the government allocated most of the available credit to them to suit national policy purposes. Since credits were allocated under government direction, banks neither checked the creditworthiness of *chaebols* nor progressively monitored the soundness of their loans to *chaebols*. Banks also did not require *chaebols* to provide them with consolidated financial statements. Under these circumstances, together with *chaebols*' insatiable demands for funds, reckless overlending by banks to *chaebols* was bound to take place.[4]

Responding to pressures from foreign economic partners and in its bid to join the OECD, the Korean government significantly liberalized and internationalized the financial sector from the early 1990s, and allowed banks access to the international financial market. However, the supervisory structure of banks did not adapt to changes in the financial sector. The lack of proper prudential supervision of banks encouraged them to borrow excessively from offshore financial markets, especially since domestic interest rates were substantially higher than those in the international market and large corporations presented an apparently insatiable demand for funds. Korean banks relied heavily on short-term borrowings from abroad, which were denominated in foreign currencies (mainly in US dollars), because of the lower interest rates on short-term borrowings and the perception of no risk with banking operations. They then lent out such funds for the long-term projects of *chaebols* or foreign projects, creating maturity mismatches. The extent and characteristics of banks' foreign debts and their lending practices led the banking sector to become one of the key causes of the 1997 financial crisis in Korea.

9.2.2 Reform of the Banking Sector

Reforms of the banking sector were aimed at rectifying its structural weaknesses, as discussed above, and concentrated on a number of core aspects:

- establishing effective prudential supervision;
- restructuring and consolidation of bank and non-bank financial institutions;
- eliminating non-performing loans (NPLs);
- enhancing transparency and accountability of banking operations; and
- improving corporate governance, credit risk management and operational efficiency (Jwa and Hahn 2003).

To provide effective prudential supervision, a new Financial Supervisory Commission (FSC) and its executive arm, the Financial Supervisory Service (FSS) were established on 1 April 1998 under the Office of the Prime Minister – not under the Bank of Korea. The new Commission has consolidated and strengthened the hitherto fragmented financial supervision of the banking, securities and insurance sectors, and has also gained substantial autonomy from government. It was then the FSC that undertook the restructuring of all financial institutions. These institutions were categorized into two groups – those that were viable despite financial difficulties and those that were simply non-viable – based on diagnostic reviews conducted by internationally recognized accounting firms. The latter group were quickly liquidated. The FSC directed surviving institutions to submit to it their recapitalization and self-rescue measures. Under the self-rescue plans, the government provided 168.3 trillion won – 30 per cent of the 2000 level of GDP – to purchase non-performing loans, undertake recapitalization and make guaranteed deposit repayments (Bank of Korea 2007a: 34). Those that survived the cull were forced to consolidate; weaker banks merged with stronger rivals or combined to form new entities. Surviving commercial banks and non-bank financial institutions were required to raise their capital adequacy ratio to the minimum 8 per cent set by the Bank for International Settlements (BIS). Through the restructuring and recapitalization process using public funds, the government nationalized eight banks, although later it privatized them all except two (OECD 2005: 174).

To enhance the transparency and accountability of banking operations, the banking sector was forced to adopt international accounting standards and public disclosure to enable shareholders, creditors and others to gauge financial institutions' performance accurately. To improve corporate governance, the sector was required to appoint outside directors for more than half of the total board membership and to adopt an audit committee system comprising outside directors for at least two-thirds of its membership (Bank of Korea 2007a: 35). To reduce the risk resulting from large credit exposures to a single entity, the ceiling on banks' credit extending to a single entity was lowered to 20 per cent of the bank's assets.

As a way of sharing the pain of restructuring, the number of employees in the commercial banking sector declined by 41.2 per cent over the period 1997–2005, from 113 933 in 1997 to 66 888 in 2005 (Korea Federation of Banks 2008). The restructuring and consolidation altered the configuration of the financial sector remarkably. As shown in Table 9.1, the number of commercial banks fell from 33 at the end of 1997 to 18 at the end of 2007.

Table 9.1 Changes in the number of financial institutions, 1997–2007

	Institutions at end of 1997	Type of resolution			Newly estab-lished	Institutions operating end of 2007
		exit	merger	total		
Banks	33	5	10	15	–	18
Merchant banking corporations	30	22	7	29	1	2
Securities companies[a]	36	8	7	15	20	41
Asset management companies[b]	31	6	7	13	33	51
Insurance companies[c]	45	11	6	17	9	37

Notes:
[a] Branches of foreign companies are excluded.
[b] Investment trust management companies have been classified among asset management companies since 2004.
[c] Excludes postal insurance.

Source: Bank of Korea (2007b: 66).

The banking sector reform in the wake of the 1997 crisis was closely related to the internationalization of the financial sector, which was in turn an integral part of the liberalization of the capital account. Although the government started to liberalize the capital market from the 1980s, it was only after the 1997 crisis that the capital market was fully liberalized for both inflows and outflows of foreign exchanges. As a result, foreign investors were allowed to purchase stocks and bonds in Korea, and to undertake M&As of Korean companies, including banks. As of the end of 2007, there were 71 foreign banks, branches and representative offices engaged in banking business in Korea. Their total assets amounted to 9.3 per cent of the total assets of the Korean banking sector (FSS 2008). By 2004, foreign capital accounted for more than 30 per cent of market shares of Korean banks and more than 50 per cent of ownerships of seven major commercial banks.

The government legislated in 2000 for a financial holding company system as part of its goal to improve the banking sector's global competitiveness (Bank of Korea 2008d).[5] Under the new system, various financial institutions such as banks, securities and insurance companies can be placed as subsidiaries under the same financial holding company which can provide core and non-core financial services.[6] As of August 2008, four financial holding companies had been established: Woori Financial Group, Shinhan Financial Group, Hana Financial Group and Korea Investment Holdings (Bank of Korea 2008d).

To enhance synergy effects and economies of scope among financial institutions, the government launched the so-called 'Bancassurance' in 2003. This allows banks, securities companies, mutual saving banks and credit card companies to sell insurance products on their own or through joint ventures with insurance companies. Banks are also allowed to sell equity-related financial products (Bank of Korea 2004b).

9.2.3 Assessment of the Reforms of the Banking Sector

The reform of the banking sector should be assessed on its longer-term health such as its stability, profitability and productivity. Non-performing loans of all domestic banks have declined remarkably from 8.3 per cent of total loans in 1999 to 0.6 per cent in 2007, comparable to their counterparts in other countries (Table 9.2). Table 9.2 shows that the BIS capital-adequacy rate of all domestic banks increased to 12.3 per cent by 2007, much higher than the minimum required rate of 8 per cent. These data show that banks now have a buffer against risk, an indication of their improved financial soundness and stability. With their stronger asset quality and capital base, together with universal banking operation, Korean banks are in a better position to cope with the macro-business environment than in the past. According to a 'stress test' by the Bank of Korea (2005a),[7] the Korean banking sector is better placed than before the crisis to handle isolated shocks.

As indicated by the liquidity ratio in Table 9.2, domestic banks are quite prudential in the sense that short-term loans and deposits are balanced. Related to the global financial crisis in 2008, it should be noted that the ratio of won-denominated loans to deposits gradually increased from 74.6 per cent in 2002 to 123.7 per cent. The ratio of 123.7 implies that domestic banks are funding home lending with foreign borrowing. However, as certificates of deposit (CDs) are deposit-like in nature, the ratio of won-denominated loans to deposit plus CDs was 104.4 per cent in 2007, indicating that domestic loans were funded by domestic deposits.

Table 9.2 Performance indicators of Korean banks, 2002–07

	2002	2003	2004	2005	2006	2007
NPL ratio (%)	1.9	2.0	1.6	1.0	0.7	0.6
Bank BIS capital ratio (%)	11.33	11.16	12.04	12.95	12.75	12.28
ROA (%)	0.6	0.17	0.85	1.27	1.11	1.10
ROE (%)	10.91	3.41	15.16	18.42	14.64	14.60
Liquidity ratio in won (%)[a]	106.0	104.7	111.1	109.8	107.8	104.9
Loan/deposit ratio (%)[b]	74.6	94.4	95.4	101.0	109.0	123.7
Loan/(deposit+CD) ratio (%)[c]	70.9	88.2	88.5	91.1	95.6	104.4
Foreign reserves ($bill.)	121	155	199	210	239	262

Notes:
[a] Ratio of won-denominated assets to won-denominated deposits with maturities less than three months.
[b] Ratio of won-denominated loans to won-denominated deposits.
[c] Ratio of won-denominated loans to won-denominated deposits plus CDs (certificates of deposit).

Sources: Financial Supervisory Service (FSS) (2008); for foreign reserves: Bank of Korea (2008d).

The entry of foreigners into the financial sector and the penetration of foreign investors in the management of Korean banks have ended government interference with the banking sector. Greater autonomy and universal banking operations, together with intensifying competition against foreign banks, have enhanced banks' operational efficiency (OECD 2005: 173; Y.S. Kim 2005; Kang and Kim 2005). The profitability of the banking sector has also improved through enhanced asset quality, retrenchment of employees and the closure of a large number of branches, and the increased scale of the banking system. As shown in Table 9.2, the rates of return on both assets and equity, though fluctuating, have increased substantially in the recent past (FSS 2008).[8] Another indicator of the soundness of the banking sector is that a number of Korean banks have listed on the New York Stock Exchange (Song 2003). These listings indicate international approval of the management and accounting standards of Korean commercial banks and will have positive effects on attracting foreign direct investment into the banking sector.

There is considerable evidence that the banking sector has been reformed successfully and that operations, stability and profitability within this sector have improved remarkably since 1997. Yet some unfinished issues of reform remain and there is room for further improvement. Through the bank reform process, some banks were effectively taken over by the government. To eliminate government interference in the banking sector and to eradicate the lingering legacy of 'banks never fail', commercial banks in which the government holds substantial shares should be privatized.

Some concerns have been expressed about the lack of competition in the banking sector. Soon after the financial crisis, the number of banks decreased markedly through financial consolidation (Table 9.1). As of the end of 2004, the concentration rate in Korea was significantly higher than that in the United States and Japan, but similar to that in Canada (Bank of Korea 2005b). The Bank of Korea (2008c) shows that the concentration ratio increased from 31.1 per cent in 1996 to 59.6 per cent in 2007, and argues that a persistent low rate of competition would have negative effects on the efficiency and stability of the banking system.[9] The high concentration is attributable to highly prohibitive regulations on entry into the banking industry and government influence on M&As among banks.[10]

To further raise their stability and profitability, banks should further diversify their operations and develop into universal banks.[11] They should expand their business scope toward non-traditional banking areas such as selling insurance and equity-related products and undertaking securities underwriting and securitization. The lack of competitive pressure in the banking industry diminishes the motivation to increase profits or to develop innovative banking products. This is reflected in unchanged banking business practices. Over the 1997–2007 period, the proportion of banks' traditional loans based on collateral and guarantees remained more or less unchanged at about 60 per cent of total won-denominated domestic loans, and the proportion of interest income of banks also remained more or less unchanged at about 84 per cent.[12] This indicates that banks still have limited profit opportunities, which adversely affects their competitiveness in relation to those of advanced countries.

To enhance its competitiveness against global counterparts as well as its business efficiency, the banking sector should be further internationalized. Korean banks should expand their operations to foreign countries through their branches and subsidiaries and localize their operations. Since the liberalization of the capital market, the government has been encouraging domestic banks to expand overseas by simplifying the establishment process of overseas branches or subsidiaries. In 2004, overseas lending of funds raised by Korean banks was only 1.6 per cent, as compared to 21.5 per cent by large US banks and 15.4 per cent by Japanese banks. Overseas branches of Korean banks accounted for 1.2 per cent of the total number of branches, compared to 28 per cent by large US banks (H.Y. Kim et al. 2005). This may indicate the lack of skills and expertise required for international operation of Korean banks.

The corporate governance of banks also has room for further improvement. There is still a significant proportion of internal directors on the audit committees of Korean banks, by comparison with US and European banks that fill their audit committees completely with external directors. Although more than half of Korean banks' board members are external, many of these board members are not professionals in the banking business, but are academics, former politicians or highly ranked civil servants. Graham (2005) argues that Korean banks and other financial institutions lack staff with skills and talent by global standards. Many of the best and brightest of Korea's university graduates in the social sciences work for the government, and those who work for the private sector tend to prefer large *chaebols* over financial institutions. Korean banks have been reluctant to hire foreigners for positions requiring specialized skills. Exacerbating this is the fact that the labour market for the Korean financial sector lacks flexibility and its unions are strong and militant compared to their foreign counterparts.

9.3 THE SECURITIES MARKET

9.3.1 The Korean Securities Market prior to 1997

Korea sought to develop a securities market from the 1950s as it recognized its importance for economic development by pooling capital and allocating it to appropriate investment projects, monitoring management of firms and diversifying risk.[13] An important advantage of market-based financing over bank-based financing is that the former, in general, provides long-term capital to the corporate sector and in particular to venturesome projects. Jin et al. (2004) argue that the market-based financial system is more conducive to economic development based on high-technology industries. As the Korean economy has to rely on high technologies for its future development, the Korean financial system should move further toward a market-based system. The market-based financial system is increasingly becoming a global standard, so adopting a market-based financial system helps Korean corporations improve their international competitiveness.

During the early development stage (1956–71), a number of important institutions were established to harness the stock market. They included the Korean Stock Exchange (KSE), the Securities and Exchange Law and the Korea Securities Finance Corporation, and the Law on Fostering the Capital Market. In spite of government efforts to develop the stock market, Korea experienced four market crashes – in 1958, 1959, 1962 and 1970 (Kim and Yoon 1992: 23) – indicating the shallowness and narrowness of the market.[14] In conjunction with embarking on the heavy and chemical industrialization policy (1972–80), the government further introduced a number of new policy measures and institutions to develop the stock market. Over the period 1972–77, the Korean Composite Stock Price Index (KCSPI), the Public

Corporation Inducement Law, the Korea Securities Settlement Corporation, the Korean Securities and Exchange Commission (KSE) and its executive body, the Securities Supervisory Board, were established (Kim and Yoon 1992). Over the period 1981–96, a series of important events occurred related to the stock market. The new Korea Composite Stock Price Index (KOSPI) was introduced in 1983, replacing the KCSPI. In 1996, a secondary segment of the Korean securities market was established mainly to support the financing of new ventures and small business. The stock price index for this secondary is known as KOSDAQ (Korean Securities Dealers Automated Quotations).

Table 9.3 Key statistics for listed stocks and bonds, 1963–2007

Year[a]	No. of listed co.	Amount of new stocks issued	Turnover value (trill. won)	Market capital-ization (trill. won)	Turnover ratio (%)	Market capital-ization to GDP (%)[b]	Public bonds issued (trill. won)	Corporate bonds issued (trill. won)
1963	15	–	–	–	223.2	2.0	–	–
1970	48	–	–	0.1	45.7	3.7	–	–
1980	350	0.2	1.1	2.5	44.9	7.0	0.9	1.0
1990	669	2.9	53.5	79.0	67.6	54.6	33.6	11.1
1995	721	6.3	142.9	141.2	101.2	35.4	55.6	23.7
1996	760	5.3	142.6	117.4	121.5	26.2	49.4	29.9
1997	779	3.4	162.3	71.0	228.6	14.5	49.7	34.3
1998	748	14.3	192.8	137.8	139.9	28.5	394.1	5.6
1999	725	41.1	866.9	349.5	240.0	66.0	112.3	30.7
2000	704	14.3	627.1	188.0	333.5	32.5	137.3	58.7
2001	689	12.2	491.4	255.9	220.7	41.1	119.0	87.2
2002	683	9.9	742.2	258.7	248.9	37.8	46.8	77.5
2003	684	11.2	547.5	355.4	193.2	49.0	155.7	61.8
2004	683	8.4	555.8	412.6	148.3	53.0	215.4	50.4
2005	702	6.8	786.3	655.1	154.4	80.8	258.2	48.1
2006	731	6.4	848.5	704.6	128.7	100.1	246.5	40.9
2007	745	17.2	1362.8	951.9	156.7	105.6	273.8	45.2

Notes:

[a] For the period 1963–70, values are in bill won.

[b] The ratio of market capitalization to GDP for the period 1995–2007 was calculated by the author.

Sources: for the number of listed companies: KRX (2007); for the rest: Bank of Korea (2008a).

Over the period 1972–96, the number of listed companies increased from 66 to 760, and market capitalization increased 477-fold, reaching 117.4 trillion in 1996 (Table 9.3). However, despite a series of policy measures and incentives, the stock market played only a minor role in mobilizing funds for

Korea's industrialization policy. This happened for a number of reasons. Because Korean companies were predominantly family-owned and managed, they were highly reluctant to go public out of concern for dilution of ownership and loss of control. In the absence of healthy underwriters, companies were uncertain about successful distributions of their issued shares and proper pricing. From the beginning of the first five-year economic plan in 1962 until the mid-1980s, debt capital was readily available for *chaebols* as policy loans. In addition, laws allowed subsidiaries of a corporation (*chaebol*) to cross-guarantees of debt-payments, thereby facilitating the raising of bank loans and the shifting of funds among subsidiaries. There was a prevailing perception until the 1997 crisis that *chaebols* were too large to fail. Under perceived low risk, businesses prefer debt capital to equity.

The major investors in Korea's stock market were individuals rather than financial institutions (KSDA 2005: 176). Trust in listed companies and in shares as long-term investments was low because of past market crashes, prevalent rumours of insider trading and low levels of ethics in Korean business. Market supervision lacked independence from government and political manipulation. Management of listed companies was undertaken and controlled by the principal shareholders and their family members, and management transparency and financial disclosure were left wanting. In addition, neither a transparent accounting system consistent with international standards nor proper credit rating agencies had developed. Due to poor corporate governance, minority shareholders were not well represented on corporate boards, nor had they adequate means to monitor and discipline the management of *chaebols* (Hwang and Seo 2000). Korean companies had a minimum dividend payout policy, as they were inclined to reinvest their profits as part of their growth strategy. Thus, individual investors did not usually expect steady flows of dividends from their shares, but pursued short-term capital gains on the stock markets. Individual investors in Korea did not hold shares for more than three months on average (Hwang and Seo 2000).[15] Because of the herd effect, individual investors overreacted to movements in the stock market, rendering the securities market vulnerable to volatility and risk.

Institutional investors did not play an important role in the Korean securities market, as they were not allowed to exercise their voting rights at shareholders' meetings (Akama et al. 2003). There were various legal limits on the shares of assets that financial institutions could hold (Hwang and Seo 2000). Many of these institutional investors such as non-bank financial institutions were owned by *chaebols*, and thus could not influence the corporate governance, financial disclosure and operational transparency of listed *chaebols* and their subsidiaries. Public funds in Korea could not, in principle, purchase stocks by law until the Pension Act was amended in 2004 (KSDA 2008: 41).[16] Furthermore, the government utilized public funds for various policy purposes rather than for meeting the interests of fund members. With no mandate of upholding the interests of fund members, public funds did not influence corporate governance, nor did they play a significant role in the securities market.

Table 9.4 Securities transactions and ownerships and outstanding bonds, 1963–2007

Year*	Securities		KOSPI (annual average)	Foreigner's ownership of stocks (%)	Individual ownership of stocks (%)	Public bonds listed (trill. won)	Corp. bonds listed (trill. won)
	Stocks (trill. won)	Bonds (trill. won)					
1963	–	–	n.a	n.a	n.a	66.0	n.a
1970	–	–	n.a	n.a	n.a	26.7	n.a
1980	1.1	1.0	108.8	2.0	56.0	0.4	n.a.
1990	53.4	3.3	747.0	1.9	51.6	29.0	22.1
1995	142.9	1.4	934.9	10.1	36.4	69.5	56.5
1996	142.6	1.4	833.4	11.6	34.3	102.4	73.1
1997	162.3	4.0	654.5	9.1	39.8	138.1	86.0
1998	192.8	15.5	406.1	10.4	38.8	214.6	119.4
1999	866.9	293.6	806.8	12.4	39.0	253.3	111.1
2000	627.1	27.2	734.2	30.2	20.0	296.8	127.9
2001	491.4	14.2	572.8	36.6	22.3	363.5	141.2
2002	742.2	47.2	757.0	36.0	22.3	422.6	141.3
2003	547.5	214.9	679.8	40.1	19.7	471.2	136.1
2004	555.8	384.1	832.9	42.0	18.0	545.9	115.5
2005	786.3	362.8	1073.6	39.7	18.4	614.6	107.4
2006	848.5	294.9	1352.2	37.3	17.9	677.7	101.2
2007	1362.8	351.3	1710.3	32.4	21.8	736.1	94.8

Note: * For the period 1963–70, values are in million won.

Sources: For stocks, bonds, KOSPI, public bonds listed, and corporate bonds listed: Bank of Korea (2008a); for foreigner's ownership of stocks: KRX (2007); and for individual ownership of stocks: KRX (2008).

For a variety of reasons, the bond market was underdeveloped and remained the primary market until 1997 (Table 9.4). Public bonds issued did not grow significantly until 1997 because of the strong fiscal positions the government maintained over time. In 1997, the ratio of public bonds issued to GDP was only 10.1 per cent, well below the average of about 70 per cent in other OECD countries (OECD 1999: 101). Over a long period, effective yields on government bonds were kept below free-market levels as part of the government strategy to use financial markets to promote real sector development. Hence, most public bonds were allocated to government-controlled financial institutions rather than being purchased by individual investors. The public bond market remained highly inefficient, as several categories of bonds were traded with different maturity dates, and bonds with similar maturities had different interest payment schedules and irregular issuing dates (OECD 1999: 101). Therefore, relatively little trading of public bonds took place, and most investors tended to hold them until maturity. Because of its small size and its high inefficiency, the government bond market could not lay a foundation for the development of a corporate bond market by providing a benchmark yield curve for the valuation of corporate bonds.

For many years, few corporations issued bonds on the open market. A corporate bond guarantee system was introduced in 1972, under which commercial banks, merchant banks, insurance and securities companies, and sister subsidiaries of *chaebols* guaranteed bonds with relatively short maturities (KSDA 2005: 75). Such a guaranteeing system was required due to underdevelopment of credit rating agencies for private companies. The final buyers of these bonds were usually investment trust companies and bank trust companies which held on to their bonds until maturity (OECD 1999: 102). Few long-term bonds with more than a three-year maturity or transferable bonds were issued. Therefore, there were no divergences in default risk, and different yields of corporate bonds by credit risk did not develop. With the lack of a spectrum of different corporate bond yields together with the lack of benchmarking of government bonds, the secondary bond market could not develop. In the absence of a secondary market, banks and other financial institutions, who were major buyers of bonds, had their funds tied up and suffered from liquidity squeeze. Similarly, issuers of corporate bonds could not find an opportunity to buy back bonds they had issued.

Foreign investors could not participate in the Korean bond market until recently. Liberalization of the bond market started in 1994, allowing foreign investors to purchase bonds under various constraints and limits (J. Kim et al. 2003). This was attributable to government concerns about a dramatic increase in foreign capital inflows due to substantially high domestic interest rates compared with international counterparts. In essence, the government planned to delay opening the long-term bond market until interest rates significantly converged. However, Korea has since recognized the banking sector as one of the main culprits of the 1997 crisis, and the importance of the securities market for the economy. The government has sought earnestly to develop the securities market further, and has undertaken structural reforms accordingly.

9.3.2 Structural Reform of the Securities Market since 1997

To develop the securities market for its conventional role of pooling capital and allocating it to appropriate investment projects, not only the securities market itself but also the corporate sector have to undertake reforms to improve their corporate governance, transparency and accountability. To this end, a variety of institutional reforms have been undertaken in both areas after the 1997 crisis. The new Financial Supervisory Commission (FSC), with greater strength and autonomy, replaced the Securities and Exchange Commission. In addition, the Securities and Futures Commission (SFC) was established under the FSC to oversee the futures market (KSDA 2008: 35).

As part of the corporate restructuring in 1998, the government sought to strengthen corporate governance with four main purposes related to the securities market: to improve management transparency, to strengthen minority shareholders' rights, to introduce outside directors for the board and to clarify the management responsibility of *chaebol* owners (Hwang and Seo 2000). As discussed in Chapter 8, *chaebols* were required to adopt international accounting standards and produce group-wide consolidated financial statements comprising all affiliates. Circular equity investment, cross-debt guarantees, and unfair trading among affiliates of *chaebols* were prohibited.[17]

To enhance minority shareholders' rights, a cumulative voting system was introduced to amplify the voices of minority shareholders in electing board members. Shareholder proposal rights were introduced. The minimum number of shares required to file suits or submit proposals to general shareholders' meetings was reduced from 1 per cent, to 0.01 per cent of total shares in 1998. In the same year, institutional investors were allowed to exercise their voting rights at shareholders' meetings (KSDA 2008: 33). To improve corporate governance for all financial institutions as well as for listed private companies, at least three outside directors have to be appointed to make up over half of total board membership, and an audit committee has to be set up with outside directors forming at least two-thirds of its membership (Bank of Korea 2004a: 32). To enhance the accountability of *chaebol* owners, they were forced to assume overt director status representing one of their *chaebol* companies. Also, to enhance market control over *chaebols*, various restrictions on M&As including hostile takeovers were eliminated, and the bankruptcy system was reformed to facilitate and expedite bankruptcy procedures.

Securities firms went through structural reforms, just as banks did after the crisis. They had to increase their capital ratios, and non-viable firms were liquidated. Fifteen securities companies were closed down following exits or mergers in the period between 1998 and the end of 2007 (Table 9.1). Over the same period, 20 new securities companies, excluding foreign companies' branches, were established, and by the end of 2007, 41 securities companies were operating in Korea (Table 9.1). Securities firms became subject to more intense competition. Deregulation allowed security firms to set brokerage commissions freely, thereby engendering fierce price competition and lowering profitability across the industry (S.H. Cho 2007). Another pivotal development was online trading, the value of which, including stocks, futures and options, grew at a phenomenal rate (KSDA 2005: 175). Online trading strengthened the position of retail investors by providing them with convenient and easy access to a wealth of financial information on a par with that available to professional traders. Retail investors could easily scrutinize services and commission fees of securities firms, leading them to compete with each other for better services and lowered commission fees.

Another pivotal development in the Korean securities market since the 1997 crisis has been the introduction of futures and options. Prior to 1997, the phenomenon of futures was virtually non-existent as a risk management tool. Because of government protection, hedging against future risk was not seriously considered, but it has become a necessity after the crisis. Finally, the Korea Futures Exchange (KOFEX) was established in 1999, and the trading of futures and options of financial and commodity products commenced in earnest (KSDA 2008: 35). In 2005, to improve the efficiency and international competitiveness of the securities market, the Korea Exchange (KRX) became Korea's sole exchange through the consolidation of Korea's three main exchanges: the Korea Stock Exchange, the KOSDAQ and KOFEX (KSDA 2008: 28).

The government bond market developed quickly after the crisis. High government budget deficits resulting from funding restructuring costs necessitated issues of public bonds. To further develop the bond market including the secondary bond market, the government has issued a variety of bonds with different maturities, including a 20-year bond in 2006 (KSDA 2008: 42). The three major bonds are treasury bonds, national housing bonds and foreign exchange stabilization bonds. The government, with its focus on three-year maturity treasury bonds, has established a benchmark yield curve with which to value corporate bonds and to develop the secondary bond market (EAAU 1999: 329). This has led private companies to issue large sums of corporate bonds on a non-guaranteed basis. By the end of 2006, 99.7 per cent of outstanding corporate bonds were non-guaranteed bonds (KSDA 2008: 127).

The Korean securities market was fully opened to foreign investors from 1998 (KSDA 2008: 189). Foreign investors are allowed to purchase stocks of listed companies freely on the KSE and KOSDAQ without being subject to investment ceilings for either individuals or aggregate of foreigners, with the exception of a few state-owned corporations. They are also allowed to participate in bonds and derivatives without being subject to ceilings. Foreign investors can purchase up to 49 per cent of shares in securities companies, and are also permitted to establish representative or branch offices, joint-venture securities companies or subsidiaries in Korea. Liberalization of the capital account has also allowed any type of local investor to invest in foreign securities that are listed on foreign stock exchanges. As of the end of 2007, Korean securities companies had established a total of 44 overseas operations in ten cities around the world (KSDA 2008: 204).

9.3.3 Assessment of the Reforms of the Securities Market

Since the 1997 crisis, the Korean securities market has undergone a remarkable transformation in its configuration and improved substantially in attracting foreign and domestic capital. As shown in Table 9.3, the securities market has expanded markedly in terms of the number of new stocks issued, turnover rates, market capitalization and public and corporate bonds. For instance, the amount of new stocks issued jumped from 3.4 trillion won in 1997 to 17.2 trillion won in 2007, although fluctuating over time. The market capitalization value increased its ratio to GDP from 14.5 per cent in 1997 to 105.6 per cent in 2007 (Table 9.3). The amount of public and corporate bonds increased from 84 trillion won in 1997 to 319 trillion won in 2007.

The introduction of online trading has contributed to the high trading volume and the popularity of day trading among individual investors who have become the main traders on the stock market. In 2007, individual investors were responsible for about 91.5 per cent of total stock trading on the KOSDAQ, and for 52.9 per cent of the Korea Stock Exchange (KRX 2007). With day trading prevalent, retail investors were drawn into short-term gains, thereby exacerbating the volatility in stock prices and exposing themselves to potential price and market distortions caused by speculative trades and herd mentality. This may be reflected in a wide fluctuation in the trading value of the KOSDAQ (Table 9.5). Soon after its commencement in 1996, the KOSDAQ increased markedly with the expansion of venture industries, but plummeted in the wake of the bursting of the information technology (IT) bubble in 2000 until it recovered substantially from 2004 (Table 9.5).

Since the commencement of the Korea Futures Exchange (KOFEX) in 1999, futures and options markets have expanded much more rapidly than the share market. Trading value of KOFEX products amounted to 1.7 times that of the Korea Stock Exchange (stocks and bonds) in 2000 and to 5.2 times in 2007 (Table 9.5) The upsurge in the futures market is attributable to the necessity for and greater understanding of the need to hedge against the increased volatility risk in stock prices, exchange rates and interest rates. In particular, the underlying asset in the KOFEX has been the three-year government treasury bond introduced in 1999, which accounted for 19.6 per cent of the total trading value of KOFEX products in 2007 (KRX 2007). Korea treasury bond futures have deepened the bond market and contributed particularly to the development of the secondary bond market. The secondary bond market has markedly expanded in the post-crisis era. As shown in Table 9.4, trading value of bonds increased from 4 trillion won in 1997 to 351.3 trillion won in 2007 – an 88-fold increment, a much faster increment than that in the trading value of stocks.

Table 9.5 Annual trading values in the Korean securities market, 2000–07 (trillion won)

Year	KSE		KOSDAQ	KOFEX*	Total
	Stocks	Bonds			
2000	627.1	27.2	578.9	1107.5	2340.7
2001	491.4	14.2	425.2	2270.1	3200.9
2002	742.2	47.2	294.1	2564.7	3648.2
2003	547.5	214.9	266.4	4121.1	5149.9
2004	555.8	384.1	155.7	4058.7	5154.3
2005	786.3	362.8	446.4	4560.2	6155.7
2006	848.5	294.9	427.5	5491.2	7062.1
2007	1362.8	351.3	500.7	7154.5	9369.3

Note: * Monthly trading values were multiplied by 12.

Source: KRX (2007).

Under the fully internationalized securities market, foreign investment in Korean securities has increased most remarkably and has become a dominant force. The number of foreign investors registered with the FSS increased from 9954 in 1999 to 22 993 in 2007. In 2007, 70.8 per cent were institutional investors such as investment companies, pension funds, banks, securities companies and insurance companies (KSDA 2008: 195). Foreign ownership of Korean stocks rose to 42.2 per cent in 2004 and declined to 32.4 per cent in 2007 (Table 9.4). Foreigners also held 4.5 per cent of the total amount of bonds listed in 2007 (KSDA 2008: 197).

After the 1997 crisis, the Korean government has sought to transform its financial system from a bank-based system to a market-based system by developing the securities market, and has made some progress. However, it appears that the government has failed to achieve tangible results, and the securities market has continued to play only a minor financial intermediary role. As shown in Table 9.6, no strong trend has been set in terms of the sources of funds for corporations since 1997. Over 2004–06, the proportion of direct financing increased substantially, but declined markedly in 2007, with the average proportion over the 2000–07 period being quite similar to that of 1997. The stock market has failed to maintain stable growth since 2000 with annual issuance of new stocks amounting to about 10.8 trillion won over the 2000–07 period (Table 9.3), which accounted for only 4.9 per cent of gross fixed capital formation.[18]

Table 9.6 Sources of funds for corporations, 1997–2007 (%)

	1997	2000	2003	2004	2005	2006	2007
Indirect financing	36.0	31.8	38.6	4.3	21.8	35.8	53.7
Direct financing	35.4	37.5	32.4	43.1	48.5	42.1	25.3
(shares)	13.1	18.2	36.5	43.6	32.6	20.5	15.4
(bonds)	22.3	19.3	–4.1	–0.2	15.3	21.2	9.5
Foreign sources	10.9	10.8	5.3	12.8	5.2	3.1	3.0
Others*	17.7	19.9	23.7	39.8	24.5	19.0	18.0

Note: * Commercial credit, borrowing from government, and payment arrears.

Source: Bank of Korea (2008e).

Another indicator for the languishing stock market is the continuous decrease in the number of companies listed on the Korean Stock Exchange (KSE) between 1998 and 2004, although this figure rose again over the 2005–07 period probably attracted by the rise in the KOSPI (Table 9.4). Similarly, the ratio of market capitalization to GDP reached 66 per cent in 1999, then declined significantly until 2005 when the ratio started to increase, reaching 105.6 per cent in 2007 (Table 9.3), comparable to the ratios in leading OECD economies (World Federation of Exchanges 2008).

The bond market has shown a trend similar to the stock market but did not rebound in 2005 and 2006. Corporate bonds issued peaked at 87 trillion won in 2001, and declined to 45.2 trillion won in 2007 (Table 9.3).[19] It is argued that there is a tendency to undervalue bonds issued by small and medium-sized companies because of underdevelopment of the credit risk analysing industry (SERI 2005a). Trading values of bonds has recently remained quite volatile (Table 9.4), indicating unhealthy signs in the bond market.

A series of developments on both the supply and demand sides of the securities market have prevented sustained growth in the market. To protect their management from takeover attempts by foreign investors, corporations have shunned issuance of new shares and bought back their existing shares. After the full opening of the domestic capital market, not only foreign financial institutions but also private equity investment funds advanced into Korea. An increasing number of Korean companies are exposed to a potential threat of management takeover by foreign investors or equity funds.[20] Under a high level of foreign investment, reaching 42.2 per cent of Korean stocks, Korean companies cannot help but stress strategies to fend off the threat of foreign takeover at the expense of their business strategy.[21]

Individual investors have been increasingly turning away from the securities market. In 1999, individual investors held 39 per cent of the total market capitalization of KSE-listed stocks, and then their holdings continuously declined to 21 per cent in 2007 (Table 9.4). This is due to ebbing of investors' trust in the securities market. Since 1999, this trust has run low due to a series of developments such as alleged scandals associated with the market and manipulations of stock prices, the bursting of the IT bubble in 2000, and a number of credit card defaults in 2003. The credit risk analysis industry has not fully developed and world-renowned credit risk analysis companies have not yet arrived in Korea. Financial disclosure and operational transparency of listed companies have not adequately improved due to inefficient corporate governance (Hwang and Seo 2000).

There are some rising concerns in Korean society about the rapid advancement of foreign capital and its implications for corporations in Korea. It has been argued that foreign investors stress high dividend payout, rather than improving the competitiveness and long-term business strategies of Korean companies.[22] These concerns have weakened public support for foreign investment in the market. All these developments have hindered the transition of the Korean financial system toward a market-based one.

9.3.4 Financial Investment Services and Capital Markets Act (FSCMA)

It has been globally recognized that the provision of a wide range of innovative financial investment services through capital markets is one of the strategic areas for economic development. A number of advanced countries and some East Asian emerging countries have restructured their capital market framework to develop their investment services industries further (KSDA 2008: 19). However, the Korean investment services industry could not develop on a par with those of advanced and neighbouring competitor countries due to its multitudinous and complex laws and regulations. Korean laws allowed only very narrowly defined investment products and services, and regulatory firewalls existed between investment services institutions, and between particular types of investments services. For example, futures trading firms could not engage in securities businesses, and brokerage and asset management were also strictly separated entities (S.H. Cho 2007). As a consequence, financial investment companies had little incentive to develop innovative new products and to achieve economies of scope, a crucial success factor. In 2008 only five kinds of derivatives were traded on the KRX (KSDA 2008: 96). Against this background and to enhance the competitiveness of securities industries, the FSCMA was enacted in 2007 and implemented in February 2009, as originally scheduled (KSDA 2008: 21).

The main features of the FSCMA include the following. The FSCMA consolidates six existing laws regulating capital markets and the investment services industry (S.H. Cho 2007).[23] In terms of investment products, the FSCMA changes from the positive system to the negative system together with a new broad definition of investment products. This will expand the scope of investment products greatly, including derivatives and securities. The financial regulations change from institution-based to function-based. This amounts to relocating the firewalls from between institutions to between functions. Under the old Act, different institutions were supervised by different supervisory rules, while under the FSCMA the same regulation is applied to the same function regardless of the institutions that provide it. Hence, a single investment company with a single license can carry out six functions such as dealer, brokerage, collective investment schemes, investment advisory, discretionary investment, and trusts. The FSCMA also allows financial investment companies to provide asset transformation services, money transferring, banking and foreign exchange functions, and to participate in the payment settlement system. In addition, investors may establish their consolidated asset management accounts with financial investment firms, which work as accounts in commercial banks (KSDA 2008: 23; Bank of Korea 2008b: 87). Investor protection is expected to be strengthened by introducing a new know-your customer rule, the suitability principle, the product guidance rule,[24] and by preventing misleading advertisements and solicitation. Also, the strong firewalls between different functions will prevent misuses of information, manipulations of the market or conflicts of interest arising from cross-functional business (Bank of Korea 2008b). All this is in addition to the existing investor protection mechanism of the Financial Supervisory Service (FSS) and two self-regulatory organizations, the Korea Securities Dealers Association (KSDA) and the Korea Exchange (KRX).

The FSCMA is a timely and appropriate reform of the securities industries in Korea. It will assist the development of diversified, sophisticated and innovative financial products that meet the needs of a variety of customers – the typical roles of the capital market. This will enhance the capital-raising function of the market, thereby increasing the size of the Korean capital market which is relatively small and underdeveloped (S.H. Cho 2007).[25] The FSCMA will help meet the challenges of knowledge-based economic development that requires more venturesome and innovative projects and the development of risk-hedging skills. All this will transfer financial funds from banks to the investment services industry. As financial investment companies play more active roles as risk bearers and conduct multiple functions, there will be strong incentives for financial investment firms to expand through M&As and through overseas expansion to spread risk and to achieve economies of scope. As a result, a limited number of surviving financial investment firms will evolve into true investment banks comparable in scope and function to major international players. This process appears to be the intent of the Act.

With the FSCMA implemented, the financial sector will consist of banks, insurance and financial investment firms. There is a variety of apprehension about the new terrain of the Korean financial sector. Korean financial investment companies will have to compete against leading global investment banks in advanced countries. Since Korean financial investment companies are not well equipped to compete against their global competitors in terms of product development know-how, experience, human and capital resources, risk-taking behaviour and global networking, there is a risk that foreign investment banks may take controlling positions in the Korean financial investment market. This leaves the Korean financial sector vulnerable to the financial activities of foreign investors. As witnessed in the September 2008 US financial crisis, a big loss incurred by one financial investment company is highly likely to spread to other related financial firms, leading to a crisis in the financial system. The world has witnessed that self-regulation in the financial service industry has not worked properly. There is no guarantee that the self-regulatory mechanism such as the know-your-customer rule, the suitability principle or the firewalls between products would work appropriately in Korea. Again, as witnessed in the United States, function-based regulations under the negative list system may not keep up their oversight with ingenious developments of new products.

The 2008 US financial crisis and ensuing global financial turbulence provided an opportune time for the Korean authority to reflect on the FSCMA before its implementation and supplement it with some new schemes to forestall possible crises. In view of the sources of problems with the US capital market, the following suggestions could be made. Leverage taken by a financial investment company should be limited to a certain level to curb excessive risk-taking. Although the self-regulation system is in place as a risk management tool, the extent to which the system will actually monitor and supervise the rapidly rising areas of derivatives and other innovative products remains a concern. To manage risk from financial investment products, including asset-backed securities like mortgage-backed securities, their database should be developed to include all information on those products issued in the market, including the risks involved and their transactions, thereby improving disclosure and monitoring. Also, the sellers of financial investment products should be properly qualified and licensed.

9.4 ASSESSMENT OF THE OVERALL FINANCIAL SECTOR REFORMS

9.4.1 Comparative Assessment of the Financial Sector

As the Korean economy is widely open to the global economy and aspires to that of advanced countries, it is imperative to undertake a comparative evaluation of its financial sector. Both the International Institute for Management Development (IMD) and the World Economic Forum (WEF) measure the extent of financial market sophistication, efficiency and openness as part of their measurements of national competitiveness. According to the IMD (2008), out of 55 countries Korea ranked 41.2th in 2008 as an arithmetic average of its rankings in ten different financial service areas.[26] A number of East Asian countries such as Hong Kong, Singapore, Taiwan, Japan and Malaysia, let alone advanced countries, fared better in most of the ten financial areas. Quite similar results are shown for Korea by the WEF (2007), although rankings of the two institutes cannot be easily compared. In 2007, out of 131 countries studied by the WEF, Korea ranked 31.4th as an arithmetic average of its rankings in seven different financial service areas.[27] A number of East Asian countries such as Hong Kong, Singapore and Malaysia ranked higher.

The relatively poor rankings for Korea convincingly indicate that the Korean financial sector has not kept up with the rest of the world and has to improve itself across the board. In particular, Korea's poor rankings with 'soundness of banks' (69th of 131 countries by WEF), 'banking regulations' (53rd of 55 countries by the IMD) and 'transparency of financial institutions' (48th of 55 countries by the IMD) indicate clearly that Korea has to improve regulations and supervision of the financial sector.

9.4.2 Assessment of the Financial Regulatory and Supervisory Systems

The world has lately witnessed many developments in the global financial industry. They include: financial globalization; expansion of the size and business areas of financial organizations; liberalization of the financial industry; developments of innovative financial products; and the proliferation of various types of funds such as private equity funds, hedge funds and mutual funds. The Korean financial sector has fallen behind with respect to these global trends mainly due to its burdensome regulations. As examined in

Chapter 10, Korea still has a large number of economic regulations in general. Related to the financial sector, there are two broad categories of regulations: one group directing financial organizations and their activities, and the other group controlling aberrations. For the banking sector under the former set of regulations, the types of business that banks can conduct are not specified by law and regulations, rather they are determined by the Minister of Finance and Economy, thereby creating a positive list of banking activities. It is therefore difficult for the banking sector to diversify and specialize. Without specialization it is difficult for medium-sized banks to survive and provide funds to SMEs (KERI 2007).[28] It was also pointed out earlier that entry barriers into the financial industry are high, and the concentration rate has been rising in the recent past (KERI 2007). Hence, to advance the banking sector, further regulatory reforms should be undertaken, whereby the entry barriers are lowered and the positive system of banking activities is replaced by a negative system.

Korea should undertake further deregulation or liberalization of the securities market. A maze of regulations had previously compartmentalized the securities market and restricted the types of financial products, thus rendering the market inefficient and prohibiting developments of innovative products. Recognizing the dysfunction of the securities market, the government has enacted the FSCMA. The detailed regulations for the implementation of the FSCMA have yet to be introduced, and it is too early to properly assess the Act. Yet, it is expected that, through the FSCMA, about 40 per cent of about 300 regulations on the securities market will be deleted, modified or simplified (KERI 2007).

Korea has to improve its financial supervisory regulations and institutions. The financial supervisory framework changed after the 1997 crisis, consolidating and strengthening the fragmented financial supervision. The basic mandate of the financial supervisor is to maintain a stable financial sector and at the same time to protect financial consumers. The supervisor should maintain independence from the government and possess the required expertise, and transparency should be maintained in the supervisory process. From an institutional perspective, the FSC which was established in 1998 lacks independence from the government, although it is a statutorily independent government agency under the authority of the president. This is evidenced by the fact that the FSC was in charge of undertaking the restructuring and consolidating of the financial sector under government directions soon after the 1997 crisis, which was beyond its basic role.

The lack of FSC autonomy results from its membership structure. The FSC consists of nine members: the Chairman, one Vice-Chairman, three ex officio members representing relevant government agencies, three part-time members, and one professional full-time member appointed by the Chairman for a three-year term. The Chairman and Vice-Chairman who are appointed by the President for three-year terms are also full-time members. Out of the nine members, only one or two would not be associated with government agencies.[29] Another indicator of its lack of independence is that the Chairman has changed four times over five years since its establishment in 1998, even though the Chairman is appointed for a three-year term (B.Y. Kim 2003). The MOFE has maintained the role of law drafting, interpreting supervisory laws and regulations, while the FSC has held only a supervisory role, limiting its freedom in implementing supervision. Such a separation of policy-making and regulatory powers not only diminishes the supervisory independence but also duplicates supervision of financial organizations. In addition, a practice has been in place which allows FSC staff to move to and from the MOFE, undermining the credibility of supervisory independence. The lack of independence of the FSC in turn weakens its accountability.

Transparency, which also goes hand in hand with accountability, has to improve in supervisory policy and practices. The IMF (2003) and S.W. Lee et al. (2007) point out that there is a lack of transparency and consistency in supervisory laws and their implementation processes. There is also a perception in the market that violations of applicable regulations are often overlooked or weakly sanctioned and that prudential supervision is not applied equally, generating a perception of inconsistency and unfairness in implementation (IMF 2003). The law related to financial supervision has been revised 11 times from the time of the enactment in 1998 to 2007, clearly indicating a lack of legal stability (KERI 2007). Finally, there is a lack of expertise in supervision, leading to supervisory inefficiency. Only one or two members of the nine FSC members would be professional experts in the area. The ex officio members would have some difficulty in developing expertise as they are involved in two types of duties. Also the frequent reappointments prevent the development of expertise.

Recognizing the lack of independence of the Financial Supervisory Commission (FSC), the Lee Myung-bak government replaced the FSC with the Financial Services Commission, which is now assigned with policy-making power as well as the implementation role (KSDA 2008: 43). At the time of writing in mid-2009 it is too early to assess how efficient the new supervisory structure is in terms of independence, transparency and expertise. However, the composition and method of appointment of the new Financial Services Commission members has not changed significantly. Out of the nine members, four ex officio members (instead of three) and two persons (instead of one) are recommended by the Chair, and the majority of members are still government-affiliated. Another serious issue is the relationship between the Financial Services Commission and its executive arm, the Financial Supervisory Service (FSS), and the *raison d'être* of the two separate institutions. Under the institutional framework of the former FSC, the Chair of the FSC had a plenary power over the work of FSC and the FSS, as the Chair of FSC was also the Governor of the FSS. Under the new 2008 system, the linkage between the two organizations was cut, thereby losing the coordination between the supervisory policy-maker and the implementer. With the introduction of the FSCMA which requires efficient coordination and feedback between the policy-maker and implementer, it is suggested that the new Financial Services Commission and FSS should be unified as one organization and its independence further enhanced.[30]

9.5 CONCLUSION

This chapter has examined the transition in the Korean financial sector in the wake of the 1997 crisis and suggests ideas for the financial sector's future agenda with a focus on the banking sector and securities market, the two major pillars of the financial sector. The Korean government adopted a bank-based financial system and used the banking sector as a conduit for financing the government-led national industrialization policy over three decades from the 1960s. The government firmly controlled and protected the sector without implementing proper prudential supervision, causing moral hazard and a lack of transparency and accountability in the banking sector. As a result, the banking sector did not perform its principal responsibilities of risk assessment, credit allocation and monitoring debtor companies, particularly *vis-à-vis chaebols*, its primary customers.

These flaws and weaknesses within the banking sector contributed to the 1997 crisis and attracted substantial structural reforms thereafter. A new cabinet-level FSC was established. A number of banks and non-banking institutions were liquidated or consolidated, non-performing loans were purchased, and some banks were recapitalized with public funds. New systems were introduced to improve corporate governance and achieve greater transparency and accountability in the banking system. The financial sector and the banking sector were internationalized as an integral part of the liberalization of the capital account by 1997. As a result, foreign investors have penetrated the Korean banking sector as equity holders as well as management participants.

The reform of the banking sector has been largely successful when the health of the sector is assessed in terms of stability and profitability. Nonetheless, there remain outstanding issues and room for improvement. To eliminate government interference with the sector, it should privatize all of its holdings of shares in banks. Korean banks should have a global perspective and expand their operations beyond domestic boundaries and toward non-traditional banking areas. There is also room for further improvement in the corporate governance and risk management of banks.

The Korean securities market played only a minor role in funding for economic development until the crisis. Korea failed to develop a proper regulatory and institutional framework for the securities market, and its stock market had not developed on a par with the counterparts of advanced countries with respect to its traditional roles. Similarly, the bond market remained small and inefficient and only as a primary market until the mid-1990s. Although the securities market was more or less fully opened to foreign investors in conjunction with capital account liberalization, it did not attract significant foreign capital until 1997.

In the wake of the 1997 crisis, Korea has recognized the importance of the securities market and has sought its development in conjunction with its drive for knowledge-based economic development. In addition, the market-based financial system is increasingly becoming a global trend, necessitating Korea to develop its securities market in line with global standards. To this end, a series of reforms have been undertaken related to the securities market. As a result, Korea's financial system has substantially improved and the securities market has undergone a remarkable transformation in its configuration. The liberalization of foreign investment in the securities market was accelerated, leading foreign investors to be dominant leaders in the Korean securities market.

Despite the post-1997 reforms and relative success in attracting foreign and domestic capital, the securities market has failed to maintain stable growth and still plays only a minor financial intermediary role. This indicates that the government has failed to achieve tangible results in transforming the financial system toward a market-based system. The main cause of this failure may be found in the Korean financial investment services industry, the weakest area of its securities market. To boost this industry on a par with those of advanced and neighbouring competitor countries, the FSCMA was enacted in 2007 and implemented in February 2009.

The FSCMA liberalizes the Korean capital market by consolidating six existing laws regulating capital markets and the investment services industry, thereby reducing these regulations by 40 per cent. It has changed financial regulation from an institution-based system to a function-based system. In terms of investment products, the FSCMA has changed from the positive system to the negative system, together with a new broad definition of investment products, thereby expanding the scope of investment products. It also makes it easier for financial investment companies to enter specialized business areas. All this is to align the Korean financial sector to financial globalization, particularly for its financial investment service industry.

The FSCMA is a timely reform in the Korean securities sector. Despite its reforms after 1997, the Korean financial system is far behind advanced countries in terms of financial market sophistication, efficiency, transparency and openness. Therefore, Korea should further open and liberalize its financial sector, align it to global trends, and improve the financial investment services industry through the FSCMA. The new Act could enhance the capital-raising function and revitalize aggressive investments in the market. There is, however, some apprehension about the new terrain of the Korean financial investment service industry under the FSCMA, such as a risk of the Korean financial investment market being controlled foreign investment banks and a high vulnerability of the financial sector to crisis.

At this juncture, Korea has to improve, above all, its financial supervisory regulations and institutions. Korea's Financial Supervisory Commission (or the new Financial Services Commission) lacks both independence from the government and expertise, largely because of the high involvement of government bodies in the membership structure of the Commission. Frequent and irregular reappointments of the FSC members in the recent past have undermined its consistency and credibility. In this respect, it is suggested that all members be professional experts in the area and appointed by the President with the consent of the National Assembly, and have staggered and legally guaranteed terms. Transparency and stability in supervisory laws and their implementation processes have to improve. The lack of independence and transparency weaken the accountability and effectiveness of the supervisor. Finally, with the introduction of the FSCMA, that requires efficient coordination and feedback between the policy-maker and implementer, it is suggested that the new Financial Services Commission and its executive arm, the Financial Supervisory Service (FSS) be unified as one organization.

NOTES

1. There is a broad literature on the linkage between the financial system and economic development. See for example Allen and Gale (1997), Levine (1997) and Thakor (1996). M.H. Lee (2005) has found that causality runs from the development of financial system to economic development in Korea – not the reverse.
2. The four pillars of the financial market include, in general, banks, securities, insurance and trust. As examined in section 9.3, trust will be part of the securities market. The insurance market has played only a marginal role for Korean economic development, and it is not dealt with in this chapter.
3. For empirical evidence of the positive contribution of the banking sector to real economic growth in Korea, see Choe and Moosa (1999). For a chronological development of financial institutions of Korea, see P.J. Kim (1997).
4. One indicator of this overlending is the 1996 average debt ratio of 387 per cent for the 30 largest *chaebols* (Jwa and Yi 2001).

5. Establishment of a financial holding company by industrial entities, and of an industrial holding company by financial institutions, are prohibited. A holding company cannot manage or supervise the operation of its subsidiaries, nor can it engage in any other business of its own. A financial holding company must hold at least 50 per cent of the shares of a subsidiary (in the case of a listed subsidiary; 30 per cent otherwise) (*Invest Korea Journal* 2005).
6. The principal advantage of the financial holding company system is the scale and synergy effects it can create, such as the reduction of management costs through common ownership of infrastructure and information, joint marketing and product development, and efficient management of organizations and human resources.
7. A stress test measures the stability of the banking sector's profits or losses in response to 'exceptional but plausible events' such as drastic changes in macroeconomic variables including domestic production and exchange rates (Bank of Korea 2005a).
8. The FSC (2008) argues that the profitability of Korean banks is better than that of their peers in the advanced countries.
9. M.S. Kim et al. (2006) point out that the concentration rate of 70 per cent is a danger level.
10. Jwa and Hahn (2003) claim that in the United States and United Kingdom, the minimum capital requirement for establishing a bank is $1 million and £1 million respectively, while the Korean requirement is 100 billion won (or about 80 times that of the United States).
11. In the wake of the 2008 US financial crisis, Goldman Sachs and Morgan Stanley have become commercial banks combining investment and traditional commercial banking activities. This indicates the global trend toward a universal banking system.
12. These numbers are calculated by the author from FSS (2002, 2008).
13. There is a broad literature on the relationship between securities markets and economic development. It includes, to name a few, Harris (1997), Levine and Zervos (1998) and Singh and Weisse (1998).
14. For a further detailed list of developments of relevant events and institutions, see Korea Stock Exchange (2000).
15. According to the Securities Exchange Law, the minimum holding period required for shareholders to enable them to exercise important shareholder rights is six months. Thus, individual investors holding shares for less than six months could not make use of their shareholders' rights (Hwang and Seo 2000).
16. In 1995, for instance, only the four largest public funds invested in stocks (Hwang and Seo 2000). As of 2007, 57 pension funds invested 15 per cent of their funds in equity (KSDA 2008: 41). For a chronology of securities market development, see KSDA (2008: 43–6).
17. Immediately prior to the 1997 crisis, the cross-debt guarantees among affiliates of the 30 largest *chaebols* reached nearly half of their net worth. This, together with the absence of consolidated financial statements, made it extremely difficult to determine the risk profiles of *chaebols* (Akama et al. 2003).
18. SERI (2005a) points out that some companies bought back substantial amounts of their shares in the market and net capital raised from the stock market was much less than 10.8 trillion won per year.
19. SERI (2005a) points out that corporations have bought back matured bonds with proceeds of new bonds, and thus net bonds issued have been substantially less than the total amount of corporate bonds issued.
20. Up to 1996, there were only eight cases of hostile takeovers in Korea, while there were 25 such cases over the two-year period 2002–03 (SERI 2005b).
21. It has been argued that Korea's financial regulations make it more difficult for local companies to maintain management control against foreign takeover than those of developed countries such as the United States (SERI 2005b).
22. There was a highly publicized case of the takeover of an ailing Korean commercial bank (the First Bank) by a foreign equity fund at a bargain price, and its sale after its market value recovered. There was another incident of a takeover bid of one of Korea's *chaebols* by foreign investors without legally changing its investment purpose from 'generating profits' to 'influencing management' (SERI 2005b).

23. The six laws that are consolidated into the CMISA were the Securities Exchange Act, the Futures Trading Act, the Collective Investment Act, the Trust Service Act, the Korea Exchange Act (KRX) and the Merchant Banking Act (S.H. Cho 2007). Banking and insurance are governed by their own laws and regulations.
24. All sellers of financial products need to explain so that the investor understands the nature of the products and the risks the investor is taking, and to get the investor's oath of such understanding.
25. The ratio of market capitalization of shares to GDP was 100.1 per cent in 2006, although it increased to 116 per cent in 2007 due to an unusual surge in market capitalization. In 2006, those for Hong Kong, Singapore and Australia were, respectively, 903 per cent, 281 per cent and 152 per cent. Another indicator of the relative small size of Korean financial assets is that the ratio of the stock of all financial assets to gross national income (GNI) increased gradually from 7.20 in 2003 to 8.88 in 2007. The same ratio for the United States and Japan in 2007 was, respectively, 10.25 and 11.92 (Bank of Korea 2008e).
26. They are: ease of credit flows, investment risk, venture capital availability, efficient financial services, banking regulations, financial risk, adequate stock market financing, transparency of financial institutions, international portfolio investment assets and international portfolio investment liabilities.
27. These include: financial market sophistication, local equity market financing, access to bank loans, venture capital accessibility, freedom of international capital flows, soundness of banks, and securities market regulations.
28. This is reflected in banks' current practices of traditional loans based on collateral and guarantees and the majority of their income (84 per cent) being interest income, as pointed out earlier.
29. Although the President of the United States has the power to appoint all five commissioners of the US Securities Exchange Commission (SEC) with the advice and consent of the Senate, none of the commissioners has been fired in the wake of the September 2008 financial crisis in the United States, indicating their independence from government.
30. Australia introduced its financial sector reform with the introduction of the Financial Service Reform Act 2001. The Australian Securities and Investments Commission (ASIC) is one unified implementer of financial supervision. The Australian financial reform and its implementation have been acclaimed as a success. The size of the securities market has doubled over five years since the reform (H.T. Kim 2006), and more importantly in 2009 the Australian financial market seems well placed to withstand the global financial crisis.

REFERENCES

Akama, H., K. Noro and H. Tada (2003), *Financial and Corporate Restructuring in South Korea*, Bank of Japan, http://www.boj.or.jp/en/ronbun/03/data/ron0306b.pdf.

Allen, F. and D. Gale (1997), 'Financial markets, intermediaries, and intertemporal smoothing', *Journal of Political Economy*, **105** (3), 523–46.

Bank of Korea (2004a), *Financial System in Korea*, Seoul: Bank of Korea.

Bank of Korea (2004b), 'Major contents of financial structural adjustments in 2003', (in Korean), *Monthly Bulletin*, February, 42–58.

Bank of Korea (2005a), 'Analysis of the stability of the Korean banking sector through a stress test', (in Korean), *Monthly Bulletin*, January, 31–56.

Bank of Korea (2005b), *Financial Stability Report 2005*, April, Seoul: Bank of Korea.

Bank of Korea (2007a), *Financial System in Korea*, Seoul: Bank of Korea.

Bank of Korea (2007b), *2007 Annual Report*, Seoul: Bank of Korea.

Bank of Korea (2008a), *Economic Statistics Yearbook 2008*, Seoul: Bank of Korea.

Bank of Korea (2008b), 'Summarised contents of the Financial Investment Services and Capital Markets Act and other finance-related acts', (in Korean), *Monthly Bulletin*, February, 81–96.

Bank of Korea (2008c), 'Assessment of the competition extent of the banking industry', *Monthly Bulletin*, August, 23–49.

Bank of Korea (2008d), 'Introduction of financial holding companies: their impacts and prospects', *Monthly Bulletin*, September, 23–58.

Bank of Korea (2008e), *Flows of Funds in 2007*, (in Korean), Seoul: Bank of Korea.

Cho, Sung-hoon (2007), '"Big bang" on Korea's capital markets: reform legislation and its impact', *Korea's Economy 2007*, Korea Economic Institute and Korea Institute for International Economic Policy, **23**, 19–23.

Choe, Chongwoo and I.A. Moosa (1999), 'Financial system and economic growth: the Korean experience', *World Development*, **27** (6), 1069–82.

East Asia Analytical Unit (EAAU) (1999), *Asia's Financial Markets: capitalising on reform*, Canberra: Department of Foreign Affairs and Trade (DFAT).

Financial Supervisory Service (FSS) (2002), *Bank Operation Statistics 2002*, Seoul: FSS.

Financial Supervisory Service (FSS) (2008), *Bank Operation Statistics 2008*, Seoul: FSS.

Graham, John M. (2005), 'Will Korea become a hub for international finance?', *Joint US–Korea Academic Studies*, **15**, 57–76.

Harris, R.D.F. (1997), 'Stock markets and development: a re-assessment', *European Economic Review*, **41**, 139–46.

Hwang, Inhak and Jung-Hwan Seo (2000), 'Corporate governance and *chaebol* reform in Korea', *Seoul Journal of Economics*, **13** (3), 361–89.

International Institute for Management Development (IMD) (2008), *World Competitiveness Yearbook 2008*, Lausanne: IMD.

IMF (2003), *Financial Sector Assessment Korea*, Joint IMF–World Bank Financial Sector Assessment Program, Washington, DC: IMF.

Invest Korea Journal (2005), 'In the wake of Korea's "big bang"', *Invest Korea Journal*, **23** (2), 74–7.

Jin, T.H., D.Y. Kim and J.H Ham (2004), 'Development direction of the Korean financial system', (in Korean), *Quarterly Economic Analysis*, Bank of Korea, **10** (2), 1–31.

Jwa, Sung-Hee and G.S. Hahn (2003), 'Korea's strategy for financial reform: a new institutional economics perspective', in O.Y. Kwon, S.H. Jwa and K.T. Lee (eds), *Korea's New Economic Strategy in the Globalization Era*, Cheltenham, UK and Northampton, MA, USA: Edward Elgar Publishing, pp. 113–29.

Jwa, Sung-Hee and Insill Yi (2001), 'The Korean financial crisis: evaluation and lessons', in O.Y. Kwon and W. Shepherd (eds), *Korea's Economic Prospects: from financial crisis to prosperity*, Cheltenham, UK and Northampton, MA, USA: Edward Elgar Publishing, pp. 73–98.

Kang, Jong-Gu and Hyun-Ui Kim (2005), 'Effects of foreign capital penetration on domestic banks', (in Korean), *Financial System Review*, **13**, 114–31.

Kim, Byung Yoon (2003), 'A study on the independence and accountability of the Financial Regulatory Agency in Korea', (in Korean), *Korean Journal of Securities Law*, **4** (1), 109–43.

Kim, He-Yeon, J.K. Lee and Y.M. Seo (2005), 'Estimates of competitiveness and development direction of Korea's large banks', (in Korean), *Review of the Financial System*, Bank of Korea, **12**, 159–81.

Kim, Hyung-Tae (2006), 'Expected effects of the Financial Investment Services and Capital Markets Act (FSCMA)', (in Korean), mimeo.

Kim, I. and T. Yoon (1992), *An Investor's Guide to Korean Capital Market*, London: Quorum Books.

Kim, J., H. Kim and Y. Wang (2003), 'Macroeconomic effects of capital account liberalisation: the case of Korea', *Review of Development Economics*, **8** (4), 624–39.

Kim, Myung-Soo, Ji-Young Kim and Hoon Tae Ryoo (2006), 'Restructuring and reforms in the Korean banking industry', *BIS Papers*, **28**, 259–68.

Kim, Pyung-Joo (1997), 'Financial policies and institutional innovation', in D.S. Cha, K.S. Kim and D.H. Perkins (eds), *The Korean Economy 1945–1995: performance and vision for the 21st century*, Seoul: Korea Development Institute, pp. 186–237.

Kim, Yoon-soo (2005), 'Foreign ownership of banks and its effect on bank performance: the case of Korea', *Korea Observer*, **36** (2), 229–63.

Korea Economic Research Institute (KERI) (2007), 'The financial sector', *Comprehensive Analysis of Regulatory Reform*, **4-2**, 176–436.

Korea Exchange (KRX) (2007), *KRX Fact Book 2007*, Seoul: Korea Exchange, http://eng.krx.co.kr/index.html.

Korea Exchange (KRX) (2008), 'Shareholding by investor group – stock', http://eng.krx.co.kr/sns/sta/sta_1_077.jsp.

Korea Federation of Banks (2008), 'Industrial structure', http://www.kfb.or.kr/kfb_eng/.

Korea Securities Dealers Association (KSDA) (2005), *Securities Market in Korea 2005*, annual, http://www.ksda.or.kr/english/dataroom/publication_annual.cfm.

Korea Securities Dealers Association (KSDA) (2008), *Securities Market in Korea 2008*, annual, http://www.ksda.or.kr/english/dataroom/publication_annual.cfm.

Korea Stock Exchange (2000), 'Information brochure on Korea stock development', www.kse.or.kr/upload/pub/kse2000.pdf.

Lee, Myung-Hoon (2005), 'Does financial development contribute to economic development', *Financial System Review*, **13**, 69–88.

Lee, Siwook, W.H. Lim, J.H. Suh and M.J. Tcha (2007), 'Designing a new economic framework', in J.H. Suh and D.H.C. Chen (eds), *Korea as a Knowledge Economy: evolutionary process and lessons learned*, Seoul: Korea Development Institute, pp. 53–77.

Levine, R. (1997), 'Financial development and economic growth: views and agenda', *Journal of Economic Literature*, **35** (2), 688–726.

Levine, R. and S. Zervos (1998), 'Stock markets, banks, and economic growth', *American Economic Review*, **88** (3), 537–58.

OECD (1999), *OECD Economic Surveys: Korea*, Paris: OECD.

OECD (2005), *OECD Economic Surveys: Korea*, Paris: OECD.

SERI (Samsung Economic Research Institute) (2005a), *Korea Economic Trends*, 22 January, 1–20.

SERI (Samsung Economic Research Institute) (2005b) *Korea Economic Trends*, 9 April, 1–24.

Singh, A. and B.A. Weisse (1998), 'Emerging stock market, portfolio capital flows and long-term economic growth: micro and macroeconomic perspectives', *World Development*, **26** (4), 607–22.

Song, J. (2003), 'Shinhan close to NY listing banking', *Financial Times*, 24 September.

Thakor, A.V. (1996), 'The design of financial system: an overview', *Journal of Banking and Finance*, **20**, 917–48.
World Economic Forum (WEF) (2007), *The Global Competitiveness Report 2007–2008*, Basingstoke, UK and New York, USA: Palgrave Macmillan.
World Federation of Exchanges (2008), 'Statistics', http://www.world-exchanges.org/WFE/home.asp?menu=436&document=4822.

10. Public sector and regulatory reforms: a critical evaluation

10.1 INTRODUCTION

Chapter 1 demonstrated that excessive government intervention was one of the principal causes of the 1997 financial crisis. Reform measures undertaken by the government in response to the crisis included structural reforms not only to the financial and corporate sectors but also to the public sector. In 1998, President Kim Dae-jung initiated a new focus on public sector reforms with the objective of 'a small and efficient but better serving government', based on market-oriented, performance-oriented and customer-oriented principles (K.H. Lee 2004; Y.S. Ha 2004). This aimed at creating a competitive, efficient and highly productive government by slimming down the public sector and applying principles of competition and performance in public sector administration. Nonetheless, the Korean public sector is still regarded as bloated, concentrated, inflexible and inefficient (Jwa 2001; P.S. Kim 2000; Yang 2004).

This chapter examines and evaluates public sector reforms in Korea undertaken in the wake of the crisis. Two overarching issues of the public sector are whether public policies are consistent with citizen preferences, and whether public services are provided efficiently. The first question is concerned, in essence, with the political process of policy-making that was discussed in Chapter 3. The latter concerns the management of public administration for the efficient and effective performance of public functions. For its management efficacy and efficiency, the scope of the public sector is broad and includes its organizational structure, expenditure, revenue (taxation), regulation, quality of services and service delivery modes. This chapter chooses to narrow its scope to public administration and regulatory reform, excluding fiscal issues and privatization of state-owned enterprises. It is important to deal with regulatory reform, not only because it has a direct impact on the economy, but also because it provides an appropriate framework of governance to enhance national competitiveness and attract foreign capital to Korea.

The scope of management of public administration and regulatory reform is extremely broad. Following Ostrom (2005), an institutional approach is employed in analysing and assessing the management system of public administration and regulatory reform in Korea.[1] This system of public administration and regulations involves the organizational structure and the operational process. The organizational structure includes organizational goals and strategy, governance, and actions with administrative and regulatory tools, all within given social, political and economic environments. The operational process includes interaction among stakeholders, problem-solving resolutions and enforcement of the resolutions.

For the management of public administration, this chapter focuses on public governance, a crucial aspect of the institutional approach. Recently the concept of public governance was introduced to conceptualize appropriate forms of public management in terms of its effectiveness, efficiency and responsiveness. This has become a key concept for public management reform (Mimicopoulos 2007). In addition, a number of cross-country empirical studies have been undertaken in the area of public governance, based on which Korea's public sector management is assessed in comparison to the counterparts of advanced countries. This chapter also includes a critical examination and assessment of the regulatory reform management – not an examination of individual regulations. To this is added an international comparative evaluation of Korea's regulatory regime.

10.2 CRITERIA FOR GOOD PUBLIC GOVERNANCE

An extant literature exists on public sector and regulatory reforms undertaken in Korea after 1997 as well as their evaluation.[2] Yet, the mechanism and processes through which public sector reforms affect the economy are not adequately articulated, and the criteria for evaluating these reforms are not appropriately established. For this chapter, the criterion chosen is public governance under the institutional framework. Public governance refers to the formal and informal arrangements that determine relationships among stakeholders, how public decisions are made, and how public actions are carried out from the societal perspective (Mimicopoulos 2007). Good public governance means that the needs of the public are served effectively, efficiently and fairly. This is achieved via appropriate public decisions and actions implemented through suitable structures and processes for all aspects of executive management. Good public governance helps strengthen democracy, and promotes economic prosperity and social cohesion, as pointed out by a number of empirical studies (Mimicopoulos 2007). The framework for good public governance for this study is focused on economic perspectives.

Consistent with Korea's strategic economic goal of achieving the status of an advanced market-oriented, knowledge-based economy, the following interrelated dimensions of good public governance are selected:

- effectiveness;
- efficiency;
- predictability;
- transparency; and
- participation.[3]

Effectiveness refers to the extent of the achievement of the overall strategic goals. Effectiveness implies consistency, as no programme will be effective unless consistently pursued. Consistency requires public management in line with the overall strategic goals and their consistent pursuit over time or over political regimes. Effectiveness of public governance in Korea may be measured by the quality of public services, competence of civil servants, and citizens' participation.

Efficiency in the implementation of public administration should be one of the requisites in that the same output should be obtained with a reduction of inputs. Efficiency may be measured by the size of the public sector, which is in turn measured by the extent of public expenditure relative to GDP, the number of civil servants compared to overall employment, and wages rates for civil servants compared to employees in the private sector.

Predictability in the management of the public sector is the most important criterion for private businesses (Mimicopoulos 2007). Unpredictability increases risk in the business environment and produces large disincentives for investment. Predictability and consistency reinforce each other. Without an adequate level of consistency in public management, it is difficulty to maintain predictability. Predictability may be measured in part by political stability and the volatility of budgetary expenditures.

Transparency is increasingly considered a basic operating requirement for any government. Transparency requires unobstructed flows of information between the government and the public. Government should also be accountable for its actions and procedures. Accountability goes hand in hand with transparency. Transparency and accountability improve the credibility of government actions, enhance the rule of law and minimize corruption. They can thus be measured by the extent of the public's respect for laws and rules, and by the level of corruption.

Success of public management depends on how comprehensively the government incorporates the aggregate social interest or the 'encompassing interest' (McGuire and Olson 1996). As discussed in Chapter 3, government stakeholders are a diverse mix of citizens, businesses and special interest groups, often with widely divergent values and objectives. It is up to the government to drive these conflicting viewpoints down to a single set of strategic administrative procedures that best serve the public interest and achieve the strategic goals. This involves participation of stakeholders in decision-making and implementation of policy measures. Increased participation can be achieved by strengthening the freedom and pluralism of the media, and establishing consultative councils to facilitate the transmission of information between the public and private sectors. Public participation also implies the decentralization and devolution of the provision of public services. Participation may be measured by the extent of involvement of consultative councils in public management, the extent of the use of e-government, or the number of NGOs.

Kaufmann et al. (2008) produce the World Governance Indicators that measure perceptions of the quality of cross-country governance, synthesizing the views and reports of diverse sources, including the World Economic Forum (WEF), the International Institute for Management Development (IMD), the World Bank Business Environment Surveys and the Gallop World Poll. To mitigate the challenges of aggregating numerous cross-country indicators, Kaufmann et al. (2008) identify six fundamental dimensions of governance:

1. Voice and accountability: the quality of citizens' participation in politics and freedom of expression, association and media.
2. Political stability and absence of violence: the likelihood that the government will be destabilized by unconstitutional or violent means, including terrorism.
3. Government effectiveness: the quality of public services and bureaucracy, competence of civil servants, independence of civil service from politicians.
4. Regulatory quality: the quality of policy and regulations to permit and promote private sector development.
5. Rule of law: perception of the likelihood of crime and violence, society's compliance with rules, the enforcement quality of laws and contracts by the judiciary.
6. Control of corruption: the level of corruption by exercises of public power for private gain.

The measured score of each indicator ranges between –2.5 and 2.5, with a mean of zero, with higher scores corresponding to better governance. The percentile rank ranges from zero to 100 out of 212 countries and territories surveyed.

Against these six interrelated conditions for good public governance, the first part of this chapter examines and evaluates Korean public sector reforms since 1997. This will be done in a global comparative context. To this end, the World Governance Indicators and other cross-country indicators will be employed. Section 10.3 provides a brief descriptive overview of the major reforms undertaken in the area of public management since 1997.

10.3 ADMINISTRATIVE REFORMS

10.3.1 Government Structural Reforms

Korea was engulfed by financial crisis just weeks before the 1997 presidential election. The cumbersome size of government ministries and their inefficient organization was held to be one of the major reasons why the government did not foresee and deflect the crisis (Yang 2004). It quickly became obvious to the new President that widespread government restructuring should take place beyond what would normally occur under a new political administration. In addition, the IMF rescue conditions required drastic fiscal austerity measures, implying the reduction of some ministries and agencies. The election of Kim Dae-jung marked a watershed as the first peaceful transfer of power in Korean politics from the ruling conservative government to a liberal-democratic opposition party. It was thus expected that the new government would undertake drastic reforms of the public sector not only to meet the IMF rescue conditions but also to change the bureaucratic culture. Shortly prior to the inauguration of the Kim administration, the National Assembly passed the Administrative Procedure Act that provided the legal foundation for public sector reforms (APEC 2007). Reforms took place in February 1998, May 1999 and January 2001.

The first restructuring of the public sector commenced immediately after the new government was in place, with the stated objectives of: the rationalization of state functions to create smaller, more efficient government; the enhancement of efficiency by incorporating competition into public sector functions and among civil service personnel; and cultural change toward a more customer-oriented public service (Choi 1999; Jeong et al. 2005). To achieve these objectives, three basic directions for structural reform were established (Choi 1999):

- elimination and consolidation of redundant functions while maintaining or expanding services in areas of increasing demand (that is, welfare, environment);
- reductions in government regulations and the privatization of SOEs to stimulate private sector competition; and
- devolution of central authority to local governments.

A variety of structural reorganizations were undertaken under the Kim Dae-jung government. Noticeable among them were the establishment of the Office of Budget, and the Planning and Budget Committee under direct presidential authority, with a commensurate reduction of functions of the Ministry of Finance and Economy (MOFE). Primary responsibility for international trade negotiations was transferred from the Ministry of Trade and Industry to the Ministry of Foreign Affairs, which became the Ministry of Foreign Affairs and Trade (MOFAT). To remedy the lack of prudential supervision of the financial sector, supervisory roles were withdrawn from the Bank of Korea and MOFE and transferred to a new Financial Supervisory Commission (FSC) under prime ministerial authority. To enhance policy coordination and evaluation, and to eliminate redundant functions, the former Administrative Coordination Office was upgraded to the Office of the Prime Minister (Jeong et al. 2005).

The second restructuring of May 1999 adopted a more robust approach to rationalization of the public sector and sought specifically to reduce its workforce. The first restructuring of 1998 had focused more on structural change than on operational systems. Despite the relatively large changes in the 1998 reforms, public opinion held that the government had protected itself from the dramatic restructuring in the private sector, and that the pain was not being shared equally across society. Hence, the second restructuring sought directly to address public concerns, pressing for reductions in the workforce and transferring some service delivery responsibility to the private sector and local government (Jeong et al. 2005; Yang 2004).

A third restructuring, which took place in January 2001, was intended to reinforce certain social and economic policies expected to be important in the future. The position of Minister for Economic Affairs was upgraded to Deputy Prime Minister in response to criticisms that the lack of a central figure coordinating economic policy was making reform more difficult. The Minister of Education and Human Resources was upgraded to Deputy Prime Minister in charge of human resource management, due to the emergence of sensitive post-crisis issues such as the re-education of displaced workers and the development of human capital. The establishment of the Ministry of Gender Affairs was the final major development in the third government restructuring (Yang 2004; Chung 2000; Jeong et al. 2005).[4]

10.3.2 Government Managerial Reforms

Government managerial reforms were undertaken alongside structural reforms to enhance public sector efficiency (Lim and Hwang 2002; Jeong et al. 2005). The newly established Office of Budget introduced the 'total operational expense system', whereby the Office set a budgetary ceiling, under which each ministry and agency determined the priority and amount of specific expenditures (Choi 1999). This provided ministries and government agencies with greater flexibility and discretion in expenditure decisions. It was also intended to promote efficiency in the budget process by conditionally offering public servants a portion of any savings that they helped to create. Budget funds were also allocated to ministries and agencies in accordance with their achievements in implementing managerial reforms (Chang and Chae 2004). Another important reform to the budgetary process was the establishment of a budget advisory board to solicit expert advice from a wide spectrum of public and business specialists (Choi 1999).

As part of its second reform, the government sought to reduce the workforce and transfer some service delivery responsibility to the private sector and local government (Jeong et al. 2005). Each ministry was given one year to lay off a certain number of employees, and was prohibited from all recruitment and promotion during that time. Subsequently, the government capped its workforce numbers permanently, although some priority occupations such as teachers were excluded (Jeong et al. 2005). The number of government employees was reduced significantly during the post-crisis era. As shown in Table 10.1, the total number of civil servants at the end of 1997 was estimated to be 934 000 (including the central, provincial and local governments). This had been reduced to 868 000 by the end of 2001.

To improve efficiency further in government service delivery, codes of conduct, performance guidelines, incentive schemes and merit-based personnel management were introduced. A new Civil Service Commission (CSC) was established in 1999 to promote transparency, merit and neutrality in civil service personnel appointments (Chung 2000; P.S. Kim 2000; Yang 2004; Jeong et al. 2005). After 1997, the government has allowed the hiring of civilians for the top three civil service grades, thereby bypassing the high civil service examinations. Government pay scales were adjusted more in line with the private sector, and various pay incentives were introduced. The civil service has moved away from seniority-based salaries, toward a system where remuneration is differentiated within each pay grade relative to performance.

To improve the accountability and performance of civil servants, nearly 600 Public Service Charters were published by nearly 300 agencies from central and local governments, presenting performance targets and standards (Jeong et al. 2005). To prevent corruption, the Presidential Advisory Council for Anti-Corruption was established in 1999, and the Anti-Corruption Act was enacted in 2001. Under this Act, the Korean Independent Commission against Corruption (KICAC) was established in 2002 (Kwon 2008: 178). The Commission has set the direction for anti-corruption policy, establishing the Public Service Ethics Act and the Code of Conduct for Public Officials, and providing protection for whistle-blowers.

Table 10.1 Number of civil servants and government expenditure, 1992–2007

Year	Number of civil servants			Public expenditure		
	No. of civil servants (000s)	Growth rate (%)	Population (%)	Expenditure (trill. KRW)	Growth rate	GDP (%)
1992	886	–	1.99	45.5	9.5	18.5
1995	905	–0.24	1.97	71.6	18.6	19.0
1997	934	0.91	2.00	100.3	18.8	22.1
1998	887	–5.10	1.89	115.4	15.1	26.0
1999	878	–1.00	1.85	121.0	4.8	25.1
2000	872	–0.64	1.83	129.3	6.9	24.8
2001	868	–0.46	1.81	136.8	5.8	25.1
2002	890	2.52	1.85	136.0	–0.5	19.9
2003	916	2.92	1.89	164.3	20.8	22.7
2004	936	2.23	1.93	173.5	5.6	22.3
2005	931	–0.57	1.91	187.9	8.3	23.2
2006	957	2.81	1.95	205.9	9.6	24.3
2007	975	1.88	2.01	209.8	1.9	23.3

Source: For the number of civil servants for 2007: KNSO (2009); for public expenditure: KNSO (2008).

To improve transparency, a new Government Information Disclosure Act was introduced which provided the public with the right to request any government documents, except those related to national security. At the same time, public institutions had to create their own information management systems, through which information could be properly kept and speedily searched by making full use of information technologies (Jeong et al. 2005). In this context, the government initiated 'e-government', which uses the Internet as a 'one-stop processing' point for routine administrative procedures and applications, public provision of information, public feedback, government procurement, and liaison between central, regional and local governments (Yang 2004; Jeong et al. 2005).

Serious efforts were made by the Kim government to enhance public participation in government affairs. The Administrative Procedure Act of 1998 was designed to ensure the participation of citizens and civic organizations in the policy-making process through preliminary announcements on legislation and government policies and public hearings (APEC 2007). Citizens' participation was also promoted with the introduction of the above-mentioned online system, through which citizens and the government could exchange information and ideas. Management consulting was introduced in mid-1998 in all central government departments. Eight firms, including foreign companies, were selected through open tenders (P.S. Kim 2000). Finally, as part of its managerial reforms, the government attempted to change the culture of bureaucracy toward more customer-oriented public services. This was an attempt to cultivate the idea that the government is a service provider that must serve the public, rather than the traditional idea of 'top-down' government.

The Roh Moo-hyun government, inaugurated in February 2003, did not have the same mandate for public sector reforms as its predecessor. The Roh government identified five goals – efficiency, customer satisfaction, transparency, decentralization and participation – as key elements of its administration (APEC 2007). This was to fulfil Roh's political pledges of an 'effective and serving government', 'a participatory government' and 'regionally balanced development' (K.B. Kim 2007). To this end, the Roh government pursued continuous reforms over its five-year tenure. However, Roh did not undertake structural reforms beyond what would normally occur under a new political administration. Instead, he introduced continuous reforms in public administration and personnel management to foster effective, though not necessarily smaller or more efficient, government. The Roh government attempted to establish a 'reform culture' by coordinating, consolidating and networking reform processes across individual ministries. It also introduced the concept of the team and the business management system into public sector management (S.B. Kim 2007).

'Participatory government' aimed at social cohesion and voluntary cooperation with the state by fostering civil society organizations and establishing a large number of commissions and committees under the President, ministers and agencies. In 2005, there were 381 committees with 3100 committee members under the central government, and 1391 committees with 3292 members under provincial governments (Hwang 2007). In undertaking incessant reforms, the number of civil servants increased from 890 000 in 2002 to 936 000 in 2004 and further to 975 000 in 2007 (Table 10.1). In addition, the Roh government initiated the dispersal of central government ministries to the regions as part of its regionally balanced development plan.

10.3.3 Evaluation of Government Structural and Managerial Reforms

A number of Korea observers have argued that reforms introduced by the Kim and Roh governments have contributed to the effectiveness of governance. The Kim government attempted to improve governmental effectiveness by enhanced policy coordination, and targeting budgetary allocations toward the emerging needs of the public. Moon and Ju (2007) find that expenditure areas of emerging social demands, such as education, infrastructure and income distribution, increased relatively faster than other areas. The Roh government also made continuous efforts to respond to the needs of the public by encouraging civil participation. S.B. Kim (2007) argues that the business management system and the team concept introduced by the Roh government helped achieve the targets of administrative reform. Because of the similarity in ideology under the Kim and Roh administrations, relative consistency was maintained by carrying out reforms in the same direction, contributing to overall governance effectiveness.

It appears, however, that overall the public sector reforms undertaken by the Kim and Roh governments are not highly regarded. Jwa (2001) points out that public sector reform progressed quite slowly. Yang (2004) argues that by the time of the third reform by the Kim government in 2001, political expediencies appeared to have won out over the initial goals of reform, as indicated by the de-emphasis on the downsizing of government and by emphasis on quality of service. Lim and Hwang (2002) point out that there was no significant change in the public sector. They argue that overlapping functions among government agencies were not coordinated and that the government organization was still full of redundancy, corruption, red tape and a peace-at-any-price principle.

The weakest link in the public sector reforms undertaken by the Kim and Roh administrations was the lack of consistent coordination, evaluation and monitoring of the reform process. As discussed in Chapter 3, President Kim lost the capacity to pursue reform as he lost public support and credibility due to his lack of coordination skills, and corruption cases involving his associates. A variety of drastic reforms introduced by the Kim government lacked consistency over the first and third structural changes, and by the time of the third structural reform his government appeared to have lost the vigour of persistent reform. The Office of Budget and the Planning and Budget Committee played a key role in the reforms. However, they were weakened in their ability to push the reforms forward and to continue the policy coordination role when they were merged into the Ministry of Planning and Budget (MPB) in the second restructuring. The Kim government attempted to strengthen the responsibility for policy coordination by upgrading the role as part of the Prime Minister's office. However, the Prime Minister is appointed by the President and carries out presidential directives with no autonomous or real power.

The aggressive pursuit of multiple goals by the Roh government undermined his government's coherence and consistency in the process of policy-making and implementation, thereby losing public support and credibility, as attested by the crushing defeat of the government party in the 2007 presidential election. President Roh pledged to strengthen the role of the Prime Minister during his election campaign, but did not delegate any real power to the Prime Minister. In practice, prime ministers changed a number of times during the two administrations, indicating the lack of a policy coordination and evaluation role in the position of Prime Minister.

Given a single five-year term, the Presidential Office cannot perform the role of consistent coordination, evaluation and monitoring of reforms over time. Hence, an organization under direct presidential authority, with a legal foundation of substantial independence and autonomy will be needed to pursue public sector reforms in a consistent and coherent way. The organizational structure and operational process of this suggested organization may be modelled after the Regulatory Review Committee which will be discussed shortly. The lack of consistency is reflected in Korea's poor ranking in policy consistency. It ranked 49th and 47th, respectively, in 2006 and 2007 on the consistency of government policy direction out of 55 countries estimated by the IMD, although it improved to 37th in 2008 (IMD 2006, 2007, 2008).

Attempts to change the culture of the bureaucracy toward a more customer-oriented public service are not highly regarded. P.S. Kim (2000) points out that those civil servants who enjoyed privileges in the past were known to oppose the directions of the Civil Service Commission. Civil servants also suffered from reform fatigue due to constant pressure to undertake changes by the Kim and Roh administrations. The Roh government constantly introduced reforms based on a strong ideology which became controversial and, as a result, the government lost its political base and public support for its reforms, as well as engendering resistance among civil servants to their implementation.

In terms of the 'effectiveness' criterion of good public governance, as examined above, the World Bank regards the improvement in effectiveness of Korea's public governance quite highly, although it is still far behind the OECD average. As shown in Table 10.2, Korea's government effectiveness score on the World Governance Indicators had improved more or less steadily in the recent past. In 2007, Korea's government effectiveness score reached 1.26, compared with an OECD average of 1.57 in 2006. Over the 1996–2006 period, Korea's average value for government effectiveness was 0.88, while the OECD average was 1.67. Korea ranked 86 percentile for government effectiveness in 2007, indicating that 86 per cent of the countries surveyed were less effective than Korea.[5] This is compared to the OECD average of 90 in 2006. Insofar as maintenance of the rule of law is part of public administration, Korea's performance is quite poor relative to OECD countries and has not improved significantly. Table 10.2 shows that Korea's index of the rule of law remained more or less unchanged at an average value of 0.72 over the period 1996–2006, while the OECD average was 1.54.

Table 10.2 Governance indicators: Korea and OECD, 1996–2007

	1996	1998	2000	2002	2003	2004	2005	2006	2007
VA									
Estimate	0.50	0.62	0.61	0.74	0.75	0.71	0.75	0.61	0.66
Percentile rank	67.3	66.7	67.6	68.6	66.2	70.0	68.1	70.7	67.0
OECD: estimate	1.21	1.31	1.30	1.29	1.32	1.46	1.41	1.36	n.a
OECD rank	87.7	89.5	89.6	90.1	90.4	91.9	91.4	90.6	n.a
PV									
Estimate	0.15	0.11	0.17	0.31	0.32	0.48	0.55	0.38	0.45
Percentile rank	40.6	43.4	51.9	54.7	51.9	61.8	60.8	60.1	62.0
OECD: estimate	0.89	1.01	1.06	1.06	0.96	0.86	0.85	0.85	n.a
OECD: rank	80.1	84.0	85.1	84.1	79.9	76.7	76.2	76.4	n.a
GE									
Estimate	0.92	0.36	0.77	0.95	0.92	0.94	1.00	1.14	1.26
Percentile rank	77.6	70.8	76.1	81.3	79.9	78.5	78.9	82.9	86.0
OECD: estimate	1.76	1.64	1.66	1.72	1.72	1.69	1.60	1.57	n.a
OECD: rank	91.2	90.9	90.8	91.4	91.6	91.0	90.9	90.0	n.a
RQ									
Estimate	0.46	0.33	0.58	0.78	0.68	0.79	0.79	0.70	0.88
Percentile rank	72.1	53.7	67.5	74.9	70.9	73.4	71.8	70.7	79.0
OECD: estimate	1.07	1.23	1.38	1.41	1.45	1.46	1.38	1.38	n.a
OECD: rank	87.5	89.5	89.7	89.8	90.3	90.2	90.0	89.6	n.a
RL									
Estimate	0.70	0.71	0.74	0.79	0.65	0.70	0.78	0.69	0.82
Percentile rank	78.0	71.6	67.8	75.0	67.8	69.2	72.5	72.9	75.0
OECD: estimate	1.59	1.55	1.53	1.52	1.55	1.56	1.52	1.54	n.a
OECD: Rank	91.8	91.2	91.2	90.5	91.2	91.1	90.1	90.0	n.a
CC									
Estimate	0.32	0.10	0.19	0.37	0.29	0.29	0.50	0.29	0.36
Percentile rank	76.6	64.2	67.2	67.2	64.2	59.3	69.0	64.6	68.0
OECD: estimate	1.71	1.71	1.73	1.73	1.73	1.71	1.66	1.67	n.a
OECD: rank	90.6	90.5	91.3	90.3	90.8	90.4	90.3	90.2	n.a

Notes:
VA: voice and accountability;
PV: political stability and absence of violence;
GE: government effectiveness;
RQ: regulatory quality;
RL: rule of law;
CC: control of corruption.

Sources: Estimates for Korea: Kaufman et al. (2008); percentile rank for Korea for 1996–2005: Y.J. Lim (2006); percentile rank for Korea for 2006–07: World Bank Institute (2008); and estimates and percentile ranks for OECD: World Bank (2007b).

In terms of effectiveness in the provision of public services, particularly in the area of social welfare, Korea has performed quite poorly. The Korean public sector is substantially smaller than those of advanced countries. As shown in Table 10.1, the ratio of public expenditure to GDP was 23.3 per cent in 2007, significantly lower than the OECD average. In terms of the number of civil servants, Korea had 18.5 civil servants per 1000 population in 2004, compared to an OECD average of 51, and 26.4 in Japan (S.B. Kim 2007). In particular, the number of civil servants for public welfare was only 0.2 per 1000 population, compared to an OECD average of 12.2, and 2 in Japan in 2004.

To improve 'efficiency' in public governance, the Kim government introduced a variety of measures. However, a number of Korea observers have pointed out the failure of these measures in improving efficiency. As shown in Table 10.1, the number of civil servants gradually decreased from 934 000 in 1997 to 868 000 in 2001. K.B. Kim (2007) argues, however, that decreases in the civil service were undertaken without accompanying streamlining of the administrative apparatus or increases in productivity, and has simply resulted in the hiring of part-time workers. Measures to enhance the performance efficiency of civil servants fell short of achieving their intended targets because of the lack of a coordinated and determined push for it (K.B. Kim 2007). The Kim and Roh governments did not seriously pursue the new system of hiring talent and expertise from both the private and public sectors through competition (Lim and Hwang 2002).

It appears that the Roh government de-emphasized efficiency in implementing multiple reforms. Efficiency, measured by the number of civil servants and their salary, declined significantly during his tenure. The number of civil servants increased substantially from 890 000 in 2002 to 975 000 in 2007 (Table 10.1). As a percentage of the total population, the number of civil servants decreased gradually and consistently during the Kim government up to his third reform and then increased during the Roh administration. The ratio of civil servants to the population declined from 2 in 1997 to 1.81 in 2001, then increased steadily to 2.01 in 2007 (Table 10.1). As compared to other countries, Korea ranked 3rd and 4th, respectively, in 2004 and 2005 in public sector employment as a percentage of total employment out of 55 countries estimated by IMD (2006, 2007). Also, during the Roh administration, salary for civil servants increased remarkably. Table 10.3 shows that the ratio of civil servants' salary to GDP jumped from 1.6 per cent in 2003 to 2.1 per cent over the 2004–07 period. As a proportion of total government expenditure, salary to civil servants increased from 9.7 per cent in 2003 to 13.7 per cent in 2004, and slightly declined over time to 12.5 per cent in 2007. Salary per civil servant increased at an annual rate of 10.4 per cent over the 2002–07 period, while the wage level of all non-agricultural industries increased by only 6.8 per cent over the same period (KNSO various years).

Table 10.3 Expenditure on civil service salaries (personnel expenses), 2001–06

	Total salary (trill. won)	Salary expenses/ GDP (%)	Salary expenses/ total government expenses (%)	No. of civil servants (000s) (Table 10.1)	Salary/ civil servant/ year (000 won)
2001	n.a.	n.a.	n.a.	868	n.a.
2002	10.7	1.6	9.8	890	12 022
2003	11.4	1.6	9.7	916	12 445
2004	16.2	2.1	13.7	936	17 309
2005	17.2	2.1	12.8	931	18 475
2006	18.2	2.1	12.6	957	19 018
2007	19.2	2.1	12.5	975	19 727

Sources: KNSO (various years).

It is doubtful that 'predictability' has improved significantly in public management, because of the lack of consistency in the series of reforms undertaken, as discussed above. This is reflected in the volatility of budgetary expenditure and of the number of civil servants. Similarly, annual growth of public expenditure varied widely (Table 10.1). The lack of policy consistency reinforces the lack of predictability which in turn increases the risk factor in the business environment and produces large disincentives for investment. This may account for Korea's sluggish investment in the recent past. As shown in Chapter 1, gross investment as a percentage of GDP decreased from more than 35 per cent during the 1990s to about 30 per cent from 2000, and fell below 30 per cent over 2006–07. 'Political stability and the absence of violence' would have helped to enhance the predictability and consistency of public management. As shown in Table 10.2, the index of political stability and absence of violence improved substantially in Korea from 0.17 in 2000 to 0.45 in 2007. However, Korea's index lagged far below the OECD average throughout the period 1996–2006.

'Transparency' in Korean policy and public administration has improved and yet remained far behind the levels of advanced countries. Korea ranked 38th and 34th, respectively, in 2006 and 2007 on the transparency of government policy out of 55 countries estimated by the IMD (2006, 2007). As examined above, both the Kim and Roh governments made significant efforts to enhance transparency in public administration. In spite of all these efforts, the level of transparency in Korea, as measured by corruption levels, remains remarkably low, compared to the OECD average. As shown in Table 10.2, the control of corruption score is estimated to be about 0.29 over the 1996–2006 period, compared to the OECD average of about 1.71. Over the same period, Korea ranked about 65 percentile, compared to a more than 90 percentile for the OECD average. Korea also ranked quite poorly on the Corruption Perceptions Index by Transparency International (Table 10.4). Korea's rank has ranged from 40 to 50 on the index and has not improved in the recent past. The lack of transparency and accountability in the public sector is also reflected in the relatively low index score for the rule of law. As shown in Table 10.2, Korea's index of the rule of law was an average value of 0.72 over the period 1996–2006, compared to the OECD average of 1.55.[6]

Table 10.4 Korea's ranks in economic freedom, globalization, and corruption, 2000–08

	2000	2001	2002	2003	2004	2005	2006	2007	2008
HF	24	25	30	40	35	38	38	36	41
Kearney	n.a.	31	31	28	32	30	29	35	n.a.
TI	48	42	40	50	47	40	42	43	40

Sources: Heritage Foundation (HF) (2009); A.T. Kearney/*Foreign Policy* (2007); Transparency International (TI) (2009).

In terms of participation, the Kim and Roh governments made serious efforts to enhance popular participation in government affairs. Public participation measured by the voice and accountability indicator in Table 10.2, which represents the perception of the quality of citizens' participation in politics and freedom of expression, has improved somewhat in Korea in the recent past. However, Korea's average value for voice and accountability of 0.66 over the 1996–2006 period was well below the OECD average of 1.33.

The success of the public sector reforms undertaken by the Kim and Roh governments may be regarded as mixed. Government effectiveness has improved. However, Korea's value of government effectiveness has remained far below the OECD average. Efficiency has also improved, although with room for improvement, particular under the Roh government. Predictability and consistency have remained low because of the continuous introduction of multiple reform programmes with poor coordination. Serious efforts were made to enhance citizens' participation in public administration with some evidence of improvement. From the above analysis and assessment, the keys to success in public sector reform include a strong and consistent commitment by the President, participation of the key stakeholders, and public support for government reform measures. An organization with the legal authority for undertaking consistent coordination, evaluation and monitoring of public sector reforms is needed.

10.4 REGULATORY REFORM AND DEREGULATION

The lack of prudential supervision over the financial sector resulting from an inefficient regulatory structure was one of the causes of the financial crisis. Excessive regulations from the state-led development period intervened extensively in enterprise and market operations, lowering market efficiency and productivity. They also hindered incoming foreign direct investment (FDI) foreign investment in the Korean securities market. Therefore, in conjunction with the IMF rescue plan, regulatory reforms were pursued from the earliest days of the financial crisis and are a key element in the shift to a more market-oriented economic system.[7]

The scope of regulations is extremely broad in Korea, with 8083 regulations at the end of 2006 in the economic, political and social areas (KERI 2007). Hence, an analysis of individual regulations and their reforms is beyond the scope of this chapter.[8] Instead, the regulatory reform management system is analysed and assessed by an institutional approach. Then, the Korean regulatory regime is assessed and compared to other countries. Regulatory management is a central instrument in promoting competitive markets. Many countries have undertaken regulatory reforms to promote national advantages under globalization (Conway et al. 2005). In particular, regulations that raise unnecessary obstacles to competition, innovation and growth are being reformed by many countries. Hence, the Korean regulatory regime must be comparatively evaluated.

10.4.1 The Regulatory Reform Management System

The legal foundation of all regulatory reforms after the 1997 financial crisis is the Basic Act on Administrative Regulation (BAAR). This was introduced in the last days of the Kim Young Sam government, and provides the specific organizational structure for regulatory reforms and their detailed management process. The BAAR specifies the following legal requirements (KERI 2007):

- Establishment of the Regulatory Reform Committee (RRC).
- Registration of all regulations with the RRC and its public announcement.
- Mandatory Regulatory Impact Analysis (RIA) of all new and existing regulations.

- Comprehensive regulatory improvement plan by each ministry every year.
- Regulations based on adequate legal authority.
- Incorporations of opinions of ministerial policy-makers, the general public and interest groups.
- Introduction of sunset clauses for new regulations.
- Monitoring and evaluation of regulatory reform.
- Publication of annual reports of regulatory reforms.

The Regulatory Reform Committee (RRC) was established by the Kim Dae-jung government in April 1998. The RRC is located administratively under the President and is co-chaired by the Prime Minister and a civilian. It consists of 20 members, seven of which are cabinet ministers, and 13 civilian members consisting of academics, industry leaders and consumer advocates who are appointed by the President for two-year terms. The major functions of the RRC include the basic direction of regulatory policy and procedure across government, and the implementation of the regulatory reform process as delineated by the BAAR. In doing so, the RRC requires all individual ministries and local governments to establish their own regulatory review and reform committees; makes proposals for regulatory review to individual ministries and local governments; undertakes reviews of regulations; and monitors and evaluates regulatory improvement in each ministry and local government.

The guiding principles for regulatory reform undertaken by the Kim government include (Choi 2001):

- eliminating all anti-competitive economic regulations;
- reforming of regulations so as to minimize protection of suppliers and to enhance users' benefits; and
- benchmarking of global regulatory standards.

These principles are consistent with the government's strategic goals of gearing the economy toward a market-oriented, knowledge-based economy under globalization. The RRC undertakes review of regulations based on the proposals submitted by individual ministries and local governments. All proposals for new regulations and those that strengthen existing ones must be attached with a Regulatory Impact Analysis (RIA). The RIA is used to determine the efficiency of regulations by subjecting them to cost–benefit analysis. Through this process, the RRC makes the initiating ministry justify its regulatory proposals. All regulations now have a five-year 'sunset clause', and must be explicitly renewed or will lapse (Yang 2004). The RRC attempts to align Korea's regulatory system more closely with WTO and OECD frameworks, eliminating those regulations that are contrary to the international framework and global standards (Choi 2001). To improve transparency, overlapping regulations are to be combined into a single, unified regulation, and excessive discretion by field-level bureaucrats is to be reduced. Finally, the RRC has the authority to monitor and evaluate regulatory improvements in each ministry by establishing the assurance system of compliance and enforcement, and a post-evaluation system.

The Roh Moo-hyun government carried on the same regulatory reform policy as that of its predecessor until 2004 when it established the Regulatory Reform Task Force (RRTF), not under the BAAR but by presidential decree (KERI 2007). The RRTF is a body comprised of government ministers and chaired by the President. The RRTF supplements the function of the RRC, dealing with individual regulations by focusing on the practical problems identified by business groups and overlapping regulations and policy measures under multiple ministries. The RRTF adopts a whole-of-government approach by coordinating relevant regulatory reforms across multiple ministries. Also in 2004, the Business Difficulties Resolution Center (BDRC) was established, providing a one-stop ombudsmen service to resolve the regulatory difficulties of business (KERI 2007).

10.4.2 Progress in Regulatory Reform

Too many poor-quality regulations with a broad scope of application were some of the main issues identified in the wake of the 1997 crisis. Most regulations had long been established as part of the state-led industrialization strategy. They protected suppliers by minimizing competition through the licensing process and other high entry barriers. The underlying tenet of these regulations was to restrict some activity with a principle of 'restricted in principle, allowed as exception'. Some regulations were established not by law but by administrative guidance. They lacked clear standards, procedures and outcomes and there were many overlapping regulations under multiple ministries. As a result of these excessive regulations and their poor quality, the burden on business was high (KERI 2007).

Deregulation was pursued by the Kim Dae-jung government under the proviso that all regulations which hinder market competition are to be eliminated, except for those required for the preservation of the environment, public safety or health (Choi 2001; Yang 2004). All regulations were scheduled to lose their status by the beginning of 1999, and were then required to be either eliminated, or reconstituted on a proper legal basis. The number of regulations decreased from 11 125 in 1998 to 6308 by the end of 1999, 43.3 per cent of the initial number (KERI 2007). However, the number of regulations had since increased to 8083 as at the end of 2006.

To enhance competition further, the government has taken action to prevent monopolies and oligopolies, and has also been empowered to protect small businesses and consumers since 2000 (OECD 2007: 30–31). Competition policy has turned more toward core competition problems related to efficiency goals and away from its historic focus on conglomerate financial structure and governance. To allow market forces to determine market composition, competition policy has been applied uniformly since 2002, ending a practice of specifically monitoring the top 30 *chaebols* (OECD 2007: 31). The government also reduced the number of business lines where entry of larger firms was restricted, from 88 to 45 by 2001. It planned to eliminate them all by 2007 as a way of removing protection and levelling the domestic playing field while also enhancing international competitiveness.[9]

10.4.3 Evaluation of the Regulatory Reform System

Although substantial progress has been made in the regulatory management system, further efforts at improvement should be made. First, Korea still maintains the positive regulatory system in which all activities are 'restricted and controlled and allowed as exception' (KERI 2007). This system should be transformed to a negative system, whereby all activities are allowed unless listed as restricted. Second, the governance and independence of the RRC has to improve. Although the RRC is established under the President as a permanent organization, its operation is still subject to other government agencies for its personnel and budget, rendering the independence of the RRC questionable. With its budget controlled by another agency, it would not be easy to staff the RRC with required experts. The strategic function of the RRC should not be weakened by establishing parallel institutions. A new organization (the RRTF) established under the Roh government, although supplementary to the RRC, may create some overlapping of authority and risk fragmented and inconsistent implementation of reform. The role of the RRTF should be subsumed into the RRC.

Third, the cooperation of front-line bureaucrats should be enhanced. Since it is individual ministries and local governments that identify regulations to be reformed, their cooperation is critical for any success. Beyond this, the relationship between the RRC and individual ministries is vertical, although consultation between them is required within a specified period.[10] The RRC directs individual ministries and local governments with regard to regulatory reforms and review. The top-down approach hinders the cooperation and involvement of field-level bureaucrats. This dilutes the effectiveness of reforms and their implementation. An incentive scheme should be introduced for field-level bureaucrats to encourage their proactive involvement.

Furthermore, local governments are under the jurisdiction of the Ministry of Administration, which in turn monitors regulatory reforms at the local government level. This indirect relationship between the RRC and local governments appears to be ineffective for the regulatory reform process. Because the cooperation of all stakeholders is vital, the RRC requires continuous commitment of the President for its successful pursuit of regulatory reforms. This is not always the case, as attested by President Kim Dae-jung's lacklustre support for the reform during the later part of his regime.

Fourth, it is critical to improve the cooperation of non-government stakeholders, particularly those interest groups who may lose from regulatory reforms. The BAAR specifies the relationship and consultation process between the RRC and government agencies, while no specific consultation mechanism has been established between the RRC and interest groups and the public (OECD 2007: 43). Part of the reform principles is to enhance competition and users' benefit at the expense of suppliers or interest groups, including professional organizations such as lawyers, accountants, medical practitioners and so on. Any regulatory reform that lessens existing privileges will face resistance from interest groups, thereby obstructing the reform. This could be the reason why, as pointed out in Chapter 5, there are still a large number of regulations imposed on the service sector. To enhance cooperation from these interest groups, the regulatory review process of the RRC should improve its objectivity, professionalism and fairness by incorporating peer review, consultation with professional experts and *ex post* evaluation.[11]

Fifth, the mechanism of providing information on the scope and contents of regulations should be improved to enhance the cooperation of relevant stakeholders. The system of registration of regulations with the RRC is meant to provide information to relevant stakeholders including interest groups and citizens as well as government agencies. KERI (2007) points out that some regulations still remain unregistered and some multiple regulations are registered as a single one. Hence, KERI (2007) argues that the registration system does not provide an adequate level of information on the scope and content of regulation. It also argues that Korea should establish a comprehensive electronic database for regulatory management as a condition of registration of regulations, which is accessible to both the government and the public on the Internet.

Sixth, the jurisdiction of the RRC should be expanded. Under its current mandate, the RRC does not include policy areas such as taxation, subsidies, and industrial and regional development policies. Also, the RRC is not empowered to reject laws passed by the National Assembly.[12] Recently a growing number of bills have been introduced by the National Assembly without going through the regulatory quality process of the RRC (KERI

2007). Hence, strong cooperation with regard to regulatory reviews should be institutionalized between the RRC and the National Assembly. Alternatively, the National Assembly should establish an institution to ensure the regulatory quality of laws initiated by members.

Seventh, a more systematic review of regulatory reform should be undertaken by fully implementing the RIA and the sunset clause. The RIA will provide valuable information with which to persuade the relevant stakeholders of the need for regulatory reform. Unfortunately, it has become a routine formality rather than an instrument for regulatory decision-making, mainly because of the lack of required experts and political support at national and local levels. Similarly, the Sunset Clause has not worked efficiently, as shown by the rising number of regulations in the recent past (KERI 2007; OECD 2007: 28–9). Through training and staffing of experts, the policy-making culture of civil servants should change to integrate RIA and sunset clauses into the policy-making process.

Finally, Korean culture has to change. A hierarchical relationship exists between government officials and the general public where bureaucrats employ their discretion and administrative guidance, and the public complies. This remains a serious issue that creates uncertainty for foreign firms (OECD 2007: 57–8). Negative perceptions still prevail in the media and among the public on imports, foreign firms and foreign investment, fuelled in part by nationalistic sentiment. Foreign firms still complain that local officials interpret and apply regulations more strictly for them (OECD 2007: 37). Such a negative perception is incompatible with globalization, and efforts should be made to curtail it.

10.4.4 Comparative Evaluation of Korea's Regulatory Regime

There is no doubt that Korea has made impressive progress in undertaking regulatory reforms in a very short time period, and as a result the economy should have benefited from it greatly (OECD 2007).[13] Nonetheless, Korea should undertake a further across-the-board regulatory reform to achieve its strategic economic goals. Korea still has excessive regulations that place a heavy burden on business. The number of regulations decreased markedly from 11 125 in 1997 to 6309 in 1999, although rising lately to reach 8083 in 2006. However, this deregulation was based on numerical rather than issue-oriented targets, and the government did not undertake reform of those sectors that needed urgent and drastic reform, nor did it address 'bundle regulations' which are more difficult to be reformed due to the required coordination among multiple ministries.

The quality of Korean regulations is not sufficiently high. The OECD (2007: 11) points out that some Korean standards differ from international references. Transparency is lacking in how the regulations are created, imposed and implemented, and consistency is compromised by arbitrary interpretation of regulations by front-line government workers. This is reflected in Korea's low score for global regulatory quality. As shown in Table 10.2, Korea's regulatory quality has fluctuated at around 0.72 out of the range of –2.5 to +2.5 over the 1996–2006 period, compared to an OECD average of 1.54. As shown in Tables 10.2 and 10.4, the lack of regulatory transparency and consistency increases the uncertainty in conducting business and the risk of corruption.

Korea has relatively more economic regulations than other advanced countries. For instance, the ratio of economic regulations to the total number of regulations was 45.7 per cent in 2004 in Korea, compared to 14 per cent in the United States (Y.K. Kim 2007). Excessive regulations particularly in the economic area and their poor quality are reflected in a relative lack of economic freedom and heavier burden on business. As shown in Table 10.4, Korea's Index of Economic Freedom deteriorated significantly under the Roh government, ranking below 35th position between 2003 and 2007. With respect to product market regulations, which includes all regulations on product and services markets, Korea still lags behind many OECD countries in terms of regulatory reform. Table 10.5 shows that overall product market regulation in Korea improved from 2.5 in 1998 to 1.5 in 2003, equal to the OECD average. Yet, the extent of product market regulations in Korea remained the 11th-highest among OECD countries in 2003 (Conway et al. 2005). In particular, as shown in Chapter 5, it should be noted that the service sector, which should be the main engine for Korea's economic revitalization in the future, still remains constrained by a large number of regulations, thereby impeding competition and productivity growth.

Regulatory barriers to entrepreneurship are substantially higher in Korea than the OECD average, for which Korea's values were estimated to be 2.5 and 1.7, respectively, in 1998 and 2003, compared to OECD averages of 2 and 1.5 (Table 10.5). Table 10.5 also shows that the higher level of barriers to entrepreneurship in Korea is attributable to a higher administrative burden on start-ups, and barriers to competition, both of which are substantially higher than OECD averages.

Costs and procedures involved in starting up companies in Korea are substantially higher than in neighbouring countries and OECD averages. The World Bank estimated that Korea ranked 116th out of 175 in overall company start-up costs in 2007 (Table 10.6). Corresponding ranks for Japan, Taiwan, Thailand and the United States were all significantly lower than that of Korea (Table 10.6). Company start-ups in Korea take 12 procedural steps, taking 22 days, while OECD averages are 6.2 steps, taking 16.6 days. Start-up costs as a percentage of per capita GDP are 15.2 per cent in Korea compared with an OECD average of 5.3 per cent. Start-up costs on this measure in Japan, Taiwan, Thailand and the United States are all lower than in Korea. The minimum capital required in starting up a company was 299.7 per cent of per capita GDP in Korea, which is well higher than neighbouring countries and the OECD average (Table 10.6). All this will raise business entry barriers and lower competition in Korea and its international competitiveness.

Table 10.5 Product market regulations (overall and sub-domains), OECD average and Korea, 1998–2003 (values ranging from 0 to 6)

	OECD average		Korea	
	1998	2003	1998	2003
Product market regulation (overall)	2.1	1.5	2.5	1.5
Barriers to trade & investment	1.5	1.0	2.2	1.3
Barriers to entrepreneurship	2.0	1.5	2.5	1.7
Sub-domains for barriers to entrep.				
1) Admin. burden on start-ups	2.1	1.8	2.2	2.2
2) Regulatory & admin. opacity	2.3	1.4	3.8	1.2
3) Barriers to competition	1.1	0.8	1.3	1.0

Source: Conway et al. (2005).

Table 10.6 Company start-up costs and procedures 2007: Korea and OECD average

	Starting a business (rank)	Procedures (step)	Start-up period (days)	Start-up costs (% of per capita GDP)	Minimum capital (% of per capita GDP)
Korea	116	12	22	15.2	299.7
Japan	18	8	23	7.5	0
Taiwan	9	8	48	4.6	200.0
Thailand	28	8	33	5.8	0
US	3	5	5	0.7	0
OECD	n.a.	6.2	16.6	5.3	36.1

Source: World Bank (2007a) and for OECD, Y.K. Kim (2007).

Korea has to improve its market opening and harmonization with international standards further, although substantial progress has already been made. There still is a perception among the international business community that certain Korea-specific standards and labelling requirements are unjustified and potentially discriminatory (OECD 2007: 38). As examined in Chapters 5 and 6, Korea's barriers to trade and investment were significantly higher than the OECD average with values at 2.2 and 1.3 respectively in 1998 and 2003, compared to OECD averages of 1.5 and 1 (Table 10.5). Similarly, Korea ranked poorly on the Globalisation Index, at 35th position in 2007 (Table 10.4).

10.5 CONCLUSION

This chapter has examined reform of the public management and regulatory regimes in Korea since 1997. Reforms were then assessed from an institutional perspective and in comparison to other countries. Both the Kim Dae-jung and Roh Moo-hyun governments undertook reforms in the public sector with the objectives of rationalizing state functions to create a smaller, more efficient government; the enhancement of efficiency by incorporating competition into public sector functions and personnel; and cultural change toward a more customer-oriented public service. To this end, the Kim government downsized the public sector and introduced a new budgeting system. Both governments introduced structural reorganizations, merit-based human resource management and a new information system. They both developed schemes for public participation and implemented anti-corruption policy.

The success of the reforms undertaken by the Kim and Roh administrations are mixed. Government effectiveness has improved, and yet Korea's value in this domain remains far below the OECD averages of recent years. Government efficiency has also improved, although there was room for improvement, particularly under the Roh government. Predictability and consistency have been low, particularly compared to advanced countries, mainly because of the continuous introduction of multiple reform programmes with poor coordination. Serious efforts have been made to improve citizens' participation in public administration with some evidence of improvement.

Korea has made significant improvements in the regulatory reform management system since 1997. The Kim Dae-jung government established a permanent regulatory reform organization, the Regulatory Reform Committee (RRC) and reform mechanisms including the RIA and sunset clause. The information system and transparency of regulations have improved. All this has aimed at aligning Korea's regulatory system with the WTO and OECD framework. The Roh government introduced a new Regulatory Reform Task Force (RRTF), supplementary to the RRC, and undertook further regulatory reforms.

This chapter has pointed out a variety of weaknesses of the regulatory management system and proposed suggestions for improvement. They include a transition from a positive regulatory system to a negative one; an enhancement of the governance and independence of the RRC; an introduction of incentive schemes to encourage proactive involvement of front-line bureaucrats; an improvement in cooperation between the RRC and non-government stakeholders as well as the National Assembly and other government agencies; and an improvement of procedural transparency and the information dissemination system of regulations for all stakeholders.

Korea has made impressive progress in regulatory reform. Nonetheless, Korea should undertake further, across-the-board regulatory reform to achieve its strategic economic goals. Korea still has a relatively large number of economic regulations, particularly in the services area, and the quality of regulations is low. Excessive economic regulations and their poor quality have raised the burden on business including entrepreneurial initiatives and company start-ups. They have also contributed to Korea's high level of corruption and its low economic freedom score, compared with competitor countries. All this lowers Korea's national competitiveness. Hence, a more systematic review should be undertaken by fully implementing the RIA and sunset causes. Korea should also improve regulations to improve its market opening and harmonization with international standards. Finally, some facets of Korean culture such as the hierarchical relationship between government officials and the general public and nationalistic sentiment against foreign goods and investment should be curtailed to expedite regulatory reform.

A few important success factors for public sector and regulatory reforms emerge from this critical analysis and assessment of Korea's reforms to public administration and its regulatory framework. They include a strong and consistent commitment of the President, participation of citizens and key stakeholders, and public support for government reform measures. Also, an organization based on a legal authority with strong presidential and political support is needed for successful coordination, evaluation and monitoring of public sector reforms and the reform process.

NOTES

1. Ostrom (2005: 3–31) proposes 'action arena' as a core unit of institutional analysis. The action arena includes 'action situations' and 'participants'. An action situation refers to the social space where participants interact, exchange goods and services and solve problems under exogenous variables including attributes of the society, rules and material conditions. Through interactions within the action arena, outcomes are generated, which are in turn evaluated in light of the exogenous variables.

2. For instance, see Yang (2004), Jeong et al. (2005), P.S. Kim (2000) and OECD (2007).
3. Various organizations have come up with different sets of dimensions for good public governance which comprise basic principles of human rights protection, democracy, transparency, participation, decentralized power-sharing, sound public administration, accountability, rule of raw, effectiveness, equity, strategic vision and so on. For the basic characteristics of measurements by those organizations, see Mimicopoulos (2007) who proposes three criteria: efficiency, transparency and participation.
4. For other structural reorganizations undertaken by the Kim Dae-jung government, see Yang (2004) and Jeong et al. (2005).
5. It should be noted that the World Governance Indicators as shown in Table 10.2 measure the perceptions of the quality of overall governance, including not only public administration as examined above, but also other areas such as regulation, taxation, management of state-owned enterprises and politics.
6. It should be noted that the level of corruption and the rule of law are determined not only by public governance but also by poor corporate governance of private business, both of which need to improve to lower the corruption level.
7. Soon after the 1997 crisis, four major sectoral reforms (financial, corporate, public sector and labour market) were launched. These four sectoral reforms were regulatory reforms in a broad sense.
8. The Korea Economic Research Institute (KERI), jointly with the Federation of Korean Industries, undertook an extensive analysis of about 5000 regulations (KERI 2007).
9. For the regulatory reforms related to FDI, M&As and foreign exchange markets, see Chapter 6.
10. The minimum period allowed for consultation is relatively short in Korea at 20 days, compared to 60 days in the United States (OECD 2007: 35).
11. In Table 10.2, the voice and accountability index is 0.68 on average for Korea over 1998–2006, compared to an OECD average of 1.3. Although the scope of this index is much broader than voice and accountability related to regulations, the significantly lower value for Korea than the OECD average indicates a general lack of consultation between the government authority and the public, and a resulting lack of accountability of bureaucrats.
12. A growing number of bills are initiated by National Assembly members, representing about 55 per cent of bills over 2000–04, and 69 per cent over the 2004–07 period (OECD 2007: 35).
13. Hlasney (2008) cites that GDP increased by 8.6 per cent and consumer prices decreased by 7.2 per cent over the last ten years since 1997–98 due to regulatory reforms.

REFERENCES

Asia–Pacific Economic Cooperation (APEC) (2007), 'The Republic of Korea: developments in public sector governance', *2007 APEC Economic Policy Report*, Singapore: APEC Secretariat, pp. 83–7.

A.T. Kearney/*Foreign Policy* (2007), 'Globalisation index rankings', www.foreignpolicy.om/story/cms.php?story_id=4030.

Chang, Dae-oup and Jun-Ho Chae (2004), 'The transformation of Korean labour relations since 1997', *Journal of Contemporary Asia*, **34** (4), 427–48.

Choi, Daeyong (2001), 'A radical approach to regulatory reform in Korea', paper presented at the Annual 2001 Conference of the American Society for Public Administration at Rutgers University, USA.

Choi, Kwang (1999), 'Public sector reform in Korea', *Korea Focus*, **7** (5), 66–77.

Chung, Jang-ryul (2000), 'Fading promise of small government', *Korea Focus*, **8** (1), 30–36.

Conway, P., V. Janod and G. Nicoletti (2005), 'Product market regulation in OECD countries: 1998–2003', Economic Department Working Papers No. 419, Paris: OECD.

Ha, Yeon-Seob (2004), 'Budgetary and financial management reforms in Korea: financial crisis, new public management, and fiscal administration', *International Review of Administrative Sciences*, **70** (3), 511–25.

Heritage Foundation (HF) (2009), 'Index of economic freedom', http://www.heritage.org/ research/features/index/search.cfm.

Hlasny, V. (2008), 'Regulatory climate change', *Korea Policy Review*, January, 55–8.

Hwang, Soo-Yeon (2007), 'How to reduce the number of government committees', (in Korean), in Jeong-Ho Kim (ed.), *2007 Policy Proposals*, Seoul: Institute for Free Enterprises, pp. 299–306.

International Institute for Management Development (IMD) (2006), *World Competitiveness Yearbook*, Lausanne: IMD.

International Institute for Management Development (IMD) (2007), *World Competitiveness Yearbook*, Lausanne: IMD.

International Institute for Management Development (IMD) (2008), *World Competitiveness Yearbook*, Lausanne: IMD.

Jeong, Hakyung, Dae-Ki Kim, Kookhyun Kim and Jeff Rinne (2005), 'South Korea', *World Bank Administrative and Civil Service Reform Country Reform Summaries*, http://www1.worldbank.org/publicsector/civilservice/rsSouthKorea.pdf, accessed 26 July 2005.

Jwa, Sung-Hee (2001), *A New Paradigm for Korea's Economic Development: from government control to market economy*, Basingstoke, UK and New York, USA: Palgrave.

Kaufmann, D., A. Kraay and M. Mastruzzi (2008), 'Governance matters VII: aggregate and individual governance indicators 1996–2007', World Bank Policy Research Working Paper 4654, http://ssrn.com/abstract=1148386.

Kim, Kwan-Bo (2007), 'Government reform and vision for Korea's advanced government', (in Korean), paper presented at the Conference of the Korean Advancement Policy, 7 November, Seoul, Korea.

Kim, Pan Suk (2000), 'Administrative reform in the Korean central government: a case study of the Dae Jung Kim's administration', *Asian Review of Public Administration*, **12** (2), 81–95.

Kim, Sun-bin (2007), 'Government reform and efficiency of public finance', (in Korean), paper presented at a Symposium for Exploration of Renaissance of the Korean Economy, Samsung Economic Research Institute (SERI), Seoul, Korea, 10 July.

Kim, Yong Kee (2007), 'Big bang of regulations', (in Korean), paper presented at a Symposium for Exploration of Renaissance of the Korean Economy, Samsung Economic Research Institute (SERI), Seoul, Korea, 10 July.

Korea Economic Research Institute (KERI) (2007), *Comprehensive Analysis of Regulatory Reform: issue one: overview and summary*, (in Korean), Seoul: Korea Economic Research Institute.

Korea National Statistical Office (KNSO) (various years), *Korea Statistical Yearbook*, Seoul: KNSO.

Kwon, O.Y. (2008), *International Business in Korea: the evolution of the market in the globalisation era*, Cheltenham, UK and Northampton, MA, USA: Edward Elgar Publishing.

Lee, Kang-ho (2004), 'Reforms and new governance of public bodies in Korea', *Korea's Economy 2004*, **20**, Korea Economic Institute (KEI), 33–40.

Lim, Hyun-Chin and Suk-Man Hwang (2002), 'The political economy of South Korean structural adjustment: reality and façade', *African and Asian Studies*, **1** (2), 87–112.

Lim, Youngjae (2006), 'National governance in Korea's vision 2030: crossroads for the future', mimeo, 4 December, Korea Development Institute.

McGuire, M. and M. Olson (1996), 'Economics of autocracy and majority rule', *Journal of Economic Literature*, **34**, March, 72–96.

Mimicopoulos, M.G. (2007), *Public Governance Indicators: a literature review*, Department of Economic and Social Affairs, New York: UN.

Moon, M.J. and K.W. Ju (2007), 'A comparative study on government size, scope of function, and strength of government in three administration', (in Korean), *Korean Journal of Public Administration*, **45** (3), 51–80.

OECD (2007), *Korea: progress in implementing regulatory reform*, Paris: OECD.

Ostrom, E. (2005), *Understanding Institutional Diversity*, Princeton, NJ: Princeton University Press.

Transparency International (TI) (2009), 'TI corruption perceptions index 2007', http://www.transparency.org/.

World Economic Forum (WEF) (2007), *The Global Competitiveness Reports 2007–2008*, Basingstoke, UK and New York: Palgrave Macmillan.

World Bank (2007a), *Doing Business 2007: how to reform, comparing regulation in 175 economies*, Washington, DC: World Bank.

World Bank (2007b), 'Worldwide governance indicators projects', http://info.worldbank.org/governance/wgi2007/home.htm.

World Bank Institute (2008), 'World governance indicators for 2007 and 2006', Washington, DC: World Bank Institute.

Yang, Junsok (2004), 'Public sector reforms', in Charles Harvie, Hyun-Hoon Lee and Junggun Oh (eds), *The Korean Economy: post-crisis policies, issues and prospects*, Cheltenham, UK and Northampton, MA, USA: Edward Elgar Publishing, pp. 120–42.

PART IV

Labour and social welfare

11. Reforms of the labour market and industrial relations

11.1 INTRODUCTION

There is a general consensus that Korean economic growth during the three decades from the 1960s was attributable mainly to the abundance of diligent and well-educated human capital, and the government's ability to utilize it (Kim and Lee 1997). With a limited industrial base and high population together with high unemployment, Korea initiated export-led industrialization with a surplus of labour in the early 1960s. However, within less than two decades, Korea was able to change that labour surplus into a labour shortage (S.K. Kim 2001). With a rapid rise in wages in conjunction with a labour shortage, companies adopted capital-intensive technology and production methods, whereby the business sector has carried on the development momentum. Industrialization of the economy since the 1960s and ensuing urbanization has changed the demographic configuration of the population. The fertility rate has dropped to the lowest level in the world and the growth rate of the population has been steadily declining. Korea's population is quickly becoming an ageing population.

Korean labour relations have undertaken a metamorphosis in the last four decades since the 1960s. Up until the late 1980s, labour relations were seemingly peaceful and cooperative under suppression of union activities by strong authoritarian regimes. In conjunction with political democratization in 1987, labour market democratization also occurred, and government power and influence on labour management fell dramatically. Labour unions have frequently applied militant tactics for their causes. From the early 1990s, globalization forces also exerted substantial influence over industrial relations and government labour policy. Faced with growing global competition, the government and employers sought to maintain flexibility in the labour market. Trade unions, on the other hand, demanded that labour rights be strengthened in alignment with international standards.

Korea has therefore faced serious challenges related to its labour force and industrial relations. Many Korean observers argue that the difficulties the Korean economy has faced in the recent past are all attributable to labour relations management. How will the Korean labour market accommodate the demographic changes? How will Korea develop its human resources consistent with its drive toward a knowledge-based economy? How should Korea improve its industrial relations? This chapter attempts to address these critical questions.

11.2 RECENT DEVELOPMENTS IN THE KOREAN LABOUR MARKET

11.2.1 Demographic Trends

Demographic trends have important implications for the labour market. Table 11.1 shows demographic trends in Korea between 1990 and 2008, and projections to 2050. During the three-decade period of rapid economic development and modernization from the early 1960s, Korea completed the 'demographic transition' to low mortality and low fertility rates – a characteristic of the advanced world. Korea recorded a very modest population increase between 1990 and 2008 from 42.9 to 48.6 million. Population growth declined from 0.99 per cent in 1990 to a third of 1 per cent in 2008.

Table 11.1 Korean demographic changes 1990–2008 and projections 2008–50

	1990	2000	2006	2008	2010	2020	2030	2050
Population (mill.)	42.9	47.0	48.3	48.6	48.9	49.3	48.6	42.3
Growth rate (%)	0.99	0.84	0.33	0.31	0.26	–0.02	–0.25	–1.07
Age %:								
0–14	25.6	21.1	18.6	17.4	16.2	12.4	11.4	8.9
15–64 (A)	69.3	71.7	71.9	72.3	72.9	72.0	64.4	53.0
65+ (B)	5.1	7.2	9.5	10.3	11.0	15.6	24.3	38.2
B/A ratio (%)	7.4	10.1	13.2	14.3	15.0	21.7	37.7	72.0

Source: KNSO (various years).

The most striking trend is Korea's rapidly ageing population, with the proportion of those aged over 65 increasing from 5.1 per cent in 1990 to 10.3 per cent in 2008. By 2050, the proportion of those aged over 65 is expected to reach 38.2 per cent (Table 11.1). On the contrary, the working-age population is expected to decline relative to the total population. The middle cohort of the 15–64-year age group accounted for 72.3 per cent of the Korean population in 2008 and is expected to decline to 53 per cent by 2050. The dependency ratio of the elderly population to working population (the ratio of population over 65 to the working population) increased from 7.4 per cent in 1990 to 14.3 per cent in 2008. The dependency ratio is expected to increase to 72 per cent in 2050, implying one working person supporting almost one retiree. Also, the absolute size of the labour force population is estimated to decline after 2015 (T.H. Kwon 2003). These demographic trends present a major challenge to future Korean society as well as to its labour market.

One of the most important features of population ageing in Korea is its unprecedented pace. The generally accepted criterion for an 'aged' population is a share of 14 per cent or more aged over 65 years (T.H. Kwon 2003). To reach an aged population, France, the United States and Japan took, respectively, 175 years, 65 years and 40 years, while it took only 25 years in Korea. The rapidity of population ageing will necessarily require a substantive shift in care responsibilities from private households to the state and society, even before the economy is prepared for it. If not managed carefully by the government, an ageing population could result in a heavy burden on a shrinking working generation to support the elderly financially, which would lessen the disposable income available to the younger generation – a disincentive to work. From society's point of view, therefore, the trend of the rapidly ageing population would require extending the working age well beyond the current practices. To this end, government policy or incentives schemes should be introduced for the private sector to implement such a change in employment practices. It appears that the government has not taken heed of this simmering issue.

11.2.2 Supply of Human Resources

Since the 1960s, the supply of human resources increased rapidly as a result of an increasing population, the mobilization of underemployed farm labour, rising labour force participation and rising education. As shown in Table 11.3, the population grew at an annual average of 1.35 per cent over the period 1963–2007. However, a declining trend in population growth has clearly been set. The population grew at a rate of 2.56 per cent annually during the 1960s, gradually declined to 1.75 per cent in the 1970s, and declined even further to less than 1 per cent during the 1990s (Table 11.3). The fertility rate started to decline from the early 1960s, reached a level below that of replacement in the late 1980s, and further decreased to 1.13 in 2006 (Table 11.2). Taking into account the declining fertility rate, it is estimated that the population will grow to around 50 million by around 2020, and decline from thereon (Table 11.1).

Table 11.2 Major indicators of the Korean labour market, 1963–2007

	1963	1970	1990	2000	2002	2004	2005	2006	2007
Economically active pop. (mill.)	8.2	10.0	18.5	21.1	22.9	23.4	23.7	24.0	24.2
Fertility rate	5.4	4.5	1.59	1.47	1.17	1.16	1.08	1.13	1.26
Participation rate: all (%)	56.6	57.6	60.0	61.0	61.9	62.1	62.0	61.9	61.8
Participation rate: female (%)	n.a.	n.a.	47.0	48.6	49.7	49.9	50.1	50.3	50.2
Unemployment rate (%)	8.2	4.4	2.4	4.1	3.1	3.7	3.7	3.5	3.2
Share of employment (%)									
Agriculture	63.1	50.4	17.9	10.9	9.3	8.2	7.9	7.7	7.4
Manufacturing	8.7	14.3	27.6	20.1	19.1	19.1	18.6	18.1	17.7
Services	28.3	35.3	54.5	69.0	71.6	72.8	73.5	74.2	75.0
Working hours per week	n.a.	n.a.	53.8	50.6	49.8	48.7	48.1	47.9	47.1
Real wage change (%)	n.a.	n.a.	9.4	5.6	8.7	2.8	3.6	3.3	3.2
Labour productivity/hour	n.a.	n.a.	6.6	3.1	4.8	3.2	4.2	4.3	5.4
Trade unions (000s)	n.a.	3.5	7.7	5.7	6.5	6.1	6.0	6.0	5.1
Union members (000s)	n.a.	473	1887	1527	1538	1537	1506	1559	1688
Union organization rate (%)*	n.a.	12.6	17.2	11.4	10.8	10.6	10.3	10.0	9.5
Industrial disputes (000s)	n.a.	n.a.	322	250	321	462	286	138	115

Note: * The union organization rate equals the number of union members divided by total employees who are permitted to organize unions.

Sources: KNSO (2002, various years); KLI (various years). For the fertility rate: World Bank (2009).

Although the labour force (economically active population) grew at an average annual rate of 2.6 per cent over the period 1963–2000, it has grown only at about 1.1 per cent a year in the recent past (Table 11.2). As the size of the labour force population declines after 2015, as aforementioned, so it is likely that the labour force will decline thereafter. Although the labour force participation rate grew slowly from 56.6 per cent in 1963 to 61.8 per cent in 2007 (Table 11.2), it is still about three percentage points below the OECD average (Martin et al. 2004). Additionally, the female labour force participation remained low at 50.2 per cent in 2007 (Table 11.2). The number of average working hours per week declined substantially from 53.8 hours in 1980 to 47.1 hours in 2007.

Table 11.3 Trends of major indicators of the labour market (annual average over the period)

	1963–69	1970–79	1980–89	1990–99	2000–07	1963–97	1963–2007
GDP growth (%)	9.8	9.7	8.3	6.2	5.2	8.8	7.7
Pop growth (%)	2.56	1.75	1.24	0.94	0.48	1.64	1.35
Real wage increments (%)	n.a.	n.a.	7.9[c]	5.6	4.3	7.4[d]	5.8[e]
Productivity/hourly growth (%)[a]	n.a.	8.9[b]	5.2[c]	4.7	3.9	4.9[d]	4.6[e]

Notes:
[a] Labour productivity is measured as the index of constant GDP divided by the index of labour man-hour input.
[b] Indicates value for 1971–79.
[c] For 1983–89.
[d] For 1983–97.
[e] For 1983–2007.

Sources: KNSO (2002, various years); KLI (various years); for productivity of over 1970–79: Korea Productivity Centre (2008).

The qualitative aspects of labour's contribution to economic development largely depend on education, culture and work ethic. Because of the influence of Confucianism, Korean workers are generally regarded as hardworking, industrious, disciplined, well-educated, easy to train, highly motivated, dedicated and loyal to their companies.[1] Historically, education has always been highly emphasized under Confucianism, and education of the Korean labour force has increased remarkably since the 1960s. Confucian influence has led to the development of a subtle social status identified by an individual's level of education, with scholars maintaining the highest social status throughout Korean history. Koreans continue to perceive education as being directly linked not only to improved social status but also to material success, thereby establishing a special place for education in Korean society. Because of Korea's close-knit family-oriented society, concerns and wishes for economic success and improved social status are regarded in terms of the family unit rather than at an individual level. Thus, parents willingly devote large portions of their finances to the education of their children, and even siblings financially support each other's education.

The educational zeal of Koreans was suppressed during Japanese colonial rule, resulting in an illiteracy rate of 78 per cent in 1945. However, after the

Korean War, the illiteracy rate started to decrease dramatically, and by the mid-1970s it had decreased to an insignificant level. As the economy has developed, education has further expanded towards tertiary education, as university education enhances social status and employment prospects. The number of students enrolled at tertiary educational institutions increased from 101 000 in 1960 to 3 million in 2007, a 7.5 per cent annual growth over this period (KNSO various years). Korea's gross tertiary enrolment rate in 2006 was 91 per cent, compared with 57.3 per cent in Japan, 59.3 per cent in the United Kingdom and 81.8 per cent in the United States (World Bank 2008). Despite a heavy social demand for higher education, the government has long enforced a strict enrolment quota system for tertiary education. This has led to fierce competition for university positions. This competition contributes to the Korean work ethic, described above.

The zeal for education has been accompanied by heavy spending on education. The private sector accounts for a substantial portion of education expenses. The government's education expenditure accounted for 13.2 per cent of the total budget in 1974, increasing to 19.6 per cent in 2006 (KNSO various years). The ratio of government education expenditure to GDP remained more or less unchanged at about 2.8 per cent over the period 1990–2004, although it increased to 3.4 per cent in both 2005 and 2006 (KNSO various years). According to the OECD (2007b: 50), public and private expenditure on education amounted to 7.53 per cent of GDP in 2003, the second-highest after Iceland among OECD countries. The ratio of public education expenditure to GDP was 4.59 per cent, compared to an OECD average of 5.2 per cent, while that of private expenditure was 2.95 per cent in contrast to an OECD average of 0.70 per cent in 2003.

Another important source of labour supply is foreign workers. Korea was a manpower-exporting country in the 1960s and 1970s. However, since the late 1980s, the population's reluctance to engage in so-called three-D jobs (dirty, difficult and dangerous) has resulted in a labour shortage in those areas. This has exacerbated labour shortages for small firms in labour-intensive and service areas that could not match rapid wage increases in the overall economy. All this has forced the government to allow the employment of workers from foreign countries, mainly from Asia. As from 2009, SMEs are able to use foreign workers for up to five years continuously (KILF 2008). Korea has entered the advanced country syndrome by which cheap foreign workers become necessary due to acute domestic labour shortages. Such a syndrome has arrived in Korea quite early, in view of its current economic status, because in this stratified society people are highly concerned with losing face by doing demeaning work.

The number of foreign workers has risen steadily since the late 1980s, although it declined in 1998 following the 1997 crisis. Numbers increased from 129 000 in 1995 to 425 000 in 2006 (OECD 2007a: 170). Foreign workers accounted for 0.3 per cent of total labour force in 1995, while in 2005 they accounted for 0.8 per cent (OECD 2007b: 30), indicating an indispensable component of the labour force.[2] The rising importance of foreign workers raises a host of social and economic issues of fair treatment and protection of foreign workers from human rights violation. Immigration laws have not been developed adequately, rendering it difficult for companies to employ foreign workers, and many of them are illegal immigrants or are working illegally.[3]

11.2.3 Employment of Human Resources

Along with industrialization and the rapid growth of the economy, the number of employed has increased at an average annual rate of 2.4 per cent between 1963 and 2007 (KLI various years). Demand for labour expanded faster than labour supply, particularly evident during the initial stages of Korea's industrialization during the 1960s and the early 1970s. As a result, since the 1970s the unemployment rate has remained quite low, except for the period 1998–99 in the wake of the 1997 financial crisis (Table 11.2). The share of employment by industry has changed remarkably since the early 1960s, reflecting Korea's industrialization. The share of employment in the agricultural sector declined steadily from 63.1 per cent in 1963 to 7.4 per cent in 2007, while the share in the manufacturing sector increased from 8.7 per cent in 1963 to its maximum of 28 per cent in 1991, then gradually declined to 17.7 per cent in 2007. The service sector steadily increased its employment share from 28.3 per cent in 1963 to 75 per cent in 2007 (Table 11.2).

The change in economic structure has weakened its job creation capability. The employment coefficient of income (the ratio of the number of employed to real GDP), though fluctuating, has declined remarkably from 48.3 during the 1990s to 34.1 over the period 2000–07. The employment elasticity of income (the ratio of employment growth to GDP growth) also shows a discernable downward trend from 0.36 during the 1990s to 0.32 over the first eight years of the 2000s (KLI various years). The Bank of Korea (2008) shows similar results on the employment–income relationship based on its input–output analyses. It shows that the number of jobs created directly and indirectly across the economy by final demand (the sum of consumption, investment and export) of 1 billion constant won declined from 24.8 in 1995 to 14.9 in 2005, a 39.2 per cent decrease in the job creation coefficient of final expenditure. Over the same period, the number of jobs created by exports in particular decreased by 55 per cent from 24 in 1995 to 10.8 in 2005. This is due to the change in export components whereby the proportion of capital- and technology-intensive exports rose at the expense of labour-intensive exports. To this is added the shifting of factories abroad, particularly by SMEs. This has serious implications for an emerging 'jobless growth' economy in Korea.

The Korean labour market has been unique in that the mobility and adaptability of labour has been relatively free of social limitations such as social class structure, regional and religious differences. As a result, the labour turnover rate was relatively high during the rapid growth period of the 1970s and 1980s at about 4 to 5 per cent, indicating a competitive labour market. However, the turnover rate gradually declined to below 3 per cent during the 1990s, and reached 2.3 per cent in 2007 (KLI various years). The real wage rate for the economy as a whole has increased substantially, at a somewhat higher rate than increases in labour productivity. As shown in Table 11.3, over the period 1983–2007, real wages increased at an annual average rate of 5.8 per cent, while productivity growth increased by only 4.6 per cent per annum.[4] As a result, the ratio of employees' compensation to GDP increased from 40.3 per cent in 1983 to 45.5 per cent in 2007 (KLI various years).

There is a significant mismatch between job-seekers' preferences and employment demand in the economy (I.S. Park 2007). Not only do large companies provide better pay and job security than SMEs, but also a higher social status is in general attached to working for large companies rather than small ones. Graduates thus prefer to work at large companies, causing labour shortages in the relatively union-free SME sector. The worker-shortage rate for all firms with five or more employees – the ratio of the shortage of workers to the total number of workers – increased from 1.1 per cent in 1999 to 3.1 per cent in 2007 (KLI various years).

11.3 LABOUR STANDARDS AND INDUSTRIAL RELATIONS

11.3.1 Labour Standards

Labour laws, introduced at first in 1953, were revised markedly in 1987 and 1998. Up to the 1987 revision, the Korean government intervened in the labour market extensively with two policy tasks: to provide protection of workplace conditions for individual workers against unscrupulous employers, and in the collective sphere to minimize labour disputes (H.S. Kim 2005b). The Labor Standards Act, amended in 1998, provides workers' rights and labour standards up to levels close to international standards. The Act sets forth the minimum level of working conditions required to guarantee workers' dignity, safety and occupational health. It also stipulates the minimum wage and provision of social safety nets and prohibits discriminatory and unscrupulous treatment, including gender discrimination and exploitation of workers. In 2003, the Act was amended after serious contestations between employers and employees to make Saturday a non-work day, thereby reducing the number of working hours from 44 to 40 per week.

Despite the improvement in formal labour standards laws, actual labour standards still fall short of international standards because of their ineffective implementation. The laws are not properly applied for temporary workers and foreign workers. Middle and senior managers who are not protected by unions are sometimes forced to take early retirement. The Labor Relations Commission, which administers and makes judgement on unfair labour practices, has a limited capacity to settle disputes due to a lack of resources (H.S. Kim 2005a). Influenced by Confucian tradition which emphasizes loyalty toward the company, individual workers are reluctant to challenge their employers with allegations of unfair treatment. It is also too expensive for individual workers to pursue remedial and legal processes to rectify unfair labour practices by employers.

11.3.2 Industrial Relations in Transition

The rights of workers to organize unions, to bargain collectively with employers and to take industrial action are guaranteed as basic rights of Korean nationals by the Constitution. To implement these basic principles of labour relations, there were 14 laws in the areas of industrial relations and labour standards as of 2005, including the Trade Union and Labor Relations Adjustment Act (H.S. Kim 2005b). Yet, the labour market and labour relations in particular are an area in which the Korean government has intervened most extensively until the late 1980s. As part of its industrial relations policy, the government promoted the rights of management, suppressing union activities and intervening in labour disputes. Management, taking advantage of government policy and intervention, has applied an authoritarian method of labour management. Whenever labour disputes occurred, management often relied on the government to resolve the disputes instead of learning and practicing appropriate methods of dispute resolution. Therefore, although the Korean labour market appeared competitive and efficient, it was under strict government control and had not progressed towards the sort of labour market seen in advanced countries.

Korean labour relations have changed markedly since the late 1980s. The Trade Union and Labor Relations Adjustment Act was revised in 1987 to deregulate industrial relations and promote voluntary settlement of labour disputes. As a result, government power and influence on labour management fell dramatically. This, together with the shortage of labour experienced in the late 1980s, led to numerous labour disputes during the 1987–89 period. It thus became apparent that past practices of labour relations management would no longer work in Korea. From the early 1990s, globalization forces also exerted substantial influence over industrial relations and government labour policy. In particular, competitive rivals in Southeast Asia, and especially China, enjoyed significant advantages over Korea due to their lower labour costs, weak trade unions, flexibility and vast underdeveloped reserves of human resources. Faced with this growing regional competition, government and employers sought to maintain flexibility in the labour market. Trade unions, on the other hand, demanded that labour rights be strengthened in line with international standards.

After several confrontations, Korean labour laws were again amended in early 1997. These amendments lifted most of the restrictions on union activities, enhanced labour market flexibility by allowing the dismissal of workers for urgent 'managerial reasons', and introduced the concept of non-regular workers including dispatched and fixed-term workers (Lee and Lee 2003).[5] The outbreak of the 1997 financial crisis had a profound impact on industrial relations in Korea. The Tripartite Commission was established in January 1998 to promote cooperation among the three key parties – government, labour unions and employers – in implementing industrial relations and labour market reforms. This post-crisis labour market reform with its focus on greater flexibility was a full-scale revision of industrial relations and the labour market and has become the basic framework of the present labour law (H.S. Kim 2005c; Kim and Park 2006).

11.3.3 Current Industrial Relations

Unions in Korea have been predominantly enterprise-based in the past but have recently undertaken a transition to being industry-based. At the end of 2007, enterprise unions accounted for 92.4 per cent of total unions, and trade-based unions 6.8 per cent in terms of the number of unions (Ministry of Labor 2008). However, in terms of union members, the number of unions with memberships of more than 1000 accounted for 3.6 per cent of total unions and 70.1 per cent of total union membership in 2007 (H. Kim 2009). Recently, a number of large unions have approved the shift to industrial unions, setting a transition in Korea's labour movement from enterprise-based unions to industry-based unions (Eun 2007). The numbers of both unions and union members increased to their maximum level in 1989, and have steadily declined since then. As of 2007, there were 5100 unions and 1.7 million union members (Table 11.2). The union density rate increased to its highest rate of 17.2 per cent in 1990, and declined steadily to 9.5 per cent in

2007 (Table 11.2).[6] Decreases in union members are attributable to a few recent developments in the labour market such as decreases in union membership in the manufacturing sector and SMEs due to their worsening economic conditions (Cho 2007).

The number of industrial disputes has varied from year to year. It was 206 in 1980 and peaked to 3749 in 1987. Since 1990, the number of labour disputes has ranged from about 80 to 400 with 115 in 2007 (Table 11.2). Cho (2007) points out that during the late 1980s most strikes were illegal, while during the 1990s one-third were illegal, and since 2000 illegal strikes have declined to 17.4 per cent of total strikes in 2006. Large companies and unions with large memberships have more incidents of illegal strikes (Cho 2007).

The major parties involved in current industrial relations in Korea are unions, employers and the government. There are two national federations of unions: the Federation of Korean Trade Unions (FKTU) and the Korean Confederation of Trade Unions (KCTU). The FKTU had 3754 unions with 872 000 members, and the KCTU had 1362 unions and 615 000 members at the end of 2000 (Lee and Lee 2003). The two union federations at the national level are quite different in their philosophy and attitudes. The KCTU, which gained legal recognition in 1999, leans towards militant activism, whereas the FKTU shows a more cooperative stance towards the government and employers, although it has taken on a more independent and antagonistic stance in recent years (Y.Y. Lee 2006). There are five employers' associations: the KCCI (the Korea Chamber of Commerce and Industry), the KFTA (the Korea Foreign Trade Association), KFSB (the Korean Federation of Small and Medium Business), FKI (the Federation of Korean Industries) and the KEF (the Korea Employers Federation). They all participate and act together in all committees related to industrial relations such as the Tripartite Commission. The Ministry of Labor is the government body that administers labour policies. The official mediator of labour disputes in Korea is the Labor Relations Commission (LRC). To facilitate communication and cooperation between employees and employers, labour-management councils are formed by law at all companies with more than 30 workers (Lee and Lee 2003).

Since trade unions are mainly enterprise-based unions, collective bargaining at most unionized firms is conducted primarily at the firm level. Hence, neither union federations nor employers' associations can participate in collective bargaining. Nevertheless, the influence of national federations of unions on company-level bargaining has been rising in the recent past. At the beginning of every year, the FKTU and KCTU make nationwide demands for wages and other contractual changes, which serve as an influential guideline to enterprise-level collective bargaining. In response to these proposals by national union houses, the employers' associations, through the KEF, offer their own negotiation guidelines to member companies.

The 1997 Trade Union and Labor Relations Adjustment Act allowed the formation of multiple unions at industrial and national levels. At the enterprise level, multiple unions were to be allowed from January 2002 (Martin et al. 2004). In the same Act, unionized enterprises were prohibited from paying regular salaries to full-time union officials effective from January 2002. After postponing the implementation of both of these new measures up to the end of 2006, the Tripartite Commission decided in September 2006 to provide another five-year grace period until the end of 2011, to implement the recognition of multiple trade unions at the enterprise level and the deletion of full-time union officials from the payroll of enterprises (Naver 2007).

11.4 COMPARATIVE ASSESSMENT OF THE INDUSTRIAL RELATIONS

Although formal institutions related to labour relations management have advanced remarkably, it is still one of the most serious constraints in enhancing the national competitiveness of the Korean economy. Labour disputes, particularly acrimonious ones with militant tactics employed by unions, some of which are illegal, are still prevalent in Korea. This is well demonstrated in Table 11.4. Korea performs very poorly on the national competitiveness of its labour market and industrial relations compared with its overall performance. Korea's overall IMD world competitiveness ranking ranged from 29th to 38th over the period 2000–08 with an average of 31.8th out of an average of 55 countries surveyed. Korea's ranks on labour regulations, which hinder business activities, declined from 30th in 2000 to 54th in 2008, an average rank over the period of 41.3th out of an average of 54.5 countries studied. In particular, Korea's labour relations were among the very worst in the IMD survey. Korea ranked 44th out of 47 countries in 2000, and last from 2004 to 2008, clearly indicating its hostile nature. Korea's average rank for industrial disputes was 40.8th between 2000 and 2008 out of the average 54.3 countries studied (Table 11.4).

Korea's performance with the level of hourly compensation was substantially higher than with labour productivity. Korea's average rank for labour productivity was 35.1th out of an average 54.4 between 2000 and 2008, while the hourly compensation level in the manufacturing sector was an average of 29.7 over the same period (Table 11.4). This shows that wages in Korea increased faster than labour productivity and the gap in the increment between them increased relatively faster than other countries, leading to a loss in international competitiveness. Korea's hourly compensation (wages and supplementary benefits) for manufacturing workers has been consistently higher than those of all Asian countries surveyed except Japan. In 2006, for instance, Korea's wage level was $14.70 as compared to $5.16, $6.43 and $8.34, respectively, in Hong Kong, Taiwan and Singapore (IMD 2008).

11.5 CRITICAL ISSUES IN THE KOREAN LABOUR MARKET AND INDUSTRIAL RELATIONS

11.5.1 Demographic Changes: Ageing and Declining Population

One of the critical challenges faced by Korea is how to maintain its labour force in the face of an ageing and declining population. To minimize the dire consequences of Korea's rapidly ageing population, two suggestions are made:

- it has to raise the labour force participation rate, particularly of women; and
- it has to prevent waste of human resources resulting from early retirement.

Korea's overall participation rate is below the OECD average, primarily because the rate for prime-age women is the third-lowest in the OECD area (OECD 2005: 152; 2007a: 113). As shown in Table 11.4, Korea's female labour force as a percentage of total labour force ranked about 40th out of about 55 countries surveyed by the IMD in the recent past. Similarly, the WEF ranked Korea at 79th and 80th, respectively, in 2005 and 2006 out of about 132 countries studied for female labour force participation as a percentage of male participation (WEF 2007, 2008).

The low rate of female workforce participation is due to a number of reasons. A survey in 2006 found that 46 per cent of Korean women in the sample cited childcare as the main obstacle to participation in the labour force (OECD 2007a: 113). Other major obstacles were social prejudice against working women (18.5 per cent), unfair labour conditions (11.6 per cent) and the burden of housework (7.2 per cent) (OECD 2007a: 145).[7] This survey indicates that in order to raise the female labour force participation rate, the government has to improve the maternity leave system and expand the availability of affordable childcare.[8] Approximately one-quarter of children under five years are enrolled in childcare, with 95 per cent of those in private institutions. According to the OECD, however, there was a

16 per cent vacancy rate for childcare in 2005, indicating underutilization of existing facilities. With respect to maternity leave, Korea currently has a 60-day employer-paid maternity leave provision, with a further 30-day Employment Insurance Scheme (EIS)-funded extension, making for a total of three months. However, only approximately half of the workforce are actively insured by the EIS (OECD 2005: 155). The OECD cites a study showing that the average maternity benefit per birth in Korea, as a percentage of production workers' wages, is only 3 per cent, compared to an OECD average of 42 per cent (OECD 2007a: 115).

Table 11.4 Comparative assessment of the labour market: Korea's ranking on its important components, 2000–08

	2000	2002	2004	2005	2006	2007	2008	Average[c]
IMD overall	29	29	35	29	38	29	31	31.8 (55.0)
Labour regulations	30	35	44	44	46	45	54	41.3 (54.5)
Labour relations	44	47	60	60	61	55	55	53.5 (54.5)
Industrial dispute[d]	38	44	43	37	38	n.a.	n.a.	40.8 (54.3)
Labour productivity	30	13[a]	41	39	34	32	n.a.	35.1 (54.4)
Labour compensation	26	21[a]	32	32	33	n.a.	n.a.	29.7 (54.3)
Immigration	45	33	49	53	59	49	54	47.1 (54.5)
Foreign labour[b]	11[a]	32	36	32	28	n.a.	n.a.	32.4 (40.0)
Foreign skill	n.a.	23	42	27	31	48	32	33.8 (56.7)
Female labour force	32	14[a]	40	41	40	39	n.a.	37.3 (54.4)

Notes:
Total number of countries studied differs by IMD publication year.
The number in parentheses is the average number of countries studied.
[a] Subcategories of data were divided into countries with populations above and below 20 million. Korea's rankings are out of 30 countries studied with populations over 20 million.
[b] Foreign labour as % of total labour force out of those countries that accept foreign labour.
[c] Over years with available data.
[d] Working days lost per 1000 inhabitants per year.

Source: IMD (various years).

With respect to social prejudice against working women, Korean society still regards the traditional role of women as staying home and looking after children, and a high proportion of female workers withdraw from the labour force after childbirth. Because of the zeal for high educational achievement, they are expected to help their children prepare for university entrance examinations. Unfair labour conditions are also related to this social prejudice and discourage women from participating in the labour force. There is also a high gender gap in wages, although it is gradually improving. During the 1980s, female wages were about 50 per cent of the male wage, while over the period 2000–06 it rose on average to 65.5 per cent of the latter (Table 11.5).

Table 11.5 Non-regular workers and compensation, 1997–2007 (%)

	1997	2000	2002	2003	2004	2005	2006	2007
1. Non-regular/ total employees	45.7	52.1	51.6	49.5	48.8	47.9	47.2	46.0
2. Wages for non-regular/regular	n.a.	n.a.	67.1	61.3	65.0	62.6	62.8	63.5
3. Female non-regular/ female employee	37.1	42.4	42.2	42.4	42.1	41.5	40.8	40.1
4. Female wages/ male wages	62.6	64.8	64.8	65.2	65.7	66.2	66.5	66.4

Sources: 1–3: KLI (various years); 4: KNSO (various years).

Another aspect of unfair labour conditions for women is the lack of available jobs commensurate with education levels. The OECD points out that while 38 per cent of Korea's workforce is female, their share of managerial positions is only 8 per cent, compared with an OECD average of 20–30 per cent (OECD 2007a: 115). Korea is the only country in the OECD where the employment rate for female university graduates (57 per cent) is less than the overall employment rate for women (59 per cent). This compares with the OECD average of a 79 per cent employment rate for female university graduates, and an employment rate of 49 per cent for all women in 2003 (OECD 2007a: 116).[9]

One of the barriers to female labour force participation is that most jobs available to women tend to be non-regular positions which are poorly treated compared with regular workers. Over the 2002–07 period, 40.8 per cent of female workers were classified as non-regular, compared to 29.4 per cent of men (Table 11.5; KLI various years). This may indicate that women who have left a regular position in the workforce will find it difficult to return as regular workers and may take up non-regular jobs. In addition, the seniority-based wage system discriminates against women who have left the workforce to raise children, in that on their return they are locked into lower-paying and lower-status positions regardless of their performance.

Another important way of mitigating the adverse effects arising from an ageing and declining population is to minimize early retirement, which may in turn require mandatory retirement ages to be either abolished or brought into line with the official pension eligibility age. As of the beginning of 2009, the mandatory retirement age for public servants ranges from 60 years for civil servants, 62 years for school teachers and 65 years for university professors. Private companies have chosen the retirement age of 55 in company regulations, but in practice it is less than 50 (KERI 2007). The retirement age expected by employees in the private sector was 43.9 in 2009, compared to 48.4 in 2008 (*JoongAng Daily* 2009). All this indicates that the retirement age is declining.[10] The large gap between the expected retirement age and actual retirement age means that employees spend the last prime years of their careers under a cloud of anxiety and uncertainty, thereby lowering their loyalty or attachment toward their companies. To this end, government policy or incentives schemes should be introduced for the private sector to increase the retirement age.

Because of the difficulty in laying off workers for employment adjustment, employers rely more on 'honourable retirements', early forced retirement or attrition (Park et al. 2001). This type of retrenchment is an expensive mode of employment adjustment due to severance payments and could also be inefficient as it may make companies lose efficient and experienced workers. Unlike advanced Western countries, it is virtually impossible for middle managers to find new jobs once they are retired, even if they are young, due to various social and business cultural reasons. Hence, the OECD (2007a: 117) estimates that three-quarters of employees retiring from private companies enter self-employment, which in Korea is characterized by low productivity and income. Forced early retirement is thus a serious waste of human resources in the face of the country's declining population. To raise labour force participation among early-retired people and to enable them to find new jobs, the government should promote additional training and lifelong learning. Participation in lifelong learning initiatives in Korea is in the lower group of OECD countries (OECD 2007a: 117).

11.5.2 Individual Industrial Relations: Rising Non-Regular Workers

Korea's labour market has often been criticized for its lack of flexibility under stringent worker protection.[11] While labour laws allow companies to dismiss workers for urgent managerial reasons, it is in practice extremely difficult to dismiss workers in unionized companies because of stringent requirements. These include giving 50 days of consultations with the unions concerned on the dismissal plan, and 30 days' advance notification of individual workers affected (KERI 2007). The union shop system of employment in place exacerbates labour market inflexibility. Rigid employment protections are mostly found in large unionized companies with a 'regular' workforce, while dismissal is relatively easy for 'non-regular' workers and the large numbers of workers in SMEs who are not protected adequately under labour laws.

The post-crisis labour market reforms have therefore resulted in a 'dualism' in the labour market between 'regular' and 'non-regular workers', raising serious equity issues and conflicts (S.T. Kim 2007). Firms have increasingly preferred to hire new recruits on a non-regular rather than a regular basis. The share of non-regular workers increased from 45.7 per cent of total employment in 1997 to 52.1 per cent of total employment in 2000, decreasing somewhat to 46 per cent in 2007 (Table 11.5). The proportion of non-regular workers was the highest among OECD member countries in 2002.[12]

Non-regular workers are treated substantially worse than regular employees in terms of remuneration and social and statutory benefits. Over the period 2002–07, non-regular workers were paid on average only 63.7 per cent of regular employees' remuneration (Table 11.5).[13] As examined in Chapter 12, there are four social safety net programmes (Employment Insurance, Industrial Accident Compensation Insurance, National Health Insurance and National Pension Insurance), for which both employees and employers have to contribute. Many non-regular workers are not covered by these social programmes, nor are they eligible for statutory benefits by their companies such as overtime pay, paid annual leave and maternity leave. An OECD (2005) survey shows that in Korea only 34.5 per cent of non-regular workers were covered by employment insurance, only 36.6 per cent were covered by the public pension scheme, and only 37.7 per cent were covered by the national health insurance scheme. There is little chance for non-regular workers to move to regular employment status. Between August 2003 and August 2004, only 15 per cent of non-regular workers moved into regular work, and three out of five remained in precarious employment (Grubb et al. 2007). The turnover rate of non-regular workers is approximately double that of regular workers (S.T. Kim 2007).[14]

A number of proposals have been suggested to address the duality in the labour market, and at the same time to improve labour market flexibility (S.T. Kim 2007; Hwang 2007; Grubb et al. 2007; OECD 2004). A common argument of these proposals is to ease the strict protection applying to regular workers, and concomitantly to improve protection and employment conditions for non-regular workers. As shown earlier, Korea's national competitiveness is already low, due in part to the inflexibility and high protection for workers. It has also been shown earlier that hourly compensation in Korea is markedly higher than in neighbouring competitors. Hence, Korea simply cannot afford to increase protection of regular workers, as companies respond by increasing the number of non-regular workers or lowering protection and compensation for them. This is seen in the higher proportion of non-regular workers at unionized companies than at non-unionized ones, and the lower compensation available to non-regular workers at unionized companies (K.S. Park 2008).

As a way of easing the rigid protection for regular workers, S.J. Park (2007) argues that the consultation period with the union concerned should be abolished in the case of bankruptcy, and for other cases be reduced to 30 days, a common period in other countries. The union shop system, under which a worker is required to join a union when entering a company, though applicable in cases of more than two-thirds of a company's employees being union members, runs counter to market principles and should be eliminated, as is the case in most advanced countries.[15] Employers' contributions to regular employees' pension plans are also higher than in advanced countries. Korea introduced the National Pension Plan in 1988 for which employee and employer each contribute 4.5 per cent of the payment. In addition, Korea introduced a Retirement Pension Plan in 2005 for which the employer contributes 8.33 per cent of an employee's compensation, under which a large portion of non-regular workers are not covered (S.J. Park 2007). Thus, the employer contributes to two pensions for employees up to 12.83 per cent of the employees' income. This scheme is more generous than those in developed countries.[16]

As a way of enhancing protection for non-regular workers, they should be covered by Korea's four social safety net programmes. Non-regular workers feel stigmatized by not being covered by these social programmes, to which they are entitled by law. The main reason why non-regular workers are not covered is the difficulty in estimating their income, as their contribution as well as their company's contribution is proportionate to their income. However, it should not be too difficult to organize for non-regular workers to have a certain minimum amount of contribution set for each of these social security programmes. They should also enjoy equal treatment with regular workers for vocational training and other benefits offered by their companies. The minimum wage system and the wage payment guarantee system should be improved.

An Act was introduced in November 2006, though as of 2009 it has not yet been implemented, to protect non-regular workers. In effect it stipulates that a non-regular worker will have regular worker status after two years of working (I.J. Lee 2007). However, in response to this Act, companies may decide to lay off non-regular workers before the two-year term matures, contrary to the intent of the Act. There is an option to extend to four years, long enough so that most companies will be hesitant to dismiss workers. In particular, in the emerging knowledge-based economy, the dispatched workers system as part of the non-regular workers system should improve and expand. The existing positive system for dispatched workers should change to a negative list system. Dispatched workers are not permitted to be employed during a strike period or within two years after companies have dismissed workers for redundancy reasons (KERI 2007). This is not only unreasonably restrictive for companies for their survival and revival, but also inconsistent with the development of a knowledge-based economy.

Korea's non-regular workers, except daily workers, are full-time workers with markedly poor remuneration and supplementary benefits compared to regular workers. To counter this inequality, Korea should expand the concept of 'part-time employment' which refers to persons who usually work less than 30 hours per week in their main job, and remuneration and other benefits for them are pro-rated to the number of working hours. Over the period 2003–06, Korea ranked on average 33.5th on part-time employment, which accounted for an average of 8.5 per cent of total employment (IMD various years). According to OECD (2007b: 32), the proportion of part-time employment increased from 4.3 per cent in 1996 to 8.8 per cent in 2006 in Korea, compared to a 2006 OECD average of 16.1 per cent. This sort of flexible part-time employment system will work as an important incentive to female labour force participation.

11.5.3 Collective Industrial Relations

It has been generally acknowledged in Korean society that cooperative and stable collective labour relations are one of the critical prerequisites in progressing the economy to the level of advanced countries. Nonetheless, animosity and militancy still prevails in Korea's labour relations (Yoon 2005). As shown in Table 11.4, Korea ranked last from 2004 to 2008 for industrial relations out of all countries surveyed by IMD. This indicates a strong aversion to unions' confrontational tactics and militancy. There are a number of contentious issues for such confrontational relations:

- salary payment to full-time union executives;
- imbalanced power between unions and employers;
- intervention of the government in labour disputes; and
- lack of transparency, ethics and law compliance on the management side.

In 2006, the so-called Grand Tripartite Agreement for the Advancement of Industrial Relations was passed by the National Assembly (MOL 2006).[17] It appears that the basic issues underpinning the tumultuous industrial relations environment have not properly been addressed by the Agreement. Rather, the Agreement appears to be a give-and-take compromise of conflicts under tension between labour and management, dealing with minor technical adjustments in industrial relations and the dispute settlement mechanism, while postponing difficult issues for future consultations. The Agreement is unlikely to reduce frictions in labour–management relations and militant union activities.

One of the major causes of prevalent union strikes is that full-time union executives at unionized companies maintain themselves on the enterprises' payroll. Enterprises paying for full-time union executives runs counter to the basic principle of 'no work no pay'. It also creates the so-called agency problem whereby full-time union officials are not working for the owners of the companies but for union members. To justify their *raison d'être*, union executives are bound to make excessive demands at collective bargaining using confrontational tactics. Union executives have substantial privilege under the union shop employment practices, which has in turn generated moral hazard. There have been a number of scandalous incidents of hiring workers by union executives through the union shop system, through which the lack of transparency in unions' operation has been pointed out.

With respect to the imbalance in power between union and management, it is argued that part of the original principles of labour laws was based on the idea of protecting a large number of workers from the monopsonic exploitation of employers. However, now that a bilateral monopoly has in effect been established in labour markets with the union shop system, power should be balanced between union and management and run under market principles. This is also an international standard promulgated by the International Labour Organization (KERI 2007). The existing labour laws tilt the balance in favour of unions in many respects. Employers cannot hire replacement workers to keep up business operations during a strike period.[18] Obviously, the effectiveness of industrial actions will diminish if business can carry on during the strike period. However, companies, even if carrying on their operation with replacement workers, will still incur costs because they have to pay non-wage benefits such as insurance to existing employees during the strike period, and the productivity of replacement workers will be lower than regular workers. Lockouts as employers' counter-right against unions are allowed only in the case of legal strikes – not for illegal strikes (H.S. Kim 2005c). This does not sound logical and encourages illegal strikes. Lockouts should be allowed regardless of the legitimacy of industrial actions.

Another imbalance is in regard to penal provisions. In order to protect union workers, a penal provision has been established on unfair labour activities of management, such as unfair dismissal and violations of labour laws. However, when abuses of union power such as illegal strikes, occupation of business facilities or union activities during office hours result in damage to companies, employers' counter-rights to claim damage compensation or to apply provisional injunctions do not exist (S.J. Park 2007; H.S. Kim 2005c).[19]

There are still government interventions in labour disputes, which encourage both parties to push for a favourable decision by the government on their behalf rather than being forced to compromise with one another. The incumbent minister in charge of labour seeks to resolve any pending labour disputes quickly, to show off his or her competence as minister. If any labour dispute carries on for long, society argues for replacement of the minister. It is therefore understandable that, with his or her typically short tenure, the minister in charge is not seriously concerned with the ramifications of the resolutions of labour disputes by government intervention. As part of the settlement conditions of labour conflicts, unions invariably come up with demands for a general amnesty for their violations of commercial and criminal laws and wage compensation during the strike period. In such a case, typically the government coerces companies to give in to the demands of unions, as it has more influence over companies than unions.[20]

As examined in Chapter 8, corporate governance of *chaebols* is inappropriate, and *chaebol* owners wield control over their conglomerates well beyond their equity ownership. The lack of transparency of business operation has been pointed out. There have been a number of scandalous illegal activities in the recent past, including owners of large *chaebols* creating slush funds. All this has led business owners to lose respect from society as well as workers. Together with the transition of the lifetime employment and seniority system to the merit-based system, employees' loyalty toward their companies has declined. This was exacerbated by prevalent forced early retirement. Because of ill feeling from both sides, mistrust between employers and employees has been strong, which is in turn a critical constraint to the further advancement of cooperative labour relations.

11.5.4 Organizations Related to Labour Relations

There are three organizations that play important roles in developing and implementing healthy labour relations in Korea. They are the Korea Tripartite Commission (KTC), the Labor Relations Commission (LRC), and the Labor-Management Council (LMC). The Tripartite Commission, established in 1998 as a presidential advisory body, was composed of representatives from the government, the two trade union federations and two national-level employer associations, the Federation of Korean Industries (FKI) and the Korea Employers Federation (KEF). It was established to provide a forum for consultation and compromise among labour, management and government, thereby encouraging cooperation among the tripartite parties. The creation of the KTC is significant in that it showed that the government had started to regard labour as a legitimate party in the political structure.

In spite of its noble intent and important potential role, there are a number of issues to be addressed for the KTC to function effectively. As indicated by the 19 commission members, which include the Prime Minister and a number of other government ministers, chairpersons representing two trade union federations and representatives from the FKI and KEF, the social consensus-building process of the KTC is a top-down approach. With the existing acrimonious relationship between the heads of union federations and representatives of large business groups, it is difficult to come up with a consensus on any issues. The division and mistrust between the two trade federations exacerbates the onerous task of consensus building. A bottom-up approach with more comprehensive representation of society should be undertaken, including some rank-and-file workers. Workers and company representatives of SMEs which presented 87.5 per cent of total employment are not represented in the KTC (SMBA 2009), while chairpersons of two trade federations which represent 10 per cent of all workers are key Commission members.

The agenda for the KTC is too broad. With its agenda of all pending problems in industrial relations, the KTC has been criticized for using the social dialogue channel as a means of imposing control over organized labour's demands or for playing the mediation role in labour–management confrontations, rather than promoting a democratic process of tripartite consultation (*Hankyoreh* 2006). This is the reason why there have been a number of incidents of repeated withdrawals from the KTC by both labour and business representatives.[21] Since the Commission has been established as a presidential advisory organization, it should seek social consensus on basic directions and principles of mid- and long-term labour relations policy rather than on short-term problems.

The Labor Relations Commission (LRC), founded in 1953, plays an important role of adjudication and mediation of disputes arising from industrial relations. The Commission is a quasi-judicial governmental body, composed of a chairperson, and tripartite representatives from labour, business and the public. The Labor Relations Commission is two-tiered: the National Labor Relations Commission and the Regional Labor Relations Commission. The process of adjudication or mediation should be simplified.

When an industrial dispute occurs, the party concerned applies to the Regional Commission for the settlement of the case. An applicant who is dissatisfied with the decision of the Regional Commission can then lodge an appeal to the National Commission. After that, the applicant can file the case before the district civil court, and then a high court. The Supreme Court, the highest court, hears appeals from the decision of the high court not on the facts of the case but on questions of law. It takes a few years and incurs high costs to pursue this five-tiered procedure (H.S. Kim 2005a). In this respect, a twofold solution may be suggested. The five-tiered procedure should decrease to a three-tiered system, and concomitantly the legal authenticity of the National Labor Relations Commission and confidence on its decisions should be enhanced. As H.S. Kim (2005b) suggests, the decision on industrial disputes should end at the National Commission level, and appeals be heard only at the Supreme Court. To bolster the National Commission in terms of legal authenticity and confidence, the Chairperson of the National Commission should be appointed from judges of the Supreme Court, compared to past appointing practices from academics or retired bureaucrats (H.S. Kim 2005a).

The Labor-Management Council (LMC), introduced in 1963, is intended to promote workers' participation and cooperation between labour and management. The Council should be established in each company with 30 or more permanent workers and be composed of an equal number of members representing the employer and workers, the number from each being not less than three nor more than ten (H.S. Kim 2005b). The Council should hold a meeting once every three months, and undertakes consultations or resolutions on a range of issues on labour management and company operation such as production practices, introduction of new technology, performance monitoring, changes to business activities, workers' grievances, and occupational safety and health measures. Legislation guarantees the adequate provision of information to workers in advance of meetings, and also the referral of disputes in the Council to the Labor Relations Commission. Agreements reached at the Council should also be submitted to workers for agreement. Different from the KTC, the LMC is a bottom-up approach to labour peace. A survey held by the Korea Chamber of Commerce and Industry (KCCI) found that the Council contributes to improving workers' benefits and stabilizing industrial relations. Therefore, the Council operation should be further encouraged and facilitated (KILF 2006).[22] To this end, it is suggested that some flexibility in terms of frequency of consultations be introduced by changing from the current fixed number (one for every three months) to a flexible number, depending on the size and nature of the company and through mutual agreements.

11.6 CONCLUSION

There is no doubt that diligent and well-educated human resources have significantly contributed to Korea's miraculous economic development until the mid-1990s. However, Korea has faced serious challenges in many respects of the labour force and labour relations in the recent past. The labour force has remained stagnant due to a slow growth of the population and its rapid ageing process. In this regard, the government and society should take heed of the female labour participation rate. The combined result of women's high education level with the availability of only lower-skill, lower-paying, non-regular jobs discourages women from joining the labour force. Another way of mitigating the slow growth of the labour force is to prolong the retirement age. So far, government policy or incentive schemes have not been sufficient to boost female participation in the labour force or to stem the trend of declining retirement age.

The structural change of the economy has weakened its job creation capability in the recent past, indicating an emerging 'jobless growth' economy. Another issue in the labour market is a significant mismatch between job-seekers' preferences and employment demand. University graduates prefer to work at large companies and a large number of them remain unemployed, whereas serious labour shortages exist in union-free SMEs. The three-D jobs (dirty, difficult and dangerous), which Koreans shun, are filled by foreign workers, whose number has risen quite rapidly, raising a host of social, economic and diplomatic issues.

Industrial relations has transformed to a remarkable extent in the recent past, yet it still remains as one of the most contentious and critical issues in Korea. As a result of a series of revisions from the late 1980s to the end of the 1990s, laws related to labour standards have improved to the level of OECD countries, although actual labour standards in Korea fall short of international standards because of their ineffective implementation. Collective industrial relations have transformed in order to settle labour disputes voluntarily, and government power and influence on labour management has lessened remarkably. Despite the improvement of formal institutions related to industrial relations, Korea's labour market is renowned for its lack of flexibility and hostile industrial relations. Korea is regarded as one of the worst countries for both labour regulations and labour relations. Not only has Korea's inefficient industrial relations management led to hostile industrial relations but it has also raised wage levels well above neighbouring competitors, hindering its national competitiveness.

Another serious issue in Korea's industrial relations is the duality in the labour market between regular and non-regular workers. The former receive higher compensation, protection and other benefits than the latter. Due to the difficulties in labour adjustment under the strict protection for regular workers and confrontational labour relations, companies prefer to hire non-regular workers. A twofold solution is suggested to the labour market duality such that the strict protection for regular workers be eased, and protection and benefits for non-regular workers improved. As a way of easing the protection for regular workers, it is proposed to shorten the consultation period for dismissal of workers for managerial reasons, and lower employers' contributions to employees' national and retirement pension programmes. It is proposed that non-regular workers be provided with the coverage of the four social safety net programmes in the same way as regular workers.

To ease the tension and animosity in industrial relations and to develop cooperation better, four proposals are suggested. First, salary payments to full-time union officials ought to be stopped. Second, the existing imbalance in power between unions and employers ought to be addressed. A penal provision is in place against wrongful and unfair activities by management, while a similar provision does not exist against unions' wrongful activities. Employers cannot operate business during strikes as they are prohibited from hiring replacement workers. In effect, there is no check-and-balance mechanism in union activities, which appears to be the main source of the industrial relations problems in Korea. Third, the government ought to stop its intervention in labour disputes and instead implement laws against unions' illegal activities. Fourth, on the employer side, corporate governance, transparency, accountability, and compliance with the law and ethics should improve to foster trust between unions and employees. Employers should also restrain forced retirement of senior employees.

The organizations that play important roles for industrial relations should improve their structure and operations. The Korea Tripartite Commission should take a bottom-up approach to the social consensus-building process with more comprehensive representation of society. To this end, it should include workers' and companies' representatives from SMEs. The agenda for the KTC should focus on mid- and long-term policy directions on industrial relations, leaving short-term issues to the Labor Relations Commission (LRC). To enhance the efficacy of the remedial process and the confidence of decisions made by the LRC, a twofold suggestion is proposed. The long and expensive five-tiered remedial procedure of labour disputes should be simplified to a three-tiered process together with appointment of the Chairman of the LRC from judges of the Supreme Court. Finally, the Labor-Management Council (LMC), which is a bottom-up approach to cooperative labour relations, should be further promoted. Some flexibility in terms of frequency of consultations should be provided.

To maintain sustainable growth and to progress its economy to the status of advanced countries, Korea has faced daunting challenges of maintaining its labour force and developing cooperative industrial relations. A number of specific issues have been identified and ways of tackling each of these issues are suggested. These suggestions are by nature socially contentious, controversial and therefore arduous and challenging. In order to undertake these tasks successfully, Korea needs a strong political leadership, societal tolerance of different views and opinions, and the skills to compromise over the differences and build up social consensus.

NOTES

1. According to a survey of foreign business people in Korea in 2002, Kwon (2003) found that foreign businesspeople viewed Korean workers as having these characteristics.
2. Foreign workers accounted for 2 per cent of total employment in 2006.
3. *JoongAng Daily* (2007) said that there were about 400 000 foreign workers in Korea in 2006, of which 190 000 were illegal foreign workers.
4. Nam and Kim (1997) argue that real wage rates in the manufacturing sector increased much faster than increases in labour productivity over the 1964–94 period.
5. The dispatched worker system refers to hiring arrangements whereby an employer can employ workers through temporary work agencies instead of hiring them directly. Fixed-term workers refer to those whom an employer is able to hire without restriction for up to three years. After three years have passed, the provision on restriction of dismissal of the Labor Standard Act will apply to them. Managerial reasons include an absolutely unavoidable case including bankruptcy, financial deterioration, technical innovation and restructuring for an improvement of productivity and change in product line. They also include cases arising as a consequence of transfers, M&As of business (H.S. Kim 2005c).
6. The union density rate refers to the number of union members as a percentage of the total number of employed workers. Korea's union density rate was 10.3 per cent in 2005, compared to 18.7 per cent, 12.5 per cent and 26.2 per cent, respectively, in Japan, the United States and the United Kingdom (Cho 2007).
7. KLI (2008) cites two major reasons for non-participation: raising children and taking care of household matters, accounting, respectively, for 15.2 per cent and 51.9 per cent over the 2003–07 period. The latter is closely related to unfair labour conditions for women.
8. The OECD (2007a: 113) points out that parental leave provisions and childcare subsidies have had major success in other OECD countries.
9. The unemployment rate for female university graduates was on average 3.7 per cent over the period 2000–06, while the overall unemployment rate for women was 3 per cent (KLI 2007).
10. The 'retirement' age in Korea is ten years younger than the OECD average (Kim and Park 2006).
11. In 2007–08, the WEF ranked Korea 71st and 107th, respectively, for rigidity of employment, and firing costs (WEF 2007, 2008).
12. In 2002, temporary workers comprised 51.6 per cent of the Korean labour force compared with 32 per cent in Spain, 27 per cent in Australia, 13 per cent in Germany and 12 per cent in Japan (Park and Kim 2005).
13. It should be noted that responsibility, productivity and loyalty toward companies could be different between regular and non-regular workers, which results in differences in compensation between them.
14. Reflecting this increase in non-regular workers, the average job tenure in Korea is low by international comparison. In enterprises with five or more employees, tenure was less than six years under the same employer in 2000. This contrasts with average employment tenures of ten years in the European Union and 12 years in Japan (Martin et al. 2004).

15. Australia, the United Kingdom and New Zealand have removed legal support for unionized closed shops, and other advanced countries have reduced support for them (de Turberville 2007).
16. In Canada, for instance, employer and employee each contribute 4.95 per cent to the Canada Pension Plan, which is equivalent to Korea's National Pension Plan. Private companies have their own retirement plans to which, typically, employer and employee each contribute 7 per cent of the employees' income. The total contribution by employers is 11.95 per cent of the employee's income. Australia does not have a National Pension Plan corresponding to Korea's National Pension Plan to which employers contribute. Every economic organization, regardless of whether it is public or private, has its own Employee Retirement Pension Plan for which the employer contributes a mandatory minimum of 7 per cent of employee's remuneration.
17. The Agreement includes the following changes:
    a. postponement of the introduction of enterprise-level multiple unionism and ban on wage payment to full-time union officers to the end of 2009;
    b. abolition of compulsory arbitration for public utility areas;
    c. adjustment of advance notice period for dismissal of workers; and
    d. an adjustment to the union shop system.
18. The United States, Japan, Germany, Singapore and Taiwan allow replacement workers (S.J. Park 2007).
19. There is a long list of illegal activities or unfair demands by unions (S.J. Park 2007).
20. This was ascertained through anecdotal personal interviews with high-ranking civil servants and private company officials.
21. The Federation of Korea Trade Union (FKTU) has withdrawn itself from the KTC for some time.
22. The Grand Tripartite Agreement has left the regulations related to the Council unchanged (MOL 2006: 15).

REFERENCES

Cho, Seong-Jae (2007), '20 years in Korea's industrial relations: based on statistics on union structure and industrial disputes', *Monthly Labor Review*, **30**, 3–29.

de Turberville, S. (2007), 'Union decline and renewal in Australia and Britain: lessons from closed shops', *Economic and Industrial Democracy*, **28**, 374–400.

Eun, Soo-Mi (2007), 'Assessment of industrial relations in 2006 and forecasts for 2007', *Monthly Labor Review*, **47**, January, 18–41.

Grubb, David, Jae-Kap Lee and Peter Tergeist (2007), 'Addressing labour market duality in Korea', OECD Social, Employment and Migration Working Papers No. 61, Paris: OECD.

Hankyoreh (2006), 'Time to rethink labor, business, government relationship', **15** March.

Hwang, Jongyon (2007), 'Counterbalanced marketization: the Korean way of labor market reregulation and welfare reform in a comparative perspective', *Korea Journal*, **47** (1), 177–211.

IMD (various years), *IMD World Competitiveness Yearbook*, Lausanne: IMD.

JoongAng Daily (2007), 'Foreign workers' rights are as valuable as ours', *Korea Focus*, **15** (1), 49–50.

JoongAng Daily (2009), 'An average retirement age expected by workers: 43.9', *JoongAng Daily*, 2 February.

Kim, Andrew Eungi and Innwon Park (2006), 'Changing trends of work in South Korea: the rapid growth of under-employment and job insecurity', *Asian Survey*, **46** (3), 437–56.

Kim, Hoon (2009), 'Prospects and policy issues of industrial relations in 2009', (in Korean), *Monthly Labor Review*, **48**, January, 31–44.

Kim, Hun-soo (2005a), 'Settlement system of industrial conflict: Australia and Korea', mimeo.

Kim, Hun-soo (2005b), 'Labor law in Korea: history and current system', mimeo, a paper presented at Griffith University.

Kim, Hun-soo (2005c), 'Contemporary reform of industrial relations in Korea', a paper presented at the 19th Conference of the Association of Industrial Relations Academics of Australia and New Zealand, 9–11 February, Sydney University.

Kim, Sookon (2001), 'Korea's industrial relations in transition', in O. Yul Kwon and W. Shepherd (eds), *Korea's Economic Prospects: from financial crisis to prosperity*, Cheltenham, UK and Northampton, MA, USA: Edward Elgar Publishing, pp. 207–24.

Kim, Sookon and J.H. Lee (1997), 'Industrial relations and human resource development', in D.S. Cha, K.W. Kim and D.H. Perkins (eds), *The Korean Economy 1945–1995: performance and vision for the 21st century*, Seoul: Korea Development Institute, pp. 586–622.

Kim, Sung-teak (2007), 'Prospects for increasing labor market flexibility in Korea', *Korea's Economy 2007*, **23**, 29–43.

Korea Economic Research Institute (KERI) (2007), *Comprehensive Analysis of Regulatory Reform: issue 4-2, labor market and finance*, Seoul: Korea Economic Research Institute.

Korea International Labor Foundation (KILF) (2006), 'KCCI survey of current status and future improvement of labor-management consultation body', www.koilaf.org/KFeng/engCommon/openPrint.php.

Korea International Labor Foundation (KILF) (2008), 'Companies will be allowed to employ foreign workers for up to 5 years', www.koilaf.org/KFeng/engCommon/openPrint.php.

Korea Labor Institute (KLI) (various years), *KLI Labor Statistics*, Seoul: KLI.

Korea National Statistical Office (KNSO) (2002), *Major Statistics of Korean Economy, 2002.9*, Seoul: KNSO.

Korea National Statistical Office (KNSO) (various years), *Korea Statistical Yearbook*, Seoul: KNSO.

Korea Productivity Centre (2008), 'Productivity statistics', www.kpc.or.kr.

Kwon, Tai-Hwan (2003), 'Demographic trends and their social implications', *Social Indicators Research*, **62** (1), 19–27.

Lee, Injae (2007), 'Labor market policies since the financial crisis: a review', paper presented at the International Policy forum on Visions and Strategies for Employment Policy in the 21st Century, Korea Labor Institute, 4–5 October 2007.

Lee, Won-Duck and B.H. Lee (2003), 'Industrial relations and labor standards in Korea', in O.Y. Kwon, S.H. Jwa and K.T. Lee (eds), *Korea's New Economic Strategy in the Globalisation Era*, Cheltenham, UK and Northampton, MA, USA: Edward Elgar Publishing, pp. 173–91.

Lee, Yoonkyung (2006), 'Varieties of labor politics in northeast Asian democracies', *Asian Survey*, **46** (5), 721–40.

Martin, J.P., P. Tergeist and R. Torres (2004), 'Reforming the Korean labour market and social safety net: key pending issues', in C. Harvie, H.H. Lee and J. Oh (eds),

The Korean Economy: post-crisis policies, issues and prospects, Cheltenham, UK and Northampton, MA, USA: Edward Elgar Publishing, pp. 78–119.
Ministry of Labor (MOL) (2006), 'Grand Tripartite Agreement for the Advancement of Industrial Relations', Seoul: Ministry of Labor.
Ministry of Labor (MOL) (2008), 'An analysis of the 2007 status of trade unions', (in Korean), Seoul: Ministry of Labor.
Nam, S.W. and J.I. Kim (1997), 'Macroeconomic policies and evolution', in D.S. Cha, K.W. Kim and D.H. Perkins (eds), *The Korean Economy 1945–1995: performance and vision for the 21st century*, Seoul: Korea Development Institute, pp. 143–85.
Naver (2007), 'Postponement of the prohibition of salary payments for full time union officials', http://news.naver.com/.
OECD (2004), *OECD Economic Surveys: Korea*, Paris: OECD.
OECD (2005), *OECD Economic Surveys: Korea*, Paris: OECD.
OECD (2007a), *OECD Economic Surveys: Korea*, Paris: OECD.
OECD (2007b), *OECD in Figures 2007*, Paris: OECD.
Park, D.J., J.H. Park and G.C. Yu (2001), 'Assessment of labor market response to the labor law changes introduced in 1998', in F.K. Park, Y.B. Park, G. Betcheman and A. Dar (eds), *Labor Market Reforms in Korea: policy options for the future*, Seoul: Korea Labor Institute, pp. 125–50.
Park, G.S. and A.E. Kim (2005), 'Changes in attitude toward work and workers' identity in Korea', *Korea Journal*, **45** (3), 36–57.
Park, Insub (2007), 'The labour market, skill formation and training in the "post-developmental" state: the example of South Korea', *Journal of Education and Work*, **20** (5), 417–35.
Park, Ki Seong (2008), 'Non-standard employment', in R.B. Freeman, S.W. Kim and J.H. Keum (eds), *Beyond Flexibility Roadmaps for Korean Labor Policy*, Seoul: Korea Labor Institute, pp. 261–77.
Park, Seong-Jun (2007), 'Industrial relations', (in Korean), in Z.S. Rhee (ed.), *Korea's Policy toward Large Corporations (II)*, Seoul: Korea Economic Research Institute, pp. 219–62.
Small and Medium Business Administration (SMBA) (2009), 'Korean SMEs: statistics', www.smba.go.kr.
World Bank (2008), *2008 World Development Indicators*, Washington, DC: World Bank.
World Bank (2009), *2009 World Development Indicators*, Washington, DC: World Bank.
World Economic Forum (WEF) (2007), *The Global Competitiveness Report 2007–2008*, Basingstoke, UK and New York: Palgrave Macmillan.
World Economic Forum (WEF) (2008), *The Global Competitiveness Report 2008–2009*, Basingstoke, UK and New York, USA: Palgrave Macmillan.
Yoon, Bong Joon (2005), 'Labor militancy in South Korea', *Asian Economic Journal*, **19** (2), 205–30.

12. Income distribution and social welfare policy: issues and strategy

12.1 INTRODUCTION

The Korean government started its economic development strategy of 'growth-first' in the early 1960s, focusing on maximizing annual growth rates, paying little attention to policy regarding income distribution and social development until the mid-1980s. Despite this emphasis on the growth-first strategy, the World Bank (1993: 72) indicated that the distribution of income in Korea was among the most equitable in the developing world. The Gini coefficient started at 0.344 in 1965, which was one of the lowest of all developing countries, and declined to 0.279 in 1997 (Table 12.1). Absolute poverty was ameliorated to a remarkable extent as indicated by a decrease in the proportion of population below the official poverty line from 40.9 per cent in 1965 to 4 per cent in 1997 (Table 12.1).

The 1997 financial crisis profoundly transformed distribution, employment and reward structures in the economy. The immediate manifestation of this was unprecedented high unemployment and significantly worsened inequality in income and asset ownership. The Gini coefficient increased from 0.279 in 1997 to 0.296 in 1998, and the poverty rate increased from 4 per cent in 1997 to 7.8 per cent in 1998 (Table 12.1). The unemployment rate increased from 2.7 per cent in 1997 to 7 per cent in 1998. The adverse impacts of the financial crisis on income distribution and employment produced an inevitable upsurge in the demand for state welfare provision.

The Kim Dae-jung government, inaugurated in 1998, sought to improve the social welfare system as one of the top national agendas under the name of 'productive welfare'. Over the 2003–08 period, building on the Kim Dae-jung government's welfare policy, the Roh Moon-hyun government promoted the so-called 'participatory welfare' on the premise that there was no guaranteeing the nation's future economic security without first addressing and bridging the income and wealth gap (S.Y. Lee 2006). These two governments expanded Korea's social security system in the direction of the comprehensive and institutionalized welfare states characteristic of the

West. As examined in Chapter 2, economic polarization weakens social cohesion which in turn decreases a nation's 'social capital', thereby adversely affecting economic growth in the long run. In this respect, the implementation of comprehensive social security programmes is essential for sustainable economic development.

Table 12.1 Income distribution (urban employee households), 1965–2007 (Gini coefficient and %)

	1965	1970	1997	1998	2000	2005	2006	2007
1. Gini[a]	0.344	0.332	0.279	0.296	0.296	0.304	0.303	0.306
2. Poverty ratio[b]	40.9	23.4	4.0	7.8	7.0	6.8	6.3	5.9
3. Poverty ratio[c]	n.a.	n.a.	8.7	10.8	10.2	12.4	12.3	12.5
4. Decile ratio	19.5	9.1	6.41	8.01	7.48	8.76	8.43	8.55
5. Female households[d]	n.a.	n.a.	21.7	24.1	24.4	30.1	31.8	31.6
6. Elderly poor[e]	n.a.	n.a.	17.5	19.1	21.7	25.3	31.9	32.6
7. Share of labour income[f]	31.8	41.4	62.3	61.9	58.8	60.7	61.3	61.5
8. Farm income to urban wages[g]	1.30	0.76	0.86	0.80	0.81	0.78	0.78	0.72

Notes:
[a] City labourers.
[b] Households with income less than minimum costs of living estimated by government (city labourers).
[c] Households with income less than 50 per cent of median income (city labourers).
[d] Households with single mothers with income less than 50 per cent of median income of city labourers.
[e] Elderly people over 65 with income less than 50 per cent of median income of city labourers.
[f] Share of labour income of national income at factor costs.
[g] Ratio of farm household income to urban household income, and the ratio of 1.30 is for 1963.

Sources: For 1965–70 for 1, 4, 7: Choi and Kwon (1997); for 1965–70 for 2: Adelman (1997); for 1970–1997 for 1–7: KIHASA (2008); and for 1963–70 for 8: Lee et al. (2004), and for 1997–2007 for 8: Bank of Korea (2008).

Nevertheless, absolute poverty and economic polarization still remain as serious social issues. The proportion of households under the poverty line has remained around 6 per cent in the recent past. The Gini coefficient increased from 0.279 in 1997 to 0.306 in 2007 (Table 12.1). The wage ratio of the top quintile to the bottom quintile increased from 4.23 in 1997 to 5.12 in 2007 (KLI 2008). In conjunction with exacerbating poverty and economic polarization, the Korean population has been ageing at an unprecedented pace. As the population ages, the number of people who need social protection increases. The relative poverty of the elderly population has also increased (Table 12.1). Another facet of the demographic change is the rising number of female households due to increasing family break-ups and the greater survival rate of females over males (KNSO 2008). The relative poverty of female households has been worsening in the recent past (Table 12.1). Under these welfare circumstances, and repudiating his two predecessors' welfare policy as an overemphasis on distribution at the expense of growth, the Lee Myung-bak government, inaugurated in February 2008, embarked on its 'proactive welfare' plan.

This chapter examines the Korean welfare system which is intended to mitigate the most pernicious aspects of the market-based economy under globalization – persistent poverty of certain groups of people and rising income inequality. To this end, this chapter first examines income distribution before and after the 1997 financial crisis and Korea's welfare policy reforms introduced since the crisis, surveying the extant literature in both English and Korean. It analyses the underlying causes of recent developments in Korea's income distribution, and makes comparisons with selected Asian and OECD countries to put the issue into perspective. Then, social welfare programmes introduced or expanded in response to the upsurge in demand for a social safety net since 1997 are examined. This chapter will evaluate the new social welfare system in terms of macro aspects of the social welfare system and then the institutional designs of the system. By combining these two types of evaluation, the appropriateness of Korea's social welfare system and its future direction will be assessed.

12.2 INCOME DISTRIBUTION

12.2.1 Income Distribution Prior to the 1997 Financial Crisis

The distribution of income in Korea was among the most equitable in the developing world up to the 1997 crisis. As shown in Table 12.1, income distribution measured either by the Gini coefficient or by the proportion of people below the poverty line improved substantially over the period 1965–97. In comparison with countries in East Asia, Korean income distribution was more equitable until 1997 (Table 12.2).[1] The pattern of income distribution in Korea was similar to those of OECD countries. In 2001, Korea's Gini coefficient of 0.319 was slightly higher than the OECD average of 0.310 (Table 12.2).

Another facet of income distribution in Korea is the functional distribution of income. One of the core functional types of income distribution is the labour income share, which showed a long-term growth trend, with short-term fluctuations, from 31.8 per cent in 1965 to 62.3 per cent in 1997 (Table 12.1). Income differentials between rural and urban regions have always been social and political issues as well as economic concerns. The income gap between rural and urban regions did not show a clear trend due to economic and policy reasons as well as non-economic reasons such as weather. Overall, the ratio of farm household income to urban household income from wages and salaries increased from 0.76 per cent in 1970 to 0.86 per cent in 1997 (Table 12.1).

Table 12.2 Gini coefficients of selected countries, 1989/90–2002

Country	1989/90	1994	1995	1997	1998	2000	2001	2002
Australia	0.337	0.352	–	–	–	0.305	–	–
Canada	–	0.315	–	0.315	0.331	0.301	–	–
China	–	–	0.415	–	0.403	–	0.447	–
France	0.327	–	0.327	–	–	0.273	–	–
Germany	0.281	0.300	–	–	–	0.283	–	0.290
Hong Kong	–	–	–	–	–	–	0.525	–
Japan	–	–	–	–	–	0.314	–	–
Korea	0.295	0.284	0.284	0.283	0.316	0.317	0.319	0.312
Malaysia	0.484	–	0.485	0.492	–	–	–	–
Singapore	–	–	–	–	0.425	–	–	–
Taiwan	0.312	0.318	0.317	0.320	0.324	–	–	–
Thailand	–	–	–	–	0.414	0.432	–	–
UK	0.326	–	0.368	–	–	0.360	0.320	–
USA	–	0.401	–	0.408	–	0.408	0.380	–
OECD	–	–	–	–	–	0.308	0.310	–

Sources: Forster and D'Ercole (2005); OECD (2006); OECD (2007a); UNDP (various years); World Bank (various years); Zin (2005).

It should be pointed out that distribution of income in Korea does not reveal the distribution of wealth. Disparities in the pattern of asset ownership will have an important bearing on the prevailing perception of economic polarization, social cohesion and social capital. Concentration of real-estate possession has been a well-known phenomenon in Korea. The top 1 per cent of people owned 27.9 per cent of total land and the top 10 per cent had 63.6 per cent of total land in 1993 (Choi and Kwon 1997). In 1988, income distribution had a Gini coefficient of 0.404, while those for financial assets, real assets and total assets were, respectively, 0.770, 0.596 and 0.579 (Choi and Kwon 1997).

This relatively equitable distribution of income in Korea was attributable to a variety of factors. Korea successfully implemented thorough land reforms in 1947 and 1950, and in addition, the destruction of all physical infrastructure and production facilities by the Korean War forced Koreans to begin again from the same level of poverty. The Korean people are homogeneous in terms of race, language and cultural tradition. In addition, there are no strong regional or religious differences in Korean society, nor is there a deeply entrenched class structure. Consequently, the pursuit of economic opportunity was not inhibited by such factors, and the mobility and adaptation of labour was relatively free of social limitations. Koreans have keen aspirations for education and were generally provided with equal opportunities in this respect.

Korea's policy of developing labour-intensive industries, during the early stages of development in the 1960s up until the early 1970s, contributed to the equitable distribution of income by providing employment opportunities for workers with a minimum level of education. From the mid-1970s, labour income increased relatively more rapidly due to the limited supply of labour, thereby improving income distribution (Table 12.1). The expansion of labour income share and the equalization of labour income distribution in Korea were promoted by trade union activity from 1987 and by introduction of the minimum wage in 1988. Income inequality in Korea declined further in the 1990s as a result of high economic growth and rapid increases in real wages, accompanied by a fall in unemployment. The government also introduced a variety of measures to minimize income disparity between the rural and urban sectors (Lee et al. 2004: 71).

12.2.2 Income Distribution after the 1997 Crisis

Table 12.1 shows that income inequality in Korea sharply deteriorated after the 1997 financial crisis. The Gini coefficient increased from 0.279 in 1997 to 0.296 in 1998 and has since remained above 0.300 (Table 12.1). Another demonstration of the increasing income disparity is the rising income ratio of the top-decile households to that of the bottom-decile households, from 6.41 in 1997 to 8.01 in 1998, and further to 8.55 in 2007 (Table 12.1). Inequality in distribution of wealth also deteriorated after the crisis, as indicated by an increase in the Gini coefficient of net wealth from 0.600 in 1997 to 0.655 in 1998 (J.W. Lee 2002).

Increases in inequality in income distribution after the crisis are attributable to various factors. First, due to the rising unemployment rate following the crisis, labour earnings declined. The labour income share decreased from 62.3 in 1997 to 61.9 per cent in 1998, and remained less than the 1998 level until 2007 (Table 12.1). Second, lifetime employment, a characteristic of Korean working life and once virtually guaranteed by law, unravelled under the labour market reforms after the crisis. Business took advantage of the new reforms to replace regular positions with non-regular workers to save on wages. As examined in Chapter 11, the share of non-regular workers increased from 45.7 per cent of total employment in 1997 to 52.1 per cent of total employment in 2000, decreasing somewhat to 46 per cent in 2007 (Table 11.5 in Chapter 11). Non-regular workers are treated substantially worse than regular employees in terms of remuneration and social and statutory benefits. Many non-regular workers are not covered by social safety net programmes. Third, as examined in Chapter 8, the bipolarization between large corporations and SMEs has worsened in term of productivity and profitability. As a result, the wage rates at SMEs were only 55.7 per cent of those at large corporations in the manufacturing sector in 2002. As a result, income in the form of wages was the main source of rising income inequality. The contribution of wage income to income inequality increased from 83.8 per cent in 1997 to 86.4 per cent in 1998, and increased to 89.4 per cent on average during the period 2003–05 (Bank of Korea 2006).

Table 12.3 Proportion of Korea's households under the poverty line by OECD standards, 1997–2004 (%)

	1997	1998	1999	2000	2001	2002	2003	2004
Upper class	21.8	22.9	23.3	22.0	22.7	22.6	22.5	22.5
Middle class	68.5	65.4	64.7	66.2	65.2	65.1	65.5	63.9
Low class	9.7	11.7	11.9	11.9	12.0	12.4	12.0	13.6

Notes:
The low class includes households with income below 50 per cent of the median household income.
The middle class includes those with income ranging from 50 to 150 per cent of the median income.
The upper class includes those with income of 150 per cent and more.

Source: Bank of Korea (2006).

A serious problem arising from rising income disparity is the increased number of people under the poverty line. After the 1997 crisis, the proportion of households in the low-income class increased from 9.7 per cent in 1997 to 11.7 per cent in 1998, and gradually increased to 13.6 per cent in 2004 (Table 12.3). Another problem is that the middle-income class has been shrinking. As shown in Table 12.3, the proportion of households in the middle-income class decreased steadily, although fluctuated somewhat, from 68.5 per cent in 1997 to 63.9 per cent in 2004. Typically the middle-income group has played an important role for the stability of Korean society and politics. The contraction of the middle class together with the increases in the number of people under the poverty line augurs ill for future developments in Korean society, politics and the economy. The income gap between rural and urban regions has also been widening. In contrast to the insignificant income differential between them from the 1960s to the mid-1990s, the ratio of farm household income to urban household income decreased from 86 per cent in 1997 to 81 per cent in 1998, and since then has remained at about 75 per cent (Table 12.1).

Income disparities will enlarge social discontent from a number of segments of society, and cause flagging social cohesion which will in turn adversely affect the economy. Therefore, it is imperative that Korea implement a better social welfare system to ameliorate the rising income disparities and the increasing number of poor people. In this respect, Korea's social welfare system is examined in section 12.3.

12.3 GOVERNMENT SOCIAL WELFARE POLICY AND PROGRAMMES BEFORE THE 1997 CRISIS

12.3.1 Developments of the Social Welfare System Prior to 1997

From the beginning of the 1960s until the mid-1980s, the Korean government, based on its 'growth first then equity' strategy, did not pay much attention to income distribution and social welfare policy. During the period of rapid industrial development, a broader social welfare provision was the sole responsibility of the family and private sector. Korea had historically developed its own culturally ingrained 'Confucian social welfare system' by which family members looked after each other in difficult times. Besides, since the economy and employment opportunities continued to grow and unemployment remained low, no serious problem was raised by the limited social welfare programmes. Hence, no proper social safety net was introduced.

Under the Park Chung Hee regime (1962–79), a number of welfare-related laws and programmes were introduced at the embarkation stage of industrialization strategy, although they were subordinate to the objective of rapid economic growth. These included the public assistance programme for the poor (1961), the industrial accident insurance programme (1963) the medical insurance programme (1963) and the Social Security Law (1963).[2] These were introduced more for political reasons to shore up grass-roots support for the military government rather than as a serious policy attempt to improve the social security system. These programmes had very low social coverage. The Social Security Law remained a statute and was not implemented until the 1980s.

Between 1980 and 1987, with a promise of establishing a 'welfare society', the Chun Doo Hwan government revised and amended laws related to social welfare, including Welfare Acts for the elderly, the disabled and children. The legislative basis for minimum wage programmes was introduced in 1986 (Y.H. Kim 2003). These Acts were supplemented during the Roh Tae Woo regime (1988–92) with the Equal Employment Act (1987), Maternity Health Care Act (1987), Maternity Welfare Act (1989) and the Regulation for the Promotion of the Employment of the Disabled (1990).

Realizing the underdevelopment of the social security system and its emerging importance and necessity, the Kim Young-Sam government (1993–97) established the National Welfare Planning Board in 1995. In 1996, the Kim government announced the Vision of the 21st Century National Welfare Reform to enhance the quality of life in Korea, and to place the welfare system on a sound and coherent basis for the future. A number of concrete policies were proposed to develop a social security system comparable to those in advanced countries (H.K. Lee 1999). Before these policies could be implemented, the 1997 crisis occurred and starkly exposed the weaknesses of the existing social security system.

12.3.2 Individual Social Welfare Programmes before 1997

Social security systems of advanced countries typically contain three types of programmes: social insurance, public assistance (income maintenance) and social services. Social insurance is a compulsory insurance in that beneficiaries are those who have made contributions to the programme. Korea's four social insurance schemes are the national pension scheme, universal health insurance system, industrial accident insurance programme and the unemployment insurance scheme. Public assistance is to guarantee a minimum standard of living for those who cannot support themselves. Beneficiaries are those who meet strict eligibility requirements through means (income and assets) and needs tests. Social (or welfare) services are to protect and support certain target populations such as people aged 65 years and over and disabled persons. The Korean social security system, comprised of social insurance, income maintenance programmes and social services, is similar in its framework to those of developed countries.

Korea's national pension scheme was enacted in 1973 but implemented only in 1988. It was fragmented and lacked universal coverage until 1999. In 1997, only 43.7 per cent of the labour force contributed to the national pension scheme. The health insurance system, implemented from 1977, was extended to universal coverage only in 1989. The industrial accident insurance programme, financed exclusively by employers' contributions, was enacted in 1963. The programme was subsequently expanded to cover all workplaces with five or more employees, and in 1997 had the highest coverage rate at 71.8 per cent of total employees. Unemployment insurance was only introduced in 1995. Coverage was originally quite limited in that non-regular workers were excluded, and as of 1997 only 31.8 per cent of employees were eligible for benefits (Table 12.4; M.S. Kim 2003; Jacobs 2000; Shin 2000; Kwon 2001).

Table 12.4 Growth in social insurance coverage rate, 1990–2007 (%)

Year	Pension[a]	Health[b]	Unemployment[c]	Accident insurance[d]
1990	31.4	100.0	–	65.8
1997	43.7	100.0	31.8	71.8
1998	44.7	100.0	42.8	66.1
1999	49.6	100.0	47.8	55.7
2000	73.2	100.0	50.5	71.0
2001	72.4	100.0	50.6	77.5
2002	72.0	100.0	50.6	74.5
2003	74.8	100.0	50.0	73.6
2004	72.9	100.0	50.9	70.3
2005	72.1	100.0	53.1	79.5
2006	74.0	100.0	54.9	75.2
2007	75.4	100.0	56.8	78.5

Notes:
Total employees include temporary and day workers.
[a] Contributors/labour force.
[b] Contributors/population.
[c] Contributors/total employees.
[d] Contributors/total employees.

Sources: For 1990–98 Yang (2000); for 1999–2007 calculated from KNSO (various years); for employment insurance, KLI (2008).

The public assistance programme was launched in 1961 as the universal safety net for those officially designated as poor, and who were not covered under the social insurance schemes. It has provided only a very basic safety net with stringent eligibility requirements. In 1997, the public assistance programme covered only 3 per cent of the population (Y.H. Kim 2003).

Social services programmes for the elderly and disabled had not developed much prior to the 1997 financial crisis because of Korean family tradition by which the core of filial piety is to respect and care for elderly parents. The Old Age Allowance was introduced in 1991 to provide support to low-income elderly people not eligible for the national pension. In 1997, this allowance changed to the expanded Elder-Respect Pension. Although health protection and housing services are now provided for the elderly, they were limited and restrictive before 1997. The government started to pay serious attention to the disabled only from the late 1980s. The extent of public support for the disabled is generally regarded as insufficient (Choi 2002; Park and Kwon 2006; M.S. Kim 2003).

Korea had therefore implemented most social welfare programmes found in advanced countries prior to the 1997 financial crisis. However, all were underdeveloped or premature, so they did not play an important role in protecting citizens against the risks and insecurities of the market. This was also reflected in a small portion of government expenditure for the welfare system, compared to the size of the national economy, as shown below. The vast majority of the population had to find their own social security arrangements in the private sphere.

12.3.3 Government Expenditures for the Welfare System prior to 1997

The development strategy of 'growth first then equity' and minimal attention to social security issues is reflected in government expenditures for social security. Social welfare expenditures were kept low throughout the period of Korea's rapid growth, and began to increase gradually in the 1990s. Social welfare expenditure as a percentage of GDP was 3.2 per cent and 4 per cent, respectively, in 1990 and 1996, with an average of 3.5 per cent over 1990–96 (Table 12.5).

Table 12.6 shows an international comparison of social welfare payments based on OECD standards of classification. Korean public social expenditure as a percentage of GDP was less than 4 per cent until 1997, though gradually rising from 3 per cent in 1990 to 3.9 per cent in 1997. This was compared to the OECD average of 19.6 per cent in 1997, clearly indicating the government's minimal concern with social welfare up to the crisis.

Table 12.5 Expenditures for major social welfare programmes, 1997–2007 (trillion won and %)*

	1996	1998	2001	2004	2005	2006	2007
1. Unemployment insurance	0.1	0.8	0.7	1.4	1.8	2.1	2.4
2. National Health Insurance	5.9	6.8	13.2	16.4	18.4	21.4	24.6
3. National Pension Scheme	4.4	7.6	5.3	8.3	10.0	11.2	12.7
4. Basic livelihood allowance	–	–	2.0	2.4	2.8	3.2	3.4
5. Basic old-age pension	–	–	–	2.0	2.5	3.1	3.9
6. Others	6.3	12.1	14.3	12.8	14.1	15.1	n.a.
7. Total	16.6	27.2	35.4	43.4	49.6	56.0	61.4
Total public soc. exp./GDP (%)	4.0	6.1	6.5	5.6	6.1	6.7	6.8

Note: *Total expenditure, based on OECD guidelines, excludes retirement payments by private firms and welfare payments by local governments with their own revenue sources.

Sources: 1. KLI (2008); 2. 3. and 5. KIHASA (2008); 4. KNSO (various years); 6. for 1990–2003 S.K. Kim et al. (2008); for 2004–07 S.E. Choi et al. (2007).

Table 12.6 Public social expenditure of OECD members, 1990–2003 (% GDP)*

	1990	1995	1997	1998	2000	2001	2002	2003
Australia	14.1	17.1	17.0	17.0	17.9	17.4	17.5	17.9
Canada	18.4	19.2	17.7	18.0	16.7	17.3	17.3	17.3
Finland	24.5	27.4	25.2	23.2	21.3	21.4	21.9	22.5
France	25.3	28.3	28.5	28.7	27.6	27.5	27.9	28.7
Germany	22.5	26.6	26.4	26.3	26.3	26.3	27.0	27.3
Ireland	15.5	16.3	14.3	13.4	13.6	14.4	15.5	15.9
Japan	11.2	13.9	14.2	14.9	16.1	16.8	17.5	17.7
Korea	**3.0**	**3.5**	**3.9**	**5.5**	**5.1**	**5.4**	**5.4**	**5.7**
Netherlands	24.4	22.8	21.2	20.6	19.3	19.5	19.9	20.7
Sweden	30.5	32.5	30.7	30.5	28.8	29.3	30.4	31.3
UK	17.2	20.4	19.2	19.3	19.1	20.1	20.1	20.6
USA	13.4	15.4	14.9	14.8	14.6	15.2	16.0	16.2
OECD	17.9	19.9	19.6	19.6	19.6	19.9	20.5	20.9

Note: * public social expenditure excludes retirement payments by private firms.

Source: OECD (2007b).

12.4 GOVERNMENT SOCIAL WELFARE POLICY AND PROGRAMMES AFTER 1997

12.4.1 Reforms of the Social Welfare System after 1997

In response to the desperate need for public assistance in the wake of the crisis, the Kim Dae-jung government inaugurated a new welfare principle termed 'productive welfare'. The conceptual underpinnings of productive welfare were the basic human right to a decent minimum standard of life, the right to work, a recognition of the importance of social welfare as contributing to the nation's human capital, and a balanced emphasis on growth and welfare (An and Choi 2003; Kim et al. 2008: 76). Broadly, the new welfare paradigm advocated income distribution through an equitable market system and fair redistribution of wealth by government so that basic human needs were met.

After realizing its stark deficiency, the government reformed and improved the welfare system to a remarkable extent. Unemployment insurance was improved promptly due to the marked increases in the unemployment rate from 2.6 per cent in 1997 to 8.5 per cent in 1999 (KNSO 2005). The coverage of the employment insurance programme was quickly expanded. By October 1998, all employees, including part-time and temporary workers, were covered. The programme provided not only unemployment benefits but also training grants and job security grants. The actual coverage rate (the ratio of contributors to total employees) increased from 31.8 per cent in 1997 to 42.8 per cent in 1998 and further to 56.8 per cent in 2007 (Table 12.4). Duration of benefits was gradually extended from two months to one year, while the qualifying period was shortened to three months from six months of work history. Benefit payments equal 50 per cent of a worker's average earnings over the previous three months.

The national pension scheme has also improved. In 1999, the coverage was expanded to include all the economically active population aged between 18 and 59 years (Yang 2000). The minimum contributing period for pensioners to withdraw benefits decreased from 15 to ten years (Shin 2000). As a result, the coverage rate (the ratio of the contributors to labour force) has been rising quite rapidly since the crisis (Table 12.4). From its inception, however, the national pension scheme has not been based on a sound financial footing, because it is too generous and the expansion of coverage has caused further problems. As of 1996, the contribution rate was 6 per cent of wages, the income replacement rate was 70 per cent, and the pension age was set at 60 years of age (Shin 2000).[3] To improve the financial soundness of the scheme, from 1999 the contribution rates of both employers and employees increased to 4.5 per cent of monthly wages and the replacement rate was reduced to 60 per cent of previous earnings only after 40 years of contributions. The pension age will increase from the current 60 years of age by one year every five years from 2013 (Shin 2000).

Reforms to the national health insurance and the accident insurance scheme were also undertaken following the financial crisis. The national health insurance scheme had three types of health insurance programmes for different target groups, each administered by different insurance associations. In 1999, all three insurance programmes were incorporated into a single system under the National Health Insurance Act (Yang 2000). The accident insurance scheme also expanded its eligibility and coverage (Table 12.4). The scheme was expanded in July 2000 to cover both self-employed business owners and workers in small businesses (Yang 2000).

Although, as shown in Table 12.4, the coverage of all social insurance programmes has expanded significantly after the crisis, they are clearly not universal. With the exception of health insurance, all exclude significant proportions of the Korean population. Not only is the social insurance coverage insufficient, but excluding the health system, the programmes only provide benefits based on previous earnings and contributions. They were therefore insufficient and ineffective as social safety nets for the core poor who do not work. Hence, Korea urgently needed to improve public assistance programmes and social services.

To provide a decent minimum standard of life, the Kim Dae-jung administration introduced the National Basic Livelihood Security System (NBLSS) in 2000, replacing the previous Public Assistance Program. This recognized citizens' rights to a minimum living standard and provided cash benefits designed to guarantee a minimum standard of living regardless of capacity to work (OECD 2007a: 135; Y.M. Kim 2008). Although the new scheme still required means and needs tests and the non-availability of relative support, the provision of universal benefits in the form of direct government transfers marked a transition of the welfare system towards a more comprehensive and redistributive system. Productive welfare also provided for free healthcare and education programmes for the underprivileged as well as welfare programmes for the urban poor and unemployed.

The Roh Moo-hyun government was inaugurated in 2003 with its own welfare principle called 'participatory welfare', which had much continuity with productive welfare. Participatory welfare attempted to reinforce the social safety net, thereby guaranteeing minimum living standards to all citizens and enhancing citizens' participation in welfare policy formulation. Building on the newly expanded social insurance and public assistance schemes, participatory welfare placed greater emphasis on social service programmes for underprivileged people to achieve universal welfare (A.N. Kim et al. 2007: 2). To raise the living standards of the elderly, the government introduced the two pillars of a welfare system for senior citizens. One was the Basic Old-Age Pension, effective from January 2008, which was funded solely by government revenues and subject to an income test. The other was a long-term healthcare programme for the elderly who suffered from chronic illness.

To create a virtuous cycle of equity and growth, the Roh government attempted to facilitate economic growth by promoting social and economic participation and integration through investment in human resources. As part of this policy, the government introduced the Earned Income Tax Credit system to strengthen work incentives, effective from 2009. Finally, the Roh government introduced a 'one-stop' provision system for eight different services in the areas of health, welfare and employment (A.N. Kim et al. 2007: 2).

Repudiating the welfare policies of the two preceding governments as an overemphasis on equity at the expense of growth, the Lee Myung-bak government, inaugurated in 2008, introduced a new welfare principle called 'proactive welfare'. Proactive welfare is meant to be market-friendly welfare and aims at the simultaneous achievement of equity and efficiency (S.K. Kim et al. 2008: 76). Information on proactive welfare has been sketchy. At the time of writing in 2009 it is yet to be seen what kinds of new programmes or reforms in the welfare system will be introduced by the Lee Myung-bak government.

12.5 ASSESSMENT OF THE REFORMED SOCIAL WELFARE SYSTEM IN PLACE

A nation's welfare system is predicated on the welfare environment. Domestic and international welfare environments have changed remarkably in the recent past. Globalization increases the income gap between rich and poor within a country. This, together with the challenging issues of a rapidly ageing population and rising family break-ups, means that Korea needs to advance its welfare system quickly. The Korean tradition of supporting family members and elderly parents has been diminishing rapidly. Since the Kim Dae-jung government promoted the principle of a decent minimum standard of life as a basic human right, people have demanded a reasonable social safety net as their entitlement.

Yet, it appears that social culture, in terms of honesty, compliance with laws and resistance to moral hazard, has not matured enough for the efficient implementation of advanced welfare systems. The prevalence of opaque and informal economic transactions is relatively high, thus rendering the implementation of the welfare system onerous. The trade-off between equity and efficiency is well recognized; however Korean society has recognized the importance of social welfare as a contributing factor to the nation's economic development not only through human capital development but also through enhancement of social capital. In light of these welfare environments, the Korean welfare system in place will be assessed.

Under this evolving welfare environment, the government should seek to achieve the following objectives: eradication of absolute poverty, reduction of income inequality and provision of equal economic opportunities to prevent poverty inheritance. In view of the trade-off between equity and efficiency, welfare policies should be introduced with the least adverse effects on growth. Distribution schemes should also be designed to encourage motivation to work among the poor. To this is added that welfare schemes should be set up to minimize administrative costs and to provide adequate support only to target groups.

12.5.1 Macro Evaluation: Welfare Expenditure and Income Distribution

Reflecting the expansion of the social security system, government expenditures for social security programmes have expanded, and yet Korea remains far behind OECD countries in this regard. Government expenditures for social welfare programmes grew rapidly at 13.6 per cent a year over the period 1996–2007 (Table 12.5), compared to a 9.6 per cent annual growth of total government budget over the same period (KNSO 2008). As a percentage of GDP, the overall welfare payments increased a minimal extent from 4 per cent in 1996 to 6.8 per cent in 2007 (Table 12.5). By OECD standards, the ratio of public social expenditure to GDP was 5.7 per cent in 2003, while the OECD average was 20.9 per cent (Table 12.6).

With such a small amount of public expenditure on social welfare, it was unlikely that absolute poverty would be ameliorated or that income distribution would have improved significantly. In effect, income differentials have worsened since the crisis, as indicated by more or less gradual increases in the Gini coefficient from 0.279 in 1997 to 0.306 in 2007 (Table 12.1). The income ratio of the top decile to the bottom decile also shows a widening income gap between rich and poor, as indicated by an increase in the decile ratio from 6.41 in 1997 to 8.55 in 2007. Although the number of households below the official poverty line has declined somewhat since 1998, the number of households with income below 50 per cent of median income has increased significantly (Table 12.1).

12.5.2 Evaluation of Individual Programmes: Income Security Programmes

In terms of the institutional framework, Korea has been successful in transforming the four types of social insurance schemes into universal ones in law since the 1997 crisis. However, while national health insurance is a universal programme, the other three programmes have not achieved full coverage (Table 12.4). The employment insurance system still suffers from deficiencies and is far from universal, with a 56.8 per cent coverage rate in 2007. Because of the restrictive eligibility requirements and administrative complexity, a large portion of workers are still not covered.[4] Unfortunately, those who fail to meet the eligibility requirements and who decline to join the insurance scheme are the working poor such as daily workers or informal employees. In 2003, for instance, 70.3 per cent of people under the poverty line did not join the employment insurance scheme (Roh et al. 2007: 68). In addition, a large portion of unemployed, even if they have joined the scheme, do not meet the requirements for unemployment benefit payments. Hence, out of those unemployed, only 2.4 per cent and 5.9 per cent actually received unemployment benefits respectively in 2003 and 2005 (B.H. Lee et al. 2008: 22). Again, a relatively high portion of non-regular, daily and temporary workers could not meet the benefit payment requirements. It is evident therefore that employment insurance does not provide adequate income security, particularly for underprivileged, working poor people. Low-income workers are a serious social issue. The numbers of working poor have been rising and the number of families with one or more low-income earners amounted to 60 per cent of all families under the poverty line in 2006, or 16 per cent of all Korean families (Roh et al. 2007: 13)

In 1999, the national pension expanded to include every employee. As a result, the coverage rate increased from 49.6 per cent in 1999 to 73.2 per cent in 2000 and further to 75.4 per cent in 2007. The contribution rate, the contribution period, the pension age, and the replacement rate were set in 1999, respectively, at 9 per cent of pensionable income, ten years, 60 years of age, and 60 per cent of a three-year average income immediately prior to retirement based on 40 years of participation in the paid workforce. Because of its recent inception, with an insufficient coverage, and a required minimum number of years of contribution to withdraw pension income, only 14 per cent of the elderly were recipients of the national pension in 2005 (OECD 2007a: 118).[5] Therefore, the national pension together with unemployment insurance has failed to provide a social safety net for those most in need of income security.

A pending issue with the national pension is its financial soundness. To improve it, the National Pension Act was revised in 2007. However, while the income replacement rate decreased to 50 per cent in 2008 and is gradually to decrease further to 40 per cent by 2028, the contribution rate and contribution period remain unchanged at 9 per cent and ten years respectively. The 2007 revision is a politically expedient and perhaps irresponsible one whereby the contribution burden on the current generation remains unchanged, while the income of future pensioners is decreased. Nonetheless, it is expected with the 2007 revision that by 2060 the fund for the national pension will run out (Yoon 2008). It is therefore obvious that sooner or later, the National Pension Act has to be further amended to make the system self-sufficient.

Related to the national pension, as discussed in Chapter 11, Korea introduced the Retirement Pension Plan in 2005, to which employers are required to contribute 8.33 per cent of an employee's compensation. As a large proportion of non-regular workers and working poor are not covered by it, the companies' retirement pension is a source of economic polarization. Tax incentives for the retirement pension plan should be extended to non-regular workers, the self-employed and farmers. Even for the accident insurance, which has a 78.5 per cent coverage (Table 12.4), a high portion of low-wage earners are not covered. In 2003, for instance, 70.1 per cent of people under the poverty line did not join the accident insurance scheme (Roh et al. 2007: 68). Therefore, under the existing schemes, despite significant improvements, the social insurance system fails to provide an adequate level of income particularly for the working poor.

As a public assistance programme to compensate the deficiency of the social insurance system, the National Basic Livelihood Security System (NBLSS) was introduced in 2000. The dual purpose of the NBLSS is to guarantee income up to the official poverty line regardless of the recipient's ability to work; and to support people with working abilities to become self-sufficient. For the latter, the system requires those who are able to work to participate in training, public work projects or community services in return for benefits. It also provides small loans to help establish small businesses. The NBLSS has increasingly become more important than other welfare programmes. Over the period 2001–07, the number of recipients increased from 1.4 million to 1.5 million – 3.2 per cent of total population, and the total payments increased from 2.0 trillion to 3.4 trillion won – a 9.7 per cent annual increment, compared to 9.6 per cent growth of social development expenditures of the central and local governments (KNSO 2008; Table 12.5).

The NBLSS is an advanced social welfare system. However, it is a highly complex system to administer as it requires means and needs tests with no obligation for contribution. For this chapter, the system is assessed using the concept of target efficiency proposed by Weisbrod (1977).[6] Target efficiency refers to the degree to which actual redistribution coincides with the desired redistribution. Target efficiency is divided into vertical and horizontal target efficiency. The former can be measured by the ratio of total benefits received by the target group to total benefits paid out ($BT/$B), and the latter is by the ratio of the benefits going to the target group to total benefits needed ($BT/$BN). Since the system is the last resort social safety net, the target efficient of the NBLSS is critically important for that of Korea's overall social welfare system.

The target efficiency and the vertical target efficiency of the NBLSS are quite low, and as a result it fails to support the core poor and working poor people. The target group for the system is those whose income is below official minimum living costs. In 2007, the number of beneficiaries amounted to 3.2 per cent of the population, while the population under the official poverty line was 5.9 per cent (Table 12.1). In terms of household income, 12.5 per cent of households had income below the official poverty rate in 2007, while only 5.2 per cent of households are beneficiaries of the scheme (Table 12.1; KNSO 2008). To achieve high target efficiency, members of the target group should be properly identified. This is an onerous task. Since the system requires a means test, the ability to work and the level of income in the case of working recipients should be assessed. As the core poor, including the self-employed, are earning informal income, it is difficult to verify their income. For those who are not earning income, their ability to work should be ascertained.[7]

Since the system is a negative income tax, cash benefits decrease as earned income rises, generating a reluctance to report income. Once people are qualified for the NBLSS, they are also eligible for social services such as housing, education and healthcare, so it is regarded as a stepping stone to access social services (Roh et al. 2007: 8). All this creates a strong incentive for people to rely on the system, which is a disincentive to work and creates moral hazard or fraudulent behaviour. The fraud rate related to the system was estimated to be 63.5 per cent in 2007, which indicates the degree to which non-target members receive the benefits (T.J. Lee et al. 2008: 1).

The horizontal target efficiency is also quite low. The amount of the payment by the NBLSS is not adequate to maintain a minimum living standard. Over the 2001–06 period, about 55 per cent of the recipients were single-person families and this proportion has been consistently on the rise (KLI 2008). Monthly cash payment for a single-person family was set at 373 000 won per month in 2007, which amounted to 13.2 per cent of the average monthly wage for workers or 15.8 per cent of average household expenditure of a single-person family (KLI 2008).[8] In 2007, food costs alone took 25.1 per cent of the average household expense of urban working families (KLI 2008). Clearly, the NBLSS does not provide an adequate level of support for recipients. With an inadequate level of support, other social services have to be added such as education, housing and healthcare to ensure that basic human needs are met for all citizens subsisting below the minimum living standard. Once in-kind social services are added, it is more difficult to enhance the target efficiency.[9]

Another important purpose of the NBLSS is to support self-sufficiency for those recipients who are able to work. This is part of the Kim Dae-jung government's 'productive welfare' system, which seeks to link social welfare to economic growth. In 2006 out of 1.5 million recipients, 275 000, or 17.7 per cent, were regarded as having the ability to work (T.J. Lee et al. 2008: 8). In order to receive the benefits, recipients should participate in training, public work projects or community services arranged by the government. Once income earned by recipients exceeds the benchmark level, they should be deleted from the roster of benefits. It was estimated that recipients who crossed the poverty line accounted for 4.9 per cent of all recipients with the ability to work in 2005 after receiving the basic guarantee support for 34.4 months (Roh et al. 2007: 15). In other words, the success rate of the NBLSS as a self-sufficiency programme for the very poor is quite limited.

To enhance the efficiency and effectiveness in achieving the dual objectives of the NBLSS, the level of benefits should be adjusted upward, and the implementation process should be streamlined. Given the high fraudulence rate, a proper monitoring system is critically important in selecting beneficiaries (verification of income and working ability), in implementing follow-up processes and in providing self-support programmes. As a large number of ministries of the central government, local governments and welfare and self-sufficiency centres are involved in implementing the system, systematic coordination and transparent standardized procedures are vitally important in the monitoring process. H.J. Lee et al. (2008: 15) point out that a proper information infrastructure has not been established for the beneficiaries of the system. The NBLSS may also raise the perception of entitlement and disincentives for low-income people to work. It would therefore be desirable to impose a certain limit on the length of time recipients can access cash benefits over their lifetime, such as ten years.

Finally, to enhance the administrative efficiency of the NBLSS, it should be coordinated with tax administration, as the latter is effective in investigating and verifying the income of working poor and self-employed people. It is suggested that the Earned Income Tax Credit (EITC) should be expanded to all NBLSS beneficiaries with working ability. In advanced countries, social welfare policy is well coordinated with tax policy. The EITC, which is highly regarded as a combination of welfare and tax policies, is a flexible system in accommodating working incentives related to welfare payment. Currently, only wage earners whose income is higher than the official minimum living cost are eligible for the EITC (T.J. Lee et al. 2008:15). It is suggested that the EITC system expand to include all income-earning recipients of the NBLSS.

12.5.3 Evaluation of Individual Programmes: Social Services for Seniors

The elderly population has been rising rapidly and is absolutely and relatively poorer than the overall population. As shown in Table 12.1, while the relative poverty rate of the total population increased from 8.7 per cent in 1997 to 12.5 per cent in 2007, that of seniors increased from 17.5 per cent to 32.6 per cent (Table 12.1). The proportion of elderly below the poverty line was 16.2 per cent in 2007 (KIHASA 2008), while the corresponding value for total population was 5.9 per cent (Table 12.1). As stated earlier, only a small proportion of seniors (14 per cent in 2005) receive national pension. The NBLSS automatically excludes elderly Koreans aged 65 and over. Under this circumstance, Korea introduced the Basic Old Age Pension in 2008 which is funded by tax revenue and a means-tested benefit. As of 2008, about 60 per cent of elderly people over 65 were eligible for the pension, which provided 84 000 won per month (Jeong et al. 2007: 20). The monthly pension in 2008 amounted to 3.1 per cent of the average wage of all industries in 2007 (KLI

2008). Thus, the amount of benefits is well below the official minimum cost of living and is not adequate for those elderly who are not eligible for the national pension.

Another social service available to elderly Koreans is a relatively new long-term care programme which provides in-house or institutional care to eligible persons. The concept of formal long-term care, whether paid care at home or care at institutions, is new in Korea and runs counter to tradition by which siblings are expected to care for their parents. However, that kind of Korean tradition is fading quickly, and as the number of elderly has rapidly risen, so too has the number suffering from geriatric diseases. For instance, the number of elderly persons suffering from dementia was 350 000 (8.3 per cent of the elderly) in 2005 and is expected to double by 2010 (OECD 2007a: 133). Korea is facing a serious challenge in making equitable access to adequate long-term care services available for those elderly who cannot take care of themselves. The number of recipients of long-term care accounted for only 1.1 per cent of the total elderly in 2004, compared to an OECD average of 13.8 per cent. Expenditure on long-term care as a percentage of GDP was 0.3 per cent in Korea in 2004, compared to an OECD average of 1.2 per cent (OECD 2007a: 132).

12.5.4 Evaluation of Individual Programmes: Employment Programmes

It is recognized that employment training and placement programmes are an important part of social welfare policy as a way of breaking the poverty cycle. It is also an integral part of Korea's labour policy. Hence, Korea has introduced a number of social welfare programmes linked to employment programmes. In 2007, the government spent 2.8 trillion won for job creation purposes, which accounted for 4.5 per cent of the total budget for social welfare and provided 611 000 jobs, or 2.6 per cent of total employment (S.E. Choi et al. 2007: 46). Employment programmes alone, as part of social services, had a budget of 1.3 trillion won and provided 201 000 jobs in 2007, and the amount of budget increased by 60.4 per cent per year for the period 2004–07 (S.E. Choi et al. 2007: 44). Fifteen ministries and agencies are involved in operating employment programmes.

The employment insurance and the NBLSS are both linked to employment policy and it is doubtful that these programmes alone would be successful in breaking the poverty cycle of the recipients by making them self-sufficient. The dual objective of employment insurance is to provide unemployment benefits and to activate benefit recipients for employment. However, recipients of unemployment benefits have no obligation to participate in job training programmes (B.H. Lee et al. 2008: 265). Beneficiaries of the NBLSS with the ability to work have to participate in job-training programmes as a condition of receiving benefits. However, as mentioned above, only 17.7 per cent of the recipients of NBLSS benefits had the ability to work in 2006. Of them, only 12.8 per cent or 35 000 were those conditional recipients (T.J. Lee et al. 2008: 8). Of those conditional recipients, those who search for employment are trained by the Ministry of Labor, and those who seek to conduct self-employed businesses are supported by the Ministry of Health and Welfare. There is little monetary incentive for recipients to earn income, as the NBLSS benefits decreases by the amount of earned income. Finally, the viability and profitability of self-employed small business is quite low.

Another group for which the government should provide employment programmes is female households. As shown in Table 12.1, the proportion of single-mother households under the poverty line has been rising quite rapidly. This is in part attributable to a low female employment rate, which was 53.2 per cent in 2007, compared to an OECD average of 57.4 per cent (B.H. Lee et al. 2008: 257). Social services such as childcare support and maternity support as well as employment and placement programmes should be provided to activate female workers. As discussed in Chapter 11, social services for female workers are not sufficient to maintain them in the labour force.

The government has introduced a large number of employment programmes as labour policy or social service programmes. However, as compared to advanced countries, the scale of employment programmes in Korea is far less. Korea's expenditure on employment programmes as a percentage of GDP was 0.37 per cent in 2006, compared to an OECD average of 1.52 per cent (B.H. Lee et al. 2008: 284). The employment insurance and the NBLSS are not successful in raising recipients above the poverty line, because they are not properly designed to motivate the poor to work.

12.6 PROACTIVE WELFARE OF THE LEE MYUNG-BAK GOVERNMENT

The Lee Myung-bak government started with its basic economic policy paradigm underpinned by pro-growth and pro-market principles. In line with this paradigm, its welfare policy is termed 'proactive welfare' with the basic principle of creating jobs for those able to work and extending a helping hand to those in need of support. Proactive welfare is composed of four elements. The first is to expand the social safety net by reforming the national social insurance programmes and improving the benefits of the NBLSS. The second element is forward-looking family policies, by strengthening social services programmes such as family and childcare support and introducing long-term care insurance for the elderly. The third element is the protection of public health and safety by establishing a health safety net, enhancing preventative healthcare, and strengthening food safety management. The fourth element refers to the development of economic growth and health and welfare by fostering health-related industries and creating a market for welfare services (MIHWAF 2009). It appears that the first element aims at improving the existing social welfare system, the second and third elements focus on a forward-looking strategic goal of building a foundation of for lifelong welfare, and the fourth element stresses market-friendly welfare.

Although it is yet to be seen how specific measures for the proactive welfare policy would transpire, it has failed, by the end of 2008, to provide a coordinated approach to addressing the key social policy issues facing Korea: the exacerbation of socio-economic disparity, the black spots of the social security system and the ageing population. The first budget of the Lee Myung-bak government, introduced for the 2009 financial year, showed that the budget for social welfare would increase by 9 per cent, compared to a 6 per cent increment of the overall budget (T.S. Lee 2008). However, a high portion of the welfare budget is legally obligated. For instance, the legally bound portion of the welfare budget was 84.5 per cent in 2007 (S.E. Choi et al. 2007: 31). A certain increment in the welfare budget has also been incorporated in the law, while leaving a small portion of discretionary budget. T.S. Lee (2008) points out that by taking into account legal obligations, only 1.2 per cent out of 9 per cent is a discretionary increment in the welfare budget by the Lee government. It should be noted that this increment in the welfare budget is dwarfed by those during the previous administration. Over the period 2004–08, the welfare budget increased by 20.1 per cent a year, compared to a 7 per cent increase in the overall budget (S.E. Choi et al. 2007: 21). Although the evaluation of specific measures by the Lee government is still under review, its budgetary emphasis on welfare appears to be much less than that of the Roh Moo-hyun government.

12.7 CONCLUSION

This chapter has examined recent developments of income distribution and the welfare system and evaluated social security programmes in place. Korea had implemented the 'growth-first' strategy up to the 1980s and paid little attention to income distribution and social welfare. Nevertheless, income distribution in Korea was among the most equitable in the developing world, and gradually improved over the three decades up to 1997. Korea's social welfare policy has been very slow to progress, due to the cultural tradition of family members supporting each other and continuous improvements in the living standards of the general public resulting from strong economic growth.

The 1997 financial crisis profoundly transformed income distribution and social welfare issues. The 1997 crisis highlighted a number of deficiencies in the current state of social welfare policy. The crisis significantly worsened inequality and further polarized income and asset ownership. The proportion of Koreans below the poverty line increased remarkably. Economic polarization weakens social cohesion which, in turn, adversely affects the economy. In the recent past, economic polarization in Korean society has become one of the central political issues. These economic and political developments since the 1997 crisis have generated an inevitable upsurge in the demand for state welfare provision, and forced Korean society and its governments to review its social welfare policy.

As a result, Korea has transformed its social welfare system, which had evolved over three decades from a bare structure with a minimal number of programmes, into a fairly comprehensive one. The current form of the welfare system was developed largely during the Kim Dae-jung government and refined by the Roh Moo-hyun government. In terms of the framework of social security programmes, the current system is composed of the three typical types of programmes: social insurance, public assistance and social service, and is comparable to those in advanced countries. All of the social insurance programmes have improved and expanded their coverage. The NBLSS was introduced as a new public assistance programme, guaranteeing a minimum level of income as a right of all citizens. For senior citizens, the Basic Old Age Pension was introduced as a supplementary scheme to the national pension. Social services for working poor mothers were also introduced. A number of employment training programmes have been introduced. Further, reflecting the expansion of the social security system, government expenditure for social development has expanded substantially as a percentage of total government budget and GDP.

Despite all these improvements in social security programmes after the 1997 crisis, the Korean welfare system still suffers from serious deficiencies, and does not provide an adequate safety net for the entire population. Core poor people are not covered by social insurance programmes, except national health insurance, as they are based on earnings-related contributions. The NBLSS has failed to support the target group (people below the poverty line) adequately. The amount of benefits for individual recipients is set below the level of a minimum living standard, and benefits leak out to non-target groups due to poor administration and monitoring systems. Social services programmes for seniors are assessed inadequately for those who are not eligible for the national pension.

A number of employment programmes are offered as part of welfare programmes as a way of breaking the poverty cycle. However, the success rate is quite low because of inefficient coordination among a large number of government ministries and agencies involved, and a minimal budgetary emphasis on those programmes. These deficiencies are reflected in Korea's welfare expenditure in comparison to its economy, which is still much lower than the OECD average, and in worsening income differentials and rising poverty rates in the recent past. A conclusion is therefore drawn that, contrary to a strong perception prevalent in recent Korean society, the welfare system over the last decade has expanded more as a response to the financial crisis than to a mature system comparable to advanced countries.

Korea now faces the challenge of ameliorating the expanding inequality in income and the poverty rate, under the emerging welfare environments of rising numbers of seniors and single families, the diminishing cultural tradition of supporting each other among family members, and people's demand for a decent social safety net as their right. If left unchecked, economic polarization will adversely affect political stability as well as the economy. To this end, the government should further improve the existing welfare system and expand its welfare budget. It is suggested that the working poor be covered by social insurance programmes waiving the income-related contributions. The government should also take steps to enhance its target efficiency by simplifying public assistance and social service programmes and improving their administrative efficacy. In early 2009, a number of embezzlement incidents by civil servants occurred, largely because of the administrative complexity and the ineffective monitoring system arising from almost 100 different social service programmes (*Dong-A Daily* 2009).

The government should coordinate welfare policy with labour and tax policy, and take advantage of tax apparatus in implementing some of the welfare programmes. The welfare budget should also be increased up to an optimal level, which is estimated to be 14.8 per cent of GDP by 2012, compared to 7.1 per cent in 2005 (S.K. Kim et al. 2008: 108). This indicates that to achieve the optimal level, public social security expenditure should increase by about 20 per cent a year over the seven-year period 2005–12, under an assumption of economic growth of 8.1 per cent a year, as was the case over the seven years from 2000 to 2007.

NOTES

1. The Gini coefficients for Hong Kong, Singapore and Thailand were, respectively, 0.434 in 1996, 0.425 in 1998 and 0.414 in 1998, as compared to 0.283 in Korea in 1997. The 1997 Gini coefficients are not available for these countries (Table 12.2).

2. For history of Korea's welfare system, see Y.H. Kim (2003).
3. In Japan, the contribution rate, income replacement rate and pension age were, respectively, 17.4 per cent, 70 per cent and 65 years of age; and in Germany they were, respectively, 18.6 per cent, 70 per cent and 65 years of age (Shin 2000).
4. Part of the eligibility requires a history of employment over a certain length of time. Thus, school and college graduates are not covered.
5. This is contrasted to most elderly Australians who receive retirement income from their superannuation (Park and Kwon 2006).
6. Weisbrod's original concept of target efficiency has been modified in various ways (Choi and Choi 2006). A quantitative measurement of the target efficiency is beyond the scope of this chapter. For a quantitative measurement of target efficiency based on a modified Weisbrod model, see Choi and Choi (2006).
7. Reliability or credibility of medical certificates issued by medical professionals is quite low in Korea (T.J. Lee et al. 2008).
8. The NBLSS payment is well below the OECD estimate of the minimum living cost which is 20 per cent of the average income (OECD 2007a: 122).
9. Roh et al. (2007: 17) point out that it is difficult to maintain a high horizontal target efficiency particularly with housing subsidies.

REFERENCES

Adelman, Irma (1997), 'Social development in Korea, 1953–1993', in Dong-Se Cha, Kwang Suk Kim and D.H. Perkins (ed.), *The Korean Economy 1945–1995: performance and vision for the 21st century*, Seoul: Korea Development Institute, pp. 509–40.

An, Chong-Bum and Kwang Choi (2003), 'Welfare policy in Korea: issues and strategy', in O. Yul Kwon, Sung-Hee Jwa and Kyung-Tae Lee (ed.), *Korea's New Economic Strategy in the Globalization Era*, Cheltenham, UK and Northampton, MA, USA: Edward Elgar Publishing, pp. 192–214.

Bank of Korea (2006), 'Effects of changes in income distribution on consumption', (in Korean), *Monthly Bulletin*, April, 23–56.

Bank of Korea (2008), *2008 Economic Statistics Yearbook*, Seoul: Bank of Korea.

Choi, J.S. and J.K. Choi (2006), 'The effectiveness of poverty reduction and the target efficiency of social security transfers in South Korea, 1999–2003', *International Journal of Social Welfare*, **15**, 1–7.

Choi, Kwang and Soonwon Kwon (1997), 'Social welfare and distribution policies', in Dong-Se Cha, Kwang Suk Kim and D.H. Perkins (ed.), *The Korean Economy 1945–1995: performance and vision for the 21st century*, Seoul: Korea Development Institute, pp. 541–85.

Choi, Sung Jae (2002), 'National policies on ageing in Korea', in D.R. Phillips and A.C.M. Chan (ed.), *Ageing and Long-Term Care: national policies in the Asia-Pacific*, Ottawa: International Development Research Centre, http://idrc.ca/en/ev-28475-201-1-DO_TOPIC.html.

Choi, Sung-Eun, I.H. Park, K.H. Goh and S.H. Nam (2007), *An Analysis of Social Welfare Budget of 2007 and Policy Issues*, (in Korean), Seoul: KIHASA.

Dong-A Daily (2009), '100 social services civil servants in charge do not know', 23 February.

Forster, M. and Marco Mira d'Ercole (2005), 'Income distribution and poverty in OECD countries in the second half of the 1990s,' OECD Social Employment and Migration Working Paper No. 22, OECD Publishing.

Jacobs, D. (2000), 'Low public expenditure on social welfare: Do East Asian countries have a secret?' *International Journal of Social Welfare*, **9**, 2–16.

Jeong, K.H., H.S. Choi and H.J. Bang (2007), *A Study on the Measures for the Successful Introduction of the Basic Old Age Pension System*, (in Korean), Seoul: KIHASA

Kim, An-Na, J.K. Cho and K.H. Jung (2007), *Evaluation of the First Four Years of the Participatory Government – Health and Welfare Area*, (in Korean), Seoul: KIHASA.

Kim, Meesook (2003), 'Social welfare system', in Doh Chull Shin, Conrad P. Rutkowski and Chong-Min Park (eds), *The Quality of Life in Korea*, Dordrecht: Kluwer Academic Publishers, pp. 265–89.

Kim, Seung Kwon, Y.C. Yoo, T.J. Lee, N.H. Cho, Y.C. Byun and M.S. Kim (2008), *Mid-term Strategies of Health and Welfare*, (in Korean), Seoul: KIHASA.

Kim, Yeon-Myung (2008), 'Beyond East Asian welfare productivism in South Korea', *Policy and Politics*, **36** (1), 209–27.

Kim, Young-Hwa (2003), 'Productive welfare: Korea's third way?' *International Journal of Social Welfare*, **12**, 61–7.

Korea Institute for Health and Social Affairs (KIHASA) (2008), *2008 Poverty Statistics Yearbook*, Seoul: KIHASA.

Korea Labor Institute (KLI) (2008), *2008 Labor statistics*, Seoul: KLI.

Korea National Statistical Office (KNSO) (various years), *Korea Statistical Yearbook*, Seoul: KNSO.

Kwon, Soonman (2001), 'Economic crisis and social policy reform in Korea', *International Journal of Social Welfare*, **10**, 97–106.

Lee, Byung-Hee, H.W. Kim, D.S. Hwang, D.H. Kim, Y.M. Kim, W.Y. Kim and O.K. Choi (2008), *Employment Insurance and Activation Strategies in Korea*, (in Korean), Seoul: Korea Labor Institute.

Lee, H.K. (1999), 'Globalization and the emerging welfare state – the experience of South Korea', *International Journal of Social Welfare*, **8**, 23–37.

Lee, Hyun-ju, T.J. Lee, B.Y. Kim, J.M. Jin, S.N. Jeon, J.Y. Yoo and E.H. Lee (2008), *A Study of Social Assistance Monitoring System: basic ideas and practical strategies*, (in Korean), Seoul: KIHASA.

Lee, Joung-Woo (2002), 'The financial crisis and economic inequality in Korea', *Korea Journal*, **42** (1), 178–204.

Lee, Pil-dong, S.H. Park, T.Y. Kim, J.I. Seong, E.J. Shin, C.H. Kim and J.H. Kim (2004), *An Analysis of the Reasons for Income and Development Gap between Urban and Rural Regions*, (in Korean), Seoul: Korea Rural Economic Institute.

Lee, Sun-Young (2006), 'Uri Party seeks budget increase to tackle economic polarisation', *Korea Herald*, 20 January.

Lee, T.J., T.W. Kim, H.S. Cho, M.K. Kim, S.H. Woo, K.H. Park, E.Y. Park and S.N. Jeon (2008), *Monitoring and Evaluation of the National Basic Livelihood Security System and its Self-sufficiency Base*, (in Korean), Seoul: KIHASA.

Lee, Tae-Soo (2008), 'Proactive welfare: Is that all?', *The Hankyoreh*, Seoul, Korea, 6 October.

Ministry of Heath, Welfare and Family Affairs (MIHWAF) (2009), 'Vision and mission', Seoul: MIHWAF, www.mw.go.kr.

OECD (2006), *Employment Outlook*, Paris: OECD.

OECD (2007a), *OECD Economic Surveys: Korea*, Paris: OECD.

OECD (2007b), *Social Expenditure Database, 1980–2003*, Paris: OECD.

Park, J.H. and O.Y. Kwon (2006), 'A comparative analysis of the social welfare programmes for the elderly between Australia and Korea: focused on income, housing and care', Mimeo.
Roh, D.Y., E.H. Lee and I. Won (2007), *Analysis of the Effectiveness of the Minimum Living Standard Guarantee*, (in Korean), Seoul: KIHASA.
Shin, Dong-Myeon (2000), 'Financial crisis and social security: the paradox of the Republic of Korea', *International Social Security Review*, **53** (3), 83–107.
United Nations Development Programme (UNDP) (various years), *Human Development Report*, New York: UNDP and Oxford University Press.
Weisbrod, Burton A. (1977), 'Collective action and the distribution of income: a conceptual approach', in R.H. Haveman and J. Margolis (eds), *Public Expenditure and Policy Analysis*, 2nd edn, Chicago, IL: Rand McNally College Publishing Company, pp. 105–31.
World Bank (1993), *The East Asian Miracle*, Washington, DC: World Bank.
World Bank (various years), *World Development Report*, Washington, DC and New York: World Bank and Oxford University Press.
Yang, Jae-jin (2000), 'The rise of the Korean welfare state amid economic crisis, 1997–99: implications for the globalisation debate', *Development Policy Review*, **18**, 235–56.
Yoon, Seok-Myung (2008), 'Direction of the old age income guarantee system: with special reference to the relationship between the national pension and the basic old age pension', (in Korean), in Hyung-Pyo Moon (ed.), *the Public Pension System: assessment and policy issues*, Seoul: Korea Development Institute, pp. 51–85.
Zin, Ragayah Haji Mat (2005), 'Income distribution in East Asian developing countries: recent trends', *Asian-Pacific Economic Literature*, **19** (2), 36–54.

Index